Travels with tl

Travels with the Self uses a hermeneutic perspective to critique psychology and demonstrate why the concept of the self and the modality of cultural history are so vitally important to the profession of psychology. Each chapter focuses on a theory, concept, sociopolitical or professional issue, philosophical problem, or professional activity that has rarely been critiqued from a historical, sociopolitical vantage point.

Philip Cushman explores psychology's involvement in consumerism, racism, shallow understandings of being human, military torture, political resistance, and digital living. In each case, theories and practices are treated as historical artifacts, rather than expressions of a putatively progressive, modern-era science that is uncovering the one, universal truth about human being. In this way, psychological theories and practices, especially pertaining to the concept of the self, are shown to be reflections of the larger moral understandings and political arrangements of their time and place, with implications for how we understand the self in theory and clinical practice.

Drawing on the philosophies of critical theory and hermeneutics, Cushman insists on understanding the self, one of the most studied and cherished of psychological concepts, and its ills, practitioners, and healing technologies, as historical/cultural artifacts — surprising, almost sacrilegious, concepts. To this end, each chapter begins with a historical introduction that locates it in the historical time and moral/political space of the nation's, the profession's, and the author's personal context.

Travels with the Self brings together highly unusual and controversial writings on contemporary psychology that will appeal to psychoanalysts and psychotherapists, psychologists of all stripes, as well as scholars of philosophy, history, and cultural studies.

Philip Cushman, Ph.D. is a psychotherapist in private practice on Vashon Island, Washington, and retired Clinical Core Faculty member from doctoral programs in psychology at the California School of Professional Psychology (Alameda) and most recently Antioch University Seattle. He has been a member of APA divisions 24, 26, 29, and 39 and the Washington State Religious Campaign Against Torture.

Psychoanalysis in a New Key Book Series
Donnel B. Stern
Series editor

When music is played in a new key, the melody does not change, but the notes that make up the composition do: change in the context of continuity, continuity that perseveres through change. Psychoanalysis in a New Key publishes books that share the aims psychoanalysts have always had, but that approach them differently. The books in the series are not expected to advance any particular theoretical agenda, although to this date most have been written by analysts from the Interpersonal and Relational orientations.

The most important contribution of a psychoanalytic book is the communication of something that nudges the reader's grasp of clinical theory and practice in an unexpected direction. Psychoanalysis in a New Key creates a deliberate focus on innovative and unsettling clinical thinking. Because that kind of thinking is encouraged by exploration of the sometimes surprising contributions to psychoanalysis of ideas and findings from other fields, Psychoanalysis in a New Key particularly encourages interdisciplinary studies. Books in the series have married psychoanalysis with dissociation, trauma theory, sociology, and criminology. The series is open to the consideration of studies examining the relationship between psychoanalysis and any other field — for instance, biology, literary and art criticism, philosophy, systems theory, anthropology, and political theory.

But innovation also takes place within the boundaries of psychoanalysis, and Psychoanalysis in a New Key therefore also presents work that reformulates thought and practice without leaving the precincts of the field. Books in the series focus, for example, on the significance of personal values in psychoanalytic practice, on the complex interrelationship between the analyst's clinical work and personal life, on the consequences for the clinical situation when patient and analyst are from different cultures, and on the need for psychoanalysts to accept the degree to which they knowingly satisfy their own wishes during treatment hours, often to the patient's detriment.

TITLES IN THIS SERIES INCLUDE:

Vol. 46 Travels with the Self
Interpreting Psychology as Cultural History
Philip Cushman

Vol. 45 The Critique of Regression
A Psychoanalytic Model of Irreversible Lifespan Development
Gregory S. Rizzolo

Vol. 44 The Infinity of the Unsaid
Unformulated Experience, Language, and the Nonverbal
Donnel B. Stern

Vol. 43 The Mindbrain and Dreams
An Exploration of Dreaming, Thinking, and Artistic Creation
Mark J. Blechner

Vol. 42 Further Developments in Interpersonal Psychoanalysis, 1980s–2010s
Evolving Interest in the Analyst's Subjectivity
Edited by Donnel B. Stern and Irwin Hirsch

Vol. 41 Understanding the Sexual Betrayal of Boys and Men
The Trauma of Sexual Abuse
Edited by Richard B. Gartner

Vol. 40 Healing Sexually Betrayed Men and Boys
Treatment for Sexual Abuse, Assault, and Trauma
Edited by Richard B. Gartner

A full list of all titles in this series is available at:
www.routledge.com/series/LEAPNKBS

Travels with the Self

Interpreting Psychology as Cultural History

Philip Cushman

LONDON AND NEW YORK

First published 2019
by Routledge
2 Park Square, Milton Park, Abingdon, Oxon OX14 4RN

and by Routledge
711 Third Avenue, New York, NY 10017

Routledge is an imprint of the Taylor & Francis Group, an informa business

© 2019 Philip Cushman

The right of Philip Cushman to be identified as author of this work has been asserted by him in accordance with sections 77 and 78 of the Copyright, Designs and Patents Act 1988.

All rights reserved. No part of this book may be reprinted or reproduced or utilized in any form or by any electronic, mechanical, or other means, now known or hereafter invented, including photocopying and recording, or in any information storage or retrieval system, without permission in writing from the publishers.

Trademark notice: Product or corporate names may be trademarks or registered trademarks, and are used only for identification and explanation without intent to infringe.

British Library Cataloguing in Publication Data
A catalogue record for this book is available from the British Library

Library of Congress Cataloging in Publication Data
Names: Cushman, Philip, author.
Title: Travels with the self : interpreting psychology as cultural history / Philip Cushman.
Description: New York : Routledge, 2019. | Series: Pychoanalysis in a new key book series ; 46 | Includes bibliographical references and index.
Identifiers: LCCN 2018015593 (print) | LCCN 2018025556 (ebook) | ISBN 9780429468049 (Master) | ISBN 9780429886454 (Web PDF) | ISBN 9780429886447 (ePub) | ISBN 9780429886430 (Mobipocket/Kindle) | ISBN 9781138605497 (hardback : alk. paper) | ISBN 9781138605541 (pbk. : alk. paper)
Subjects: LCSH: Psychology–Social aspects. | Identity (Psychology)
Classification: LCC BF57 (ebook) | LCC BF57 .C87 2019 (print) | DDC 150.1–dc23
LC record available at https://lccn.loc.gov/2018015593

ISBN: 978-1-138-60549-7 (hbk)
ISBN: 978-1-138-60554-1 (pbk)
ISBN: 978-0-429-46804-9 (ebk)

Typeset in Times New Roman
by Wearset Ltd, Boldon, Tyne and Wear

To my Karen Ann, forever

Contents

Acknowledgments		xi
1	(2017) Introduction: strange and unexpected travels with the self	1
2	(1990) Why the self is empty: toward a historically situated psychology	6
3	(1995) What we hold in our hand	33
4	(2000) White guilt, political activity, and the analyst	39
5	(2000) Will managed care change our way of being?	51
6	(2003) Welcome to the 21st century, where character was erased: the William James lecture in psychotherapy and ethics	77
7	(2005) Between arrogance and a dead-end: psychoanalysis and the Heidegger-Foucault dilemma	91
8	(2005) The case of the hidden subway station and other Gadamerian mysteries	106
9	(2013) Flattened selves, shallow solutions: a commentary on "The McDonaldization of Psychotherapy"	121
10	(2013) Because the rock will not read the article: a discussion of Jeremy D. Safran's critique of Irwin Z. Hoffman's "Doublethinking our way to scientific legitimacy"	134

11	(2013) Your cheatin' heart: from scientism to medicalization to an unethical psychotherapy	153
12	(2015) Horror, escape, and the struggle with Jewish identity: a review of *Contemporary Psychoanalysis and the Legacy of the Third Reich*	165
13	(2015) Relational psychoanalysis as political resistance	175
14	(2015) The Golem must live, the Golem must die	204
15	(2016) The earthquake that is the Hoffman Report on torture: toward a re-moralization of psychology	223
16	(2017) Living in the politics of uncertainty: cultural history as generative hermeneutics	253

References 268
Index 300

Acknowledgments

In my 1995 book I wrote three pages of thanks to family, friends, teachers, and colleagues. It is now almost 25 years later, and I have a slew of new names to add to that list. Sadly, however, this time around I do not have the space to name everyone who deserve to be recognized; but I must mention a few.

Initially I thought of this book as discussing the hermeneutic concept of the self and then the history of the more contemporary American self. However, recently I came to realize that, unbeknownst to me, this book is not only a chronological story about *the* self, it is a story about *my*self as well. That is, it inadvertently reveals snapshots of a young person growing into his life and then growing old as a psychologist and a person.

Writing for me is like body surfing in the ocean, which I did often in my youth — being lifted up and swept along by a great and mysterious force. It is a profound sensation, a moment out of time and beyond personal will. But while the power of an ocean wave comes from the physical world, the power of writing originates from the social realm. The written word is propelled by others, and the energy originates from understandings generated by human societies and framed by historical traditions. Language and tradition and critical thought speak me when I write; sometimes I don't know where the words come from, sometimes I hardly even recognize them as my own.

Hermeneutics has helped me realize where the words come from: from people like you. The words come from generations of folks who have come before or are with me now; from my family past and present; from dear friends and beloved students; from 45 years of patients and 34 years of readers; from teachers and supervisors and classmates and teammates. I owe so much — really everything — to all of you.

In particular, I'd like to thank Donnel Stern for the wise and creative work he has gifted to all of us and for his continuing friendship with me; to Charles Bath, Mary Ann Muller, and all the folks at Routledge who helped make this book possible; to Catherine Buchanon-Richardson who miraculously secured for me Sony's permission to include the chorus of "Your Cheatin' Heart," to Jim Levine, who did the same for the extract from Da Capo/Hachette for parts of Chapter 8, and to my long-time friend Jim Cooke, who translated my family's photos into electronic cover art.

I feel deep gratitude to my family: my mother Frances, father Alvin, brother Edward, daughter Leah Corrina, and to all those who came before us, building Jewish traditions and somehow surviving pograms, persecutions, hatreds, forced immigrations, fleeing to unknown lands so that we can now live in a slightly safer place and continue to fight for freedom and critical thought everywhere and for everyone. Thanks to dear friends Bob Cuthbert, Jim Cooke, Jerry Winston, Joel Rosenberg, Terence and Melanie O'Hare, Jane Burka, Jules Burstein, Tony Stigliano, Blaine Fowers, Frank Richardson, Nathan Adler, Lane Gerber, Dan Taube, David Goodman, Rob Crawford, Merna Hecht, and Mark Russell; to my 8th grade American history teacher (and later psychologist colleague) Paul Erickson; to Judaica teachers Bill Cutter, Richard Levy, and Abraham Zygielbaum; to my first supervisor Jack Mitchell, and long-time consultants Hilde Burton and Margaret Singer.

Most of all, of course, I am forever grateful to my wife Karen, who saw something (who knows what) in me 50 years ago that I did not know I possessed. Obviously, you are the real writer in the family, and also my editor and reference librarian and partner and lover and dearest friend. Somehow, even with — or perhaps especially because of — our differences, we built a life together, and that life has saved my life.

Thank you, one and all.

Every effort has been made to contact the copyright holders for their permission to reprint selections of this book. The publishers would be grateful to hear from any copyright holder who is not here acknowledged and we will undertake to rectify any errors or omissions in future editions of this book.

The cover art was prepared and arranged by James Cooke, architect, graphics designer, furniture maker. Images are top left a Nathanson-Segal-Cushman family photo (1888, recently arrived refugees in Palestine 1888); and top right a Cushman family photo (proud store owner ca.

1926, store lost in the Great Depression). Images are bottom left kind permission granted by the Benedict J. Fernandez photo archives (1966); bottom right permission granted by Shutterstock.com.

Chapter 2 was first published as Cushman, P. (1990), Why the self is empty: Toward a historically situated psychology, *American Psychologist, 45*, 599–611. Reprinted by permission of American Psychological Association.

Chapter 4 was first published as Cushman, P. (2000), White guilt, political activity, and the analyst: Commentary on paper by Neil Altman, *Psychoanalytic Dialogues, 10*, 607–618. Reprinted by permission of Taylor & Francis Ltd, www.tandfonline.com.

Chapter 5 was first published as Cushman, P. & Gilford, P. (2000), Will managed care change our way of being? *American Psychologist, 55*, 585–996. Reprinted by permission of the American Psychological Association and Peter Gilford.

Chapter 6 was first published as Cushman, P. (2002), How psychology erodes personhood, *Journal of Theoretical and Philosophical Psychology, 22*, 103–113. The title has been changed and the text modified. Reprinted by permission of the American Psychological Association.

Chapter 7 was first published as Cushman, P. (2005), Between arrogance and a dead-end: Psychoanalysis and the Heidegger-Foucault dilemma, *Contemporary Psychoanalysis, 41*, 399–417, © the William Alanson White Institute of Psychiatry, Psychoanalysis & Psychology and the William Alanson White Psychoanalytic Society, www.wawhite.org reprinted by permission of Taylor & Francis Ltd, www.tandfonline.com on behalf of the William Alanson White Institute of Psychiatry, Psychoanalysis & Psychology and the William Alanson White Psychoanalytic Society.

Chapter 8 was first published as Cushman, P. (2005), Clinical applications: A response to Layton, *Contemporary Psychoanalysis, 41*, 431–445. The title has been changed and the text slightly modified. © the William Alanson White Institute of Psychiatry, Psychoanalysis & Psychology and the William Alanson White Psychoanalytic Society, www.wawhite.org reprinted by permission of Taylor & Francis Ltd, www.tandfonline.com on behalf of the William Alanson White Institute of Psychiatry, Psychoanalysis & Psychology and the William Alanson White Psychoanalytic Society. Also text extracts were taken from *Constructing the Self, Constructing America* by Philip Cushman, © 1995 (pp. 302–303, 321–324,

326–328). Reprinted by permission of Da Capo Press, an imprint of Hachette Book Group, Inc.

Chapter 10 was first published as Cushman, P. (2013), Because the rock cannot read the article: A discussion of Jeremy D. Safran's critique of Irwin Z. Hoffman's "Doublethinking our way to scientific legitimacy," *Psychoanalytic Dialogues, 23*, 211–224. Reprinted by permission of Taylor & Francis Ltd, www.tandfonline.com.

For Chapter 11, in both the title of the chapter and the body, "Your Cheatin' Heart," words and music by Hank Williams Sr 1952, reproduced by kind permission of Sony/ATV Acuff Rose Music, London W1F 9LD.

Chapter 12 was first published as Cushman, P. (2015), Review of *Psychoanalysis and the Legacy of the Third Reich* in *Contemporary Psychoanalysis, 51*, 423–459 © the William Alanson White Institute of Psychiatry, Psychoanalysis & Psychology and the William Alanson White Psychoanalytic Society, www.wawhite.org reprinted by permission of Taylor & Francis Ltd, www.tandfonline.com on behalf of the William Alanson White Institute of Psychiatry, Psychoanalysis & Psychology and the William Alanson White Psychoanalytic Society.

Chapter 13 was first published as Cushman, P. (2015), Relational psychoanalysis as political resistance, *Contemporary Psychoanalysis, 51*, 423–459 © the William Alanson White Institute of Psychiatry, Psychoanalysis & Psychology and the William Alanson White Psychoanalytic Society, www.wawhite.org reprinted by permission of Taylor & Francis Ltd, www.tandfonline.com on behalf of the William Alanson White Institute of Psychiatry, Psychoanalysis & Psychology and the William Alanson White Psychoanalytic Society.

Chapter 14 was first published as Cushman, P. (2017), The Golem must live, the Golem must die. In Severson, E.R. & Goodman, D.M., (Eds.) (2017), *Memories and Monsters* (pp. 23–42), New York: Routledge. First presented in a longer form as an invited address at the American Psychological Association Annual Convention, 2015. Reprinted by permission of Taylor & Francis Ltd, www.tandfonline.com.

Chapter 15 was first presented at the American Psychological Association Annual Convention, 2016 as "The earthquake that is the Hoffman Report on torture." It is also in press with *Psychoanalysis, Self, and Context* for 2018, volume 13, number 3. Reprinted by permission of Taylor & Francis Ltd, www.tandfonline.com.

Chapter 1

Introduction
Strange and unexpected travels with the self

Many cultures from many historical eras have conceived of human life as a journey. The ancient Greeks imagined the end of life as a crossing of the river Styx; in the Hebrew Bible the Israelites escaped slavery and then spent the next 40 years traveling in the desert; Don Quixote and his squire Sancho Panza wandered the countryside, looking for wrongs to make right; many a tragic hero, from Oedipus to Shakespeare's Macbeth on the heath to Captain America in the film "Easy Rider," all hit the road. "Many rivers to cross," sang Bob Marley, and Robert Frost described "two roads diverged in a yellow wood." American novelist John Steinbeck enshrined his adventures with his canine companion in *Travels With Charley*.

So yes, traveling represents a compelling symbol for living a human life. I use it for the title of this book to convey both the changes the concept of the self has undergone over time and across cultures, and the ways my intellectual travels as a psychologist and my relational travels as a therapist and a person have been enriched by my long-time travel companion, the concept of the self.

In my writing I use the self in its hermeneutic meaning, that is, the set of embodied beliefs and activities that live out what are considered by a particular culture or historical era to be the proper ways of being human and the limits and potential nobility of humans. During my early years of searching at the university, I longed for, but could not begin to articulate, the combination of history, literature, politics, and psychology that unite in that hermeneutic concept. I remember once looking for a graduate program that would help me learn about people in that interdisciplinary way. I went to a beloved former psychology professor, who said "that approach sounds interesting, but it isn't psychology. Try history." So I interviewed in the history department; they said "that approach sounds interesting, but it isn't history. Try psychology." Many years, graduate programs, and interesting but ultimately unsatisfying learning experiences later, social psychologist Ed Sampson introduced me to critical theory and philosopher Tony Stigliano to hermeneutics. That dual perspective has brought me as close to an intellectual home as I have ever had.

The title of this book, *Travels with the Self*, then easily moves us into the subtitle, *Interpreting Psychology as Cultural History*, because if there are a multitude of ways of being human, shaped by particular cultural understandings, historical traditions, and political arrangements, then the indigenous psychologies embedded in those various societies must be considered artifacts of their time and place. For that reason, a psychological theory or practice, then, can't be considered a universal science, whose subject of study is the putatively one, constant, immutable, universal human. Instead, psychology itself must be seen as a cultural artifact — in a way, it is the embodiment of the historical era that has brought it to light. In 1973 Ken Gergen wrote "Social Psychology as History," and in the same year historian Warren Susman wrote *Culture as History;* these two contributions helped me learn how to apply hermeneutics, as did psychologist Louis Sass, who in a nod to Clifford Geertz wrote in 1988 that understanding humans is not a matter of "getting inside someone's head," but more like standing behind the other and reading over their shoulder the cultural text from which they themselves are reading (Sass, 1988a, p. 250).

The idea that Western psychology is a cultural artifact has never upset me — in fact, I welcome it. It was a relief to think that I had been skeptical about the claims of a scientized psychology not because I was too stupid to appreciate the material, but because the concept itself was wrong-headed. It was in 1990, with my article "Why the Self Is Empty," that I put those ideas together and applied them to an important subject. And by 1995 I was able to better notice my overall approach to historical study and describe it through a four-part approach to the self. I suggested that we could study an era by identifying (1) the era's predominant configuration of the self; (2) the ills to which that particular self is vulnerable; (3) the designated healers for those characteristic ills; and (4) the healing practices the designated healer uses.

When using the four-part analysis, it soon becomes apparent that, because the self changes over time, so do the other items of the analysis.

They change because they are products of the social terrain in which they are embedded; they fit with the moral understandings and political arrangements of the time, and they serve particular functions within the body politic. When the terrain shifts, so do the self, its ills, its healers, and their healing practices. The self is a historical, cultural artifact. It travels.

The chapters of this book are composed of six articles I previously published and nine talks I delivered, plus this new introduction. Originally the book was designed to be twice as long, but for publication purposes half of those chapters had to be left out. I have arranged the surviving papers in the order in which they were written. I edited the published articles and unpublished talks very little. I amended the titles of Chapters 6, 8, and 12, for Chapter 9 I included a section from another talk of mine from the same conference as a further illustration of the main point, and for Chapter 15 I reinstated an important section of a talk I'd given that I had to delete when originally submitting it for publication in a journal due to limitations of space. With these few exceptions what you see here is what was originally spoken or printed. I did this in order to stay true to the intent of this project, which is to face the historical nature of our psychological practices (including *my* practices). For that reason I have also included a brief historical introduction for each chapter, trying to describe something about the social terrain from which the writing of each paper emerged, thereby letting the texts — their limitations, mistakes, and overall historicity — speak for themselves and give readers ample opportunity to interpret the material contextually. Just as the psychological theories and practices I critiqued are historically situated, so too are my interpretations. Readers get to view them, warts and all.

In the pages that follow you will find the products of some of my most difficult — and enjoyable — intellectual struggles. For many years I was uncomfortable about certain aspects of psychology, but I couldn't really explain it to my therapist colleagues and friends. However, studying with Sampson and Stigliano and talking (and talking) with philosophical psychologists Frank Richardson and Blaine Fowers helped me understand the hermeneutics of my discontent. Over time, I was able to make myself more understandable (although not necessarily more persuasive) to my therapist colleagues. But through my writing I was able to find kindred souls, in psychology and elsewhere, and our ongoing conversations have enriched my work and my life beyond measure.

All of these chapters have something to say about theory and practice. In my opinion hermeneutics speaks to the most important issues facing Americans today, so of course it holds important ideas for psychology, which, from a hermeneutic perspective, is all about meaning and the pursuit of the good.

Often I don't know much about what I am thinking until I write it, and so what you read in this book has been invaluable to my sense of sanity and my ongoing attempt to make sense out of psychotherapy, what Freud rightly called "the impossible profession," and more generally the necessity of surviving what Peter Berger (1961) called "the precarious vision." Thank God I stumbled upon writing. In truth, both the process and product of writing has enriched my life — in fact saved my life — in ways impossible to overstate.

So now I give these papers to you. I hope they help you in your struggles, as the process of creating and shaping them has helped me in mine. I am proud of them. Sometimes, when I am confused or in despair, I will read one of my papers to soothe myself, and miraculously, it usually works. I can't exactly explain why it works, but I hope it will have a similar effect on you. Ultimately, my goal is not to attack, but to point to the vague outlines of a better way. I mean to offer hope, because in part it is by drawing from historical memory — the good and the bad — that humans can make a better world. If we forget the important things — that is, the events, the mistakes, the meanings, the beloved ones, the joys, the betrayals, the cherished beliefs — we are doomed.

Ah, but how to figure out what is important? That is where interpretation comes in, and then of course that is the door through which disagreement, avoidance, self-deceit, confusion, and general messiness arrive. But that is all right; in fact really it is unavoidable. Our most important task, I think, is to learn how to better meet those moments, draw wisdom and courage from our favorite texts, teachers, and friends, and get through those challenges together, with honesty and compassion, knowing in our better moments that our understandings are, as the hermeneuticists say, always uncertain and incomplete. In a way, that is the subtext of much hermeneutic and relational psychoanalytic literature, and hopefully of these chapters as well: how to survive the inevitable and continuing difficulties of living a human life, a life with others, in cooperation and conflict with others. Let us hope that, as J.D. Salinger (1962) once wrote, we can survive with at least "some of our faculties intact" — yes, our faculties and what they produce, including our cherished ideals, our most deeply held beliefs.

It seems possible, does it not, that a critical hermeneutics — a critical cultural history — can lead us to compassion, love, and finally even hope. It is with hope that I offer this book to you. Once Ed Sampson, who was about to depart on a trip to China, gave me a reprint of his recently published 1988 article and signed it by paraphrasing Chairman Mao with the inscription "May a Thousand Mavericks Bloom." I pass that hope on to you, with good cheer and gratitude for traveling along with me.

Chapter 2

Why the self is empty
Toward a historically situated psychology

(1990 American Psychologist, 45, 599–611)

Historical introduction

I think I will never again write an article like "Why the Self Is Empty" — it was one of a kind. The empty self was an idea just waiting to happen, an event just begging to be understood and interpreted. Once I got a glimpse of it, a world of understanding opened up for me. Writing the article helped me get a sense of how to draw from hermeneutics in order to better understand the fit between psychotherapy, pop culture, history, and my political commitments both within and outside of psychology. It has been the most important academic paper I ever wrote, and I will be forever indebted to the historians whose writing pointed the way and to the teachers and friends who helped me develop and bring it to life.

It took a long time to develop the intellectual understandings that prepared me to write the article. In 1988 Ed Sampson, a former teacher of mine, published "The Debate On Individualism" in *American Psychologist*. I loved that article. It helped me see how my beginning questions about selfhood could develop into ideas, and then where those ideas could take me. Immediately after reading Ed's article, between clusters of patient hours, I began to make notes. Those notes and sketchy paragraphs eventually became "Why the Self Is Empty." It was a joy to write; in fact, truthfully, it felt as though the article wrote itself.

During the 1980s I was struggling with the meaning of American psychotherapy, its political functions and consequences. I was reading postmodern and hermeneutic critiques of the modern era and applying them to therapy and trying to figure out whether or not I could justify continuing to work as a therapist after coming to some brutal realizations about psychotherapy's history and its contemporary political functions. At that time in psychology there was little help with the moral struggles I was experiencing. Most psychotherapists I knew were not too knowledgeable about or deeply troubled by therapy's historical-political effects; critical perspectives on psychotherapy were usually written by non-therapists skeptical of or hostile to the profession. Of course, as I learned after the empty self article was published, there were therapists with questions and concerns similar to mine, but I had trouble locating them until my article helped them find me.

Complicating and compounding the struggle with my conscience was the character of the political events of those years, starting in the late 1970s. The first eight years of the 1980s were the Reagan years, followed by four years of George H.W. Bush. They were years full of right-wing posturing and the skillful and unethical use of advertising in manipulating public opinion regarding both domestic and foreign policy. Despite Reagan's simple-minded, mean-spirited comments about labor, the poor, people of color, and anti-war and environmental activists, the mainstream press continued to characterize him as friendly, good-natured, good-hearted: the Great Communicator. And let's not forget the role of a Republican Congress that wrote the deregulation laws that led to the Savings and Loan debacle and protected the administration's adventurism in Central America.

As the 1980s unfolded, opposition to Reagan and all he stood for grew increasingly difficult. He was cast as such a nice guy, and besides, because computer technology was on the rise, there was money to be made. The baby-boom cohort was in the process of being seduced into quiescence, if not conversion. The press was in a trance, and me and my psychologist colleagues were hustling to generate enough cash for a down payment and private schools and college funds for our children. George (The Elder) Bush's unconscionable use of the Willie Horton attack ads were appalling, but who had the time to write about it? We had new psychological theories to study, interventions to learn, private practices to build. And so it goes.

It was for many Americans a time of middle-class political complacency and avoidance. I bring all this up to emphasize the importance of cultural history and the usefulness of historically situating, and thus critiquing, one's own work. A generation came of age during those years: we took jobs and entered professions, formed marriages and had children, reached middle age. What were we like, how did the world in which we found ourselves influence us, and in turn how did we affect it?

Through the concept of the empty self I tried to understand, describe, and then interpret the promise, seductions, and dangers, the self-confidence and the troubledness of the era. Most of all the concept of the self helped me understand why young Americans moved so easily from activism to consumerism, blue collar workers from union and Democratic loyalty to

> Reagan worship, and how young therapists and their therapy theories mirrored those shifts. The late 1970s through the mid 1990s was a time of psychotherapeutic expansion, affluence, and cultural influence. Youthful, middle aged boomers populated the field of psychotherapy with an energetic, intelligent, articulate presence that was motivated and ambitious.
>
> But what had happened to the political activism of our younger years? That was one of the questions I was trying to address in the article. Why didn't the events of the 1980s cause massive unrest and resistance among blue collar workers and the baby boom generation?
>
> What was needed was a complex understanding of how large historical forces create trends that develop outside of consciousness, and consequently how those trends constitute one's way of being. Then compliance is experienced as a personal preference, a recognition of an obvious truth chosen freely, rather than the result of calculated coercion and forced submission. What was needed was a way of understanding large-scale historical change that conceived of the social realm as constitutive of human being and yet one that avoided a historical determinism. In other words, what was needed was a robust hermeneutic explanation.
>
> The philosophical frame that I used when writing "Why the Self Is Empty" was not the kind of philosophically complex hermeneutics I began studying as the years went by, but it was a start. I still had a lot to learn about hermeneutics, but I have never felt that my hermeneutic limitations significantly diminished the meaning or the innovations of "Why the Self Is Empty" — it will always hold a special place in my heart, and I hope in the history of critical, hermeneutic psychology as well.

From its beginnings, modern psychology has had difficulty developing a historically situated perspective on its discourse and practices. Nowhere is this ahistorical tendency more obvious than in the debate on individualism. Many researchers have treated self-contained individualism as an unquestioned value and the current concept of self — the bounded, masterful self — as an unchangeable, transhistorical entity. In opposition to a decontextualized approach, I will argue that cultural conceptualizations and configurations of self are formed by the economies and politics of their respective eras. By studying the self in this way, psychologists will be better able to understand the current era and psychology's place within that era.

I have drawn from the insights of hermeneuticists such as Faulconer and Williams (1985), Gadamer (1979), Heidegger (1962/1977), Morawski

(1984), Rabinow and Sullivan (1987), Stigliano (1989), and the authors in the book edited by Messer, Sass, and Woolfolk (1988) in order to develop an approach characterized by historical and ontological concerns. The argument is at times speculative and non empirical. It depends in part on a survey of the opinions of other social scientists and on the arguments of historians whose qualitative data is far too detailed to reproduce in an article of this size. I realize that this approach will be considered imprecise by some psychologists, but after much debate, I have decided that it is, with all its flaws, the best approach for such an elusive subject.

Even with these limits, I think the study of the self across time and cultures is an *essential* topic for psychology. If psychologists do not recognize the ethnocentric nature of psychology's discourse about the current Western self, we commit several errors. In particular, we participate in a culturally disrespectful and damaging psychological imperialism abroad and at the same time perpetuate the discourse of self-contained individualism and its attendant miseries at home.

By the *self* I mean the concept of the individual as articulated by the indigenous psychology of a particular cultural group, the shared understandings within a culture of "what it is to be human" (Heelas & Lock, 1981, p. 3). The self embodies what the culture believes is humankind's place in the cosmos: its limits, talents, expectations, and prohibitions. In this sense the self is an aspect of what Heidegger (1962/1977) called the horizon of shared understandings or "the clearing" carved out by the particular practices of a particular culture. There is no universal, transhistorical self, only local selves; no universal theory about the self, only local theories.

Studying the self of a particular era in this way allows us to operationalize a basic tenet of ontological hermeneutics: The process of studying humans is not the same as "reading" persons as "texts" (Gergen, 1988), but more like standing behind them and reading over their shoulder the cultural text from which they themselves are reading (Sass, 1988a, p. 250). In an earlier article (Cushman, 1987), I suggested that all elements of the clearing, including psychological theories about the self, are cultural artifacts and can be examined as elements of the cultural text.

That is what I am attempting to do when I describe the current configuration of self: read over our shoulders. The self is a difficult concept on which to get a perspective, precisely because it is such a central aspect of the horizon. As Sass (1988a) explained, "The horizon's concealment is intimately or intrinsically connected with the condition of being visible

… its presence is almost too obvious, too self-evident" (p. 242). It is therefore difficult for us to imagine the self as other than the way it is in our era or to consider it a legitimate subject for study. But as difficult as it is, the study of the self is a crucial element in interpreting an era. By studying the configuration of the current self, we will come to have an enlarged perspective on the forces that shape it, the discourse that justifies it, the consequences that flow from it, the illnesses that plague it, and the activities responsible for healing it. These things come in packages; unraveling one helps reveal them all.

The emergence of the empty self

Many authors have described how the bounded, masterful self has slowly and unevenly emerged in Western history. This is a self that has specific psychological boundaries, an internal locus of control, and a wish to manipulate the external world for its own personal ends. I believe that in the post-World War II era in the United States, there are indications that the present configuration of the bounded, masterful self is the empty self. By this I mean that our terrain has shaped a self that experiences a significant absence of community, tradition, and shared meaning. It experiences these social absences and their consequences "interiorly" as a lack of personal conviction and worth, and it embodies the absences as a chronic, undifferentiated emotional hunger. The post-World War II self thus yearns to acquire and consume as an unconscious way of compensating for what has been lost: it is empty.

One can see evidence of the empty self in current psychological discourse about narcissism and borderline states, the popular culture's emphasis on consuming, political advertising strategies that emphasize soothing and charisma instead of critical thought, and a nationwide difficulty in maintaining personal relationships. Broad historical forces such as industrialization, urbanization, and secularism have shaped the modern era. They have influenced the predominant psychological philosophy of our time, self-contained individualism; constructed the current configuration of the bounded self, the empty self; and developed the professions that I believe are most responsible for filling and healing the empty self, advertising and psychotherapy. Thus, the ideologies, subjects, and businesses of modern psychology have historical antecedents, economic constituents, and political consequences. They do not float suspended in time and space: They have a context.

Unfortunately, throughout the ongoing debate on the meaning and value of individualism, it has become increasingly clear that many researchers have made the fundamental mistake of decontextualizing the subject. Gergen, (1973, 1985), Giorgi (1970), Harre (1984, 1986a, 1986b), and Sampson (1977, 1981, 1983, 1988) have tried to reorient psychology's perspective. Others, such as Foucault (1980a) and Levin (1987b) also have argued that each era produces a particular configuration of self and corresponding kinds of psychopathology. Sampson's work in particular has emphasized the political antecedents and consequences of the current self.

My understanding of their historical interpretations is that an increasingly bounded, masterful self was constructed after the collapse of feudalism. It emerged at the same time that the modern state was faced with the necessity of developing justifications and techniques for controlling a modern populace. During the beginnings of the modern era in the 16th century, the Western world began to shift from a religious to a scientific frame of reference, from an agricultural to an industrial means of production, from a rural to an urban setting, and from a communal to an individual subject. These vast changes were coincident with and some say responsible for the dual triumph of the concept of Montaigne's subjective individual and the method necessary to study it, Descartes's objective empiricism (Taylor, 1988). Culminating with the Victorian era, the concept of the deep, secret, instinct-driven, potentially dangerous self was used by the state to justify its role as official controller of selves. Over the course of the 20th century, it has become apparent to cultural historians such as Susman (1973) and Lears (1983) that Americans have slowly changed from a Victorian people who had a deeply felt need to save money and restrict their sexual and aggressive impulses. Americans in the post-World War II era seem to have become a people who have a deeply felt need to spend money and indulge their impulses.

The thesis of this article is that the current self is constructed as empty, and as a result the state controls its population not by restricting the impulses of its citizens, as in Victorian times, but by creating and manipulating their wish to be soothed, organized, and made cohesive by momentarily filling them up. The products of the social sciences, and of psychology in particular, have often worked to the advantage of the state by helping to construct selves that are the subjects of control and to develop techniques that are the means of control. In the early modern period, Bentham's innovative prison, the Panopticon (Foucault, 1979), and in the current era, political polling strategies (Ginsberg, 1986) are prominent illustrations of the political utility of the social sciences.

This article supports Foucault's and Sampson's line of political reasoning and follows it into the realm of the economy. I believe that the construction of the post-World War II middle-class American self is a good illustration of how the economy and the power structure impact on personality. Since the end of World War II the configuration of an empty self has emerged in the middle classes. It is empty in part because of the loss of family, community, and tradition (Levin, 1987a; Rieff, 1966; Zaretsky, 1976). It is a self that seeks the experience of being continually filled up by consuming goods, calories, experiences, politicians, romantic partners, and empathic therapists in an attempt to combat the growing alienation and fragmentation of its era. This response has been implicitly prescribed by a post-World War II economy that is dependent on the continual consumption of nonessential and quickly obsolete items and experiences (Zinn, 1973, pp. 89–119). In order for the economy to thrive, American society requires individuals who experience a strong "need" for consumer products and in fact demand them (Henry, 1963). Such an economy requires individuals who have an uninterrupted flow of money and a continual motivation to spend it. The complex interrelatedness of social change, political forces, and cultural forms has somehow accomplished this through the dual creation of easy credit (Malabre, 1987) and a gnawing sense of emptiness in the self (Kohut, 1977).

Psychotherapy is one of the professions responsible for healing the post-World War II self. Unfortunately, many psychotherapy theories attempt to treat the modern self by reinforcing the very qualities of self that have initially caused the problem: its autonomous, bounded, masterful nature (Sampson, 1985). The patient is diagnosed as empty and fragmented, usually without addressing the sociohistorical predicament that caused the emptiness and fragmentation (Bordo, 1988; Levin, 1987c). Thus, through the activity of helping, psychology's discourse and practices perpetuate the causes of the very problems it is trying to treat.

The self is a social construct

This article is based on the type of social constructionist argument recently developed by Geertz (1973), Gergen (1985), Harre (1986a),

Morawski (1988), and Sampson (1983, 1988). Humans do not have a basic, fundamental, pure human nature that is transhistorical and transcultural. Humans are incomplete and therefore unable to function adequately unless embedded in a specific cultural matrix.

Culture "completes" humans by explaining and interpreting the world, helping them to focus their attention on or ignore certain aspects of their environment, and instructing and forbidding them to think and act in certain ways (Heidegger, 1962/1977). Culture is not indigenous clothing that covers the universal human; it infuses individuals, fundamentally shaping and forming them and how they conceive of themselves and the world, how they see others, how they engage in structures of mutual obligation, and how they make choices in the everyday world.

The material objects we create, the ideas we hold, and the actions we take are the consequences or "products" of the social construction of each particular era. They are cultural artifacts. However, these artifacts are not only the expression of an era. They are also the immediate "stuff" of daily life, and as such they shape and mold the community's generalized reality orientation in subtle and unseen ways. Consequently, they inevitably reinforce and reproduce the constellations of power, wealth, and influence within their respective societies.

The many shapes of the Western self

The self, as an artifact, has different configurations and different functions depending on the culture, the historical era, and the socioeconomic class in which it exists. For example, the Western self has gone through many permutations over the course of the last 2,500 years. We would do well to remember Foucault's (1970; Hutton, 1988) warning that the changes undergone by the Western self are not developmental changes brought on by an inner logic, the unfolding of a secret genetic code, or the peeling of layers of enlightenment. The self has undergone extreme, erratic, often discontinuous change because it is part of the larger sociohistorical fabric of its time. The self must function within a particular cultural pattern: matching, maintaining, and replicating it.

For instance, the communal, outward looking, non-sexually conflicted self of Aeschylus' Oresteia (458 BC/1953) looks vastly different from the tortured, confused "inner" self of Augustine's Confessions (397/1986). The self of the early Middle Ages was an immortal soul enclosed in the shell of a mortal body. It looked vastly different from the cynical, confused, increasingly nihilistic self of the 1920s. To get the sense of this contrast, imagine a conversation between Roland, the French knight in the 12th century epic The Song of Roland, and Zelda Fitzgerald, the quintessential 1920s "flapper."

During the last 2,000 years in Western society the self has become increasingly more individualistic, more subjective, and "deeper" (Logan, 1987; Meyer, 1986; Morris, 1972). Some scholars (e.g., Dreyfus & Rubin, 1987; Taylor, 1988) believe this individual depth was first expressed by Augustine's mistrust of self. It was later influenced by Europe's incremental steps toward capitalism and then developed by the Renaissance, the Enlightenment, and the Romantics (Baumeister, 1986, 1987; Greenblatt, 1980; Trilling, 1971) into the hypertrophied, individual self. Finally, the Western self took a major complicating turn during the ascendancy of the Victorian bourgeoisie with the overt articulation of its "hidden" sexual and aggressive content (Lowe, 1982). The individual, bounded, communally isolated self is a modern phenomenon (Rieff, 1966; Zaretsky, 1976), roughly paralleling the development of industrialization and the rise of the modern state. The belief in objective empiricism was based in part on the Enlightenment's search for the universal laws of a "pure" human nature, accomplished by studying the decontextualized individual. Lowe (1982) has shown how the particular qualities of bourgeois perception objectified and quantified everything. Taylor (1988) described how the subject-object and mind-body splits led to an increasing interest in, and the eventual hegemony of, the empirical social sciences. The social sciences thus developed at the same time as the emergence of the isolated, individual self and the modern state's need to control it through study and calculated manipulation (Foucault, 1979; Trigg, 1985).

The sexually conflicted Victorian self

More specifically, the bounded, masterful, middle-class self that has emerged in Western society during the last 200 years. The bourgeois self of the Victorian era in Europe reflected the impact of the Enlightenment and the industrial and French revolutions. The economy's need for an industrial labor force caused traditional rural communities to be uprooted, populations to become urbanized, and work to become increasingly compartmentalized and alienating. The percentage of Americans living in urban settings had grown from 3.4% in 1790 to 33% in 1900 (Blum et al., 1973, p. 441). Researchers such as Flexner (1959), Schiebinger (1987), Smith-Rosenberg (1981), and Welter (1966) have shown that in the late 18th and 19th centuries in general and the Victorian era in particular, gender roles in the middle and upper classes took on a polarized and restrictive cast unique to that time regarding both social privilege and economic function.

Lowe (1982) convincingly argued that the Victorian bourgeois self was a secular, rational, subjective, divided, sexually conflicted linear self that viewed the world as objectifiable and quantitative. The "unknown" was once thought to reside in the external world. Slowly, as the modern age dawned and developed, the self became the container for that which could be hidden from others and from oneself (Baumeister, 1986, pp. 36–50). Trilling (1971) described this as the concern for sincerity preoccupation. Foucault (1979) argued that the modern state exploited this conception of the self in order to justify its new, restrictive powers (see also Sass, 1987). By the triumph of the Victorian bourgeoisie, the unknown was understood to be unequivocally interior (see also Brandell, 1979; Taylor, 1988) and potentially dangerous. Freud (1953, 1961) postulated a self with an interiorized unconscious that contained primitive drives — sex and aggression — that had to be restricted in order for normative bourgeois society to function. Early psychoanalysis reflected these trends, describing and further constructing the modern self.

Some authors, such as Drinka (1984) and Van den Berg (1961), have suggested that as a consequence of the attempts to control "dangerous" impulses, new mental problems developed in the middle and upper classes, most notably hysteria and neurasthenia. Many other writers (e.g., Bernheimer & Kahane, 1985) have also suggested that the particular Victorian construction of gender and identity, especially the conflict between the growing ethic of modernity and the restrictiveness of women's roles was prescriptively linked to the outbreak of hysteria. Susman (1973) and Lears (1983) also argued that in the United States the strain of acting in a proper bourgeois manner took a toll on spontaneity and expressiveness. What Lears (1983) referred to as the therapeutic ethos came into being in order to alleviate derealization and reintegrate selfhood in the upper classes (pp. 11–17). New business roles developed, such as the preacher-therapist who attempted to cure these new diseases by using the ideology that Meyer (1980) called positive thinking. The advertising industry, which Lears thought was another manifestation of "the therapeutic," attempted to cure by implying that products would magically "transform" the customer's life. In order to do that, ads became progressively less informative and more evocative, associating the product with happy, clean, vigorous models (Lears 1981, pp. 4–58, 300–312; 1983, p. 19).

The early 20th century American self

During the last 90 years, psychological discourse and practice in relation to the middle-class self have changed from a focus on the Victorian, sexually restricted self to the post-World War II empty and fragmented self. The seeds of this change slowly began developing in the United States in the early decades of the 20th century. For instance, the tactics, products, and successes of therapeutic businesses such as the advertising and self-improvement industries changed from a preoccupation with restriction to an inclination for indulgence.

Susman (1973, pp. 271–285) has demonstrated how especially in America, the quest for developing a secular personality came to take precedence over building religious character. Unlike character, which is centered on personal moral integrity, advice manuals of the time taught that personality was synonymous with becoming liked by others. The self was conceived of as capable of personal change; impressing others and gaining their approval became an important aim in life, far outstripping the value of doing the morally correct act, which was dictated by one's character. Riesman, Glazer, and Denny (1953) and Fromm (1955) have also described the inner-directed, self-reliant rugged individualist who began to give way to the outer-directed, socially skilled salesperson type of individual.

After the turn of the century, popularized forms of psychology and religion began to offer advice on how to impress others, become popular, and achieve monetary success and peace of mind. Advertising began developing a highly effective strategy: By identifying the product with an "imaginary state of being" (Lears, 1983, p. 19), the ads sought to allay the customer's personal fears and feelings of inadequacy. "By the 1920s," Marchand (1985) explained, "advertisers had come to recognize a public demand for broad guidance ... about taste, social correctness, and psychological satisfaction. ... Advertising men had now become broader social therapists who offered ... balms for the discontents of modernity" (pp. 347, 360).

In the 1920s and 1930s, psychology began to forge an alliance with business management that appeared to aid psychology's emergence as an independent social science discipline. As Brammel and Friend (1981) and Gillespie (1988) have suggested, the famous Hawthorne experiments (Mayo, 1933; Whitehead, 1938) on worker productivity led the way for an alliance that has not always been as scientifically objective as historians depicted. Asch (1983) and Scheibe (1988) have intimated that this alliance has led to laboratory psychology's quick rise to power in American academia. As big business became increasingly interested in using psychology to boost profits, maximize worker productivity, and influence consumers, new subfields of academic psychology emerged. Applied psychology was used in advertising, marketing, and personnel work.

The trend toward the waning of Victorian values, which began and increased in the first three decades of the century, appeared to have slowed somewhat during the economic depression of the 1930s and World War II. The concrete economic problems of unemployment and hunger took precedence over the cynical and reckless self-absorption of the 1920s. Then, World War II effectively ended the Depression and provided an inescapable sense of realness. For a moment the ennui of the upper classes, which the therapeutic ethos had tried to cure, receded.

Slowly, the fortunes of war began to change as the managers of big business and government learned how to develop and focus America's industrial power for the war effort. There began to emerge in the national consciousness a sense of the power and affluence that the United States would generate in the unknown postwar future (Goldman, 1960). A new era was about to dawn.

The post-World War II era and its economy

In the decades immediately following World War II, the United States developed an economy that depended on the continual production and consumption of nonessential and quickly obsolete products, celebrities, and experiences (Lowe, 1988). A new era with a new self was beginning to emerge. Although the roots of this new world reach back into the earlier decades of the 20th century, its distinctive character became fully formed in the decades following the war (Goldman, 1960; Zinn, 1973).

Authors such as Blum et al. (1973) have described an America that became highly urbanized and industrialized. In 1940 the urban population comprised 77% of the whole; by 1970 it comprised 95% (Blum et al., 1973, pp. 441, 808). In the postwar era writers such as Fromm (1955) and Lasch (1984, 1978) have described a world in which flash is valued over substance, opportunism over loyalty, selling ability over integrity, and mobility over stability. The car transformed urban living, and postwar industrialization brought with it new business capacities and new technologies. The movie and music businesses became dominant, producing a new kind of star, not a hero, but a celebrity (Susman, 1973, pp. 282–284).

More and more the focus has come to rest on the individual (Bellah, Madsen, Sullivan, Swidler, & Tipton, 1985; Levin, 1987b; Zaretsky, 1976). People are living ever more secluded and secular lives, forsaking even the shrinking nuclear family. The percentage of American households of seven or more persons declined from 35.9% in 1790, to 20.4% in 1900 to 5.8% in 1950. At the same time, households with only one person rose from 3.7% in 1790 to 9.3% in 1950 — and to 18.5% in 1973. Households with two persons rose from 7.8% in 1790 to 28.1% in 1950 (Kobrin, 1978, p. 71). Coincident with the decline of the large, extended family unit, the individual self came to be seen as the ultimate locus of salvation: the evolving, constantly changing self, on a never-ending search for self-actualization and "growth" (Lifton, 1968). Personal fulfillment is seen to reside within the purview of the individual, who is supposed to be self-sufficient and self satisfied (Sampson, 1977, 1985). For this self there are supposed to be no limits to achievement and enjoyment. Middle-class Caucasians born in the baby boom era directly following World War II were told that they were the privileged generation of the most privileged and powerful country in the world (Marin, 1979).

For the United States, one of the tasks of the 1950s was to convert its powerful, international war machine into a viable, international peacetime economy. This was not an easy task, and at times the country floundered in recessions (Goldman, 1960). Eventually it found a way into postwar prosperity through the creation and use of universal, easy credit (see Friedman, 1988; Malabre, 1987). Credit made the new economy go: personal credit, business credit, and government credit. But credit for what?

The increasingly powerful print and electronic media unleashed a flood of opinions about how post-World War II families should spend their money. Countless ads, radio shows, and TV situation comedies portrayed a nation of postwar families that needed new homes. Indeed, large suburban housing developments began transforming the countryside. Advertisements portrayed a nation of new families that needed modern, electronic "conveniences" in order to stay scientific and modern (see the popular comic strip Gasoline Alley in 1949 for a good example of these themes; e.g., the *Los Angeles Times,* particularly February 27, 1949; also January 2, 1949, and January 6, 1949). New appliances appeared on the market and transformed household chores. Because the homes and products were so expensive, young middle-class families could not save enough cash to purchase them. Thus, credit became indispensable. The percentage of after-tax income that Americans have saved has decreased from a high of 25.5% in 1944 to less than 2% by 1986 (Malabre, 1987, pp. 4, 21). In contrast, the Japanese rate is currently at 30% of after-tax income. During that same span of time, the volume of consumer installment loans rose from 5% of personal income in 1949, to 15% in 1979, to a record 20% by 1987 (Malabre, 1987, p. 27).

The post-World War II era and the empty self

I believe that after the war the configuration of the empty self coalesced and finally became predominant as a consequence of the loss of community and in order to match the needs of the new economy. Without this particular self, America's consumer-based economy (and its charismatically oriented political process) would be inconceivable. New discourses and practices such as the advertising industry and the field of psychology were modified in order to respond to and further develop the new configuration of self (Ewen, 1989; Fox & Lears, 1983). Practitioners in both fields are placed in the position of being responsible for curing the empty self without being allowed to address the historical causes of the emptiness through structural societal changes.

Authors such as Gendlin (1987), Lasch (1978), Lears (1983), Lifton (1968), Rieff (1966), Susman (1973), and Taylor (1988) have observed that Americans in the post-World War II era came to need self-improvement in a form and to a degree unknown before. As the individual's growth, enjoyment, and fulfillment became the single most valued aspect of life (Baumeister, 1987), several industries grew up to minister to this newly created need. The cosmetics industry, the diet business, the electronic entertainment industry, preventive medical care, and the self-improvement industry (containing mainstream psychology, pop psychology, and pop religion) all came into prominence. The technological advances in these fields have been astronomical, as has their increasing power to influence and control the mainstream of American life (Lasch, 1978; Lears, 1983).

But how does this new self-improvement industry work? What makes this network possible? Why do Americans "need" these items and experiences now when they never did before? Again, I am speculating that it is the formation of the empty self that has made this situation possible; a sense of meaninglessness and absence feeds these businesses. The Western world and America in particular constructed a new type of bounded self that was the perfect complement to the postwar economy built on a system of universal, worldwide credit. Credit is only necessary when the individual's wish to buy outstrips his or her capital. Individuals do not wish to buy if they do not perceive a need for a product. But with an empty self people *always* need.

Inner emptiness may be expressed in many ways, such as low self-esteem (the absence of a sense of personal worth), values confusion (the absence of a sense of personal convictions), eating disorders (the compulsion to fill the emptiness with food, or to embody the emptiness by refusing food), drug abuse (the compulsion to fill the emptiness with chemically induced emotional experiences), and chronic consumerism (the compulsion to fill the emptiness with consumer items and the experience of "receiving" something from the world). It may also take the form of an absence of personal meaning. This can manifest as a hunger for spiritual guidance, which sometimes takes the form of a wish to be filled up by the spirit of God, by religious "truth," or the power and personality of a leader or guru (Cushman, 1984). For instance, one of the most au courant of New Age therapies is channeling, an experience in which an individual is said to be entered by the soul or spirit of another "entity," usually thought to be a god, who then speaks "important truths." The wish to be spiritually filled up and guided can make the individual vulnerable to the deceptive practices of restrictive religious cults (Cushman, 1986), charismatic political leaders (Kohut, 1977; Strozier, 1978), unethical psychotherapists (West & Singer, 1980), or even highly authoritarian and controlling romantic partners (Boulette & Anderson, 1986).

Psychoanalytic theory and the empty self

The empty self has become such a prevalent aspect of our culture that much contemporary psychotherapeutic theory is devoted to its treatment. Levin (1987c) and Lasch (1978) among others have suggested that disorders of the self (i.e., narcissistic and borderline personality disorders) are one of the more popular diagnoses of our time Heinz Kohut (1971, 1977, 1984) developed an entire theory of psychotherapy based on the empty, fragmented self. His theory was an attempt to explain how the self is developed in the individual and how to treat it in order to alleviate or lessen the effects of emptiness and fragmentation. In a crucial aspect of psychological development in Kohut's self psychology, the parent is psychologically "taken in" by the child and used to develop a self. He used the term *selfobject* to describe the undifferentiated nature of the parent-child relationship. In analysis it is the therapist, functioning as a selfobject, who initially fills the emptiness. Later in the treatment, the process Kohut (1977) called transmuting internalizations is said to fill the emptiness by building the self of the patient.

The other major psychodynamic theory that has recently come to prominence is object relations theory (Kernberg, 1975; Masterson, 1981). In general, object relations theory posits the prominent self of our era, the bounded, masterful, individuated self, as has Kohut. But for object relations theorists what fills the emptiness of the self is not the selfobject experience but rather a whole cast of psychological introjects: representations of others (their thoughts, feelings, and needs) and representations of the thoughts, feelings, and needs of one's self at various stages of development (Ogden, 1986). The representations interact with one another and with the external world, creating various dramas. What is important to note for the purposes of this article is that for object relations theorists the interior of the self is also an emptiness. It is a space partially filled by the stable self-representation (the "true self") and by external "part-objects" brought into the empty self through the psychological mechanism of introjection.

Kohut's method of treatment in particular can be interpreted as an attempt to undo the historical circumstances of our current isolation, to create a different context in which the growing self in the adult patient has a more nurturing environment. Kohut's work implies that our era needs this kind of therapy because children do not get enough empathic attention in the postwar world. Why is it that we currently need this particular kind of parenting, one that has previously been rare or perhaps nonexistent in Western history (Kessen, 1979, p. 815)? In this less communal and certain world, perhaps significantly more empathy and accurate reflecting is needed from parents because more traditional sources of guidance have been lost.

The construction of the empty self is, in fact, a product of a central cultural paradox (Sampson, 1985). The self of our time is expected to function in a highly autonomous, isolated way. To accomplish this it is thought that the individual must develop an ability to be self-soothing, self-loving, and self-sufficient (Fromm, 1955; Sampson, 1985). And yet in order to develop this type of self, many psychologists argue that one must have a nurturing early environment that provides a great deal of empathy, attention, and mirroring (Horner, 1984; Masterson, 1981; Stern, 1985). Who is to provide this environment? If adults are self-serving, highly ambitious, heavily bounded individuals, why would they choose to undergo the self-sacrifice and suffering necessary to be nurturing parents? Even with the best of intentions, empathic parenting is difficult to accomplish because many of the requisite traits have been constructed out of the self. According to Miller (1981), one possible result of this historical situation could be a group of parents inadequate to such a demanding role and, thus, a generation of offspring who have been narcissistically wounded.

Furthermore, this situation creates a significant gap between society's expectations of high self-sufficiency and the lessened ability of narcissistically wounded individuals to achieve it. The awareness that they are falling short of society's central expectation is a further wound to the self-esteem of young adults, increasing the dichotomy between their outward presentation of self and their internal sense of self. This dichotomy exacerbates a characteristic symptom of narcissism, g sense of personal fraudulence described as a "false self" that masks the frightened, hidden "true self" (Masterson, 1981; Miller, 1981; Winnicott, 1965). Thus, even the current dichotomy between expectation and experience appears to be used in service of constructing the empty self.

Although some of these observations are informed by Kohut's theory, I do not want to leave the impression that self psychology is somehow immune from the critique developed in this article. I use Kohut's theory to interpret the current era because, like any popular psychological theory, it is an artifact that both illuminates and distorts the social world it purports to describe (Cushman, 1987). The criticisms that follow, especially the notion that psychological discourse not only describes but also actively prescribes the empty self, apply to Kohut as well as other contemporary theorists (Ehrlich, 1985; Sass, 1988b).

More specifically, Kohut has seemed particularly vulnerable to charges that his belief in the natural, unfolding program of each unique self valorizes the individual's inner world at the expense of the external, material world. Sass (1988b) has explained how Kohut's thought is part of the Counter-Enlightenment and Romantic traditions of the expressivist form of modern humanism (p. 579). This branch of humanist thought has perpetuated what Taylor (1988) called a radical reflexivity. The danger, according to Sass (1988b, p. 589), is that such an extreme preoccupation with the inner self causes the social world to be devalued or ignored except to the degree that it mirrors and thus becomes appropriated by the self. The social thus loses its impact as a material force, and social problems lose their relation to political action. Hence one sees the bumper sticker "Visualize World Peace."

Advertising and the life-style solution

In the second half of the century the empty self has made it much easier for advertising to exert influence and control. Marchand (1985) demonstrated how advertising accepted a therapeutic role by stepping into "a vacuum of advice ... created by new social and technological complexities" (p. xxi). Writers such as Lears (1983) and Modleski (1986) have argued that ads sell by convincing the public that a certain product is indispensable to their well-being or by implicitly addressing or exacerbating a personal fear in the customer that could be reassured or soothed by purchasing the product.

Because emptiness is, in part, an absence of communal forms and beliefs, individuals in the postwar era are thus particularly vulnerable to influence from cultural forms such as advertising that emanate authority and certainty. A good case could be made that many current advertisements (e.g., regarding body odor, hair color, or life insurance) are less a type of benign guidance and more a kind of coercive attack. Ads seem to criticize and condemn the average consumer while glorifying the model, extolling a standard of beauty and mastery impossible to achieve.

24 Why the self is empty

Advertising certainly does not address itself to the political causes of the customer's problems (e.g., alienation and the loss of community); therefore, it must turn to the refuge of what I will refer to as the lifestyle solution. Unable to effect lasting change by developing political solutions to the problems of modern life, advertising must offer an illusory cure. One prominent type of ad offers the fantasy that the consumer's life can be transformed into a glorious, problem-free life — the "life" of the model who is featured in the ad. This can be accomplished by purchasing and "ingesting" the product, which will magically transfer the life-style of the model to the consumer. By surrounding themselves with the accoutrements of the model, by ingesting the proper liquid while wearing the proper clothing, all the while exhibiting the proper shape, customers seek to "become" the model. The customer's problems will simply disappear when the magical transfer takes place.

The paraphernalia of a commercial model are, of course, a poor substitute for the tools traditional cultures use for curing the sick. Geertz (1973) has described these tools as the web of meaning, the array of stories, songs, beliefs, rituals, ceremonial objects, costumes. and potions that heal by teaching and readjusting the society's cultural frame of reference. Because advertising cannot cure by invoking a workable web of meaning, I believe ads substitute the concept of life-style: the experiences and material possessions that are identified with the celebrity or model. It is a kind of mimicry of traditional culture for a society that has lost its own. In this way life-style is used as a pseudoculture — a pseudoculture that promises an instant, illusory cure, a "transformation."

This hope of substituting one identity, one life, for another is used as the sales strategy for many products today. Ewen (1989) has referred to this as "the consumable life, the buyable fantasy" (p. 85). Examples are numerous: the yuppie Lowenbrau models who lift their bottles and say "Here's to good friends"; the working-class Old Milwaukee drinkers who maintain "It doesn't get any better than this"; the upper-class version that portrays a yachting/equestrian "Cadillac style," or the ad that asks "What kind of a man reads Playboy?"; cigarette ads that feature the Marlboro Man, Camel's man-beast who is a "smooth character," or the Virginia Slims's model who has "come a long way, baby"; and of course toothpaste and deodorant ads that transform models with instant sex appeal and popularity. These customers buy life-style in a vain attempt to transform their lives because their lives are unsatisfying and (without massive societal change) ultimately unfixable. But without the option of providing a viable solution through the vehicle of structural change, advertising can only offer the illusory exchange of one life for another.

This is a powerful illusion. And what fuels the illusion, what impels the individual into this illusion, is the desperation to fill up the empty self. Currently, the self is not only suffering from feeling unreal, and thereby somewhat passively hoping for a cure, as it did at the turn of the century. It is also aggressively, sometimes desperately, acquisitive. It must consume in order to be soothed and integrated; it must "take in" and merge with a selfobject celebrity, an ideology, or a drug, or it will be in danger of fragmenting into feelings of worthlessness and confusion.

This is why the life-style solution has become such an efficient form of advertising, particularly in political campaigns. Kohutian social critics would argue that the life-styles portrayed in advertising have become larger-than-life, glamorous selfobjects. For those despairing and hopeless about their real lives, the wish to consume and take in a new identity, a new life, can be very compelling. By using the right toothpaste or identifying with the most reassuring or powerful politician, consumers are thus covertly promised a magically different, transformed self.

The late 20th century has thus become an advertising executive's dream come true: Life-style has become a product that sells itself, and the individual has become a consumer who seeks, desperately, to buy.

Psychotherapy and the life-style solution

Researchers such as Lears (1983), Wilson (1983), and Susman (1973) have demonstrated that the same historical context that gave rise to the advertising industry in the United States has also shaped the field of psychology. By using a mode of analysis similar to that which was applied to advertising, psychotherapy appears to be less a "scientific" cure and more a covert vehicle for cultural guidance and transmission. Individuals in the postmodern era, without a cohesive community, are struggling to find sense and meaning in a confusing world. There is little to guide them, and they stumble and feel despair. Failure is manifested in the particular mental problems of modern life, catalogued by the current psychiatric nosology (i.e., the Diagnostic and Statistical Manual of Mental Disorders-Revised [DSM-III-R]; American Psychiatric Association, 1987).

Psychology is the social science most responsible for treating these illnesses. But the argument presented earlier has shown that psychology is also a product of the larger historical context that causes these illnesses. Psychology cannot fully alleviate the symptoms unless it can treat the cause (i.e., the political and historical constellations that shape the era), and yet that cause is the exact subject psychology is not allowed to address. Psychological ideology ignores it, and job descriptions exclude it. Psychology, therefore, is caught in a historical bind from which it cannot escape, a bind similar to that in which advertising is caught. I believe the field's current solution to this bind is a creative adaptation of the same life-style solution advertising uses. Psychotherapy practices have subtly attuned to the empty self of our era by unconsciously allowing or encouraging patients to incorporate the personal characteristics of the therapist, including his or her mannerisms, behavioral style, and personal values. Advertising uses the life-style solution in order to sell products; psychotherapy uses it in order to initiate patients into alternative cultural practices.

Because psychotherapy grew out of the late 19th century scientific tradition, its ideology is built on the foundation of a mechanistic, rationalistic biological model (Taylor, 1988) and the bounded, masterful Victorian self (Dreyfus & Wakefield, 1988; Rieff, 1966). Current psychoanalytic practice maintains this tradition through ideas such as the abstinence principle, the concept of the economy of the libido, the self-object split, and the overriding importance of tracing the "genetic" (i.e., original internal) causes of a symptom. Other psychotherapeutic modalities, even those far removed from psychoanalytic theory such as Primal Therapy, Transactional Analysis, and Bioenergetics, also share some of these tenets.

Although much psychotherapy discourse advocates the objective, scientistic uncovering and "working through" of genetic roots and traumatic causation within the self-contained individual, I believe a strong case can be made that psychotherapy practices necessarily deviate from that theoretical stance (Dreyfus & Wakefield, 1988, p. 274; Kohut, 1977, pp. 251–261; 1984, pp. 106–110; Singer, 1981). Let me suggest that, without the therapist being aware of it, practice deviates from normative discourse by allowing the therapist to function as a model for the patient, by providing corrective emotional experiences of care, respect, and understanding, and by allowing the patient to "take in" the therapist's ideas, values, and personal style. Some theories do explicitly refer to this as the patients modeling themselves after, temporarily merging with, or introjecting the therapist. The objective uncovering of genetic causation and the goal of individuation are still the basic, consciously enacted activities of much current psychotherapy. But an alternative interpretation of what happens behind the behavioral surface is that not only does the uncovering or understanding of trauma and distortion occur, but that functions such as modeling, guiding, and relatedness also occur and are indeed primary factors in the healing aspects of the modern therapeutic hour.

In 1966 Rieff suggested that historically there are commitment therapies that cure by returning individuals to their community's sacred forms, and analytic therapies that cure by a detached, intellectual analysis of individuals who are bereft of a viable communal tradition. I believe that during the last 25 years the two therapeutic strategies somehow have been combined. It is a particular combination of analytic and commitment therapy to which I am referring as the life-style solution. Most psychotherapies claim they are healing by applying a detached, scientistic analysis that has little to do with the transmission of cultural guidance. But, by unconsciously offering the personal values and behavior of the therapist as a model to be imitated by and incorporated into the empty self of the patient, psychotherapy actually functions as a substitute for more explicit, institutional forms of cultural transmission that have been lost or devalued.

Consequently, the most important function of current psychotherapy is that it offers an alternative attitude toward life (one of confidence and hope), alternative cultural values (respect for an individual's feelings and for the importance of understanding, empathy, and psychological insight), and alternative social practices (listening to others, assertiveness, and honesty). Sometimes this emphasis on guiding and modeling is overt (e.g., health psychology emphasizes proper exercise and nutrition, and many cognitive and family therapists make straightforward behavioral assignments). Sometimes the emphasis is covert (e.g., when and with what level of emotion a Rogerian therapist ventures a reflective formulation or a psychoanalyst delivers a carefully thought-out interpretation).

The central point of my argument is that in a world sorely lacking in community and tradition, the most effective healing response would be to address those absences through structural societal change by reshaping political relationships and cultural forms and re-establishing the importance of their transmission. Because that avenue is closed for normative psychology, psychologists can only provide guidance and caring within the therapist-patient dyad. I think that this is done by employing the life-style solution. Disorders of the self are thought by theorists such as Atwood and Stolorow (1984), Horner (1984), Kohut (1977), and Miller (1981) to be caused by an interpersonal environment that is disrespectful, psychologically avoidant, unempathic, and punitive. The modeling of respect, psychological courage, and empathy therefore helps patients imitate, practice, and finally internalize the qualities they most need. Kohut has written extensively that disorders of the self produce a powerful wish to psychologically merge with admired figures, to take them into the empty self; if this is accurate, then this narcissistic wish greatly enhances the teaching-incorporating aspects characteristic of the life-style solution. So the fit is a good one.

Abuse in psychotherapy

However, there are some serious, perhaps dangerous, problems inherent in this situation. As discussed earlier, most psychotherapy discourse uses the dominant ideology of its era (the value of individualism and the transhistorical nature of the bounded, masterful, fully individuated self) even though the patient's suffering is caused in large part by that particular formulation and by the political and economic arrangements that construct it.

If this analysis is correct, therapy is helpful when it deviates from the dominant discourse of the past and adheres to the life-style solution — not because of the normative, scientistic psychotherapy discourse but in spite of it. The life-style solution carries out a small but nevertheless subversive activity (i.e., compensating for cultural deficiencies through teaching and modeling); however, psychology undermines its helpful practices when it wraps itself in the ideology of the status quo. Not only is this actually less than honest, but it undermines the most therapeutic aspects of its practice because it does not acknowledge that they exist. Although therapy succeeds because it compensates for cultural absences in our society, it usually does not admit to doing so. In fact, by outwardly adhering to the practices of an objective technology and the ideology of self-contained individualism and the bounded self, writers such as Prilleltensky (1989), Sampson (1988), Sass (1988a), and Taylor (1988) have argued that it perpetuates the social problems that caused the patient's wounds in the first place. This paradoxical situation undermines the helpful work of the therapy because it is unempathic (the therapist is choosing adherence to an ideology over the needs of the patient), harmful (it indicts on patients the discourse by which they have previously been harmed), and ultimately counterproductive for our society as a whole (it reproduces the present power hierarchy and economic structure that have caused our present suffering).

Second, the difference between discourse and practice in the life-style solution is dangerous to the patient because it increases the possibility of psychological, sexual, and political abuse within the therapeutic setting and ultimately in society as a whole. The wish to over idealize and psychologically merge with an admired figure or the experience of grandiosity and the pull to exhibit before and please the admired figure are exceedingly powerful psychological motives (Bollas, 1987; Kohut, 1977). These impulses are regressive and destructive of critical thought. Under the best of circumstances in the therapy setting these urges can be discussed, understood, and ultimately used during transference analysis in service of the healing process. However, in the hands of poorly trained or power hungry therapists, these urges can be encouraged, and the power they give the therapist can be misused.

In the post-World War II era, the potential for the misuse and abuse of the selfobject-patient merger is high. Patients with disorders of the self are empty and hungry for idealizing and merging and thus are in a highly suggestible and vulnerable state. Their wish to be guided and taken care of is one that can easily be exploited. This is particularly true when therapists have not been trained to recognize and understand narcissistic transference reactions, when their own needs for understanding and appreciation are so great that they try to elicit them from their patients, or when they themselves have been so wounded that they want to dominate and abuse their patients (Kohut, 1976).

When these conditions are present, I believe the life-style solution becomes a tool of abuse. Therapists who are hungry for adulation and power can easily create overidealization and submission (whether it be psychological, sexual, or political) within the therapeutic setting. There are certain aspects of theory and practice that increase the likelihood of an abusive dynamic: extreme forms of the decontextualization of the individual (Sampson, 1981), the devaluation of and disrespect for the patient (Kohut, 1984; Wile, 1984), a belief in a universally "true" theory and a "perfect" technology (Riebel, 1979), and the encouragement of overidealization and compliance by misusing the transference (Cushman, 1984). These techniques can be used to create or exacerbate a patient's narcissistic crisis in order to use it in service of dominance and exploitation. The occurrence of sexual exploitation of the patient within the therapy setting (Bouhoutsos, Holroyd, Lerman, Forer, & Greenberg, 1983; Holroyd & Brodsky, 1977) could be explained through this dynamic. The occurrence of emotional and financial exploitation and psychiatric damage within religious cults (Clark, 1983; Cushman, 1986; Singer, 1979) and mass marathon psychology trainings (Cushman, 1989; Haaken & Adams, 1983; Hochman, 1984; Ofshe & Singer, 1986; Temerlin & Temerlin, 1982) could be similarly understood.

Patients who experience an exploitive life-style therapy or cult training feel as though they have been "transformed." Rather than seeing themselves as historical beings, embedded within the larger communal matrix and their own personal history, they usually devalue their communal ties and believe themselves to be "emancipated" from their earlier lives and former beliefs. This reproduces the isolation and moral confusion that are among the greatest problems of our time. These ills must then, somehow, be treated. By substituting an artificially loving community and an authoritarian, self-sealing doctrine, restrictive groups and exploitive therapists soothe the problems they have created or exacerbated. Thus, exploitive forms of the life-style solution that promise personal transformation should be recognized for what they are: iatrogenic illnesses.

Fortunately, the vast majority of therapists do not misuse the therapeutic setting in this way. But any amount of abuse is too much abuse. The point is that because the life-style solution is a covert and culturally syntonic solution, the problems inherent in it, especially the opportunity for exploiting the patient, remain too often hidden, unacknowledged, and thus unaddressed. Because we cannot straightforwardly talk about the life-style solution, we cannot completely guard against its misuse.

The emphasis placed on drawing out and analyzing the transference in psychoanalysis and psychodynamic psychotherapy can be interpreted as a way of addressing some of the hidden aspects of the life-style solution, thus making them less dangerous and more easily guarded against. The patient's secret wishes for the therapist as parent, romantic partner, or mentor can be analyzed and deconstructed in order to more easily uncover idealizing tendencies and the wish to be taken care of, loved, and guided. In this way well-conducted psychodynamic therapies do in part guard against exploitive forms of the life-style solution.

I am not arguing that an ethical use of the life-style solution is wrong. I am arguing that it exists and that it exists precisely because, given our historical moment, it provides some aid and comfort to a beleaguered people in one of the few ways the present power structure tolerates. However, even in its more helpful forms, the life-style solution does not solve the larger historical bind in which psychology is caught. In fact, by ignoring the bind and outwardly accepting society's expectations and psychology's normative discourse, the life-style solution cooperates in further constructing the empty self, which ultimately exacerbates the current broken historical moment and reproduces the current political and economic arrangements of power and privilege.

Where does this leave us? The task of this article was not to devise the "correct" therapeutic technology but to do what Furumoto (1988) has suggested, to interpret the collective mentality of our era. Perhaps other studies will be able to devise more historically situated and explicit therapeutic solutions to the problems of our time. Heidegger's concept of the clearing offers intriguing possibilities. Boss (1963/1982), and more recently Chessick (1986), Dreyfus and Wakefield (1988), and Sass (1988a) have made promising steps in that direction.

Conclusion

We are witnessing an important shift in the content of the bounded, masterful self of the 20th century, a shift from a sexually restricted to an empty self. At the same time there has been a shift from a savings to a debtor economy. The dual shift has not been a coincidence. It is a consequence of how the modern nation state must currently regulate its economy and control its populace: not through direct physical coercion, but rather through the construction of the empty self and the manipulation of its needs to consume and ingest. Three beneficiaries of this narcissistic dynamic are the modern state, the advertising industry, and the self-improvement industries (including psychotherapy). All three perpetuate the ideology of the empty self, and all three profit from it.

One of the disquieting results of this constructionist perspective is the realization that our current era has constructed a self that is, fundamentally, a disappointment to itself (Sampson, 1983). We could also say that about our nation as a whole. The dynamic of our society revolves around a fundamental paradox. We are a nation whose ethical idealism has often informed its actions, and yet we are a nation that struggles with conflicting and mutually exclusive ideals. From slavery to manifest destiny to Vietnam to the struggle over reproductive rights, we are often a nation at odds with itself. Now a new paradox has arisen: one of the wealthiest nations on earth is also one of the emptiest.

Let us hope, as Sampson (1988) has, that in the years ahead we can construct a society that is less in need of suffering and a self that is less a sacrifice to the nihilistic economics and politics of our time. But such changes would require developing a distance from the current normative intellectual discourse regarding individualism, the self, and the good life. Psychology has been one of the foremost contributors to that discourse. The field's historical insistence on a scientistic epistemology has obscured the political nature of its discourse. Psychology has continued to decontextualize the individual, examining the patient as an isolated entity without considering the larger sociohistorical causes of personal distress. As a result, cultural absences and political wounds are "interiorized" (i.e., located in the self) and thus "blamed" on the victim (Ryan, 1971). While psychologists have been treating the empty self, they have, of necessity, also been constructing it, profiting from it, and not challenging the social arrangements that created it.

Could psychology now become a helpful force, assisting in the development of a perspective on the masterful, bounded self in opposition to the current system? Given the history of the Western self, and the role of psychology within that history, it is doubtful. In order to accomplish this shift, psychology would have to acknowledge the historically and culturally situated nature of its discourse and the political and economic consequences of its practices. We psychologists would have to rethink the entire way in which, to use Hales's (1986) phrase, we conduct "the business of psychology." Rethinking would necessitate a profound critique of our field and our society, and most of us do not have the training to attempt such a task. But the integrity of our profession, and possibly the viability of our society, may depend on our success or failure.

Chapter 3

What we hold in our hand

(1995 APA Annual Convention)

Historical introduction

"What We Hold in Our Hand" was written as a contribution to a two-hour symposium titled "Struggling With Relativism and Politics: Constructionist, Hermeneutic, and Feminist Approaches" for the 1995 APA convention, New York City. For this symposium we[1] invited Ken Gergen, who during this time was the most famous postmodernist at APA, and Elizabeth Fox-Genovese, a well-known feminist, to appear with us. As expected, a big crowd showed up, including seven of my students who traveled from the San Francisco Bay Area to witness the festivities. I was scheduled to present last; my task was to describe culture theory and hermeneutics in such a way as to inspire audience participation especially about the building of new hermeneutic responses to our current society-wide problems. But the other presenters took longer than their allotted time, and when I got to the podium there were only two minutes left. There was no time for my presentation and time for only one question from the audience. Afterwards, many who attended voiced complaints about the lack of time for audience participation, including my students, who were disappointed because they had been led to believe (by me) that the panel would demonstrate hermeneutic dialogue. But they complained that type of dialogic process was absent. I had to agree.

All this is to say that finally, after more than twenty years, this paper finally gets to see the light of day! By the way, that year the annual APA hermeneutic party the three of us always threw was a smashing success, a real brawl. In fact it was without doubt our proudest moment yet. We always held our hermeneutic parties in a hotel room, and that year our revelers were shoulder to shoulder and way out into the hall. The historians, feminists, and philosophical psychologists mixed, talked, and shared hopes of working together in the future. Blaine and Ken got into a long argument

> — about relativism — and others chimed in. But here's what was really great: the hotel finally had to call the cops on us! We were ordered to lower the volume on our music, laughter (which was uproarious), and arguments (which were many), all of which I think expressed our delight in finding and enjoying one another amid the over-serious professionalism of our usual academic world. Sadly, we were forced to bend to the pressure and quiet down a bit. But imagine that: a bunch of academic psychology professors had too much fun and were far too loud on a Saturday night in a big hotel in the theater district of NYC. We were so proud.

The Amish have a saying: "What you hold in your hand, you carry in your heart." This is why they do not allow community members to carry guns or use machinery: they believe that what they use, they will become. This reminds me of Martin Heidegger's and Hans-Georg Gadamer's ideas about "engaged activity." We know things in the world when we engage with them, when we are active in the world, trying to do things, make things, build things. Heidegger's famous example of engaged activity is of a hammer, for good reason: human life is a matter of being thrown into an already constructed world, which we constantly reproduce through the actions of everyday life, according to the rules and moral understandings of that world.

Halachah — Jewish law — says that one should never eat until one has fed the family animals. Why? Because the animals are incapable of getting their own food, and so to eat in front of them would be cruel. The Law is created, it is thought, to help humans live a more humane life, and by so doing to transform the world. What one holds in one's hand, one carries in one's heart.

Halachah says that when hunting for bird eggs, one should first chase away the parent bird, for the same reason that one should never cook a calf in its mother's milk.

Why? Because although sometimes animals must die so that humans can live, it would be intolerably cruel to allow the parents to see their offspring being killed.

The ways we engage in the world, what we do each day with others, what we comply with or resist, the world we help construct, make us who we are.

The word for Jewish law, *Halachah*, comes from the root "to walk." It means "the path;" the path of one's life. The path lays out a proper way to live. There are 248 positive commandments, and 365 negative commandments. The 248 positive commandments, explained the rabbis, correspond to the number of bones and organs in the human body; the 365 negative commandments correspond to the number of tendons and ligaments. As we walk the path of life, the social practices we perform become embodied by us: we become our values. We are what we *do;* what we do comes to constitute us.

However, Gadamer has pointed out that the world each of us are thrown into is not made up of just *one* way of hammering, not just one idea of what a building — or a life — should look like, not just one set of rules about how to conduct oneself while building. If it were, then there would be no change, no arguments, no resistance, no revolution. Each of us lives, Charles Taylor argued, at a point of intersecting moral traditions, traditions that are always contending with one another as new problems appear and choices are made. They are inescapable traditions, they constitute us, and then we have a hand in reshaping ourselves, each day, a thousand times each day, by the words we use, the actions we take, the way we listen or don't listen, the honesty or dishonesty with which we examine our actions, by the opportunities we see or the opportunities that do not appear, the moments we seize or the moments we lose.

Yes, language speaks us; and by being spoken, we develop a voice. Yes, the positions we take are made available to us by the particular configuration of the cultural horizon that brings us to light; but then, *we* have to stand in that place, we look out at other persons in other places, we reach out or hold back, we resist or comply with governmental policies and political regimes. How? By sifting through the traditions that have constituted us, the traditions that frame for us what is right and wrong, good and bad, just and inequitable. We sift through them while standing on them, we speak while being spoken, we see by virtue of the light that they supply.

We stand, Reb Nachman taught us, on a very narrow bridge between two eternities, the past and the future. Our task is to continually reconstruct the bridge we have been given, the one upon which we stand. It is a strange, absurd, noble, crazy condition, our human condition, and we really cannot begin to put into words the beauty, frustration, and majesty of it all. And yet we are called upon to keep living, keep constructing, keep being spoken. We must go on, even though we don't exactly know how to go on. The hammer is in our hands. Where does our hand end and the hammer begin? Are we the same after we have hammered as before? We know the hammer by using it, it appears to us *as* we use it, *we* appear differently to ourselves *as* we use it. We try to learn about others, but in the process the first thing we learn about is *the world* that has constituted *us*. Reaching out to others is the way we learn, first, about ourselves. It is through engaged activity that otherness comes into view, and it is through otherness that *we* come into view. And then, what do we do together, so that through mutual activity, relationships and communities come into view?

What, indeed, *do* we do together? We live out a tradition, and by doing so we influence it. We use one part of a tradition or a neighboring tradition to modify our tradition, shift it slightly, sculpt it a little, without really realizing it. By living and making everyday choices, a life — our life — emerges: and as it lives us, we live in it; we act automatically, we question, we complain, rebel, and comply: we subtly reshape it.

I think this is how therapy works, when it works. Patients and therapists engage in social practices that help them get in contact with and draw from alternative traditions previously unavailable to them. By engaging with one another, in particular ways given them by their traditions, they encounter one another, see themselves from a different perspective, and develop new, slightly shifted ways of being.

But, as psychologists, it is a mistake to limit our social vision to the parental or therapeutic dyad, or even the family. Our definition of our role must not be defined solely by the mainstream understandings of the discipline of psychology. Those understanding influence us mightily, of course. Initially, they set the horizon for us. Traditions, including academic traditions, are very important to us, but they are not sacred. They should be continually questioned, historically situated, politically interpreted, and compared to other traditions. Placing them in their historical context will help us decide whether or not we think they are worthy of our allegiance. We will realize that the mainstream, hypermasculine, scientistic traditions in psychology are not the only traditions in our field. Women psychologists, such as Mary Calkins, who began developing an interest in the self; African American psychologists, such as W.E.B. Dubois, who could see through the racist assumptions of the highly popular eugenics movement; philosophical psychologists such as William James, who noticed the "bloomin', buzzin' confusion" of the world if it would be devoid of culture and history; cultural historians, such as Kurt

Danziger, who could see through the Whiggish, positivist historicism of E.G. Boring and began the reinterpretation of Wilhelm Wundt; lefty psychologists, such as Howard Gadlin and Joel Kovel, who won't let us forget the inequities of class; Ken Gergen, Ed Sampson, Alan Buss, Rachel Hare-Mustin, and Jeanne Marecek, who had the courage to begin writing and talking about social constructionism; Laurel Furumoto and Jill Morawski, whose courageous and intrepid historical research continues to bring creative feminist understandings to light; probably some of you in the audience — all of these people have worked or are working to develop and keep alive alternative traditions and interdisciplinarity in our profession. We can notice these traditions, and let ourselves engage with them.

I don't know what will happen, as more of us do that. One thought I have is that our sense of what constitutes the social realm will grow. And therefore our moral understanding about what is our proper role in our society — the good — will shift along with it. I think we might begin to conceive of our work as community psychology. We might be moved to speak out directly about moral and political issues. If we take seriously the idea that social practices constitute the self, we might turn our attention to the everyday activities that everyday people engage in. How many hours do people in the U.S. watch violent, boring, anti-intellectual, racist and sexist television programing? How much poverty and homelessness do people have to ignore or dismiss as they travel to work each day? How much violence against women do we all avert our eyes from, out of fear, disinterest, or despair? How many times in our day do we feel compelled to overwork, trick, or cheat others because we are terrified by the ultra-competitive, capitalist world we have been thrown into? How often do psychotherapists resort to the slick, ultrasmooth, humanistic-sounding, scientistic, reductionistic, reifying, mechanistic jargon of the brave new world of HMOs, in order to survive another year in private practice?

What kind of impact do these everyday social practices have on us? This is what we hold in our hands, each day. These are the practices that constitute our world, and ultimately our selves. What are we, as psychologists, going to do about it? How are we going to shift traditional understandings about what a psychologist does — about the good — so that we can address these issues in our work?

Of course, if we try to do something about it, we will be faced with some basic hermeneutic dilemmas, which we will be terrified of and feel immediately defeated by. How, we will ask ourselves, can we possibly decide questions of right and wrong, good and bad? And how can we possibly declare ourselves justified in speaking to these issues, and claiming that we have ideas about what to do? And just how do people develop ideas about what to do, anyway? We can remember that the ethic of objectifying the subject and erasing the researcher's values — the Enlightenment-era "view from nowhere" — is itself a moral stand, disguised though it is. Lyotard's deconstructionist admonition, to mistrust all metanarratives, is itself a statement about the good. That is what we do in our work. We are always taking a moral position in our work, whether we recognize it or not.

Perhaps this thought will help us gain some courage for the difficult times ahead. Some will say we should only critique, never construct; as proof, they will point to Heidegger's monstrous, unforgiveable mistake of turning to and never renouncing the Nazis. Will we make mistakes? Of course, we are always making them. It is just that when the physical science model sets the frame, it's easier to cover them up.

The biggest mistake, of course, is that as psychologists we cover up our mistakes by claiming that what we do is objective, politically neutral science. Our everyday social practices as psychologists enable this world to run: we normalize the morally disgusting stratifications of our economic system, the waste and destruction, the despoliation of our environment, and the organized hatreds of "the other" by dismissing them as that which is beyond our influence, and at the same time we medicalize — and thus depoliticize — the unbearable suffering of our people.

What does this gigantic cover up, which is an everyday social practice in our work, do to us and the people we are supposed to be serving? Remember, the everyday rules one follows constitute one's bones, ligaments, and organs. Should we not direct our work to the little moments of everyday life? The ordinary acts of one's life become one's self, and one's self builds one's life path. What one holds in one's hand, one carries in one's heart. What kind of a heart is our profession going to shape for our nation, in the years ahead? The hammer is in your hand.

Note

1 The symposium was designed by Frank Richardson, Blaine Fowers, and me.

Chapter 4

White guilt, political activity, and the analyst

(2000 Psychoanalytic Dialogues, 10, 607–618)

Historical introduction

One interpretation of the late 20th century in the United States is that the country went through a struggle over civil rights and the Vietnam War that had cultural similarities to the Civil War. It was also suggested that the remainder of the century was likewise similar to Reconstruction — or rather to the tokenism and ultimate failure of Reconstruction — which led to the Jim Crow era of brutal repression, sharecropping (a kind of economic slavery), and a new, insidious kind of institutional racism. The foreign policy deceitfulness and domestic political realignments begun in the Nixon presidency and intensified during the Reagan years resembled the broken promises and political realignments from which the country suffered in the post-Civil War decades.

The George H.W. Bush and Bill Clinton presidencies continued the (sometimes) subtle oppression of Black America, the uses of celebrity spectacle, and the inevitable economic boom-and-bust cycles of consumer capitalism. Prominent during the Bush and Clinton presidencies — the eras directly preceding this article — were Bush's shameless use of the racist Willie Horton commercial, Clinton's Work-For-Welfare plan, and his cancelation of crucial banking and investment regulations. The Clinton boom years, fueled by the meteoric rise of the electronic digital industry and the euphoria of quick and prodigious Wall Street wealth created by digital start-up companies, saw the growth of gentrification in the big cities and thus the growing displacement of the working middle classes and the continuing damage done to the urban dispossessed.

But, in general, negative aspects of those years usually appeared below the surface. There were plenty of warnings, of course, if one wanted to notice: the multitude of feature films about financial and political corruption or racial and sexual violence (e.g., *Wall Street* [1987], *Mississippi*

Burning [1988], *Cocktail* [1988], *Glengarry Glen Ross* [1992], *In the Time of Fire* [1993], *Ghosts of Mississippi* [1996], *L.A. Confidential* [1997], *Any Given Sunday* [1999], *Boys Don't Cry* [1999], *Mumford* [1999]), or occasional news events that momentarily highlighted environmental damage, racial conflict, and sexism (e.g., the Rodney King beating, the O.J. Simpson murder trial, Clinton's sexual misconduct and impeachment). And yet, discomfort and suffering about racial, sexual, and financial inequality, let alone political critique and resistance, was often difficult to locate in mainstream America during those years.

In the second half of the 20th century, psychotherapy had become a popular and generally well-respected profession. Although during the late 1980s and throughout the 1990s Managed Care Organizations began vying for control of the processes by which treatment was described, delivered, and paid for, generally psychotherapy in the post-World War II decades was relatively quiet and in control of the practitioner. However, by the early 1990s, psychotherapists had begun to be challenged about race and gender in the therapy hour. What traditionally had been an occasional opportunity for discussing what was distorted or pathological about patients of color was slowly becoming a discussion about the subtle limitations, if not outright prejudices, of white therapists and how their unconscious actions compromised treatment. Multiculturalism was slowly becoming a movement to be taken seriously, both in the academy and in the clinic. Neil Altman (e.g., 1995) was one of the first psychoanalysts to write honestly and without victim-blaming about race and the vicissitudes of racial transference-countertransference dynamics. I thought Altman's article ("Black and White Thinking: A Psychoanalyst Reconsiders Race") was a brave and honest attempt to face racial issues in the therapy hour. My contribution in my commentary, as I saw it, was to identify some of the damage often done through avoidance, denial, and scapegoating, and to bring a more explicit political focus to the clinical conversation.

Thank you, Dr. Altman, for your willingness to discuss the difficult topic of race and ethnicity and to offer his work, and himself, as a subject of study. His article provides an opportunity to explore certain issues that I would like to discuss hermeneutically — that is, historically and politically — and by doing so advance values to which I know both of us subscribe.

Psychologists tend to over-psychologize the origins and effects of racial oppression. Mainstream psychologists usually understand prejudice or racism as a universal occurrence caused by natural processes or inherent structures of the mind activated by a putative universal human tendency to create in-groups and out-groups by generalizing about others and creating stereotypes. In their minds, the social realm enters the picture as only one "causative factor" among many. Although this academic tradition has had a long lineage and has served important functions in the ongoing attempt to secure a place for psychology in 20th-century U.S. society, lately it has been encountering opposition from some multiculturalists and from what is called the linguistic or interpretive turn (see Rabinow and Sullivan, 1987). How this debate plays out in psychoanalysis will constitute an important aspect of the movement's historical legacy. Altman's work is an important contribution to that debate.

The universal-feature argument, the position Allport (1954) popularized, is one much beloved by psychologists of most theoretical stripes, but its accuracy has recently been called into question. As Gaines and Reed (1996) pointed out, W.E.B. DuBois's (1903) position is much preferable to Allport's. Racial oppression, DuBois argued, is a product of social, material arrangements — a matter of history and politics — and therefore is local, not universal; voluntary, not inevitable; and changed primarily through large-scale political activity. The belief that racial oppression is political does not mean that individual struggles don't matter or that psychotherapy can't help in the fight against oppression. It does mean that we should not delude ourselves by thinking that psychotherapy alone is the answer, or that as therapists we have done all we need to do in opposing racism if we have become more sensitized and knowledgeable about the intricacies of race and ethnicity in the transference-countertransference interactions of our clinical work.

There are strikingly few examples of over-psychologizing in Altman's paper. However, I address one point in order to raise a larger issue that will frame my commentary. With regard to the case of Mr. A, Altman uses a postmodern argument about linguistic dichotomies to suggest that psychoanalytic theory reflects an Enlightenment-era idea — the binary rational-irrational — that has played a central part in the oppression of people of color. Now, the belief that language has a profound, in fact constitutive, effect on a configuration of the self (i.e., on local understandings about what it means to be human) is extremely important. The ideal of Western rationality has justified many a racist act and framed many a racist policy. But by emphasizing linguistic dichotomy as the main problem (the initial, causative factor in Western racism), some postmodernists, although arguing that racism is not a universal, essential feature of all humans, imply that racism is caused by a universal, essential feature — the tendency to create linguistic binaries. This strategy seems to run the risk of carrying on the very process it claims to be discrediting.

In other words, if racism is thought to be a naturally occurring event, caused by either the natural workings of the mind (e.g., the urge to generalize and stereotype), the natural structures of language (e.g., the tendency to think in terms of dichotomous forms), or the natural effect of inherent psychological processes and structures (e.g., splitting, projection, the bad breast), then racism will be thought of as an inevitability among all humans. When theorists believe that they have solved the mystery of racism's source — by locating it in the natural world — they run the risk of implying that nothing can be done to eradicate it. It is obvious that postmodern writers do not want to aid racism, but I am concerned about how some writers combine a summarized form of postmodern theory with aspects of Kleinian theory in ways that appear to argue against the very point they are trying to make. Instead, I prefer a hermeneutic perspective, one that I think causes fewer problems than other forms of the linguistic turn in the human sciences.

The racism that concerns us in the United States is not universal, ahistorical, or inevitable. It is the product of an intersection of local customs, power relations, and institutions developed in Western Europe and then in the United States during the modern era (which began ca. 1600). Racism is the product of various political arrangements, and currently it serves many rather specific political purposes. It facilitates the exploitation of "Third World" and domestic labor and natural resources, the continuing destruction of the urban dispossessed, the manipulation of working-class labor and middle-class consumers, the control of voters, and the neutralization of resistance movements.

Unfortunately, Altman's discussion of the origins of racism gives us a bit too much Allport and not enough DuBois. For instance, Altman explains that people "construct [in-groups and out-groups] ... in order to deal with difference and similarity." Racial categories "draw lines between those who are 'me' or 'like-me' and those who are 'not-me' or 'unlike-me.'" His approach seems to attribute racism to psychological, natural causes (however socially constructed after being put into motion). This seems upside down from DuBois's perspective. According to

DuBois, political ideologies and institutions such as racism are produced by existing political arrangements and by political motivations, such as financial greed or the wish to accumulate power, not by abstract psychological motivations such as the "need" to "deal" with difference. The attempt to "draw lines" between those who are me and those who are not is not for DuBois a universal cause of racism, as it is for Altman. Instead, DuBois believed that "lines" demarcating groups were drawn and maintained for political reasons (e.g., economic greed produced slavery, which then had to be maintained through law and military might). First, lines are drawn to separate groups; individuals then respond to them psychologically.

As Foucault taught, culture is "always, already" encoded in us; it becomes part of one at the same time we learn there is a one. And racism is perpetuated because it is such a fundamental aspect of the ways the U.S. economy is structured, power is exercised, and the good is understood and practiced. If we want to combat racism effectively, we would do well to think about it like this — as a complex product of the sociopolitical terrain — and not as the inevitable result of biochemical, cognitive, or psycholinguistic structures and processes. Psychoanalysis can help us understand more about how cultural meanings about race affect us psychologically, and as a result we can better understand how racism has affected each of us and how individuals contribute to ongoing oppressions based on race. But psychotherapy alone cannot change a political system. It is a step in combating racial oppression, but it is only a step. It is not the whole journey.

If we were to study racism hermeneutically, we would focus on the moral understandings and power relations that frame U.S. society and allow and encourage racist practices. We would ask: what understandings of the good would have to be in place in order to bring racist practices to light? Hermeneuticists remind us that, until we understand the frame, we cannot understand fully why specific practices come to be and what functions they serve. When we understand some of that, we can begin to dispute those understandings and offer alternative understandings, which could bring different, antiracist practices to light.

The case material

Obviously, the two cases Altman writes about — the case of Mr. A and Leary's (1997) case of Ms. C — are discussed for a particular purpose, which is to identify certain transference-countertransference issues with which he struggled in order to discuss certain issues that arise when the analytic dyad struggles with issues of race and ethnicity. Primary among these issues is the matter of white privilege; the way racism, in the language of postmodernism, "speaks" whites; and how all this might manifest itself in the consulting room during psychoanalysis.[1] I appreciate Altman's willingness to do this, to offer his occasional inelegant or imperfect behavior for critique, so we can learn more about these issues. So, I do not ask about all the things we do not know about Mr. A, things about which, as therapists, we are probably curious-things such as the state of Mr. A's marriage (his initial reason for seeking treatment), his feelings and conflicts about women, trust, and betrayal (which might have been important aspects of his marital struggles), the nature, content, and progress of his treatment, whether his work life had any relation to why he missed so many sessions and bounced so many checks, and so on. Altman chose to focus on the more problematic aspects of his own racial countertransference, and in this way he calls on white therapists — no, all therapists — to spend more time attending to their racial countertransference. I follow his lead in this commentary, but I do not want to forget that there was a real-life patient involved in this case of Mr. A, and I hope none of us lose sight of him or think him unimportant.

White guilt

One way to think about the case of Mr. A is to place white guilt at its center. Altman's honesty about the case illustrates how counterproductive white guilt is, how in the case of Mr. A it prevented, or at least postponed, the analyst from being direct and authentic — something that of course bodes ill for an analysis. Altman's guilt about being white seemed to stop him from confronting Mr. A earlier because he wanted to avoid getting angry and thinking racist thoughts, hurting his African American patient by unintentionally giving voice to those thoughts, facing Mr. A's possible anti-white attitudes or anti-Semitism, and reproducing the anti-Semitic stereotype of an African American Jewish American relation. Altman's ability to interpret and learn from his own countertransference about race is obviously unusual for a white therapist, and it is helpful for him, potentially for his patient, and especially for his readers.

It seems striking that Altman found it difficult to be direct, confrontive, and self-protective with Mr. A. It is only in discussing the second case (from Leary, 1997) that he allows himself, vicariously, to experience more direct anger and confrontation. He reports how Leary made a few responses to a white patient that could be thought of as foreclosing the expression of potentially offensive material.

Altman's interpretation of her intervention is that she was being properly self-protective and confrontive. Perhaps she said to her white patient some of what he wishes he had said to Mr. A. In effect, she said: You are attacking me right now, in this room, by indulging your racism. I recognize it, and I will not be destroyed by it. I realize your statements are about you, not me. So, let's explore them, which means let's explore you. And don't try to accuse me of countertransference distortion, because other African Americans would agree with me; we have experienced this kind of behavior before.

But Altman did not allow himself this type of response to Mr. A, even though he believed that Mr. A was silently accusing him of — and, in fact, might be unconsciously inviting him to enact — being a stingy, bloodsucking Jew. Altman explains that, because of his guilt, he didn't respond aggressively or self-protectively to Mr. A. But what is the guilt about? Surely it is not guilt about the conduct of his family or the Jewish community during the time of slavery, the Civil War, or Reconstruction, because his family were poor Jews in Russia, Poland, and Lithuania, and his people were generally poor, hounded, and scattered throughout Europe, so oppressed that they finally fled in desperation to the New World. Surely it is not guilt about the conduct of his parents, who — although probably benefiting from the pecking order of racism, located as they were slightly above African Americans in the capitalist food chain — were certainly in no position to create, control, or even greatly affect racist institutions.

So, what is the source of his guilt? He mentions in passing that his guilt is in part caused by his identification as white. But I would argue that, for Jews, this is less an identification than a wish, a wish fostered by the late 18th-century French proposal that Jews be allowed, for the first time, to enjoy the rights of modern-era citizens (e.g., the equal protection of the law) if and only if they agree to give up what was most essential to their sense of self — their communal identity. Jews would be allowed to pass as white if they agreed to give up their communal, group-self identity and embrace a Western, highly individual identity, including foreign ideas such as the Western, modern-era distinctions of mind-body, rationality-irrationality, individual-society, and especially culture-religion. As several historians (e.g., Rudavsky, 1967; Kates, 1990; Biale, Galchinsky, & Heschel, 1998) have described, the Jewish community in Europe did gain admittance into modern-era Europe and then into 20th-century U.S. society, but at the cost of its communal identity, its purpose, its soul. It was a tragic mistake, not only because of the obvious — even the betrayal of 4,000 years of tradition and commitment, complete with name changing, the baptism of children, and cosmetic surgery, could not forestall the slaughter — but also because of the culture that was lost, perhaps never to be reclaimed.

I (1995, pp. 385–387) have suggested that abandoning the Jewish communal self in order to indulge in the fantasy of passing as white is in general emblematic of the dilemma of European American ethnic groups in the modern era, and to varying degrees (depending on physical characteristics or language), the dilemma many American immigrant minority groups face. Embedded in this interpretation of Jewish history is the suggestion that whiteness is first and foremost a political signifier about socioeconomic power that in actuality few people possess; therefore, most whites are in the position of trying to pass. "Power," Dyer (1993) suggested, "habitually passes itself off as embodied in the normal as opposed to the superior. This … works in a particularly seductive way with whiteness" (p. 142).

Recently, Thandeka (1999), in a study about the harmful effects of being considered "white," found that children have to be trained to be white. She suggested that part of that training consists of being taught to despise and disown parts of oneself, to project those qualities onto people of color, and then to consider oneself superior to them. This training creates a deep shame in whites, a shame that profoundly harms them at the same time that it grants them important socioeconomic advantages. We might say that whites are marked, oedipally, by the process of becoming white. We could, in fact, read Freud's Oedipus story as an unintentional description of how some oppressed groups "become" white (see Ignatiev, 1995; Brodkin, 1998) by complying and identifying with the oppressor (see Curtis-Bowles, 1997). If this is the case, then Altman is Everywhiteperson, and the guilt he speaks of is the guilt of all persons who try to identify as white, who are deluded into thinking they *are* white, and who are then haunted by a secret shame. It is the shame of abandoning historical traditions and important values of their people, abandoning important aspects of themselves, then countenancing and to some degree perpetuating the abandonment and oppression of others in order to live on the banks of what Kurt Vonnegut (1965) called "the Money River."

If white therapists unknowingly embrace this form of ethnic-group self-hatred and indulge their wish to pass as white (manifested in an embodied sense of guilt and shame), then how will they be able to help their patients of color, who are themselves probably struggling with their own form of ethnic-group ambivalence — an aspect of what DuBois called doubleness? How, for instance, will Mr. A be able to freely explore race and his relation with his analyst if his analyst does not in a way let himself go into and face his own countertransference; even though some of it, when it leaks out, may be unintentionally provocative, hurtful, or indirectly racist?

But there is something potentially useful in the unusual "place" Jews have inhabited in the European modern era, and especially the 20th-century cultural terrain of the United States.[1] Jewish struggles with assimilation and particularity, with being simultaneously insider and outsider, have provided a potentially liminal space (see Biale et al., 1998). Within this space, if Jews can grasp the opportunity, the insider-outsider predicament can bring to light the struggles of race, ethnicity, class, and gender in a highly instructive and insightful way. This takes a fair amount of study and soul-searching, but, if it is done honestly, Jews can confront their own struggles with the seductions and self-loathing that constitute the wish to pass as white (i.e., to escape the fate of being Jewish) and develop a critical yet meaningful understanding of their own Jewishness. When individuals can do this, the effects of doubleness can help Jewish therapists develop a slightly shifted perspective on the injuries of race, class, gender, and sexual orientation, both the hidden (see Sennett & Cobb, 1993) and the obvious (see Boskin, 1968). I imagine that this — perhaps especially insider-outsider issues related to class — holds true for some other European white ethnics as well. It might also hold true for some alienated white intellectuals, whose political commitments distance them from an unproblematic insider identity as white.

In other words, whiteness signifies a kind of political power that few in U.S. society actually hold. It confers various degrees of socioeconomic privilege on certain groups, provided they remain silent about what they have given up and how others have to be degraded and destroyed in order for them to be so entitled. But privilege, especially such a tainted and tenuous privilege, is not necessarily power.

And without power, privilege is just a kind of passing — anxiety provoking, shame-inducing, and ultimately chimeric. It induces the kind of white guilt that undermines the treatment of a patient of color and destroys meaningful political reform in a society that has been seriously wounded by hatred and injustice.

It is my belief that, ultimately, beyond all the theories — ideas about psychological integration and cohesion, working through, achievement of the depressive position, expansion of the true self, comfort with multiple subjectivities, ability to live in intersubjective space — it is also what Martin Buber called meeting that helps patients. Help comes from the opportunity to face the other with honesty and directness, to learn about and be understood by others, to tolerate ambiguity and uncertainty, to face the random nature of misfortune and death, and to become more skilled at opening oneself to difference. Psychotherapy, ultimately, is a kind of moral discourse (see Doherty, 1994; Cushman, 1995; Greifinger, 1995; Messer & Woolfolk, 1998; Richardson, Fowers, & Guignon, 1999).

That won't happen unless analysts are willing to take chances, to make mistakes and pick themselves up again, to face the worst of what pops into their minds and out of their mouths. That takes the capacity to grant oneself the freedom to be human and make mistakes, to recognize one's mistakes, to understand them, admit them, learn from them, and continue in relationship with others. It takes the capacity to be open to others, to let them teach you something you don't know about them and something you don't know about you, to come to understand something about the world of others, which will in turn help you learn something new about your world. This is the process hermeneuticist Gadamer (1975) called genuine conversation, or dialogue (see also Warnke, 1987; Stern, 1991, 1997; Richardson, Rogers, & McCarroll, 1998), and I believe it is the most helpful description of psychoanalysis that has yet come out of the linguistic turn. None of this can happen if analysts are plagued by ethnic, racial, or class self-hatred or are counterphobic or too afraid of making mistakes to be honest and relatively free in their own responses. Nothing will deaden an analysis more quickly than an analyst terrified of saying the wrong thing.

Back to white guilt. Probably, white guilt can be attributed not to the past but to the present, especially to the therapist's complicity in the present. Ironically, most whites, although guilty about what they didn't do, are remarkably myopic about the privilege they enjoy, the advantages from which they benefit, and the ways they protect that privilege — and thus the racist acts that they allow others to commit or the everyday omissions and slights that they themselves commit. All whites (those who know they are trying to pass and those who don't) should feel guilty about their current complicity with the political status quo. The ever poisonous demographic stratifications, political oppressions, and economic injustices of our world — no matter their origins — are kept in place by the current silences and absences of political resistance in white communities. It is probably a good thing to feel some guilt, or at least sadness, about the despicable acts one's ancestors committed, especially those committed ostensibly for the good of their descendants. This seems like a type of communal guilt or responsibility that is reasonable and helpful, that can guide us in the political decisions that currently confront us as a nation.

But ultimately, it is not so much the behavior of their ancestors that should make whites feel guilty today, but their own actions today — the socioeconomic conditions we allow, the overt racism we avoid facing, the corruption we do not really challenge, the covert racism (in ourselves and in others) that we do not comment on, the personal paralysis we tolerate in ourselves and in our communities. I know most of us don't know what to do about institutional racism today, but it is that very not knowing that must be challenged, in ourselves and in our communities. Until we break through that inaction, and live in the world in ways we approve, we will continue to feel guilty, and guilt will paralyze us and freeze us and keep us from genuinely meeting our patients of color, and all our patients.[2]

In other words, white analysts will not be good-enough analysts until they take political action against racism and economic injustice in their everyday lives. It is not enough that analysts think about matters of race only in terms of what they do or don't do in the consulting room. Of course, what one does in the consulting room is important, especially if one combines that with a commitment to better integrate one's practice or volunteer time to an agency serving minority communities. But it is not enough.

I am not advocating a passive, generalized white guilt. I'm suggesting that white guilt and shame are, among other things, covers for ethnic group and class self-hatred and for the consequences of abandoning aspects of oneself and degrading others in order to "become" white. I'm suggesting we embrace an honest, direct awareness of our political responsibilities, and get to work. What can we do about the institutions that drive racism? What can we do to change the political structures and cultural practices — including psychotherapy practices — that have created and continue to perpetuate racism? We must ask these questions, and develop answers, or our work in the analytic dyad will be corrupted by the ill-defined, wanna-be guilt and shame of ethnic group and class self-hatred and will be haunted by the guilt that should be present and won't go away, and both feelings will severely limit our work. We can do better than that.

Notes

1 Undoubtedly, this was an important source of Freud's insights (e.g., see Gilman, 1993).
2 One of the traps caused by thinking about psychoanalysis and race in ways limited by the guilt and shame of the past is that most of the professional literature is about the difficulties encountered when a white analyst treats a patient of color. Much less often do we explore what goes on with an analyst of color and a white patient, or an analyst of color and a patient of color, or perhaps most to the point, a white analyst and a white patient. What is said and done, especially in the context of the last dyad mentioned, that perpetuates the racial status quo? What is it, when both analyst and patient are white, that remains unsaid or undone? What is it that protects economic injustice, and thus the pitiful scraps of white privilege that both horde? If we care about undoing racism, then isn't it precisely the political meanings of the interactions in that dyad that must not be ignored?

Chapter 5

Will managed care change our way of being?

Co-author Peter Gilford
(2000 American Psychologist, 55, 985–996)

Historical introduction

This paper was a result of years of discussion and research by Peter Gilford and me that began when Peter, as a graduate student, showed up at my office to ask if it would be possible to write a dissertation about the self in managed care. Many hermeneutic courses, in depth research, and innumerable discussions later, we began to write an article about that subject. We submitted it to *American Psychologist*, and much to my surprise it was rejected. We cut that version in half, refocused the detailed sections about the historical shift from the empty self to the multiple self, and submitted that version — titled "From Emptiness to Multiplicity" — to *Psychohistory Review; they* accepted it happily and included it in a special issue titled The Self At the Year 2000. Then we recast the remaining material about managed care, still using a hermeneutic framework as our guide, and submitted the new paper to *AP*. Fortunately, this time around the renown psychologist Ken Gergen accepted the role of action editor. He understood the importance of our project and appreciated our approach. Given the disciplinary politics of that moment, if Ken had not been action editor this paper probably would not have been published by *AP*.

The effects of neoliberalism (both in economic arrangements and as a way of being), were reflected in the actions of managed care organizations; by the early 1990s they were being felt by American psychotherapists with mounting intensity. What at first was thought to be just an annoying inconvenience was over time revealed as a major challenge to the way therapists described their work, conducted their business, even thought about their practices. In hindsight it was a crucial step in the corporate takeover of the profession of psychotherapy, but in the longer view just another step in the development of the ongoing isolation, instrumentalism, and technicism of the society. Although it was difficult to recognize at first, we were witnessing a growing anti-labor corporatism, complete with forms of anti-communalism, racial and gender scapegoating, and a merging of religious fundamentalism and political authoritarianism. Now, at the end of the second decade of the 21st century, that way of life has become hegemonic. The crassness, greed, and hunger for spectacle that can be witnessed in a typical day of pop culture can be can be traced in part to the events and forces described in this article.

These were changes Peter and I were trying to document through the detailed textual analysis necessary in hermeneutic research. In particular, we applied the cultural history approach I introduced in *Constructing the Self, Constructing America* (1995) that featured a four-part analysis: a description of the predominant self of an era, the ills to which that self is vulnerable, the designated healers of those ills, and the healing technologies they utilized.

The results of our research were quite clear, relatively easy to understand, and we thought terrifying. Especially salient was our conclusion that managed care not only instituted changes in the self but also was a reflection of changes that had become pervasive in U.S. society. Surprisingly however, this article has generated only a few comments, either positive or negative, in what is now approaching its 20th year. Unlike "Why the Self Is Empty," my first *AP* article, which to this day is still being read and commented on, this 2000 article has generated extremely few reactions. There have been few reactions except, importantly, from students, who are forced to start out in psychology caught in the binds of and burdened by the continuing sociopolitical effects brought on by the processes and regulations that we identify in this article. The silence continues.

Although much has been written and debated about the finances, efficiency, and ethics of the corporations that currently control mental health services in the United States, one question remains unexamined — in fact, unseen — in the professional literature: What impact are the discourses and practices of managed care having on societywide understandings of the good and thus on our everyday way of being as the new century dawns?

Whoever controls the delivery of mental health care — by determining such things as the definition of mental disorder, triage criteria, and the nature and length of proper treatment — inevitably and deeply affects society-wide understandings of health and illness, abnormality and healing, the possibilities and limits of human nature, and thus what is believed to be proper and good. Managed care organizations (MCOs) now dominate these processes.[1] In this article we inquire into what the recent shift in power from private practitioner to insurance company to MCO means about the emerging historical era and the people who inhabit it.

To address these issues, we focus on the discourse related to the treatment philosophy and practices commonly used in MCOs.[2] We use a cultural-history, hermeneutic approach, stressing the historicity of human being, the importance of power relations, and the centrality of interpretive and moral processes. We believe that culture clears a space for a social world to emerge and that then, within that world, certain things, understandings, and relationships can come to light. Social practices enact these understandings, which are "inescapably" moral understandings (see Taylor, 1989) that have political consequences, and eventually they become embodied by those who inhabit the space. These practices reflect and develop shared understandings about many things, including what it means to be properly human. Hermeneuticists call these embodied understandings *the self* of a particular time and place. Therefore, although we are aware of the power imbalance between therapist and patient, we believe common understandings about the self have framed these two roles and the meaning and delivery of treatment so that these roles and activities all fit well with one another and with the larger social terrain.

The relationship between the exercise of power and the configuration of the self is a profoundly entangled and reciprocal one. Foucault (1980, 1987) maintained that control is diffuse and exercised through synchronistic processes that produce compliance by appealing to what is understood to be commonsensical or natural. Because local norms and customs have been embodied, self-understandings and the sense of what is proper and improper tend to reinforce the dominant political arrangements of a society. Thus, power is exercised not so much by coercion but by fitting with, influencing, and profiting from the shape of the cultural frame of a particular time and place.

Without that fit, the activity called psychotherapy and now psychotherapy under managed care — could never take place. However, managed care is a recent development, and many things are still in question. In this article, we inquire about how managed care discourse is developing new understandings of illness, the patient, the therapist, and therapy. We also speculate on the political impact these understandings may have. Then, in turn, we examine how these understandings and practices not only shape the pre-dominant way of being but also reflect it.

Managed care

In past years, one of us has applied these ideas to prominent psychoanalytic theories and practices (see, e.g., Cushman, 1990, 1994, 1995). In this article, we focus on a different, competing psychotherapeutic technology: the treatment philosophy and practices of managed care. We realize this is a difficult task, given how persuasive are the claims to scientific progress in current U.S. society and in the field of psychology. For late-20th-century Western society in general, the intersection of mainstream psychology and market values reflects several deeply held cultural beliefs, such as the importance of efficiency, pragmatism, and objective reasoning. This vision is especially appealing to psychologists, representing as it does the allure of science and the promise of an ongoing march of rational, technical progress that have both been central to psychology's historical self-understanding. It captures in particular one of psychology's most profound commitments and hopes: the achievement of an effective practice attained through unimpeachable scientific procedures. Yet, even as the profession makes claims that it is approaching this milestone (see, e.g., Orlinsky & Howard, 1986; Persons & Silberschatz, 1998, pp. 126–127), it would be wise to inquire into the impact of these beliefs.

In the past decade, what is commonly called managed care — that is, large, for-profit corporations specializing in the management and control of health care delivery through the exercise of a bureaucratic rationalism — has become the dominant force in mental health care. Although each corporation conducts business in a slightly different way, their regulations and practices and the arguments they use to explain and justify them are often quite similar (see Gilford, 2000). Managed care corporations usually favor behavioral descriptions of patient symptoms, treatment formulations focused on symptom relief, psychotropic medication, and concrete, opportunistic, directive interventions within a radically short-term format. All of this is carried out with adherence to specific — and inaccessible — bureaucratic guidelines (Miller, 1994, 1996) that MCOs claim are determined by the use of actuarial tables, cost-benefit analyses, outcomes studies, and cost-cutting regulations designed to generate profits. The intense corporate secrecy with which MCOs conduct business makes it extremely difficult for researchers not in their employ to collect evidence about the exact nature of their practices. It is also difficult for clinicians and subscribers to the plans to know exactly what their benefits really amount to. Yet it is precisely this information that must be studied to better determine whether MCOs live up to their professed ideals and advertising claims.

Configuring the client in managed care

What in managed care discourse helps configure the shape, meanings, and functions of the early-21st-century self? Examples of managed care ideology and practices can be found in or inferred from the literature about the definition, determination, treatment, and justification of psychotherapy in managed care environments. It seems inevitable that managed care practices would have a significant impact on the understandings about the proper way of being human held by patients, practitioners, clerks, administrators, supervisors, and CEOs (see, e.g., Austad & Berman, 1991, p. vii). Consider first the ways in which such practices affect conceptions of the client.

In managed care arrangements, emotional distress and psychological problems must necessarily be framed by the definitions and solutions developed by positivist method in coordination with economic formulas. A government-sponsored report explained that "HMOs consider clinical care management to be an objective process. ... Written clinical guidelines and protocols have been developed by the HMOs to add a formal framework for organizing the data and facilitating objectivity in the decision making practice" (Lourie, Howe, & Roebuck, 1996, p. 36).

There has always been the hope that the myriad components of psychotherapy practice could be tied to an objective, formal framework, and originally there was much optimism regarding the quantitative measure of diagnostic and therapeutic processes and techniques. Yet researchers studying the impact of therapist variables on outcome have run into problems. As Beutler, Machado, and Neufeldt (994) explained, "Efforts to identify the therapist attributes that account for ... systematic variations [in outcome] have often been unproductive ... because therapist characteristics interact in complex ways with the characteristics of the client, the situation, and the type of therapy practiced" (p. 229).

In diagnosis, similar problems have been encountered. Kirk and Kutchins (1992, pp. 221, 224) noted that despite attempts to make

> diagnosis more objective and technically rational — they fail to eliminate subjectivity from psychiatric diagnosis. ... [T]hese processes are easily distorted by the clinician's past personal experiences, expectations, emotions, and by illogical thinking, unfounded inferences, selective attention, stereotypes, and all sorts of other subtle biases.
>
> (cf. Loring & Powell, 1988)

Despite these obstacles, diagnosis continues to be thought of as being produced relatively unproblematically when a properly normed, previously designed evaluative form or interview has been correctly applied.

> It is essential to conduct inter-rater reliability studies by having multiple providers use the assessment tool to rate various patients. ... This is the only means to establish the soundness of the assessment tool. ... [It establishes] the validity of the treatment recommendations generated by the expert system.
>
> (Pigott, 1997, pp. 253–254)

Diagnostic practices take for granted several understandings about human being, including the following: Forms of inquiry and observation can be constructed so that all aspects of bias and prejudgment are removed from the process; how a patient is feeling or acting can be accurately observed by such unbiased predetermined forms of inquiry and observation; human distress and psychological life are constituted by concrete, ahistorical, acultural mental categories composed of specific patterns of behaviors and emotions, which can be quantified and confidently known by scientific experts; these categories can be communicated to other workers, such as therapists and utilization review clerks, who can use them in the course of treatment; these categories can be studied objectively by experts to determine the proper planning and administration of treatment techniques that are to be applied to the particular diagnostic category; the therapist can apply predetermined techniques to the patient suffering from a particular diagnosis within a predetermined time period and achieve a predetermined result; this result can be obtained by the therapist's proper application of the appropriate technique within the authorized time period, as long as the patient fully cooperates with the treatment; the behavior thought to indicate the predetermined outcome can be unproblematically observed by the therapist and evaluated by oversight personnel; and the predetermined outcome, once achieved, is an adequate solution to the patient's distress.

The putatively unproblematic nature of diagnostic and treatment procedures in managed care indicates that psychological ills are thought of as relatively simple to understand, easily identified, and easily fixed. The existence and nature of diagnostic categories are rarely questioned; it is assumed that they represent universal and ahistorical phenomena readily available for study and use. The monocultural assumptions that inhere in this view are particularly troubling. Of course, these tendencies are not unique to managed care; they have a long history in most treatment settings (see, e.g., Fowers & Richardson, 1996; Sue & Sue, 1999). In this view, the self is thought to be composed of concrete behaviors and thus seems almost mathematical in its orderliness. Descriptions of psychological illness in managed care have split into two seemingly disparate poles — one a highly anecdotal, behaviorally driven, developmental, antipathology view (see, e.g., Budman & Gurman, 1988, pp. 97–119, 1992; Cummings & Sayama, 1995, pp. 11–16) and the other a medicalized, biochemical view (see, e.g., Institute of Medicine, 1997, p. 19; Kisch, 1991, p. 82; Mohl, as cited in Vallenstein, 1998; Whittington, 1993, p. 27). However, they both share a highly concrete, psychologically uncomplicated, behavioral, monocultural self.

In the process of therapy mandated by managed care, patients further become compliant recipients of expert knowledge and technique, and their records are available on the computer network at corporate headquarters. Knowledge and technique are dispensed by the therapist and always monitored through various oversight procedures by supervisory personnel. "The planned action and the outcome should recursively influence each other. Plans cannot be evaluated without feedback, and feedback is impossible without some precision in defining outcomes" (Johnson, 1995, p. 50).

Implicit in this view is the idea that the patient should accept the therapist's evaluations; use the therapist's opinions, guidance, or behavioral directives; and carry them out as instructed. L.M. Richardson and Austad (1991) explained that

> resistant or noncompliant clients can cause difficulties for managed-care systems because clients who refuse or do not comply with treatments that are preventive or provide early intervention may develop more severe problems that require more aggressive or costly treatments. Some HMOs require their clients to sign treatment contracts that state that noncompliance can be grounds for dismissal from the HMO treatment benefit. For example ... the protocol for noncompliant persons is that noncompliance is first documented in the individual's chart and discussed with the client, then a letter is sent to the client referring to the "termination for cause" section of the member's service contract, and finally the matter is referred to the Medical Director, who attempts to meet with the client and family members to discuss the situation and offer possible solutions, with the last resort being termination of the client.
>
> (p. 57)

Although there is considerable thought given to the creation and maintenance of a teamwork alliance between patient and therapist, a prime reason for this emphasis is the attempt to maintain patient compliance. "Homework," Cummings and Sayama (1995) explained,

> is at the heart of targeted, focused psychotherapy. It is the critical feature that convinces patients that they are truly partners in their own treatment. ... [The therapist often forgets] that understanding is not measured by what the patient says, but by demonstrable changes in behavior and attitudes."
>
> (p. 97)

Certain forms of case formulation, such as cognitive behavioral formulations, are often favored by MCOs. Those formulations, Tompkins (1997) explained, are "particularly helpful in ensuring that the patient complies with treatment recommendations, homework assignments, and other aspects of the therapy that increase the likelihood of a positive outcome" (p. 50).

When working within this type of therapeutic frame, the therapist comes to view the patient as naturally compliant, adjustable, and willing to follow directions. If patients display independent thought, confusion, disagreement — let alone resistance — their behavior may lead the clinician or MCO oversight manager to invoke a diagnosis such as the pejorative Axis II borderline personality disorder or other ongoing, long-term maladaptive patterns of personality or character. This fulfills two functions: First, it medicalizes, and thus depoliticizes, deviance from the approved role of docile patient. Second, it threatens noncompliant patients with a withdrawal of benefits because managed care companies rarely pay for the treatment of Axis II diagnoses (Goodman, Brown & Deitz, 1996; Tuckfelt, Fink, & Warren, 1997; Weisgerber, 1999). Alternatively, because dependency and transference are discouraged, independence of thought can also be interpreted as an indication that treatment is no longer necessary. Either way, these interpretations threaten the withdrawal of treatment authorization.

The definitions, descriptions, and treatments of disorder — elements of the technology of the self (see Foucault, 1987) of a particular time and place — are crucially important in the ongoing construal of the patient. The above two elements that configure the patient in managed care — psychological simplicity and compliance — are made possible in part by a third element: a belief that symptoms constitute psychological life. In the emerging era, MCOs are requiring practices that influence oversight managers, therapists, and patients to believe that symptoms in some way *are* mental illness. Discrete behavioral symptoms, it is thought, can be attacked, manipulated, altered, substituted for, or erased through strategic technique and psychotropic medication. Symptoms are thought to indicate that a "developmental crisis" (Budman & Gurman, 1988, pp. 102–104; Cummings & Sayama, 1995, pp. 11–15) has appeared; they require direct, concrete therapeutic attention, but only long enough to remediate the crisis, cause the symptom to disappear, and thus return the patient to a previous (and approved of) level of functioning.

"Patients," Austad and Berman (1991) wrote, "usually wanted help in solving these problems quickly and efficiently in order to return to their prior lifestyle" (p. vii). The patient, in other words, is conceived of as a figure who wants to — and should — be reconstituted and returned to his or her personal and work life as soon as possible. Many patients seek therapy, Budman and Gurman (1988) explained, "because their sense of being 'off time' with their contemporaries was becoming more acute and severe" (p. 104). It seems that managed-care-oriented therapists are not to entertain the idea that one's prior lifestyle, the social and financial objectives of one's peers, and the material or cultural conditions of one's life might be partly the sources of one's psychological problems.

Thus, patient behavior is defined as a problem when it interferes with work or prevents individuals from acting and achieving like their peers. "The objective in all cases," Bennett (1989, p. 352) explained, "is to mitigate the obstacles to adaptation." Difference is medicalized and thereby considered something to be eradicated in the name of science. In this vision of human being, compliance and adaptation, because they are not thought to be symptoms, cease being the subject of psychological inquiry and then cease being thought of as linked to psychological problems. Soon, they disappear from view: they are thought to be normal and thus blend into the taken-for-granted cultural background and become unproblematic. But difference shows up as a problem — a medical problem — and therefore must be eradicated.

The claim that patients seek treatment to stop being different and to conform is particularly troubling when the patient is struggling with matters of cultural, racial, or religious assimilation; ethnic group or class identity; gender prescriptions; physical disabilities; or sexual orientation. There is little discussion about the possibility that being different has a political meaning or that being different might, in various circumstances, be considered something positive that therapy should encourage. The obliteration of difference is a remarkably monocultural — and thus dangerous — trend.

If therapeutic attention is granted only to emotional problems constituted by concrete behavioral symptoms that prevent the individual from conforming, then other forms of psychological issues — such as suffering that is thought to involve personality formation rather than discrete behavioral symptoms — no longer come to light. This may explain why in the future, Axis II disorders will probably not play as prominent a role in therapeutic discourse as they did in the last third of the 20th century. At first, therapists did not use Axis II as the primary diagnosis on claim forms because MCOs would not reimburse for them. Then, later on, perhaps due to self-image management (see Hales, 1985), therapists began limiting discussion about Axis II with their supervisors, consultants, or peers, and, eventually, they stopped considering Axis II altogether. This illustrates how institutional discursive practices, in combination with other sociopolitical forces, gradually can erase a way

Will managed care change our way of being? 61

of being. The notion of character then simply disappears or is limited to those who can afford to have one.

For all of the above reasons, the nature of psychological experience — and thus the self — is becoming flatter and less nuanced. Emotions and identities seem to be located on or near the surface of a thin self, where they can be easily accessed and maneuvered in service of attacking symptoms and normalizing patients. This shift in the self in managed care is in sync with important changes in the overall social terrain. In an earlier article (Cushman & Gilford, 1999), we suggested that the deep, complicated interior of the post-World War II era, what Foucault referred to as a "richly furnished interior" — is being overtaken by a concrete, exteriorized, and unreflective self — what we called a "multiple self." This new self, we believe, facilitates the emerging socioeconomic arrangements of the new era.

Configuring the therapist in managed care

Approaches to therapy that focus primarily on symptom reduction, such as cognitive-behavioral therapy, solution focused therapy, or brief strategic therapy, are thought to be particularly well suited to managed care. This has implications on how the therapist comes to light. In managed care environments, the therapist is often pictured as equipped with predetermined, structured practices that are so precise they can be managed through computerized monitoring and regulation. For example,

> The preexisting highly structured and topic-delimited approach of cognitive-behavioral therapy is ideal for translation into a computer program. The rules are already explicit (in contrast to the practice of most psychotherapy where the rules are implicit), and the process is perceived by patients as conducting therapeutic work.
> (Gould, 1996, p. 44)

In this environment, the therapist appears to be a rather impersonal — although potentially personable — dispenser of a predetermined set of technical maneuvers. Therapy is seen as an instrumental activity through which techniques are used by the therapist-expert to help alleviate difficulties presented by the patient.

However, this does not mean that the therapist is necessarily unempathic; for instance, if it is determined that the proper (i.e., most efficient) response in a given moment with a particular patient in a specific diagnostic category is an empathic response, the therapist is expected to deliver empathy (see Cummings & Sayama, 1995). At other times, the therapist is expected to be "active," "intensively alert," or "selectively focused" (Binder, 1977, pp. 235–237). Also, a "quick perceptiveness" can aid in the therapist's "willingness to take risks" (Hoyt, 1995, pp. 226–227), another necessary trait. The therapist seems to be understood as active, incisive, perhaps at times even impulsive, and yet at other times controlled, careful, and compliant with the protocols and procedures stipulated by the corporate office.

What do these seemingly contradictory descriptions mean about managed care understandings that characterize the therapist? One way to interpret the above descriptions is to conclude that the therapist is thought to be a psycho-technician, ever alert and quick to act, trained and monitored to provide the prescribed and consistent intervention even in highly contradictory situations, and open to being overruled as necessary during administrative or supervisory oversight reviews.

One indication of the extent to which this technical or instrumental approach is succeeding in regulating the therapist's role is in how managed care discourse understands variation in therapeutic intervention. Differences in interventions — between one therapist and another when treating patients with the same diagnosis or between the clinical practices a therapist might use with two patients with the same diagnosis — are thought of as one of the major problems in all mental health treatment settings, especially managed care environments. "Variance in clinical practice," Pigott (1997) explained,

> results in widely varying types and costs of care, as well as clinical outcomes, for patients with similar conditions. Such wide variance is due to the historical failure by the behavioral health professions to systematically link patient assessment data, and their analysis, to actual clinical decision making. ... To address this issue and decrease such variance, expert software systems have been developed by managed care companies to ensure consistency in their case managers' level of care authorization.
>
> (p. 247)

For managed care systems to function properly, the therapist's opposing inclinations and opinions as to treatment, technique, and duration must be kept out of the therapy (for some disturbing examples, see Gerber, 1996). Managed care treatment philosophy implies that therapy is most efficient when the therapist's personal idiosyncrasies and theoretical preferences are bracketed off or at least made secondary to standardized goals and objectives. The individual characteristics of the therapist are thought to be simultaneously both measurable and unimportant to successful treatment processes. Discourse relating to the computerization of mental health care, including therapy, assessments conducted by or through a computer interface, or clinical-decision support systems, implies a therapeutic endeavor that requires a precisely calibrated therapist and a uniform patient. This way of functioning is thought to be possible because the work of the therapist is understood by MCOs to be formulaic and predetermined: the human variance inevitably present in the therapist's performance is to be studied and minimized as much as possible, and treatment protocols are to be scientifically derived.

"Managed care companies," Woods and Cagney (1993) explained,

> are looking for providers who are "committed to goal oriented therapy." Preferred providers are selected based on a demonstrated ability to diagnose a problem and return the patient to a functional level. There is an increasing focus on outcome, and it relates to functioning. MCOs are looking for providers who understand that insight alone does not equal outcome. An average target for MCOs is to have 80% of outpatient work completed within 8–10 sessions.
> (pp. 38–39)

Although concerns about the effects of managed care often focus on the patient, this section touches on the effects of managed care on the therapist. Leyerle (1994), for instance, discussed at length the effects of the increasing surveillance tactics of managed care on clinicians. "Through the collection of this data," Leyerle noted, providers as well as patients "are placed under surveillance by utilization review agencies" (p. 187). It may be, she speculated, that "the major goal never has been to cut health care costs, but to institutionalize the surveillance and control mechanisms themselves" (p. 190).

In summary, the therapist in managed care tends to come to light as a technical worker whose personal biases, opinions, and conclusions are less valuable than the standardized procedures determined by management. Therapeutic practices are thought in large part to consist of determining which scientifically derived techniques to use, at which prescribed pace, to produce predetermined results related to concrete symptom relief in a replicable and consistent manner. Therapists become something like psychotechnicians, monitored and sometimes corrected or overruled by superiors during review sessions, and then "profiled" over time through various surveillance techniques to determine their efficiency and thus their cost-effectiveness.

The therapeutic relationship in managed care

The belief that the patient's ills can be located unproblematically in a discrete diagnostic category, which then dictates a specific set of detailed therapeutic guidelines, requires a rather mechanistic — and primarily intrapsychic — view of therapeutic process. "Problems and symptoms," Tompkins (1997) explained, "result from the activation of underlying core beliefs by stressful life events. Cognitive therapy focuses on altering the cognitive structures and processes that cause and/or maintain problematic behaviors" (p. 38). This common attitude about the patient's subjectivity and the therapeutic encounter, although sometimes described in interpersonal[3] and reformist terms, often cannot overcome an allegiance to conceiving of therapeutic activity as unilateral and unidirectional. This stance seems to reflect a terrain in which the therapist is not so much a person as a removed, unaffected, faceless expert, one who provides the predetermined intervention to the patient and then recedes into anonymity to let the putatively unidirectional effect take place. Stiles and Shapiro (1989) called this the "drug metaphor" vision of psychotherapy.

Of course, drug treatment in MCOs is not only a metaphor — it is also an important element of the treatment plan. Medication not only has reduced the number of treatment sessions in symptom-reduction therapies, it also has affected how therapists and patients understand therapy. For instance, some critics (e.g., Bollas & Sundelson, 1995, p. 99; Walls, 1994, 1999, p. 7) think treatments regulated by managed care rely too heavily on medication. Overreliance, in turn, has tended to influence practitioners to aim at quieting rather than resolving symptoms, thus attenuating the patient's capacity and motivation for tolerating pain and uncertainty, which some think are needed to achieve a psychological resolution of psychological ills. An overreliance on medication also affects theoretical notions about the very meaning of treatment, health, and illness.

The drug metaphor and the increasing reliance on medication are both causes and reflections of the emerging era. There appears to be little time in managed care's arrangements of psychotherapy for an examination of the therapist-patient relationship: disagreements, complaints, arguments, the voicing of hurt or angry feelings, the exploration of misunderstandings or puzzlements, or the challenging of monetary arrangements, roles, and power distributions within the hour. As a result, the development of the type of alliance found in longer term therapy — predicated as much on conflict as on agreement — is precluded in such an environment. In its place is an alliance that seems manufactured and forced, based primarily on procedures and aims usually identified with consumer-satisfaction survey research, such as postsession rating devices (see, e.g., Johnson, 1995).

Significantly, proponents of managed care often conflate therapeutic alliance with "agreement" between therapist and patient or feature agreement as a central aspect of the alliance. *"The Working Alliance Inventory,"* Johnson (1995, p. 43) explained, "measures ... the therapy bond, agreement on goals, and agreement on tasks." But a therapeutic alliance can also be built on other kinds of processes, such as those that grow out of disagreement or confrontation. Conceiving of alliance as primarily the product of agreement, many psychodynamic and family therapists would argue, runs the risk of creating a fragile or false alliance that must by definition avoid disagreement or disagreeable feelings. Indeed, it seems that alliance based solely on agreement reduces the concept to a consumer-satisfaction dynamic. In this respect, it resembles the purchasing of a refrigerator or used car. What does that do to the integrity of the treatment? What is to stop the managed care therapist from protecting his or her position within a managed care panel by colluding with, rather than confronting, the patient to secure high consumer-satisfaction scores? Conversely, what is to stop the therapist from pressuring the patient into complying with the therapist's directives to maintain the agreements, the therapist's good will, and finally a good case write-up and nonpejorative diagnosis?

"Time constraints," Austad and Berman (1991) explained, "are incorporated as a working ingredient of psychotherapy. Assessment is early and accurate. Intervention is prompt. By definition, therapy is goal-directed and focal" (p. 9). In what form, then, given such a strategic environment, does the therapeutic alliance appear? "Rapport, or a good working alliance between patient and therapist," Austad and Berman reported, "must blossom promptly" (p. 9). *Blossom* is a curious verb to use in describing the manner in which an alliance develops in managed care. Given managed care's usual emphasis on positivist science, the reliance on a naturalized, organicistic metaphor is a romantic move found surprisingly often in the discourse of proponents of managed care. For instance, the belief that the need for treatment appears naturally, bubbling up at various times throughout the life span, especially during moments of "developmental dysynchrony" (Budman & Gurman, 1988, p. 104), seems to be a romantic concept that naturalizes social processes. Austad and Berman's implication is that a therapeutic alliance is something that just appears naturally — and quickly, too, if one needs it or wills it to. But what is it that naturally blossoms: alliance or compliance?

Indeed, how can the therapist tell the difference between alliance or compliance without careful attention to the meaning of disturbances in the therapeutic relationship? Among some practitioners who conceive of their work in part as a kind of political resistance in the broad sense, the process of unraveling and demystifying power relations such as doctor-patient, expert-novice, and male-female is at the center of therapeutic activity. If patients have no time to complain, argue, discuss, test, and explore their relationship with the therapist, there is a concern that therapy is reduced to an unchallenged power relation, either that of powerful expert over passive, ignorant, and/or sick patient or, conversely, of domineering, accusatory, manipulative patient over insecure, compliant therapist.

One danger that comes from diminishing an exploration of the therapeutic relationship is that therapy runs the risk of becoming increasingly instrumental. For instance, Tompkins (1997) explained that "the success of cognitive behavioral therapy depends on the quality of the collaboration between therapist and patient. The dilemma for the therapist is how to ensure compliance while maintaining a collaborative alliance with the patient" (p. 50). In this passage, collaboration shows up as an effective way of creating compliance; collaboration (or the appearance of collaboration) is a tool the therapist uses when necessary to get the patient to act in the preferred way within the therapy setting. "A common therapy-interfering behavior is homework noncompliance. The cognitive-behavioral case formulation can help the therapist understand possible reasons for homework noncompliance and generate strategies to deal with it" (Tompkins, 1997, p. 51). Here, we see a therapist strategizing unilaterally to influence the patient to comply. But what if the patient's noncompliance means something important about the process in which they are both engaged? What if it means the particular homework assignment is not helpful for the patient? What if the whole process of homework itself is not best for a particular patient? What if noncompliance reflects something about how the patient feels about how therapy as a whole is being conducted? These questions, evidently, are not typically asked by this type of therapist. The meta-plan, the larger frame of the treatment, is set in advance of meeting and getting to know the patient. From the beginning, this type of therapy seems to be a somewhat unilateral process, tempered occasionally when the therapist uses interactions that appear to invite collaboration, but often these interventions seem instrumental, calculated to create compliance.

Instrumentally-oriented therapists could counter by highlighting the many ways they enlist the patient's agreement and creative "input" regarding a particular therapeutic strategy, and this is a good point. However, we believe this point also demonstrates a common mistake psychologists have made over the course of the 20th century: the substitution of subjectivity for political freedom. Often, psychologists have equated the opportunity to feel, emote, or choose among a predetermined and limited set of alternatives with meaningful political freedom. Expressing oneself emotionally about various alternatives, events, or desires is a paltry freedom if their number, kind, or meaning is crafted by groups and processes from which one is excluded. Expressive subjectivity does not necessarily indicate the presence of egalitarian, democratic processes. It just means that one is free, after the fact and without any real influence, to be emotionally expressive. In the late 20th century, the easier it has been to convince citizens that emotion — especially emotional consuming — is the essence of political freedom, the easier it has been to exert political control. Similarly, in psychotherapy, if the therapist asks the patient for emotional expressiveness and input about various treatment goals and strategies, the patient may well characterize the therapy process as nonauthoritarian and respectful, thereby overlooking the fact that therapeutic goals, strategies, and overall processes were determined without his or her involvement. In this way, therapy is reduced to the procedural requirements of consumer protection standards.

Of course, such a unilateral, instrumental approach to intervention is not the sole prerogative of any one treatment modality — therapists from all modalities are capable of acting this way. The point here is that managed care arrangements *institutionalize* formulaic approaches — it seems inevitable given the ontological understandings that inhere in managed care practices.

Is evidence the answer?

One of the professed ideals of MCOs is to provide quality care and thereby protect the patient by tracking and determining therapeutic outcome, thus holding the therapist accountable for effective and efficient treatment. The philosophical problems and methodological dilemmas that are involved in attempts to evaluate psychotherapy practices have confounded the profession throughout its history (Strupp, 1996). Many researchers have attempted valiantly, but with limited success, to create ways of describing and evaluating psychotherapy to determine what works, what causes harm, and how to tell one from the other (see Bergin & Garfield, 1994; Garfield, 1992; Lambert & Bergin, 1994; Strupp & Howard, 1992). For psychotherapy evaluation, the 20th century ends as it began, with mainstream academic psychology and medical science laying claim to an exclusive ability to determine the truth through positivist method, with romantics claiming the metaphysical (and transpersonal) high ground, and with celebrity therapists making extravagant claims about revolutionary techniques and miracle cures.

In any case, the initial promise of evaluative studies, including especially the emphasis on positivist methodology applied to outcome, has not lived up to the profession's high hopes. Outcome studies have both champions and critics, but one thing remains a concern: Outcome research is beset by what critics of scientism call the "problem of circularity" (e.g., see Smedslund, 1985; Stancombe & White, 1998). That is, the way researchers conceive of rigorous research necessarily affects how they define symptom, illness, treatment, goals, and effectiveness (Strupp, 1996, p. 1023). Thus, the process of determining what counts as a positive outcome in therapy encompasses numerous factors that involve the expression of diverse and incommensurate concerns — the patient's, the therapist's, the researcher's, and now that of the corporate bottom line. Under managed care, it is the latter that prevails.

Through the ideology of accountability that underlies the concept of managed care, preference is given to a definition of clinical evidence that relies on the objectification of emotions so that an exchange value can be placed on states of mind (see Kovel, 1980). This is consistent with capitalism and modern bureaucracy, wherein accountability is linked to a belief in objectivity, measurement, and the value of efficiency as ends in themselves. Positivist-based approaches intended to verify the efficacy of mental health treatments are founded on this ethos of efficiency and must thus be predicated on a mechanistic, simplified, and efficient configuration of the self. Other forms of research based on dialogical or interpretive methods become marginalized because of their allegedly inefficient complexity.

In the discourse of managed care, there is little acknowledgment that privileging one conception of evidence over another, through the production and management of a specific form of therapeutic effectiveness, does not so much discover the "one" truth as it privileges a particular truth compatible with the political needs and moral understandings of the group doing the research. This is Foucault's point regarding knowledge and power: in the human sciences, there can be no unbiased evaluative processes that lead to one unassailable truth.

If this hermeneutic argument makes sense, then expecting, for instance, interpersonal, relational, or existential practices to be evaluated according to positivist measures is like evaluating a baseball team according to how many touchdowns it scores. The two playing fields look similar enough, but the two games are fundamentally incommensurable.

Managed care's reliance on the evidence of effectiveness and on its enforcement through bureaucratic surveillance has an additional, unseen side effect: accountability institutionalizes distrust at the most basic level. It reduces relational reality to a simple, mechanistic, cost-output calculation and renders irrelevant the moral dialogue required in any shared social and community life. The result is the managed care belief that there is such a thing as an empirically verifiable relationship.

In this, one can see traces of the centuries-old power strategy launched in the early modern era: the slow but inevitable overcoming of the church's authority by the new science. Science's triumph eventually attenuated some of the abuses of the church, but that triumph was part of larger historical movements that also developed self-contained individualism and the idealization of the free market and unrestricted competition. As

Western society and Western capitalism evolved, the individual came to be understood as someone without communal obligations, moral commitments, or personal limits except those based on individual self-interest (see Taylor, 1989). It is only the power of the state — in the case of health care exercised through bureaucratic regulation — that is thought to keep one person or guild from cheating and defrauding others. As a result of this understanding of the self, the West eventually produced the alienation and lifelessness characteristic of the late-modem-era self (Levin, 1987b; F.C. Richardson, Fowers, & Guignon, 1999). There are various problems with ceding moral authority to disengaged procedure, including especially that, in the end, nothing is left for the individual but a cynical, avaricious emptiness: "We are the hollow men," T.S. Eliot intoned, "we are the stuffed men" (Eliot, 1925/1971, p. 56). Ironically, it turns out that some of the ills modem psychology set out to cure (e.g., narcissism), it had, and has, a hand in creating.

The contention that objective scientism not only is not foolproof and is sometimes unhelpful but also is part of the problem presents psychologists with a dilemma many are intellectually and professionally unprepared to deal with. How can the profession proceed ethically if it cannot depend on objective, procedural method to safeguard patients and determine the best care? One way to proceed is to undo the prohibition against engaging in moral discourse. Not only does moral authority not have to be ceded to disengaged procedure, in fact it cannot be: moral discourse does not get bracketed off, it just gets disguised (see, e.g., Bernstein, 1976). Indeed, most psychotherapy theories are good examples of disguised morality (e.g., see the valorization of interior locus of control, separation individuation, self-actualization, the true self-false self dichotomy, and the privileging of cognition over affect). Rather than trying to disavow or erase one's moral nature, one could embrace it and become better at exercising it.

The necessity of moral deliberation

As the preceding suggests, we believe that discussions about managed care and psychotherapy are unavoidably and necessarily moral discussions. In this respect, neither the attempt to develop a cost-controlled, cost-efficient health care system nor the use of positivist method to attain that goal can be accepted as mere matters of fact. That goal and its

Will managed care change our way of being? 71

accompanying method obviously are expressions of a set of historically developed moral values that emphasize instrumentality, efficiency, and conformity. Because we believe that values can never be determined through scientific method, it seems more fitting to evaluate psychological care by examining these issues thoughtfully and critically through moral dialogue.

What values do Americans want to use to direct their health care system? Why is it that corporate competitiveness and profit-seeking currently shape health care, and that health care practices fail to embody other values, such as economic justice, equal access, critical thinking, and individual attention and care, that would bring to light a different set of social practices? More important, what kind of vision of the good do Americans hope to develop through their health care system? How are the nature of persons and relationships to be defined?

After reading a great deal of literature about managed care, we see the values that inhere in its theories and practices begin to emerge. It is instructive how often certain terms or qualities show up in the literature: clarity, activity, speed, concreteness, solutions, practicality, realism, efficiency, systemization, replicability, consistency, functioning, adaptation, specificity, and parsimony. Although there is an implicit disapproval of attachment and interdependence, beliefs about the importance of the patient's autonomy, independence, and self-responsibility appear as unquestioned values; in turn, they are used to justify the belief that therapists should absent themselves from their patients as soon as possible once the solution to a specific problem has been found. There is an abhorrence of ambiguity, complexity, uncertainty, perplexity, mystery, imperfection, and individual variation in treatment.

These qualities, although implicit, show up everywhere in managed care discourse. Where do they come from? For one thing, they seem reflective of the modem era's broad agenda. Slowly, beginning in the 16th and 17th centuries, humans began to be conceived of as arrangements of matter and, as such, best understood and controlled not by the spiritual practices of the church but by the secular use of scientific knowledge. As the material world became disenchanted, so too did humans, who were transformed from placeholders in God's divine plan to self-contained individuals who made up the vast sea called "labor." The marketplace inherited the sanctity and status of the church, and its workings became the updated equivalent of God's plan. Laborers, thought to be part of the calculus of profit and loss that drove the new system, were to be relocated and exploited under the poorest working conditions possible to produce the most financial profit. Labor was thought of as a kind of natural resource, one that should be colonized, managed, and exploited by the economic elite.

The modem-era, European focus on calculation, instrumentalism, logic, and profit became transformed into 20th-century practices when catalyzed by such quintessentially American virtues as pragmatism, optimism, rugged individualism, and systematic control. These American elaborations on modem-era values obviously fit well with 20th-century industrial capitalism and the propitious alliance between psychology and corporate business in the areas of personnel management, marketing, and advertising. Therefore, it was only a matter of time before a highly scientized psychotherapy would appeal to corporate insurance companies, always alert for new sources of income.

Are these values the only values through which a national health care system can be arranged? We do not believe so. In the interests of inviting further deliberation, we propose a hermeneutic or interpretive alternative to the prevailing instrumentalism (see, e.g., Rabinow & Sullivan, 1987; F.C. Richardson & Fowers, 1998; Taylor, 1985, 1989). A hermeneutic conception of psychotherapy would necessitate quite different arrangements of care. First of all, a hermeneutic perspective would encourage psychology to understand humans as moral and historical beings, rather than as the human equivalent of machines that can be best refashioned and "tuned up" through the use of technicist procedures produced by physical science methodology. This would necessitate conceiving of therapy as a kind of moral discourse that attempts to aid in developing what Heidegger thought of as an encounter with mortality and an examination of the moral trajectory of one's life (see, e.g., Guignon, 1993). Gadamer (1975) believed this is best achieved through the processes of engaged dialogue, what he called "genuine conversation" (see Cushman, 1995, chapter 9; Gilford, 1997, 1999; Greifinger, 1995; F. C. Richardson, Fowers, & Guignon, 1999; Warnke, 1987).

In this hermeneutic vision, psychological symptoms of distress are understood in part to be products of political arrangements and particular moral understandings developed by macro- and micro-cultural frames and thus are aspects of the social rather than a putatively isolated inner or behavioral realm. Therefore, the attempt to reduce human being to hyperconcrete, quantifiable behaviors, and treatment protocols to the dictates of outcome studies, would be understood as an impossible — and counterproductive — task. The cost-benefit analysis and time restrictions justified by positivist studies would be of limited value to the practice of a hermeneutic psychotherapy. Other ways of allocating the health care dollar and protecting the public from exploitation and harm — ways more fitting to psychotherapy as a moral and critical activity — would have to be devised.

Second, a hermeneutic perspective would encourage a historical, critical examination of therapy practices. Included especially would be an extended interrogation of the taken-for-granted assumption that health care in general, and psychological care in particular, should be the responsibility of employers.

What practical structure could be used that would be fitting for a hermeneutic understanding of psychotherapy? There is much in this that is still unclear to us. However, we can say that disengaged diagnostic practices, although not dismissed, would not be accorded the unquestioned value they now enjoy. The activity of peer consultation, perhaps supplemented with periodic supervision, could substitute for bureaucratic decision making regarding dispersal of benefits. In other words, oversight that protects patients and reinforces the ethics of the profession would require not a product but a process: not a disengaged *Diagnostic and Statistical Manual of Mental Disorders* number but an ongoing, cooperative, challenging intellectual and affective engagement with one's colleagues. If peer consultation groups composed of practicing therapists could furnish the opportunity for meaningful and responsible dialogue about cases, therapists would be engaged in ongoing, challenging feedback from their peers regarding diagnosis, treatment, and case management. Of course, there is no ultimate guarantee against the entanglements of self-interest, guild affiliation, and theoretical allegiance in these peer consultation processes, but there never is. There are only the hard-won understandings that well-meaning but flawed human beings develop together, in dialogue.

Conclusion

We have come to realize that managed care alone is not the problem. Our primary purpose in writing this article is to deepen understandings of the sociohistorical context in which positivism, parsimony, instrumentalism, and managed care have arisen and to examine their potential political consequences so that the decisions the profession makes about the responsibilities and practices of therapists can be more fully informed. We have tried to articulate some of the moral consequences of arranging psychotherapy so that cost-output calculations, as well as the societywide instrumentalism that frames those calculations, are the major determinants of our national health care system. For the purposes of this article, the issue is not whether managed care causes either fiscal efficiency or medical abuses but rather how its practices affect society's sense of what is health and sickness, normal and deviant, healing and quackery — in short, what it means to be human.

We are aware of the arguments of managed care proponents claiming that MCO regulations develop a more equitable service-delivery system. However, we believe managed care proponents – by failing to critically investigate the current life-world that they attempt to return the patient to — do not realize that their practices have the effect of subtly influencing patients to renounce difference and to conform to a problematic way of being. Managed care seems to advance a removed, disengaged practice for a compliant patient, a practice that produces a politically conservative kind of treatment — a normalizing and homogenizing practice that reinforces the political status quo. It does not help the patient question or resist the sociohistorical, material conditions from which he or she suffers.

Of course, throughout its varied history, psychotherapy has usually served normalizing functions simply by the way power relations are obscured and political suffering is medicalized in its worldview (see Kovel, 1980; Rieff, 1966; Rose, 1989). However, in managed care, the normalizing function of psychotherapy becomes its *defining* characteristic: In managed care, the act of complying with rules, procedures, and cultural prescriptions comes dangerously close to *constituting* successful treatment.

In other words, managed care is and is not changing our way of being. It is in that its practices and theories are inevitably affecting and intensifying this surface-oriented way of experiencing oneself, one's capacities and limits, and one's place in the world. But managed care is not changing the predominant way of being because U.S. culture has already been shifting, and managed care is a product — as well as a producer — of that shift. Managed care alone is not the problem; the problem resides in how people live, respond to the power relations of their social world, distribute resources, and conceive of and pursue the good.

The therapeutic practices valued by MCOs mirror recent sociohistorical changes: Living has become faster and shallower, action preferable to critical reflection, parsimony better than generosity, superficiality valued over complexity, image preferable to substance, solutions prized above questions. Life for many has indeed become digital, ones and zeros in infinite regress — boring, alienating, occasionally dangerous, often heartbreaking, and ultimately empty of meaning. Psychologists must fight against this way of being, but they cannot do so by appealing to scientistic notions of objectivity and disengagement, because it is those notions (and the political arrangements that benefit from them) that helped create the conditions under which people are currently suffering.

Fortunately, the profession of psychology has other streams of Western and non-Western traditions to draw from besides the ahistorical, technicist scientism currently used by managed care. The hermeneuticists encourage psychologists to fight against the trends of their time, including the way of being that is emerging, when it violates their sense of the good. They suggest that this can be done by using an awareness of the historicity of human being and its inescapable moral nature, by turning to and learning from the historical traditions that have constituted Western society and from neighboring traditions that have influenced it, and, through them, by devising therapeutic and political practices that are more in keeping with one's best values and commitments.

That will be difficult. But remember that some streams of Western tradition suggest that people seeking help deserve respect and care by virtue of their intrinsic worth as human beings, not because they can be made into tireless workers or more acquisitive consumers. The fight against instrumentalism and technicism is a long and complicated one, but one from which we psychologists can ill afford to absent ourselves. "And if not now, when?"[4]

Notes

1 Managed care has many meanings in the literature. We use the term *managed care organization* because it is inclusive of the variety of regulatory administrative processes and financial strategies currently found in the management of mental health care.

2 Managed care discourse is defined as textual materials that have arisen as a response to the growing hegemony of managed care. This includes journal articles, textbooks, and treatment manuals, and selected preexisting texts that underlie managed care's emphasis on efficiency and brevity (e.g., texts on brief therapy and manualized treat approaches). Quotations were chosen because we believe they are illustrative of managed care ideology and treatment philosophy; they embody the ethic of managed care, not necessarily the ethic of the specific authors.
3 For an example, see Safran and Segal (1990).
4 This is part of a saying of the Jewish sage Hillel (first century BCE–first century CE): "If I am not for myself, who will be for me? And if I am for myself alone, who am I? And if not now, when" (see Hertz, 1945, p. 25).

Chapter 6

Welcome to the 21st century, where character was erased

The William James lecture in psychotherapy and ethics

(2002 University of Nevada, 1st Annual William James Lecture in Psychological Ethics)

Historical introduction

I wrote a shorter version of this paper for a 2001 APA symposium titled "Does Psychology Erode Personhood?" which was published in Journal for *Theoretical and Philosophical Psychology* under the symposium's title the following year. The next year I gave this expanded version for the William James Lecture and Workshop in Psychological Ethics at the University of Nevada, Reno. Writing the paper gave me an opportunity to continue my ongoing commitment to using the four-part analysis of the self in order to better understand historical eras and especially more contemporary eras. By studying the history of the Diagnostic and Statistical Manual (DSM) I was able to notice an important change in a diagnostic category, relate it to changes in the cultural terrain of the early 21st century, and illustrate the way a healing technology (in this case a diagnostic system) not only reflects the political arrangements of its time and place, but also reproduces those arrangements.

As the 21st century began, psychotherapy, under the increasing influence of the corporatization of the profession, was becoming more dependent on quantifiable measures and behavioral practices, and on justifying those moves by claiming a physical science warrant. Some of us had been arguing that trend had serious political consequences for U.S. society, but to no avail. The forces at work on the society to roll back civil rights advances, militarize the police, and incarcerate disproportionate numbers of young males of color found a willing but politically naïve partner in an ahistorical, scientistic psychology. This paper discusses how seemingly innocent, technical changes in a diagnostic category can serve damaging political ends, yet all the while proclaiming its objectivity.

In 2002 the Bush administration's war on terror was ramping up, as were its efforts to secretly develop legal justifications for the military's use

> of torture in the Middle East and the detention center in Guantanamo, fight against campaign contribution reform, and increase the number of conservative judges in federal courts and the Supreme Court. Right-wing politics was in the air, and psychology was certainly not immune from its influences.

Thank you, Dr. Bruce Moran, for the opportunity to be here today and to be part of the first William James Lecture and Workshop in Psychology and Ethics. I am pleased to be with you.

I am also worried. You and I are undertaking a complex topic and probably one that will be challenging to our audience. Challenging because it is not easy for therapists to examine therapy practices through a cultural, historical perspective. We tend to be somewhat uncritical about our most beloved theories, if not somewhat true believers. That kind of certainty is helpful in one respect: it sometimes serves to comfort and reassure our patients. And of course it especially soothes our doubts.

Ah, but there's the rub: Our work is not supposed to soothe us, it's not supposed to quiet our anxiety, it's not supposed to make us feel good. We get paid, that's supposed to be enough. In other words, theoretically at least, the therapy isn't supposed to be for us, it's supposed to be for our patients. So, then, why are we anxious about our work? Why is it so difficult for us to think critically — that is, historically and politically — about our work? Why do many of us suffer from a nagging sense, like Doc Mumford in the recent film *Mumford*, that we are pretenders, frauds, or at best incompetents? And when we aren't self-doubting, then we tend to err in the opposite direction, and have an overblown, grandiose, somewhat arrogant sense of our work.

Why, indeed. Freud was right: ours is an impossible profession. It is impossible, I have come to think, because we think we should be doing one thing, but we can't. We are really doing something else, and we think we shouldn't be. To make matters worse, the thing we aren't supposed to be doing but are doing (and parenthetically, the only thing that really, honestly, in the long run, helps) is something we are not trained to do or even helped to do. And furthermore, it is probably something that is extraordinarily hard to do, it is probably not something you can exactly be taught how to do, and it is not something that can be planned out ahead of time. No wonder we're so nervous.

Most of our work as therapists is not the application of universal scientific truths won during long years of objective research. Therapy, I think, is not scientific in the sense of a modern-era physical science model. Instead it is a kind of moral discourse, and worse yet, one that has political consequences. Given that most of us have been trained to believe we should bracket off our moral preferences and banish our political commitments when entering the consulting room, the hermeneutic argument I'm about to deliver might seem frightening and dangerous.

But today I do hope you will be able to think about that argument, and consider it carefully. This is not an easy subject for me to think about, either, let alone talk about in public, and I suspect it will not be an easy one for you to listen to. But perhaps we can struggle along together, and try to make some sense out of this most perplexing of subjects.

Goodbye, character

Over the course of the last 115 years or so in the U.S., cultural historians have noticed that character has been slowly disappearing — like a fading image of a very old photograph weakened by the light. Once a picture of an important family member, a great grandparent, perhaps, or a group photo of the extended family assembled for an important occasion, the image is now undone, eased into insignificance, indistinct and finally unrecognizable.

Who were those people? How can they look so much like us and yet be so completely different? It is obvious, we could say, that they have a great deal of character — maybe too much, certainly too much rigidity and self-righteousness for us! We want none of that. And yet ... they are the ones who did the heroic deeds, such as immigrating from far-away continents or surviving slavery, and we are the ones who complain that our cappuccino has too much foam. What is character, the good and the bad of it? And what do we have instead? Our hipness, looseness, and youthfulness seem far superior, until you hear how many hours the average American watches television, or remember that George W. Bush is the current President. We can't go back to the Victorian era, of course, but how can we learn from it in order to make our world better?

As the 21st century dawns, psychotherapy is embedded in a fast-paced society in which market values are increasingly hegemonic; these elements influence psychology to strive toward ever-faster and more efficient brief therapy practices, more concrete and specific DSM categories, and more quantifiable therapeutic outcomes, all in order to better technicize and industrialize therapeutic practices. These trends can be seen throughout U.S. society; for instance, George Ritzer (1993) has referred to this trend as the "McDonaldization" of America.

From character to multiplicity

We stand at an important moment in U.S. history. The post-World War II boom has come and gone, and the Cold War has evaporated. The last fifty years have brought many changes to U.S. society, for both good and ill. What do we think about these changes, what meaning do we make from them? And most importantly, what do we do with them: what do we do next? Perhaps the first thing we can say about ourselves as a nation at this moment is that we really don't know what to do next. We seem confused, somewhat dazed, almost reeling from the activities and events of the last fifty years, and especially the tragedies and scandals of the last three years.

Perhaps historians won't think that we have entered the 21st century until we develop some consensus about who we are and what we choose to do next about the problems facing us as a nation. Or perhaps, unfortunately, the dazed and confused look many of us exhibit is, itself, our new way of being.

The early 21st century self

It was historian Warren Susman (1973) who first noticed that around 1890 advice manuals stopped talking about character as the central ingredient of the predominant way of being (i.e., the self), and began touting the importance of what they called personality. Personality was thought to be a cluster of unique qualities that made one stand out from the crowd, that made one successful at impressing and attracting others. Victorian character, composed of moral rigidity, steadfastness, and commitment, was sliding into insignificance in the face of a new, urban, more secular, faster-paced, ambitious, alienated world of corporate, industrial capitalism. Victorian character stole, conquered, and then settled a continent, built communities, and produced heroes; early 20th century personality created new personal identities — think for instance of Jay Gatsby

— and produced celebrities. Character sacrificed for the common good; personality spontaneously seized the moment and acted impulsively in order to achieve personal fame and fortune. Character was good; personality was famous.

As the 20th century moved forward, the taken-for-granted components of the self continued to shift away from character and toward personality. Of course this was not a smooth and consistent change, but over time it surely happened. With the development of the post-World War II era, and especially with the advent of the 1960s, the qualities that constituted character got fainter and fainter. The spontaneous, colorful, self-centered, gratification-seeking, perennially immature, youth-worshipping self arrived on center stage. As American life became increasingly commodified, and advertising became the primary avenue of entertainment, a new understanding developed: the self became emptied of much of its substance in order to be hungry for and constituted by ever-new purchases of products and experiences. The commodity came to be viewed as that which would transform the consumer into the kind of personality she or he longed to be. Purchasing and consuming became the transformative acts for a way of being I called in a 1990 article "the Empty Self."

This emphasis on personality and emptiness happened not only in pop culture but also in intellectual and professional circles. In the Academy, psychology developed a subfield called Personality Psychology; several theories emerged and many measures were developed to define and evaluate personality traits and determine how pathology resulted from them. More recently, some postmodernists have argued that Victorian character, the major ingredient of the centered, unified, coherent Victorian self, is one of the significant cause of modern-era racism and misogyny, because it cannot tolerate otherness in itself and therefore creates a despised other, in order to project (and then attack) one's internal differentness onto the external other. In clinical psychology, narcissism — a disorder distinguished in part by a pervasive sense of emptiness — and other disorders of the self became the diagnoses of the day, and new theories, such as Kohut's self psychology and British and American object relations theory described human development, parenting, and therapy through the use of consumerist metaphors, and defined and explained the putatively universal nature of emptiness, the differences between pathological and healthy narcissism, and the distinction between the False and the True Self.

The empty self of the post-World War II era fits hand-in-glove with and seamlessly facilitates our highly consumerized era and the people who profit from it. The psychotherapy theories that achieved popularity describing, explaining, and treating the empty self, in turn, legitimated and normalized it and thereby played an important, albeit unintentional, political role.

In 1999 Peter Gilford and I (Cushman & Gilford, 1999) speculated that a new self, a possible "multiple self," seemed to be emerging. We think this new self might "be marked by a propensity to gather about itself a number of identities that are located around the outside of the self, external to but identified with the individual..." (Cushman & Gilford, 1999, p. 16).

We think that one of the identifying aspects of this multiple self is the tendency to believe that nothing can be changed by facing up to authority and directly opposing it, that the only way to survive difficult situations and enhance one's life is to morph, to shape-shift, into someone *else*: To escape, to always be a moving target. If these observations sound familiar, the U.S. might be

> witnessing a shift from a self that had a wish for what Foucault called a "richly furnished interior" to a self with a need for many, varied exteriors that one can quickly select from and present to the world; from a self that should be singular and unified, to a self that should be multiple and decentered; from a self that had a deeply felt yearning to experience an interior, essential change, to a self that yearns to have many exteriors to change into; from a self that hoped to be fundamentally transformed, to a self that hopes to present the most effective and attractive identity at the most propitious moment; from a self whose understanding of the good was to consume in order to live the good life, be enlivened, or soothed, to a self whose understanding of the good is to consume in order to develop more identities and thus be more alluring, effective, and elusive [and therefore, momentarily safe].
>
> (Cushman & Gilford, 1999, pp. 17–18)

Here are two examples from television ad campaigns: the first is from a soft drink commercial, and it illustrates the empty self. A senior citizen's center and a college fraternity both throw parties on the same day.

Unfortunately, the respective soft drink orders are mistakenly switched and subsequently delivered to the wrong parties. The seniors receive the highly invigorating, youth-inducing Pepsi, and the frat boys receive the Coca-Cola, which causes boredom, stupidity, and an early onset of old age. The seniors daringly ride skateboards, dance the latest dances, use the latest youth language, and generally look ecstatic. The frat boys have been transformed into dull, napping, senile old folks, trying to stay awake during their bingo game. The commodity is all-powerful; by purchasing and consuming it, the very nature or essence of the consumer is transformed.

The second example illustrates the multiple self: A young man is driving a very fast sports car over a winding road. He has a kind of grungy look about him, he's playing loud hard-rock music, and he has a young, sulking, arrogant expression on his face. A middle-aged, sour-looking motorcycle cop, hiding behind a billboard, spies the kid and takes off after him, sirens sounding. The grungy guy slowly pulls over, and in the process changes the music station to classical, puts on a tweedy sport coat, innocuous glasses, and quickly shaves with a portable electric shaver. By the time the cop walks over and confronts him, he is transformed. The cop is speechless, staggers away, and just gives up. The kid, looking straight ahead, smiles an inscrutable smile, and drives off. The prevalence of the shape-shifting, morphing, and doubleness often featured in pop culture today might well indicate that contemporary Americans do not believe they can make themselves understood by and develop a fair and mutually satisfactory agreement with those in positions of authority. They seem to think the only solution to cultural and political differences and conflicting interests is to deceive and escape. The self is configured in that image.

When Peter and I first noticed that the empty self seemed to be on the wane and a new self was beginning to come to light, it was 1996 or so. At that time what was most prominent about the newly emerging self — or rather about the social world that was constituting the emerging self — was its rapid pace and its boom-town style, a product of the giddy — and arrogant — affluence of the dot.com "New Economy." But in the last three years the boom has gone bust, the 9/11 attack has happened, and the CEO-Accounting Scandals and California Energy Crisis have hit with shattering effect. The earlier affluence and arrogance seem to have covered up other aspects of the multiple self, which are now coming to light. These are characteristics such as the essential political hopelessness that grows out of a fundamentally unjust, intolerant, and immoveable world. It is a world morally confused, continuing to lose community and tradition, and dominated by a scientistic technicism that has denigrated moral discourse and threatened it with extinction.

The DSM as a carrier of the new self

The DSM has been influenced by market-driven imperatives regarding speed and efficiency, framed the emerging multiple self, and in return has contributed to its growth. The format of the DSM has undergone significant changes, from its inception in 1952, through the first monumental change in 1980 with the unveiling of the DSM-III, and finally with the most recent iteration, the DSM-IV. DSM-I was concerned primarily with links between patterns of complex behavior and holistic conceptions of characterological styles, couched often in psychoanalytic language. The focus on patterns and styles has shifted over time to the scientistic and hyperconcrete outlines and decision trees of DSM-IV, couched in behavioral language.

Of course, the shift to a hyperconcrete, behavioral, and symptom-driven understanding of human being has been influenced by the attempt to adapt to and fit with the demands of managed care arrangements of psychological treatment. Of this there can be little doubt. But I would like to examine these changes through a broader historical perspective. I am interested in how both managed care and the DSM have been affected by and are reflections of the social world of our time and place. I want to explore how the understandings of the good and the broad sociopolitical and material arrangements of our social terrain have brought to light both the changes in the DSM and the recently concluded power grab successfully accomplished by the multinational insurance and pharmaceutical corporations that have culminated in what we now call managed care.

The change from DSM-I to DSM-III

The shift from DSM I to DSM III could be interpreted as a reflection of a particular understanding of human being: A more complex, messier, holistic description of humanity, haunted by the dark urges and unconscious conflicts of a classical psychoanalytic vision, has given way to a focus on delimited, highly concrete and specific bits of observable, unproblematic, straightforward behavior. The shift implies a self that is made up of data points of public, observable, behavioral acts, which are declared symptoms and signs by the DSM experts, not complex interactive patterns of holistic personality styles. The DSM-IV self is a kind of Lego-like self, composed of concrete, singular behaviors that can be easily disconnected and reconnected to one another in order to form larger — but momentary — self-configurations. There is little that is complex, indeterminate, and ambiguous, let alone anything that refers to deeper, especially unseen forces that form a larger pattern or style of personality or type of character.

The DSM-IV self is a self of parts, not wholes; behaviors, not characters; concrete observations, not artistic interpretations; conscious speech, not unconscious dreams; surfaces, not depths; putatively incontrovertible data points, not ambiguous narrative; cleanliness, not messiness.

The creation of Axis I and Axis II

It was with the introduction of DSM-III that the distinction between Axis I and II was instituted. The influence of psychoanalysis was deliberately undermined by the authors of DSM-III, who argued that the category of neurosis was far too ideological and vague to be helpful diagnostically, and in fact was part of the problem rather than the solution. The DSM III's authors systematically disassembled the neuroses, and their symptoms re-described and then relocated into new categories — such as Anxiety Disorders, Mood Disorders, Dissociative Disorders — characterized by their specific, observable behaviors rather than their hypothetical personality styles. With the new behavioral categories came the claim that the disorders clustered in Axis I could be more easily identified, treatment plans devised and carried out more efficiently, and outcomes coded quantitatively and thus evaluated more accurately. Emotional struggles unable to be parsed into such easily observable and countable elements — those still thought to be organized around personality styles rather than discrete behaviors – were called Personality Disorders, and thereby banished to the Axis II category. A personality disorder was thought to consist of a problem of character, "an enduring pattern of inner experience and behavior ... [that] is stable over time, and leads to distress or impairment" (DSM-IV, p. 629). Therefore, they were thought to be qualitatively different from Axis I disorders.

Now, one of the most significant effects of the division between Axis I and Axis II is the body of theoretical justifications used by Managed Care Organizations (MCOs) to explain why they will not pay for the treatment of Axis II disorders. They claim that Personality Disorders are not the same critters as Axis I disorders (which are the true mental illnesses), and this explains why personality disorders take a long time, or even forever, to treat. Instead, the literature produced by MCOs speculated that Personality Disorders might not be mental illnesses at all, but rather "problems in living," or dilemmas better left to philosophical discourse or religious practice. In other words, length and type of treatment for Axis II are not cost effective — so they have been banished to a non-psychological realm. What matters is to get troubled workers back to their jobs, consumers back in the stores, and borrowers back in the banks as quickly as possible. In any event, the MCO literature argues, the treatment of these types of problems were never, and should never, be thought of as the financial responsibility of the real clients of MCOs: not the employees, but the employers who pay for the benefits.

The consignment of Personality Disorders to the category of Axis II, and the subsequent decision of MCOs to refuse payment for Axis II, has had several consequences, including two that are important for the topic of this paper. One, diagnoses that presuppose a self that is relatively unified and thought to be consistent across time (i.e., composed of a coherent character type), are separated from and distinguished qualitatively from the other categories. This move fits well with the aforementioned historical shift from 19th century character to 20th century personality, and more recently from the empty self to the multiple self. The second consequence is that, because MCOs do not pay for the treatment of Axis II disorders, clinicians tend to avoid acknowledging them unless or until they can also make an Axis I diagnosis. In their paperwork for the MCOs delineating the diagnostic descriptions and treatment goals for specific patients, clinicians uniformly feature only or primarily the Axis I diagnoses and downplay the Axis II diagnoses in order to protect themselves against criticism and then financial reprisals from their MCO superiors.

Over time, this will lead to moral conflicts in the therapist, and probably she or he will come to selectively inattend to the fact that she or he is lying or at least not disclosing the whole truth to the MCO in order to get some treatment for the patient and also some payment for her or his work. The pattern works like this: At first, for pragmatic reasons, therapists greatly limit their use of Axis II diagnoses. Later on, perhaps due to self-image management (see Hales, 1985), therapists ... [begin] limiting discussion about Axis II diagnoses with their supervisors, consultants, or peers, and eventually, they stop ... [using and then even thinking about] Axis II altogether. This illustrates how institutional discursive practices, in combination with other sociopolitical forces, gradually can erase a way of being. The notion of character as an ongoing ... [pattern] then simply disappears or is limited to those who can afford to have one" (Cushman & Gilford, 2000, p. 989).

What effect does it have for a proportion of an entire profession, a profession that prides itself on its ethical code, and is based on the importance of honesty, to consistently lie to the corporate bureaucracies to which they have legally promised to tell the truth? Once again we see the influence of current trends on our capacity to think morally and act honestly: to have character.

A case study: the case of the disappearing sociopath

I have studied the description of DSM-I's Sociopathic or Psychopathic Personality Disorder, which were excluded from DSMs III and IV, and compared them with DSM-IV's description of what is now called Anti-Social Personality Disorder. The authors of DSM-I and II, with their more narrative, complex, darker vision, were able to describe a type of person who was glib, charming, and smooth. This type of patient was thought to be raised in upper class intact homes by parents who placed great value on appearance over substance. Politicians, charismatic business and religious leaders, and highly effective but unethical salesmen were some of the examples used in a popular text book from the DSM-I era (Coleman, 1964). Examples of patients with the Anti-Social diagnosis in a currently popular, abnormal psychology textbook (Seligman, Walker & Rosenhans, 2001) were more violent and dangerous, criminals who committed armed robberies, murder, and mayhem.

The authors of DSM-IV instituted changes that over time have tended to criminalize the Anti-Social category. That is, they have narrowed the category so that the distinguishing characteristics are more violent, crude, and pertain to those who commit what might be referred to as "blue-collar," as opposed to "white collar," crime. They did so in particular by making it mandatory that when the patient was a youngster she or he must have been diagnosed Conduct Disordered. Although the link between sociopathic adults and delinquent children or adolescents was recognized in each of the DSMs, it was not a requirement until DSM IV.

I think Conduct Disorder itself is a highly problematic category, and I fear that this diagnosis, especially in inner city schools, will suffer a fate similar to that of ADD/ADHD: it will be a way that political suffering is medicalized and then medicated into silence. Often in the 1990s members of a minority group — in the case of ADD/ADHD poor young inner city males of color — were diagnosed and medicated far out of proportion to their numbers, blamed and pejoratively diagnosed for learning the skills and adopting the way of being needed to survive the dangerous and dehumanizing world in which they are forced to live. By making Conduct Disorder mandatory for the adult diagnosis, DSM IV creates a situation in which Anti-Social Personality Disorder could become a depository for the economically disadvantaged and dispossessed, for poor whites and people of color. This is accomplished while at the same time the new category excludes the children of the affluent and powerful; they are excluded from the new category even though their psychopathology when reaching adulthood is ultimately much more damaging to society. One of the results of this trend is that Anti-Social PD no longer recognizes as pathological the more subtle crimes that indicate pathology among the wealthy and powerful.

I find the shift from sociopathic to anti-social, and from white collar to blue collar crime, significant. Consider that during the time this change in DSM categories occurred, the Savings and Loan fiasco and the Iran-Contra Drugs-For-Arms scandal of the Reagan Presidency were committed, the 2000 Presidential Electoral scandal in Florida was perpetrated, the California Energy Crisis of 2001 burst on the scene, and the contemporary Accounting and Stock Option scandals have destroyed the retirement funds of millions of hardworking citizens. These white-collar deceptions and scams have cost state and national governments — and thus deprived schools and social service agencies — of untold millions of dollars. And consider that these recent white collar crimes against the body politic have been committed by supposedly upstanding, highly successful, wealthy people in positions of trust and power. They willfully and consciously conspired to defraud and rob the governmental coffers and deprive everyday workers and retirees of staggering amounts of money. And they accomplished this task first of all by paying the highest of elected officials to pass laws that would allow them to perpetrate those crimes legally.

What does it mean that the most dangerous criminals in our current society have been effectively excluded from the diagnostic category "anti-social personality disorder?" It could mean that American society is becoming more and more sanguine about — in fact perhaps openly supportive of — deviousness, deception, lying, and trickery when it is in service of profit. The old saying "All's fair in love and war" might now need an addition: love, war, and profiteering.

It could also mean that the hermeneuticists are right: there is no way to prevent our moral and political prejudices from affecting our psychological practices, no matter how persuasive the claim that scientific method is "guaranteeing" objectivity. In this case the subtle racism and classism still deeply embedded in American customs and laws have leaked into the health care decisions of DSM-IV. Contemporary moral understandings about the good (in this case the virtue of pursuing large profit through any means necessary), have profoundly, but invisibly, affected the decisions of the DSM authors.

If the case of the disappearing sociopath is any indication, it appears that attenuating human being and reducing it to a remarkably thin and superficial self composed of observable behaviors and interchangeable symptoms has neither stopped psychology from reproducing the racism and classism of the status quo, nor from opposing and treating the greed and power hunger that might well have driven them. In fact, perhaps it has greased the wheel of political collusion. Perhaps eviscerating the more complex, holistic, style-oriented formulations of DSM-I and II, and erasing the concept of character in favor of a thin, behavioral, procedural self has caused us to constitute human being in ways that are harmful beyond our imagining. Perhaps, ironically, by doing away with the concept of what DSM-I in the Sociopathic PD called "moral insanity," the DSM-IV authors have played a part in further reinvigorating and valorizing it.

Is personhood being eroded?

By being uncritically accepting of the social forces pushing psychology toward ever-more market-driven and scientistic diagnostic and therapeutic practices, perhaps we are in the process of unknowingly shaping a psychology that is reproducing the multiple self and eroding the one quality of personhood that is indispensable to humankind: the ability to think of oneself as a moral and civic being and to practice moral discourse, self-reflection, and have the capacity for moral action.

In this way psychology might well be eroding our ability to experience guilt, the presence of which is thought to be one of the main characteristics of what was once called neurosis. What have we lost, and what have we created, by attenuating, eviscerating, and thinning out our moral capacities in the name of objective science, speed, efficiency, and multiplicity? What has our society lost in its rush to erase character and embrace first personality, then the empty self, and now the multiple self? What have we lost, and will we be able to recapture part of it somehow, and adapt it into a contemporary shape? And if recapturing and reinvigorating our moral capacities and our willingness to act on those morals in the public commons — in other words, our personhood — is not the true goal of psychotherapy, then what good is it?

Chapter 7

Between arrogance and a dead-end

Psychoanalysis and the Heidegger-Foucault dilemma

(2005 *Contemporary Psychoanalysis, 41*, 399–417)

Historical introduction

Those who know me will recognize this article as a product of many years of struggle with the philosophical issues that were prominent in the humanities and social sciences during the modern era in Western society. My first foray into the serious interdisciplinary study of humans was an undergraduate course, titled "Culture and Psychology," at UCLA in 1964. It was an elective course, and a nervous, chainsmoking graduate student had been assigned to teach it. Sadly, it was a lousy course, but for me it served as a beginning. Little did I know that 20 years later I would be consumed by the topic; or that 40 years later I would write this article, which among other things could have been a philosophical foundation for my imaginary version of that 1964 course.

Since 1981 I had been studying the two intellectual streams that make up the Interpretive Turn: postmodernism and hermeneutics. Although many therapists have neither the time nor inclination to delve deeply into the philosophical aspects of the Turn, I came to realize that it was necessary — in fact indispensible — to do so. Postmodernism was the hipper of the two streams; it was cool, seemingly streetwise and hard-edged, and better connected to the Left. Hermeneutics, on the other hand, seemed less cool, more academic, and perhaps, some critics argued, even quietly conservative. However, as the years went by I came to realize that hermeneutics had fewer internal contradictions and made more sense philosophically. I sensed that hermeneutics was misunderstood by the Left and ultimately was a crucial ingredient in the Turn's development in the new century.

This article was an attempt to put into plain words why therapists and psychological researchers needed to learn more about the philosophical concepts and arguments that constitute the Interpretive Turn. I learned a lot by writing this paper; it helped me as a therapist, teacher, and supervisor.

During my one and only sabbatical in 2000 I hoped to develop a deeper understanding of Heidegger's *Being and Time* (which lead me to explore his involvement with the Nazis), Foucault's body of work, Gadamer's *Truth and Method*, and the horrific historical situation of the first 50 years of the 20th century. I came to realize that both streams of the Interpretive Turn had their good and problematic aspects. And if the Turn was to have anything meaningful to say it would have to be said from those who could critique and embrace both streams, tolerate the paradoxes involved, and come to some sort of philosophically solid framework for understanding the mystery that is human being.

Concurrent with researching these issues was the historical moment: in 2000 George W. Bush had been appointed by a bitterly debated decision of the Supreme Court; in 2001 the 9/11 terrorist attack on the U.S. was carried out; in 2003 the Bush administration crafted explanations and legal protections for its use of torture in military prisons; Christian fundamentalists and evangelicals became a significant political force; and a continuation of the Republican Party's attack on voting rights increased in intensity. And in 2004 President Bush was elected to a second term.

All this helped me realize and mention in the article the importance of the type of subtle political resistance that could be exercised by psychologists, if only we could get our philosophy straight. It would be ten years before that idea became the article "Relational Psychoanalysis as Political Resistance" (Chapter 13), but "Between Arrogance and a Dead-End" was its beginning.

I'd like to point out that in the years after this article was published, I came to realize that my characterization of Heidegger's concept of "authenticity" was not correct. I had conflated it with an aspect of what Gadamer called "dialogue" and what Foucault thought was a valued result of historical study. I stand by the overall point of my critique of Heidegger, but "authenticity" wasn't quite the good political guidance I had originally thought it to be. For reasons of historical accuracy, I didn't change the original text.

The interpretive turn (in both its postmodern and hermeneutic forms), the intellectual movement in the humanities and social sciences that has become so important — even commonsensical — in Europe and the United States, has of course been applied to psychotherapy. Interpretive ideas have had an impact especially in existential-phenomenological, feminist, object relations and family therapy and interpersonal and

Lacanian psychoanalysis. Out of the mix of postmodernism, hermeneutics, interpersonal, and object relations has come relational psychoanalysis, which, at the turn of the century, has assumed a leading role in psychoanalysis.

But how much, really, do therapists know about the interpretive turn? What are its strengths and weaknesses, its factions and especially their consequences? In this paper, first delivered at a 2001 APA symposium titled "Otherness and Dialogue," I examine two of the most important 20th century figures in the interpretive turn, Martin Heidegger — the founder of ontological hermeneutics — and Michel Foucault — identified prominently with postmodernism. Psychoanalysts have often stayed clear of discussions such as this. But the continuing success of relational psychoanalysis, given its indebtedness to the interpretive turn, necessitates a detailed exploration of its the philosophical foundations.

Occasionally psychoanalysts have taken up these issues. For instance, *Psychoanalytic Dialogues* has from time to time taken up philosophical debates (e.g., v. 3, n. 2, 1993) about the fit between hermeneutics and psychoanalysis, and *Contemporary Psychoanalysis* once dedicated an entire issue to the postmodern concept of multiplicity (v. 32, n. 4, 1996). Most recently, *Bringing the Plague: Toward a Postmodern Psychoanalysis* (Fairfield, Layton & Stack, 2002) featured contributions from many prominent relational psychoanalysts. Today, more than ever in a world threatened by extreme and ever-increasing economic stratification, militarism, terrorism, family violence, racism, sexism, and homophobia, we need to continue the conversation. The questions in this paper are questions that address the political and moral climate psychoanalysis belongs to and helps perpetuate. Of course, analysts not only apply theory; they also explain, justify, and create new theory. By doing so they have an impact on social practices, thereby affecting interpersonal interactions, undermining or shoring up social institutions, and shifting the larger social frame.

The dilemma

Both hermeneuticists and postmodernists attempt to stay true to a vision of human being that we might today call "historical" or "cultural." They do this while at the same time trying to avoid a historical determinism in their theory and their research — that is, resisting the influence of the inevitable hatreds and narrowness of vision of their particular time and place. This perspective is thought to encourage critical thinking and political resistance. Hermeneuticists often attempt political resistance by emphasizing the concept of intersecting traditions and the process of what Heidegger called "authenticity." Postmodernists often attempt political resistance by focusing on the center-periphery distinction and valorizing what Foucault called "the insurrection of subjugated discourses."

In this paper I examine these two strategies by discussing Heidegger's involvement with National Socialism and thus his collaboration with the violent "othering" and then genocide of the Jews, and by asking questions about Foucault's valorization of the periphery and his limited vision of and then contradictory statements about the moral. I argue that both positions are flawed. Heidegger's flaw was the arrogance of monoculturalism and intellectual monologism. Foucault's flaw was the reduction of moral discourse to the exercise of power, a move that painted him into a philosophical corner from which all of us informed by his work continue to suffer.

The dilemma that confronts us today in American psychology grows explicitly from the above two flaws: how can we find a way to ground our practices in a historicity without arrogance and develop political critique without sabotaging our own projects through a refusal to engage explicitly with the moral. I suggest that this dilemma is being addressed by an emerging North American project that extends Gadamer's concept of dialogue while also emphasizing a critical, but philosophically more modest, Foucaultian dimension.

This is not an arcane, esoteric issue. The philosophical foundations of interpretive therapeutic ideology, and its goals, practices, and consequences, are all of a piece. They fit together like a jigsaw puzzle, mutually affecting and constituting one another. Because one's therapeutic ideology has far-reaching implications for one's therapeutic practices, we owe it to our patients, students, colleagues, and our own best political commitments to learn about and struggle with these issues as fully as possible.

The problem with Heidegger

While studying Heidegger and his involvement with the Nazis, I have been struck by his heartlessness and lack of remorse, but also by the blindness of some of his apologists and the hysteria of some of his accusers. It has been heartbreaking and sickening to read Heidegger's speeches and personal correspondences and match them with the political events of their moment. The Nazi's military revaunchism and public promises to dominate Europe did not seem to bother him, nor did their hateful and increasingly violent anti-Semitism move him to public (or private) condemnation. Heidegger claimed that he was innocent or misunderstood, but the lack of evidence to the contrary is staggering. His excuses and defenses seem without merit.

There are many who have tried in various ways to explain away Heidegger's complicity, and there are those who have tried to account for it by finding proof that his philosophy inevitably led to Nazism (e.g., Rockmore, 1997; Wolin, 1990). Neither of these approaches seems persuasive. There is no doubt that Heidegger collaborated with the Nazis much more than we knew until recently, and that he and some of his supporters suppressed and denied the truth. Also, there is no doubt that some of Heidegger's ideas reflected the taken-for-granted anti-Semitism that was prominent in Christian Europe for over a thousand years before the Nazis came to power. It also seems obvious that some of Heidegger's ideas were reflections of German chauvinism and were probably attempts on his part to prove his dedication to the party; often he did this by elaborating on philosophical concepts that for two centuries had reflected and justified German anti-Semitism (see Sluga, 1993). But that does not mean that *all* of Heidegger's philosophy, especially its most central ideas, lead to Nazism.

Although Heidegger's involvement with the Nazis and his explanation of why he was involved might not condemn his entire philosophy, they do illuminate two important flaws. *Flaw number one*: Heidegger's conception of the German people and their historical destiny excluded important minorities within the German population. The belief that Aryans were destined to dominate Europe and usher in a new golden era was rarely challenged in Germany in part because ethnic groups such as Jews and Roma ignored by the cultural conversation and had little influence. Heidegger wrote about the transcendent importance of German culture, but it was a monocultural tradition to which he referred. Other traditions within Germany and Central Europe, such as Jewish traditions, which were meaningful and potentially helpful in the resistance to the modern era, were excluded out of hand.

In retrospect it is easy to explain away Heidegger's involvement by suggesting that he was simply a bigot, and noticing that in fact nearly all of Europe was awash in a virulent anti-Semitism. But when racism is voiced by one whose job it is to think, and by one whose theory focused on history and the vicissitudes of social conformity, it is particularly frightening. It is especially important to remember the irony in all this: Heidegger's philosophy, although obviously ethnocentric, also contained a hard-won antidote for the ethnic hatred and Aryan supremacy that was so prevalent at that time. Heidegger's use of the hermeneutic circle and especially his concept of authenticity, often currently misunderstood and maligned by postmodernists, require an ability to engage in dialogic, critical processes that, if followed, might have made it more difficult for Heidegger to collude with the Nazis.

Flaw number two: Hannah Arendt and Karl Jaspers (see Olson, 1994), and more recently Bernstein (1991, pp. 79–141), have noted that there is a poverty of human caring detectible in Heidegger's later work, a poverty reflected especially in his lack of appreciation for the intensely interpersonal nature of the social realm. In Heidegger's post-World War II writings in particular he withdrew from a certain type of emotional involvement with and then intellectual interest in the social. Also Scheibler (2000, pp. 99–170) referred to this when she noticed Heidegger's emphasis on the overwhelming power of impersonal Being and on the work of the isolated poet and intellectual as the "saving powers," rather than interpersonal relatedness, dialogic practices, and political activism. Bernstein suggested that Heidegger's withdrawal from the social realm into an intellectual monologism was caused in part by his inability to face and respond meaningfully to the horrific details of the Holocaust and his collusion with it.

Ironically, there is a way that the first and the second flaws are linked together. Jewish tradition was, for the most part, denigrated and finally violently silenced during Europe's dominant cultural conversation through more than 1,000 years of one of the supreme acts of "othering." Yet, Judaism has much to say about humility, respect, and dialogue. Unlike Heidegger's turn away from relatedness, some Holocaust survivors, like the then-young journalist Elie Wiesel, applied Judaism's regard for the interpersonal even after being tortured in the Nazi death camps:

> To say 'I suffer, therefore I am' is to become the enemy of man. What you must say is 'I suffer, therefore you are.' Camus wrote

somewhere that to protest against a universe of unhappiness you had to create happiness. That's an arrow pointing the way: it leads to another human being. And not via absurdity.

(Wiesel, 1964, p. 118)

Heidegger, it turns out, cooperated in the near total destruction of a tradition that contained a belief in human caring and wisdom about the healing nature of the interpersonal realm. It was precisely the absence of such values that motivated or at least enabled Heidegger's collusion with the Nazis and later contributed to his emotional breakdown and then near complete social isolation.

Dialogue

One of the reasons why Heidegger's Nazi involvement and then lack of remorse is so disturbing is because he had previously developed ideas that described how one can resist social and political conformity. Heidegger thought that only by fully facing the historicity of human being, and thereby the "nothingness" that is human life without culture, an individual can grasp how deeply dependent and constituted one is by one's culture. But Heidegger thought that one can also learn how to understand and honestly face the limits and dangers of one's culture, as well as its grandeur. By doing so, the completely involuntary nature of cultural membership at birth, and thus the accidental nature of cultural and familial identity, becomes more obvious. Its accidental nature helps us realize that even though our historicity constitutes us, it does not have to completely control us — precisely because human being is historical, it is (slightly) changeable. And indeed, we can be affected by other cultures, ideas, and ways of being. In other words, history is constitutive but not monolithic. Heidegger called the product of this process "authenticity," the ability to be aware of one's own historicity and yet not be completely determined by it.

Hans-Georg Gadamer, one of Heidegger's former students, must have watched as Heidegger's integrity was destroyed by his inability to practice successfully the process of authenticity. I imagine that in response to witnessing his country's embrace of National Socialism and his mentor's willing collaboration with them, Gadamer was able to develop an understanding of what went wrong, both nationally and personally. As a result he came to appreciate the importance of political resistance, and especially the capacity to respect and be curious about the other, a quality he came to recognize as an indispensable element of resistance. In response, he expanded upon and made more accessible Heidegger's concept of authenticity, and called it dialogue. Recently, a few North American philosophers such as Charles Taylor (1985a & b, 1989, 1991), Richard Bernstein (1983, 1991), Charles Guignon (1985), David Hoy (1978), James Risser (1997), Tony Stigliano (1989), and Georgia Warnke (1987) – and psychologists Blaine Fowers and Frank Richardson (Richardson, Fowers & Guignon, 1999), Jack Martin and Jeff Sugarman (1999), Brent Slife and Richard Williams (1995), and Donnel Stern (1991; 1997) have interpreted and expanded upon Heidegger's and Gadamer's concepts, making them more compatible with early 21st century Western psychological culture.

Briefly, Gadamer described what happens during an encounter with difference. Two people meet and notice that they have a radically different opinion, value, or way of being. They struggle to come to some common agreement about their difference, but mostly just defend their own position and argue or accuse. But if both have good will toward the other and are genuinely interested in finding respectful agreement, they begin to try to understand the other by opening themselves to the other's point of view. That is, being willing to place in question one's most cherished beliefs and commitments by comparing it with the other's point of view. This is done not in order to develop a false agreement or to pretend that somehow one can, through empathy, feel what the other feels. It is done by imagining the kind of world the other lives in that would bring their opinion or value or way of being to light in the way it is. The other, Gadamer argued, can never be known in some unproblematic way, but one can learn something about the other by trying to understand the cultural framework that brings the other to light.

When that happens, it usually comes in a flash of understanding, something Gadamer called a "fusion of horizons." This fusion only lasts for a moment or so, but it means that the participants' perspectives have shifted slightly. Standing in a slightly shifted location, they are then able to ask "If their world brings them to light in the way they are, what kind of world is it that brings me to light in the way I am" (see Cushman, 2001)?

In other words, dialogue, when entered into in good faith, can help participants realize that the political arrangements of their social world are imperfect and sometimes seriously flawed; their cultural frame is not the only frame possible; their cultural truths are not the only truths available. By contextualizing cultural understandings, participants can come to realize that they live at a point of intersecting traditions, and each of these traditions has some good aspects and some bad aspects. By doing so, it might be possible to get more proficient at identifying and then evaluating the good things and the bad things about particular traditions, including one's own. By facing difference and opening oneself to the other in this way, one can let oneself be taught something new by the other. This concept has many applications in psychology, and especially psychotherapy (see for instance Cushman, 1995, ch. 9, 2001; Greifinger, 1995; Richardson, Fowers, & Guignon, 1999, ch. 9; Stern, 1991, 1997).

Now, this does not mean that the power relations of one's society are somehow magically erased by dialogue. It does not mean that through dialogue partners can come to some sort of putatively perfect, or objective, or even accurate understanding of the other or the other's social world. It does not mean that difference is erased, that fragmentation or incoherence are healed, that lack is undone, or emptiness filled. It does not mean that dialogue is easy, simple, or achievable unproblematically. It means that power and prejudice and bias are always with us, that imperfect and unproblematic perception of the other is our human lot, never to be transcended. It means that, even though we are fragmented, incoherent, or at least constituted of multiple voices and influences, we can still think, be curious, have creative moments, feel compassion for, cooperate with, and love another. We can come to common understandings — at least for a few moments — but they will always be incomplete and uncertain. Hermeneutics is not interested in perfection, objectivity, cleanliness, comfort, completeness, simplicity, or certainty. It embraces messiness, imperfection, not knowing, and mystery.

The problem with Foucault

Whereas Heidegger's problem was an inability to critique the dominant ideology and power relations of his time and place, we might say that Foucault's problem was an inability to do anything else. Foucault's work was brilliant; the human sciences own him a tremendous debt of gratitude. His work brought a creativity, verve, and driving moral force to history and philosophy. The last chapter of *Discipline and Punish*, for instance, is one of the most beautiful, chilling, and ultimately inspiring examples of historical research ever written.

On the other hand, Foucault's work suffered from exaggeration and occasional fabrication (e.g., Scull, 1993, pp. 5–8). Despite his relentless campaign against an Enlightenment-style "view from nowhere," some critics think Foucault's work contains a similar type of unexamined — and unquestioned — perspective (e.g., Taylor, 1986). Most importantly, although he articulated ruthlessly how ideology disguises its beliefs in the protective coloration of the "truths" developed by science, religion, philosophy, and folkways, he mostly avoided a recognition — let alone a discussion — of how the moral traditions of his own era affected him and his work (e.g., Bernstein, 1991, pp. 142–171; Jay, 1986, pp. 175–204). And he only hinted at evaluative statements regarding various practices or events of other eras or how to draw upon them in order to aid in deciding the moral decisions confronting us all in the present.

An in-depth examination of Foucault's life (see e.g., Macey, 1993) helps make the paradoxes of his work more understandable. Foucault grew up in a small French town. He was embedded in the conservative, bourgeois, Catholic tradition of the French countryside (the small city of Poitiers, which he was later to call "provincial" and "narrow-minded"), only to witness at 13 years of age the Nazi invasion and cultural domination, then five years later the allied victory, the slow rebuilding of the Marshal Plan, the independent de Gaulle presidency, the rigidities, hypocrisies, and nuclear terror of the Cold War, and the homophobia of the colorful and affluent 1960s, 1970s, and early-1980s. He saw several cultural regimes come and go, each with their own truths and epistemologies, heroes and villains. No wonder his focus on the evanescence of truth, the importance of power, the arbitrary nature and historical relativism of moral understandings. He lived in highly volatile, changeable, and often deeply hypocritical times, and in retrospect it is not difficult to see the origins of what Foucault brilliantly grasped and explained: the historical effects behind the warrants of science and religion, the power disguised as truth, the radically profound influence of the cultural frame. Perhaps he can be best understood as the historical figure who was deeply affected by Hegel's concept of the master-slave dynamic and most actively put Heidegger's radical notion of historicity to use in the detailed study of history. He was the radical employer of the most radical theory of the 20th century.

In his last years he appeared to become slightly more explicit about moral understandings, but we received precious little from him even then; his opinions about the good remained opaque, at best, to the very end. For instance, it is true that Foucault's last two books (*History of Sexuality*, volumes 2 & 3) were not directly about the periphery (although they can be interpreted to be in service of justifying current peripheral communities and their practices). They do seem to be an attempt to make an argument in favor of a certain way of being, even though the particular statement seems vague and indirect. But in his last published article — "What is Enlightenment?" — he again lapses back into a view from nowhere and a somewhat confused or self-contradictory style in reference to the good, as he does in his last interview, "The Return of Morality" (in Kritzman, 1988, pp. 242, 254).

Foucault's overall avoidance of explicit and detailed moral discussion created a certain kind of philosophical incoherence, limitation, and concealment in his work. His emphasis on power to the exclusion of the moral made it increasingly difficult for him to (1) imagine sustained political cooperation and change, and (2) make nuanced evaluations and suggestions based on moral deliberation. This one dimensional vision created some remarkable insights but also a kind of intellectual dead-end, both for himself and his readers.

However, I believe Foucault's practices are only a dead-end if we think of them as fully complete in themselves. If we understand them as a step in a larger process, new possibilities arise. For instance, both Martin Jay (1986) and Charles Taylor (1986) suggested that it is not possible to only critique, expose, and attack, which Foucault proposed in his concept of genealogy. Perhaps every attack requires a political and moral alternative or at least evaluative, background assumptions about the good in order to be an attack. To see X as a problem necessitates a different perspective than the one that approves of X; if this perspective isn't acknowledged, it is disguised (see Crawford, 1999). Thus, ironically, without a discussion of the moral understandings that bring its perspective to light, Foucault's genealogical praxis that reveals disguised ideology runs the risk of itself becoming a disguised ideology. Genealogy is not an ahistorical, neutral tool, but an aspect of larger moral-political traditions that are located in a broader horizontal space that itself must be examined in order to be understood and situated.

The absence of explicit moral direction from Foucault leaves his practices open to the by now familiar charges of relativism. But even more important is where Foucault's line of reasoning ultimately takes him — and, by implication, us. Without an ability to draw explicitly from the moral traditions of his time, and situate and measure his own ideas within as well as against those traditions, and without any goal but the search for the hidden locations of power, Foucault must turn elsewhere in order to find alternatives and develop political resistance.

The force of Foucault's moral rage and the logic of his concerns finally moved him to suggest that researchers must look to the cultural periphery and especially to the subjugated discourses located there in order to learn about the dominant society, locate alternatives to it, and organize resistance against it. There is no question but that difference, subjugated discourses, and groups located on the periphery can be extraordinarily helpful in learning about, interpreting, and changing a society, as I suggested in the above section on Germany and the Jews.

However, there is an important problem here: If all that researchers have at their disposal is the periphery, how are researchers to think about and interpret a peripheral group, its people, and its discourses? How are researchers to evaluate what is found there? What are researchers to do with a better knowledge of the periphery once it is studied? And how do researchers apply what is learned there to those not on the periphery?

Foucault's work brings to mind the old saying "If your only tool is a hammer, everything looks like a nail": If your only criteria is power, everything looks suspicious and dangerous. And then critique — endless, repetitive critique — is the only blameless activity, and the only criteria for choosing allies is the appearance of powerlessness and victimhood. Authority, effectiveness, generativity, continuity, success — all these are thought to be dangerous, because they will lead to influence and then to power and then to the abuse of power, and thus are to be avoided at all costs.[1]

Foucault's solution raises more problems than it solves. In particular, what is most important about those on the periphery if not their culture, the moral understandings embedded within that culture, and the meanings they make of the oppression from which they suffer? How will Foucault have us discuss and evaluate those moral understandings, when they are the very same phenomena he avoided when studying those closer to the center of power. The same issues abide, wherever the attention of the researcher is focused. How can a political movement — a thus political change — emerge out of such suspicion and fear of oneself?

If this was all there was to Foucault's genealogy then it would, finally, seem in danger of leading to a dead-end. But genealogy is not a dead-end if one thinks of it as an aspect, a step, in Gadamerian dialogue: It can be thought of as an attempt to force an encounter with difference, an attempt to help difference stand out, be recognized, and engaged with.

But in order to do what? Foucault couldn't really say, because when all you see is power there is no place for openness, the attempt at mutual understanding, or for building something new. There is only suspicion, critique, attack, accusation. Perhaps that is why Foucault was sometimes so evasive and contradictory about the good. Genealogy brilliantly and forcefully opens up the possibility of an encounter with difference, but then it cannot proceed; it is incomplete without Gadamer, or at least without the emerging North American interpretation of Gadamer.

Foucault needed Gadamer in a way similar to how Heidegger needed Gadamer: neither of them could adequately avoid the potential pitfalls of their practices without the concept of dialogue. Heidegger's concept of authenticity holds most of the tools necessary for cultural humility. But Heidegger's embeddedness in a monocultural understanding of Germany and his monologic understanding of interpersonal relations overwhelmed his opportunity to adequately practice authenticity, and his integrity drowned in the chauvinisms and hatreds of his time.

Foucault's theoretical work only broke down when he tried to describe what comes after an encounter with difference. Without question, Foucault himself was able to extend genealogy into dialogue and activism, but he couldn't put the process into words for others to be guided by. And sadly, we kept asking Foucault for more, always pushing him to philosophize about his work, to extend into metatheory what had been remarkable historical research. His celebrity, in this way, caused us to demand too much, and in an attempt to give it, Foucault extended himself beyond what he was capable of. He was an absolutely brilliant historian and an energetic and highly moral political activist. But he was not quite so good a philosopher. What he gave us was truly brilliant, but we need Gadamer, and now Gadamer's interpreters, to explain what can come next, what can be built out of an encounter with difference, and how we can imaginatively interpret meaning.

Dialogue isn't automatic. It takes work that includes a willingness to struggle with the moral – otherwise an encounter with difference inevitably devolves simply into a kind of self-indulgent, self-righteous exercise in either self-satisfaction, anthropological exoticism, or a kind of overwrought "going native." This is best understood as incomplete or misdirected dialogue.

Learning from the periphery and bringing to light subjected discourses can be extremely helpful, if we can figure out what to do with the new knowledge they bring. But we must be careful not to let our anxieties, confusions, or disappointments move us to make a fetish or — more to the hermeneutic point — an unquestioned method, out of something Foucault said when he was pushed too far.

Conclusion

The flaws of these two great scholars should teach us something about the inescapable nature of moral traditions and the indispensable element of respect for the other. Heidegger, when push came to shove, was unable to exercise the best aspects of his own philosophy, and as a result joined with one of the most despicable and destructive political movements of all time. Foucault, driven by a philosophical overreaching, could not find a way out of the dead-end he had painted himself into. He chased the specter of the insurrection of subjected discourses in a never-ending search for exoticism and difference, and his followers sometimes pursue a never-ending critique and the valorization of powerlessness and victimhood.

In our world of today, we can afford neither Heidegger's nor Foucault's mistakes. Our world is calling upon us to be open to the other and yet not to abandon out of hand our own best understandings of the good, to fight against oppression and yet be willing to recognize our activities as moral activities, and therefore neither infallible nor completely arbitrary and meaningless. We need to have the courage to take a stand, as well as criticize; to discuss what is good, as well as what is bad; to build as well as tear down. Liberation is not the only good. Sometimes personal restraint, humility, the appreciation of nuance, and the postponement of gratification is needed in order to serve the common good. Without this understanding — what Woodruff (2001) has called "reverence" — postmodernism then becomes simply another form of hyperindividualism, another vision of the decontextualized, hedonistic individual over against a dangerous, oppressive society (see Gantt, 1996). As the growing fascism of our current political terrain closes in around us, we need more than ever to learn from the limitations of our intellectual ancestors, so as to use well the gifts they gave us and carry on the fight with both humility and hope.

One of the few places potentially still available for the exercise of dialogue is the psychotherapy office. I am more convinced than ever that therapy is a kind of moral discourse, and one of its most meaningful processes is Gadamer's dialogue and the self-reflectiveness and self-understandings — and the critical political perspective — that it can bring. But as therapists we still do not skillfully understand the philosophical foundations of our work, and now that interpretive theory is increasingly finding its way into our discourse, we must take care to know it well, so that we do not fall prey to its pitfalls: to neither the monocultural and monologic rigidity of the right, nor the moral phobia and valorization of powerlessness of the left — to neither arrogance nor a dead-end.

Note

1 Among other things, this too-narrow vision of proper political activity overlooks one of Foucault's most important ideas: the "positivity" of power. That is, power is exercised not solely or even primarily through coercion, but by how the larger cultural frame is shaped. Foucault also taught that the location of power is diffuse, and thus in subtle ways we all have a hand in our own oppression.

Chapter 8

The case of the hidden subway station and other Gadamerian mysteries

(*2005 Contemporary Psychoanalysis, 41*, 431–445)

Historical introduction

This chapter was first written as a response to Lynne Layton's commentary on "Between arrogance and a dead-end" (see Chapter 7); the original article, Lynne's commentary (2005), and my response were published in 2005 by *Contemporary Psychoanalysis*, although originally my response was titled "Clinical Applications" and the body of the paper was slightly modified for this chapter. Her contribution, "Notes Toward a Nonconformist Clinical Practice," focused on the importance of identifying political content in the psychotherapy hour and especially of meeting those moments in ways that reveal oppression to be pathogenic and ways that advance a Progressive politics. Her commentary gave me the opportunity to illustrate ways of utilizing hermeneutic concepts (such as the cultural clearing) in therapeutic practice and by so doing therapeutically draw out political meanings both large and small.

I thought our two approaches — both aspects of the Interpretive Turn (see Hiley, Bohman, & Shusterman, 1991) complimented one another; Lynne's emphasis on contemporary poststructuralism was a good addition to my use of Gadamer, and our mutual admiration for Antonio Gramsci's groundbreaking political ideas about culture and hegemony focused our interchange in a way that was needed. I remain an admirer of, and indebted to, her prolific and intelligent body of work.

The George W. Bush years provided many political challenges to the country, both domestically and internationally. One result was an increased interest in and development of the political effects of psychotherapy. Both streams of the Turn helped me respond to those challenges in my work as a therapist: postmodernism offered tools for political critique, and hermeneutics helped me realize also the need to create and build as well as critique and attack. As therapists wishing to contribute to political change we must live out both practices. Now, in the last two years of the second

> decade of the 21st century, the need to resist the rising tide of the far Right — growing more visible in the Trump administration — is more urgent than perhaps anytime in U.S. history since the years leading up to the Civil War. When therapists realize that they cannot escape having some kind of political effect on patients in the therapy hour, I hope they will be able to draw from the Turn in order to be more articulate and helpful to their patients and to the country.

In "Between arrogance and a dead-end" (Chapter 7) I examined the pitfalls, respectively, of the right and the left in postmodern politics. In this paper I respond to Lynne Layton's (2005b) helpful commentary on the article by sketching out and illustrating through clinical examples how, from the beginning, we might think differently about psychotherapy in order to avoid the excesses of both the right's monocultural arrogance and the left's moral relativism. My point is that the two errors can be effectively avoided only by attending to both at once, because ultimately they are expressions of the same philosophical problem and must be addressed in the same way: by a wholehearted embrace of a more fully thought-out hermeneutic vision.

Being aware of the political influences active in the therapy hour — rather than trying to banish them — is a good thing to do because, well, there is no alternative. The Interpretive Turn (Hiley, Bohman, & Shusterman, 1991) has helped me realize that political activity is always present in the clinical hour. One way or another, therapists are always challenging or colluding with the status quo — we just don't realize it. Heidegger's concept of being-in-the-world means that humans are fundamentally shaped, constituted really, by the cultural/historical worlds into which they are thrown. Psychology's goal, throughout its modern-era history, has been to discover the universal laws that determine human behavior. Heidegger's philosophy directly challenges that goal. Although it has brought psychology a certain amount of wealth and influence, ultimately hermeneuticists believe the goal cannot be achieved. The goal is unreachable, Heidegger taught, because there is only *one* important universal, ahistorical law about human being: there are none. He thought all the really important things about humans are shaped by the language, social practices, political arrangements, and moral understandings that inhere in the cultural particularities of everyday life. That is what he meant when he said that human being is historical.

Heidegger's idea is a revolutionary concept; it calls into question detailed theories of human nature, what anthropologists call indigenous psychologies (see e.g., Heelas & Lock, 1981). It is not that indigenous psychologies are wrong; it is just that they are not the one, true, universal theory about the details of human being. Behavioral psychology is an indigenous psychology, as are, for instance, cognitive psychology, Zen Buddhism, and psychoanalysis. Indigenous psychologies form part of what Clifford Geertz once called the cultural "web of meaning"; they are potentially wonderful inventions that reflect the most profound understandings of a people. As such, they can tell us a great deal about the social world in which particular psychologies are embedded, if we can develop the capacity to interpret them contextually. They just can't tell us much about the putative universal, ahistorical subject they claim to know so much about, because there is no such critter.

Negative aspects of the cultural clearing, such as what Lynne Layton (2005b) called conformist ideology, affect clinical practices even when therapists try to utilize hermeneutic or postmodern theory; it is inevitably so. Humans are continually pulled to comply and collude with problematic or destructive aspects of their social world, because the social world has constituted us, and so the inevitable seductions and common sense understandings that call to us fit us like a key fits a lock. We comply and collude, we live out and thus reproduce the shape of the cultural frame — including the political status quo — without being aware of it.

At least, that is, we live out the status quo until we begin educating ourselves. That is when a crucial aspect of becoming a human being begins: what Heidegger called "authenticity," Gramsci called "the work," and Harry Stack Sullivan called interpersonal psychiatry. It is through hard-won intellectual, emotional, and psychological change that one begins to recognize how the status quo operates through one's *own* actions (in part, for instance, through what postmodernists call gender or racial performance). It is then that one can strengthen one's capacity to understand and oppose it. Of course, we always do so imperfectly, oscillating between either being seduced/engulfed/momentarily soothed or anesthetized by a reigning ideology or occasionally by meeting the moment and resisting it.

In my life, few experiences typify that oscillation quite so much as doing therapy, when so much is to be attended to, so many pressures exert themselves, so much happens so quickly. It is then that the social key quietly turns our embodied locks, and we say things or do things that seem right at the time but in retrospect can be understood, sadly, as tools of the status quo. It is then, if we are lucky, we realize we used a reified theory uncritically, tried out an intervention that reinforced self-contained individualism, copied a metaphor or a technique that took for granted the "naturalness" of Hobbesian competition, made a remark that struck us as so clever in the moment but in the light of day turns out to be misogynist or racist, or found ourselves being spoken by a Cartesian voice dead-certain about the mind-body duality. In the literature, these moments are usually referred to as countertransference enactments, but Layton, to her everlasting credit, points out that they are much more than personal countertransference. They are political events, fueled by what she calls "normative unconscious processes." This is the connection therapists need to but often have not been able to make: countertransference moments are products of moral understandings (i.e., reflections of particular social understandings of the good) and political arrangements (e.g., the means of production, institutional racism, consumerism). Layton (2005b) is correct: for the most part psychoanalysis, often including relational psychoanalysis, has yet to make this connection, has yet to help patients develop the capacity to connect to broader social processes and inequalities. It was my contention in "Between Arrogance and a Dead-End" that Gadamer's concept of dialogue can help us understand some of what is missing in our work as therapists and what we can do to open ourselves to the world of the other and educate ourselves politically. Layton, utilizing Gramsci, suggests that the dialogue that is needed is between those in power and those not in power. That, as I see it, is what the evolving north American interpretation of Gadamerian dialogue describes: how persons, especially in a privileged position such as psychotherapist, can, through an encounter with difference, come to understand something about the world of the other, and by doing so come to understand something more about themselves and the world they inhabit.[1] Social thirdness, then, is always already present in the therapeutic dyad, for good and ill, because it is embodied by us. Of course, as Layton suggests, thirdness is apparent in enactments, because thirdness is enacted — that is, lived out — in all social interaction, including psychotherapy. When enactments reflect negative aspects of our social world including, especially, the ways psychotherapy theory and practice reproduce the status quo — those negative aspects must be "contested and articulated," in Layton's words, or all is lost.[2] It is, in fact, precisely *that* task that is an indispensable aspect of the interpretive turn; without the turn's complex political understanding, relational theory recedes into mediocrity. Without the hermeneutic insight that clinical material is moral and political, relational theory is reduced to a kind of intellectual tokenism and partakes of a particularly upsetting political kind of collusion: the kind that should know better. That is what happened, for example, to Humanistic Psychology in the 1980s and 1990s, when some of its practitioners got derailed by the quest for an asocial human potential, followed by an apolitical "spiritual" transformation, and finally in organizational psychology the depoliticizing, trivializing, and silencing of the aspirations of labor. A fuller understanding of the interpretive turn moves us to realize that human life is historical, and thus moral and political. For instance, from a hermeneutic point of view, the distinctions between subject and object, individual and society, internal and external, clinical and political, personal and political are highly misrepresentative of human being (see e.g., Westerman & Steen, 2007). These distinctions are products of perhaps the single-greatest emblem of the modern era, the Cartesian split between matter and spirit, and thus are historical artifacts of their time and place. When we use them in our work as therapists we unintentionally but necessarily reproduce the modern era understandings that under-gird late modern era institutions, such as consumerism, and render them invisible — and thus more effective — in everyday life.

Hermeneutics in clinical practice

But how are we to change that? In the following four subsections I use examples from my practice to illustrate four ways hermeneutic concepts such as the clearing and the "inescapability" of moral and political understandings can be used in everyday clinical work. How one recognizes and discusses the political in psychotherapy is a complex issue;[3] it includes not only explicit political topics such as war, poverty, racism, and sexism, but also more subtle ways that therapists usually reproduce the status quo. There is comparably little writing on the subject, and for a good reason: it is very difficult to do. But although it is a difficult task, it is not impossible. For instance, a hermeneutic understanding can help clinicians become aware of how often therapeutic practices reproduce the Cartesian split. Therapists do this whenever words like "inner" life, "inner feelings," or "introjection" are used. These types of words imply a taken-for-granted understanding of human being that reflects Cartesian distinctions such as interior-exterior that were responsible for producing modern-era self-contained individualism, and thus the current hyperindividualism that contributes significantly to our patients' suffering and the nation's decline. Our striving to achieve a therapeutic "neutrality" or "objectivity," and our claim to sometimes achieve it, is another example of the reproduction of modern-era Cartesian ideology. It reinforces the split between subject and object and encourages the scientific disengagement that hermeneuticists think profoundly misrepresents human learning and damages human relatedness. As a result, clinicians then unknowingly have a hand in reinforcing the instrumentalism and technicism of our time (see Cushman 1990, 1995, Cushman & Gilford, 2000 for more detailed illustrations). I don't think it is an exaggeration to say that many of the political problems that cause so much personal suffering today can be traced to the taken-for-granted ideas — such as the Cartesian split, interiority, self-contained individualism — that are emblematic of the modern era in Western society. It is a measure of our unquestioning acceptance of a Cartesian universe that it is so difficult for us to imagine alternatives to those concepts. What in particular has the potential to help therapists work in a less Cartesian way is Heidegger's concept of the clearing: he suggested that one's cultural world is like a clearing in a dense forest. In that clearing there is room for people, social practices, and things to appear, be understood, and interacted with. Imagine that the clearing is like a room lit with indirect lighting — we can't see where the light is coming from, but in the room people, identities, activities appear. The shape of the clearing is distinguished by its perimeter, which hermeneuticists think is formed by the moral understandings and political arrangements of the era in question. The particular rules that are prominent in the clearing are thought to be produced by understandings about the good. We are always striving to do the right thing in any given moment, even when we don't conceptualize our actions in that way. For instance, the belief that individuals in capitalist societies should pursue their own personal interests without regard for the interests or well-being of others is an aspect of a larger understanding of the good. (Just because someone's behavior is thought to be motivated by their moral understandings doesn't mean, of course, that one has to agree with it. The point is simply that we must recognize it as a moral position.) We learn these moral understandings by enacting them over and over again long before we are able to understand them or be reflective about what they mean. Social practices become embodied by us; they are us. That is why some hermeneuticists do not use the word "internalize:" it implies a fully formed, uninvolved person who stands outside of culture and is *invaded* by an idea, value, parental role model, and hermeneuticists do not believe such an isolated, asocial person exists. Such ideas, values, and models do not invade us, they constitute us.

Patients in the clearing

When I began to picture my patients and their lives as located in a clearing, the power of the Cartesian split began to have (slightly) less unconscious influence over me. When therapists imagine their patients in this way, therapists and patients can begin identifying the social world — the clearing — that they both inhabit, and this in turn might help them think in a slightly less split, more integrated way. Then they can begin to recognize and name the particular aspect of the larger clearing that the patient inhabits, including the part of the clearing shaped by the idiosyncrasies of parents, neighborhoods, socioeconomic classes, ethnicities, genders, and so forth. This is how I (Cushman, 1995, pp. 302–303) first put it into words for a patient:

> I was listening to a patient ... one of the most tortured patients I have ever worked with. ... [H]e is certain that no one will want to know how he really feels, everyone will hate him and reject him for what he thinks, and no one will allow him what he needs. And it occurred to me that day that he was describing a world to me, the world that he lived in when he was in this particular state of mind. Suddenly, I saw that world spread out before him on all sides, peopled with certain characters and voices from the past, from a time when the horizon was originally formed or significantly reordered. I thought of those pop-up books made for children: when we open them, a whole little world of mountains, cities, and individuals instantly pops up and comes to life before us. ... I told him it seemed to me as though a world had suddenly appeared before us, a world that encompassed him on all sides. In this world, the people of his young life live and interact, all according to the rules that he has described to me or

enacted with me. These rules create positions in which certain people must live, and these positions determine destinies. I described some of these rules as I had come to understand them, especially those that pertained to how he felt that day.

"Well," he said, "that's life. That's all there is." He paused, cocked his head and looked puzzled. "What do you mean — that there's some other world?" He paused, and then laughed, a relaxed, pleasant kind of laugh I have rarely heard from him.

By imagining the patient in a spatial clearing, therapists can begin to notice that what was usually thought to be located *inside* the skin of the self-contained individual — such as emotions, ideas, relations, values — can also be understood as being located in the social space of the clearing, in the space *between* people. It is the relocation of things thought to be inside the skin to the space between people that moves hermeneuticists and postmodernists to claim that human understanding is "perspectival" and to say things like "language speaks us."

A space of possibilities

Imagining patients as inhabiting a certain space in the clearing can, in turn, help therapists imagine that their patients understand their world in a certain way because they stand in a certain predetermined place in the clearing, a place that then makes certain things, feelings, and actions visible and available to them and certain things invisible, unimaginable, and thus unreachable. One way of understanding the goal of therapy is that it can give patients the opportunity to notice more of what is available in the clearing. Therapy can give patients the opportunity to see what else is possible, to imagine where else they could stand and to experience living that way for a few moments. Therapy can give patients the opportunity to explore what that new position could mean about the right way of thinking or acting in a given situation. It is important to remember that a hermeneutic concept like the clearing should not be reduced to the understandings generated by a particular family or individual. The clearing is the larger social, historical clearing we all inhabit, but there is much in the clearing that we as individuals do not see by virtue of the particular position we inhabit and the particular limitations of that position.

A patient, one who learned at the age of 34 that he had been adopted at birth, had a dream.

> He was in the passenger tunnels of the New York subway. ... [He] found an opening in the wall that had been closed up. He climbed in and found an old abandoned subway station that had been closed off for years, walled off from the public, unused and unappreciated. It was an absolutely beautiful old terminal, majestic and impressively crafted. ... And then he discovered a cluster of circular mail slots, set in a wall off to the side. In the holes were rolled-up blueprints, just what he needed. He took one out to examine it, and sure enough, it was the floor plan for the old abandoned terminal he had just located...
>
> In looking back over the dream, I think it significant that the visual image of the newly discovered room was associated in the patient's mind with his hopes and dreams for his [about to be birthed] son, and with his moral commitments to his son. ... [T]he dream speaks to us about someone who is in the process of making room for new possibilities, possibilities that are social in nature and that somehow have their roots in another, earlier time... The promise of that old majestic room had been lost forever; it had been boarded up and closed off from sight, until it was somehow reconstructed anew by my client, in ways that neither he, nor I, nor anyone, I trust, could ever adequately explain. But we do know this: the room appeared in part because a new life (perhaps two new lives) had to be served, and my client felt a moral commitment to these new lives and to the relationship between them. His commitment transcended the secrets and limitations located in a world too small for the possibilities my client could now embrace. ... My patient felt a stirring, a wish, to travel to new places and see what might happen when he got there. The dream indicates that somehow new possibilities have been opened up for my patient — the horizon has been moved back away from him, and new territory, or at least the possibility of traveling to new territory, has shown up for him.
>
> (Cushman, 1995, pp. 321–324)

Relational expectations as reflections of the good

One of the advantages of utilizing the concept of the clearing is that therapists can come to understand the strange and seemingly irrational thoughts, feelings, desires, and relations of patients as products of the embodied moral understandings and political arrangements that frame the clearing. They are brought to light by the particular way the clearing — and the particular part of the clearing inhabited by the patient — is shaped. Thus the expectations the patient has about how to act and feel, for instance, in the session, and how the therapist will act and feel in the session, can be understood as products of the political arrangements and expressions of the good that frame the clearing. A middle aged woman who once had lived for many years in a communal, highly authoritarian religious group, sought individual therapy for help with parenting problems and job-related issues. This is a composite of exchanges that came in sessions six though eight:

> Patient: I know, I know, I'm not supposed to make excuses for not doing something. I have to just go out and do it! Me: Really? Don't excuses sometimes make sense? Patient: Oh, come on, no one, especially therapists, think that way. You're just trying to trick me into saying more about how whimpy and weak I am. I know the truth, I'm just running a game when I complain. Me: A game? Patient: Look, I've been in more marathon healing sessions than you can shake a stick at. I know how this all works; I'm no good, that's all. I don't take responsibility for my own actions, I don't just go out and do things. I used to, but now I can't. There's ... there's something wrong inside of me. I'm just a whimp inside. And ministers like you, they ... I mean, therapists like you, ... hmmm. Therapists like you ... (pause) Oh, God [she starts to cry], this is about the church, isn't it? Me: How is it about the church? Patient: [She then describes the marathon sessions, the demand for psychological confession, cathartic emoting, making promises and following through on them at any price.] Me: It sounds like a pretty coercive, intimidating environment. Patient: Well, we had to comply. We thought it was good for us, but we had to comply in order for the healing to work. Me: Is it possible that what was wrong with that picture wasn't *inside* you? You're describing a pretty authoritarian world. And now you expect me to be in the "minister" position, and you in the sick, screwed up, cowardly position. What's wrong sounds more outside of you or around you than inside of you. Look at the world you describe. Is it any wonder you think I'm going to humiliate you? In that world,

that's all there was: only two places to stand the one who humiliates and the one who is humiliated. There was just humiliation and then the "escape" after a "healing." Patient: Except it never worked for long. And then it was back to the marathon again: More humiliation, and then more promises. It was exhausting. ... That's what I think this therapy will be like. Boy [she is laughing and crying], you can't imagine how much I have dreaded coming here. You don't act like him, but I'm sure you are going to start anytime now. Oh, God, I hate those feelings. Me: It sounds like it is hard to figure out which world you are in now. Patient: Hard? It's impossible. Me: Well, it sounds like that's part of our job here: to help you figure out which world you're in now.

From my point of view, the concept of the clearing affords the patient a dignity and respect that is more difficult to come by if one thinks of thoughts, feelings, object relations, and so forth as originating in and taking place within the interior of the self-contained individual. It also affords a helpful understanding about psychological change, because in Heidegger's philosophy the edge of the clearing, what he calls "the horizon," encompasses many possibilities (this is especially true in a multicultural society like the U.S.) and is, like all horizons, moveable. That is, a horizon looks like it is set in concrete, and indeed when it comes to psychological processes, opinions, and identities created by years of social repetition it at first feels like those processes are immoveable. But, fortunately, horizons are perspectival, not concrete; they move slightly when one's point of view shifts. The horizon, in other words, is not only the horizon of limitation, but also the horizon of possibility.

Of course, some of the most important determinants of these rules about behaviors, feelings, and relations are the political arrangements and institutions prominent in the clearing. These rules and conditions come to light both as products of a particular clearing and also as determinants of the shape of the clearing. Much can be learned about why patients (and therapists) act the way they do because of the politics of a clearing, although from a hermeneutic point of view the moral understandings about how to be human are the primary force that brings to light the political. But really, it is counterproductive to conceive of either of these forces as completely distinct from one another. The relation between the moral and political is dynamic and entangled, with multiple and circular influences. There is no one beginning and no final end. The point is these are all aspects of the social and are thereby best located in the social terrain.

Politics and the good

By imagining the social clearing in which the patient dwells, therapists can come to conceive of what takes place in a therapy session as a kind of moral discourse about political issues: a conscious, embodied, dynamic negotiation about the good. In a therapy framed by hermeneutic ideas therapists and patients can get a sense of how fluid or entangled or complementary are the realms of the personal and the political. The following is from the last weeks of therapy with the same patient who had the subway dream. Toward the end of a long therapy, he was struggling with a problem at work that had profound implications for his life: when to accept jobs from customers and when to turn them down. He came to realize that the moral understandings about the good in his family of origin fit well with those of the unscrupulous work world with which he was involved. He often felt placed

> in the same moral predicament from which he suffered in childhood. He is in the position of being both victim and perpetrator: He is a victim because he is forced to live in a framework he never agreed to and that he hates, and a perpetrator because in order to emotionally survive he must not care even though he has promised to care, and because he has promised to do, properly, a job that ultimately cannot be done properly, given his standards. "In other words," I responded, "you are in the middle of a moral conflict. According to the moral code of your family and the society, you should accept the double bind: detach and yet pretend to care, work conscientiously and yet know that the work is impossible to accomplish, and all the while pretend not to notice that you are feeling enraged, unsatisfied, and deadened."
>
> We came to realize that he is in the process of ... [shaping] a new understanding of what is moral. He has a sense that if he takes the job, he will be cheating the client, living a life of detachment, denial, and falseness. And now he thinks that is the wrong thing to do. But to refuse is to break the old family rules [and the rules dominant in

today's society], to act in ways that they would think immoral. He is caught in a dilemma.

...Hoping to find others to encourage him to refuse the job, my patient began asking his colleagues what they thought he should do. Contrary to his hopes, each of them, without hesitation, advised him to take the job. The money, they thought, was too good to turn down, no matter how damaging it might be to him emotionally. ... "It was like they stood up and spoke with one voice! The voice was my mother's voice, and it said 'Hey, your feelings don't count'"...

"Well," I said, "it sounds like your mother isn't the only one who thinks that money is more important than emotional well-being." My patient smirked. ... "Maybe it's everyone — hell, it's the system. That's the voice." ... "I think the voice you heard speaks through all these people, because it's sedimented in each of us. ... "My patient was silent for a moment. ... "It's speaking through everyone, he said angrily, "my buddies, my competitors, everyone. It's not just my mother, as much as I'd like to blame it on her. It's the whole system." He thought for awhile, and then he looked up and smiled. "This is going to be more difficult than I thought. How are we going to get the whole damn system into the room?" We laughed together and I said, "You know, if it's all the same to you, I'd rather you take your ideas out there, instead of bringing ... [everyone] in here.

(Cushman, 1995, pp. 326–328)

Can the members of the therapeutic dyad come to recognize and name and interpret those moral understandings? When embodied understandings can be named and interpreted, therapist and patient can engage in a kind of moral discourse, a sifting through of those understandings in an attempt to figure out which understandings are most fitting for a particular issue or moment (see especially Richardson, Fowers, & Guignon, 1999). To do so consciously and articulately, realizing that the moral understandings and political effects of each person are products of the larger historical and cultural traditions in which both persons are embedded, presents some big problems. For instance, how can therapists and patients sift through and evaluate different value systems, political positions, and activities when patients and therapists are not very experienced in explicitly doing so, and when therapists have been trained to avoid such an activity at all costs? How are differences of opinions and moral conflicts, for instance, to be handled? These are difficult questions. But it is precisely the hermeneutic point: that kind of moral and political discourse is what we are *already* doing all the time in therapy, although unknowingly and in a disguised manner. If we could do so consciously, we could better develop our skills and minimize the times we err and unknowingly support institutions and ideologies we are against. Also, as Stern (1991) pointed out, when we can put words to a pattern or recognize an alternative way of seeing an issue, a shift has already occurred, the place where we stand in the field of our life has already altered. The ability to recognize and name something, in a way, is more a product of what has already taken place than a wish for, or a goal about, future behavior.

Why do therapy?

"Living in the shadows of nuclear, societal, and environmental disasters," Lane Gerber (1990) noted,

> affects us all whether we are therapists or patients. While these horrors outside of our office doors continue to grow, they are rarely admitted into our psychotherapy hours. Should what we see and hear of the world outside of our therapy offices influence what we do as therapists?
>
> (p. 471)

Indeed, how could it not? I have come to put into words something that the combination of Gadamer's dialogue and Gramsci's socialism has incited in my thinking: the reason to work as a therapist is not, for instance, simply to help make conscious and/or attenuate the individual suffering of one's patients. The reason to work as a therapist is also to help patients become aware of the socio-political causes of their suffering, better understand the connections between the shape of their social world and the human suffering that it causes, and develop the political ideas and moral energy necessary to change that world. For me, that means assisting patients in becoming more politically progressive — to join with or encourage their allegiances and activities on the left of the political spectrum. In other words, a reason to work as a therapist is to help prepare patients to engage in effective *progressive* political activity.

We will all do this in our own ways, ways that correspond to our visions of the good and good therapy. But if our work isn't to prepare our patients to bring on and work toward a better world, what good is it? If therapists don't think in a more political — and more politically progressive — manner, and help others prepare themselves for becoming more active and effective in causes of the left, it is likely very few others will. But we will not be able to carry out this goal unless we avoid the errors both Heidegger and Foucault fell into. We must be able to open ourselves to difference and the voice of the other, and yet remain knowledgeable about and critically engaged in our own traditions, so that we know what we value, and why, and retain the courage necessary to act on behalf of others and on our own best sense of what is right. This project will necessarily entail a continuing critical evaluation of the traditions of our birth, and thus a never-completed reshaping — including, perhaps in some cases, a rejection — of aspects of those traditions. This is what Stern (2002), drawing from Heidegger, called seeking out the experience of not-at-home-ness. In our world, particularly, this seems a necessary, perhaps indispensable, step along the path to a better world.

Notes

1 Importantly, this is not all there is to dialogue in therapy; for instance, it might be the best description to date of how the mystery of therapeutic change comes about. It is also the way hermeneuticists characterize the equalitarian process of engagement, which to them is a way of conceptualizing how meaningful understanding — including self-understanding — is achieved (e.g., Stern, 1991).
2 Let us remember, however, that there are also many positive interchanges that encourage critical thinking, kindness, equalitarianism, creativity, honesty. These emanate from the social realm, just as do such negative enactments as conformity to racism, misogyny, or homophobia.
3 A few have written about the moral and the political in psychotherapy in more detail. Gerber addressed the topic in several articles (e.g., 1990, 1992), as did Greifinger (1995). I devoted a chapter to the topic, as did Richardson, Fowers, & Guignon (1999); also Stern (e.g., 1990, 1991) addressed the topic in several articles (e.g., 1990, 1991) and in his important book *Unformulated Experience* (1997).

Chapter 9

Flattened selves, shallow solutions
A commentary on "The McDonaldization of Psychotherapy"
(2013 APA Division 24 MidWinter Meeting)

Historical introduction

I was asked to write a commentary on the presentation "The McDonaldization of Psychotherapy: The Loss of Pluralism and Its Impact on Social Class" for the 2013 MidWinter Meeting of Division 24 of APA (Theoretical and Philosophical Psychology). I took the opportunity to link the political concerns of the authors — especially the effects of structural political arrangements such as racism, sexism, and classism on the delivery of psychotherapy — with the philosophical problems that inhere in the current hegemony of behaviorist, cognitivist, and quantitative measures in psychotherapy.

President Obama had been reelected to a second term, and many good things happened as a result of his first term in office, including of course the passing of the Affordable Care Act. However, as with any regime influenced by neoliberalism, governmental regulations tended to be affected by a certain kind of scientistic technicism, and mental health care under the Obama administration was no exception. Evidence-based treatments and symptom-reduction techniques, using randomized control trials and various kinds of consumer survey measures as justifications for the prescription of cognitive-behavioral language and treatment interventions, solidified their power during the beginning of Obama's second term. The APA, reflecting the cultural moment, tightened its grip on accreditation procedures, thereby intensifying its previously instituted regime of academic competencies and bureaucratic forms of proceduralism that have driven the humanities out of graduate program curricula. The result is the creation of a kind of scientistic psychology that is sealed from criticism through a series of interlocking procedures and rules.

By the early 21st century we were confronted by and had to work within a psychology that claims to be completely objective and apolitical, but when examined through a hermeneutic lens is revealed to be a tool of the political status quo. That is the concern that motivated my commentary.

122 Flattened selves, shallow solutions

I am grateful to the authors of "The McDonaldization of Psychotherapy" for their important presentation. Their concern is that treatment options for persons with few economic resources — as compared to those of the affluent — are narrowed evidence-based" and "symptom-reduction" modalities (Goodman et al., 2016). They argue that this is an inequitable situation and one that undermines the country's most cherished values. I am in agreement with their position, and feel both heartened by their argument and heartsick that it has to be made.

But of course the argument must be made. The move to Evidence Based Treatments (EBTs), Randomized Control Trials (RCTs), manualized treatments, and academic competencies has been eerily similar to some of the exploitive, empire-building, even occasionally craven movements in the history of American psychology. These practices also suffer from the same philosophical wrongheadedness that has plagued mainstream psychology in its continuing rush to claim a physical science warrant for its practices. Both of these critiques have merit and deserve to be carefully discussed. But instead, in this talk I'd like to address a larger historical and political issue, one that encompasses and in fact makes possible the McDonaldization of which Goodman and his colleagues speak.

The concept of EBT is dangerous not only because it justifies a two-tiered system of care that patronizes, cheats, and uses the oppressed and the poor for its own ends, as Goodman et al. explained — although that is more than reason enough to oppose it. EBTs are also dangerous because they are implicated in a broad and increasingly prominent way of being that degrades and politically silences Americans in all walks of life. In various ways each of us is affected by the impoverished, instrumental, technicized understanding of human being that EBTs reflect and reproduce. Goodman et al. have identified a problem that is a manifestation of the larger cultural terrain, and it is that terrain that I would like to address. Besides an unquestioned belief in EBTs, it has also produced electronic machines and their sequelae, such as computers, social networking sites, avatars, manualized therapies, and psychological graduate programs built around academic competencies. In this commentary, I briefly discuss some of their moral and political consequences.

The early 21st century self

Above all, I am suggesting that EBTs, RCTs, manualized therapies, and academic competencies are not mandated by health care corporations, blessed by mainstream psychology, and recognized by federal health care initiatives because they are better than other practices. No, they are considered to be the standard because they fit hand-in-glove with the predominant self of the early 21st century. To mainstream therapists and researchers they seem to be unquestioningly correct because they speak the predominant language of our time. The way of being of today in the U.S. has shifted from the empty self of the post-World War II era (Cushman 1990, 1995) to what in 1999 Peter Gilford and I called a multiple self, and Jacobson (1997) and Orange (2009) called a flattened self. Peter and I suggested that the multiple self is a way of being characterized by a significant attenuation of interiority. It is marked by a propensity to gather about itself a number of identities that are located around the outside of the person, external to but identified with the individual, although this identification takes on a different, less essential, or intense valance than identifications within a deep self. This is an exterior self with less complex or conflicted identities to draw from — identities that cluster on, not inside, the individual, decorating and standing ready to appear on center stage when the need arises.

Unlike the 20th century self, this new self does not feel a deep, gnawing sense of emptiness that must be filled by purchasing and consuming unneeded calories, snazzy electronic gadgets, or charismatic celebrities like politicians, actors, and therapists in what in 1990 I called the "lifestyle solution." Today the multiple, flattened self is driven by a powerful imperative to develop and present various selves for public viewing, offering them according to the social needs of the moment. A person is thought to "morph" naturally and unproblematically from one self to another as the occasion dictates. These selves, of course, are created and accessorized by consuming the avalanche of consumer products, especially online electronic goods and services that are omnipresent in American society today.

I do not mean to imply that the empty self is all good and the multiple self all bad. All understandings of the self — that is, cultural ideas about the proper way to be human — have their good and bad aspects and have particular political consequences. From a hermeneutic perspective a psychologist's job is not to take up the modern-era, scientific search for the putatively one, perfect, universally correct way to be human and the one way to treat it. Instead, it is to historically situate ways of being and their corresponding healing practices and thereby explore their moral implications and political functions. The hope is that this historical process, which includes what Gadamer (1989) called "dialogue," will help us develop a facility to encounter difference, put our own cherished professional theories and historical traditions into question, and thereby be continually involved in refining our understandings of self, other, and the good. These are understandings always thought to be provisional and in process, necessarily uncertain and incomplete (see e.g., Richardson, Fowers, & Guignon, 1999). This hermeneutic framework allows us to locate our moral understandings within the historical traditions that have constituted us — in other words to know where we stand, and yet be able to critique where we stand and be open to learning new things in relation to others.

The post-World War II baby, born in a car

In 1949, in the nationally syndicated comic strip Gasoline Alley, a baby was born in a taxi on the way to the hospital. She was named Clovia because she was graced with a small but portentous birthmark on her hand, a four-leaf clover. Clovia was emblematic of a new generation, a luckier, less restrained, privileged generation, free from the war, free from the Great Depression, free from irrational, rigid social constrictions. It was a new, post-war generation, born in a car. It was mobile, unhinged from tradition, hungry and brazen and unashamed. Gasoline Alley, the quiet, family-style, mild cartoon strip, had introduced newspaper readers throughout the nation to the post-war cultural invention that was first introduced as a new generation of hope and then a puzzling kind of critter, the post-war teenager. In time that teenager was to become the baby-boom generation, what historian Christopher Lasch later identified as a product of what he called "a culture of narcissism" (1978).

And sure enough, the self-contained individualism that slowly emerged in the last 400 years in Western society began to take a form that shaped the baby-boom cohort. America became a psychological society, consumerism became the engine that drove its economy, and a personal, inner sense of emptiness emerged as fuel for the engine.

Psychotherapy theories soon recognized and theorized about that constellation of forces: emptiness was thought to be an anomaly, something unusual or deviant. The theorists, unable to see beyond the individual's intrapsychic world, named emptiness a symptom, Narcissism (and other Disorders of the Self) the disease, parental (read maternal) mistakes and limitations the cause, and, of course, individualistic, ahistorical psychotherapy the cure. Emptiness as a central element of the post-war social world — as a natural, but anomalous, experience — could not be faced by mainstream psychology unless the profession was willing to call into question the larger political arrangements that created emptiness, such as consumerism. Ultimately, psychotherapy was unable to take that step into a more sophisticated critical vision.

The early 21st century baby, born in space

Today, beginning the second decade of the 21st century, there are new babies being born, lots of them; and like Clovia of 1949, they and the circumstances of their birth are emblematic of an emerging social world. Who are these new babies, and what can they tell us about the social relations and political meanings of the new world that is emerging around us? The new babies — and there are untold millions of them — are virtual creatures: avatars, in the language of consumer electronics. Researchers report that there are more than 15 million accounts registered in Second Life, a popular Massively Multiplayer Online Role Playing Game (MMORPG) in which at least one avatar is required. It is thought that participants in virtual worlds are increasing at a rate of 15% each month, with no indication of it slowing down.

Avatars are animated electronic images of humans or human-like creatures who can interact with other images in game-like environments in order to collaborate or compete in challenging situations and fight or make war on other images. Computer users can create as many avatars as they like, create for them various identities, genders, sexual orientations, personalities, jobs, families, friends, allies, and clothing. Depending on the rules of the game, these alternative identities can set out on terrifying and violent adventures, live quiet, mundane, everyday lives, or anything in between. Their creators can buy consumer items for their avatar, set up bank accounts, houses, neighborhoods, schools. The name of the popular game Second Life describes the experience (and perhaps the motivation) quite well. Creating and developing an avatar is a way of living an alternative life; many people, it seems, wish to do so. This new electronic space seems above all to generate the possibility for different, alternative, multiple ways of imagining and presenting oneself.

We could say that the new baby being born today, the emblem of our new social world, is an avatar, a baby born not in a car but in electronic space. But what does this mean about who we now understand ourselves to be? If we are spatial and fictive beings floating in imaginary worlds, what are our limits and possibilities, proper and improper ways of interrelating, correct and incorrect activities in work and play?

The brave new virtual world

We are now fourteen years removed from when *Psychohistory Review* published "From Emptiness to Multiplicity," and some of the meanings of the multiple self, and some of the mechanisms for how it has been developed, are clearer now. For instance, if most of one's news and information gathering is now done online, new understandings about the nature and generation of knowledge have begun to emerge (e.g., Carr, 2010). In a virtual world, knowledge becomes understood as a flashing image of a readily available data point, the smallest, uncontested, and most easily transported fact. In our computerized world, the machine does the defining, locating, and delivering of a requested fact, the human just does a quick read of what is delivered. Reading in this environment is a relatively superficial act, the rapid jumping from one flashing image, one "hit" or link, to another in a somewhat disengaged search for something interesting or attractive that will catch one's eye. In other words, the attainment of knowledge begins to resemble a detached search for what is entertaining. However, because speed and variety are of the utmost importance to this way of being, one does not linger long over a particular data point, one moves on to a search for the next entertaining fact, and then the next. One — or at least one's attention — does not stay stationary for long.

When knowledge becomes reduced to entertainment in this way, an interest in facts often leads to a focus on events, which could be defined as a cluster or linked series of data points that make up some sort of exciting moment: a celebrity happening, political uprising, sporting event, or natural catastrophe. With increased computer usage, this process of searching the internet by scanning or jumping from one image to another can comprise a significant amount of one's life. Life itself in this social world comes to be experienced as a disconnected but continuing series of mini spectacles flashing on the screen — part of a never-ending search for entertaining moments. Recently there has been research published about how internet use changes the brain of the user (e.g., Carr, 2010). Due to the life-long malleability of the brain, some researchers believe that electronic living will literately change the mental processes of thinking and experiencing.

The act of creating and living through avatars in MMORPGs such as Second Life, exaggerated or untrue self presentations in computerized dating services or Facebook, or the current adolescent obsession with fiction that features shape-shifting vampires and zombies who disguise themselves as regular humans, then become more understandable. They are simply the reflection of what human life has been reduced to: an ongoing experience of being profoundly used, exploited, or attacked by one's fellow humans. These images portray persons vicariously living through electronic symbols or movie characters experiencing in a continuing series of frightening but highly entertaining events. And the more entertaining the event the more engrossing and momentarily stimulating it appears, which in a world of exhausting, deadening, relatively meaningless work and an often unsatisfying and confusing communal and relational life, promises at least a jolt of adrenalin and thus the appearance of something important. The bite of a vampire, for instance, furnishes romance and sexual excitement, and confers differentness, specialness, the power of conquest, the promise of eternal escape.

There seems to be a connection between this state of affairs and what has recently been referred to as "internet addiction." The high that comes with experiencing a happening helps the user overlook the fact that whatever is happening is not really happening except to a computerized symbol in an electronically-animated environment. Still, it feels momentarily stimulating, which in our over-stressed, speeded up, often disappointing, even dangerous world, might appear to be all that one can hope for. If one cannot have a life, at least one's avatar might. As a recent University of Washington continuing education department advertisement in *Columns*, the alumni magazine (University of Washington, 2010, p. 18), asked: "Why keep learning? ... Because an avatar might be the next you."

The utility of an avatar as an escape might also add to its popularity. In a world in which human being comes to light as a multiple, or what Lawrence Jacobson (1997) and Donna Orange (2009) called a flattened self, the availability of an avatar — an alternative identity in an alternative universe — might appear to be exceedingly attractive. Why try to stand one's ground and fight when the adversary or the system seems overpowering or immune to reason or compassion, and escape is as near as one's computer screen.

When quantification and calculation have robbed life of spontaneity and vitality, when bureaucratic procedures have reduced and numbed work, or justified the loss of benefits or lay-offs, and when isolation and loneliness have decreased communal experiences and stripped social interaction of meaning, escape into an electronic make-believe is increasingly seductive. Tragically, of course, the more one avails oneself of escape, the less capable one is of figuring out what is wrong, working to change it, and thus living a meaningful life in a painful but real world.

In the recent spate of teenage vampire movies, the defining relation in the world of the undead is an extreme instrumentalism. The undead feast on the living, and by using the living, they turn the living into the undead. This seems eerily like what avatars, MMORPG participation, and we might say capitalism itself, accomplishes. Vampires live out the primary relation in a capitalist world: what Jessica Benjamin (1990) famously called the "doer and done to" relation.

The deprivations, confusions, and inequalities of our world can be so overpowering, and possible solutions so difficult to imagine and implement, that despair and hopelessness often result. It is this hopelessness that seems to motivate the wish to escape, and it is the recent changes in the self that make a radical escape imaginable, in fact, nearly inevitable.

As the deep self has become a flattened self, the experience of emptiness has shifted into a vague and ever-present anxiety or dis-ease — a vulnerability — somehow linked to a lack of belonging, personal significance, and especially safety. As the second decade of the 21st century unfolds, many of us attempt to quiet this anxiety by being involved with others electronically, which is accomplished by attracting others through offering images, stories, and texts about one's various selves. These emotions are also momentarily lightened by engaging in various electronic, magical adventures through participating in MMORPGs such as "Second Life" or "Farmville," or by viewing films, commercials, or computer

Flattened selves, shallow solutions 129

games built on amazing and life-like special effects and animation. These electronic stories and activities demonstrate how purchasing the proper product, possessing the magical amulet, or being implanted with the latest electronic gadget or prosthesis allow viewers or players to (1) communicate with an enormous number of electronic acquaintances who follow their every move; (2) alternatively follow an enormous number of electronic acquaintances who appear to be extremely popular and live a life of continuous, enjoyable adventures; (3) create and live through electronic representations of their various selves — called avatars — in MMORPGs, online dating services, and chat rooms; or (4) appear to achieve magical and extreme powers that enable them to achieve superhuman feats of athletic, military, magical, or criminal mastery simply by imagining and then keying in the solution to a challenge or threat or puzzle, and then watching as the solution comes to life on screen. The dynamic involved in solving a problem posed by an external (i.e., objective) threat by creating a internal (i.e., subjective) solution (e.g., designing and then identifying oneself with a powerful or invulnerable avatar) was recognized by Sampson in 1981 as pervasive in American culture. In other words, the political problem is solved through an apolitical (i.e., psychological) solution. The one who suffers thereby is prevented from engaging in activities that might actually solve the problem. Sampson realized that cognitive psychology's model for human mentation fits perfectly with that politically regressive dynamic, and therefore cognitive ideology (and the therapies that have been created out of that ideology) reproduce the political status quo. His critique is every bit as salient in the second decade of the 21st century as it was in 1981.

There are many ways contemporary electronic machines are contributing to these trends. Remember when celebrities were somewhat frightened by the press and the paparazzi? Now everyday folks seem to aspire to celebrity status — to be human means to be a minor celebrity: not only do we enjoy being exposed to others, we crave it. In fact, we are our own paparazzi: we violate our own privacy, take our own revealing photos and tell our own embarrassing stories and post them electronically for all to see. We don't seem to cherish privacy anymore, it was an artifact of the 20th century, interiorized, empty self. We live on the surface these days; privacy doesn't have much utility in a flattened, multiple, speeded up, dangerous world. By definition, avatars don't need privacy, in fact privacy is their enemy. They exist in order to be known, watched, and used.

Flattened selves, shallow solutions

Notice that each of these solutions to problems encountered by the multiple self are cosmetic in nature: behavioral dilemmas or challenges or dangers are reduced to superficiality and shallowness, products of a speeded up world lived on the surface. Lonely? Collect, entertain, and watch acquaintances found and connected to online. Confronted with a troubling or challenging dilemma? Just think differently about it — for instance, conceive of it differently, and imagine a different scenario, create in your mind a new skill or ability and imagine its use. Feel lost, insignificant, unimportant, unappreciated? Just purchase the football jersey of your favorite player, or the newest cosmetic of an admired celebrity, or the latest, most powerful smart phone, and watch as your popularity rises and personal skills soar.

Similarly, a 2013 television commercial depicts human cells being scientifically transformed electronically. The voice-over explains that after purchasing and using a Droid smart phone, the consumer will receive a "Droid DNA augmentation", which "is not an upgrade to your phone, it is an upgrade to your self." In these examples we see the individualist and subjectivist reductions that inhere in a cognitivist worldview (Sampson, 1981), updated for an electronic, shallow social world. The target of change has been relocated by cognitive theory from the world of political arrangements to the world of individual cognitive operations. World hunger, for instance, shouldn't be attacked by trying to change political structures, but instead by individuals thinking differently about how they go about providing for themselves, and if they choose for designated others. In this worldview, a new type of narcissism is coming to light, one that is less interiorized but every bit as self-centered as the narcissism of the late 20th century empty self.

Therapeutic applications

These types of solutions should sound familiar to therapists: EBTs advocate for the use of behavioral or cognitive techniques to solve the relational, financial, or psychological problems of everyday life. Therapeutic change is thought to come about, not by transforming one's deep, interior psychological character, but by changing one's behaviors through thinking differently about one's dissatisfactions or problems, or by rationally planning a behavioral strategy for difficult emotional moments.

These days a rule-bound, manualized proceduralism has become increasingly influential, if not hegemonic, in psychotherapy. What does that mean about our profession, our nation, ourselves? As psychologists, it is our responsibility to explore how and why the social world that produces the multiple self is also producing the proceduralism that is saturating current psychological practices and its moral and political consequences. If we exercise our historical memory, we will realize that EBT proponents are not courageously protecting the wellbeing of the poor, as they claim. Instead, they are involved in a political collaboration with the purveyors and profiteers of the bread-and-circuses strategy so successful in our contemporary society. Of course, a two-tiered system of service delivery (a deficient, EBT-style, brief therapy for the poor and a more nuanced, reflective therapy for those who can afford it) is criminal. But the way to attack that political arrangement is to change the arrangement, not accommodate to it by developing a professional apologetica. Our preoccupation with electronic devices that portray consumerist and cognitivist solutions to political dilemmas draw our attention away from the sociopolitical realm in which those dilemmas are properly located. In other words, we are too busy creating and managing our electronic images, private thoughts, and Facebook "friends" to notice, study, and engage with the real political world around us.

The power of proceduralism

In 1987 the historian Thomas Leahey wrote "we are all cognitivists now." Several forms of cognitive theory claim that the brain functions like a computer. This reflects and reproduces a popular belief that we function best when we are provided with the most up-to-date procedures (like a kind of software), which allow us to think and act more effectively. With good upgrades, it is thought we become smarter, stronger, faster, more powerful — a kind of "Droid DNA." The same cultural terrain that brought computing machines to light now brings to light an understanding of the human creature as a computing machine.

Currently, our world is increasingly dominated by a bureaucratic proceduralism. Look around us: voice mail decision trees, medical prescription orders, online shopping, academic competencies, psychotherapy intake and insurance forms are all structured — and thus limited — by procedures that must be strictly adhered to. Computers, let us remember, are all procedure. They are machines that unquestioningly follow orders. So, this kind of cultural thinking goes, although we function like computers, we are poor computers: slow, emotional, irrational. Therefore, in order for humans to think and perform better, human interaction must be guided by objectively derived procedures. Our everyday transactions are now the responsibility of electronic machines and the forms and procedures they provide; those procedures are thought to save us from our human limitations and foibles. For instance, therapists must follow manualized protocols because the protocols are thought to be a kind of scientifically derived "software"; when adhered to, the behavior they prescribe putatively saves us from weak, irrational, or uncontrolled human interaction.

In other words, I am arguing that EBTs and their manualized products are mandated because they fit best with the overall cultural clearing of our time — they come to light as the obvious truth. And then, by applying a physical science method, the epistemological circularity impossible to completely escape in human science research produces the putative proof of the superiority of scientific practices. As hermeneuticists have suggested, researchers who try to bracket off their prejudices only succeed in disguising them. So EBTs and Randomized Clinical Trials (RCTs) will inevitably provide a healing technology that fits with the cultural understandings — and thus the political arrangements — of our time and place. Scientistic psychotherapy research produced primarily by middle class Caucasians is based on a decontextual understanding of psychological problems that medicalizes political suffering and creates therapists who are true believers anxious to follow a manualized treatment regime in order to deliver a decontextualized, instrumental, technicist healing to the poor. It is a healing that, parenthetically, has generated handsome profits for the corporate elite. But more importantly, it keeps the dispossessed less able to make the connections between their suffering and the political forces (such as institutional racism or misogyny) that cause their suffering, thus politically silencing them and simultaneously muzzling their therapists. And all this in the name of pure science.

We cannot help ourselves

Those of us who should know better — psychologists who claim to be trained to think critically and learnedly about issues of suffering and healing — are so much the product of our time and so enculturated in the professional avoidance of historical and political perspectives that we cannot think our way out of the circularity of scientism and thus the pervasive influences of the multiple, flattened self. We are so constituted by an electronic, procedural, technicist world that we cannot see the wrongheadedness of these theories and practices. Therefore we cannot help our patients, research participants, and graduate students. We cannot help them because we cannot help ourselves. We cannot see that the technicist proceduralism we inflict on them reproduces the cultural terrain that has caused their suffering in the first place. We are trapped in the swirl of a smug paternalism that is too caught up in its own self-sealing ideology to realize that we have a hand in reproducing the very racist, sexist, and classist ills we are responsible for healing. It is an ongoing tragedy for the poor, for the urban dispossessed, for us all. But the greatest tragedy will be if, when computers decide to take over the world and come for us, they have a difficult time telling the difference between the humans and the machines.

Chapter 10

Because the rock will not read the article

A discussion of Jeremy D. Safran's critique of Irwin Z. Hoffman's "Doublethinking our way to scientific legitimacy"

(2013 Psychoanalytic Dialogues, 23, 211–224)

Historical introduction

Sometime in 2006 or 2007 renown psychoanalyst Irwin Hoffman arranged for several of us to begin an email correspondence in order to formulate an ongoing response to the increasing pressures on analysts and therapists to comply with the financial coercion being exerted by managed care corporations, the federal bureaucracy, and academic psychologists to conceive of therapeutic and diagnostic practices in a highly technicist, instrumental, procedural manner. Under Irwin's leadership several of us began writing in order to explain why a procedural, manualized approach to clinical work and the exclusive use of quantification and randomized clinical trials in research is so damaging to our patients, our profession, and our society.

One of the outcomes of our collaborative efforts was Irwin's brilliant Plenary Address at the 2008 Winter Meeting of the American Psychoanalytic Association, titled "Doublethinking Our Way to Scientific Legitimacy." Remarkably, it produced a standing ovation. That speech was published in 2009, and not long after *Psychoanalytic Dialogues* asked Jeremy Safran (2012), a well-respected analyst and researcher, to write a commentary on Irwin's article, and then four others to write a response to Jeremy. Two of the commentators, Carlo Strenger (2013) and Peter Fonagy (2013), supported Jeremy's critique of Irwin's article; two others, Donnel Stern (2013) and I (2013a), were members of the original online group and supported Irwin's position. Other papers from the group, such as two written by Gary Walls (2007, 2012), were also produced from the original group and were delivered at various conferences. "Because the Rock Will Not Read the Article" was my contribution to the *Dialogues* three part special section titled "Rethinking 'Doublethinking': Psychoanalysis and Scientific Research."

> Obviously, these issues were and remain salient elements of our contemporary social world. What is emotional distress; what can be done to alleviate or attenuate it; how is it properly addressed; who gets to be treated and who gets turned away; and how can U.S. society accurately assess what helps and what does not? — these are important questions for any society. Especially in the 21st century, when political struggles over the responsibilities of a society for the health and wellbeing of its citizens are pressing philosophical and financial questions, the above issues must be faced. And as long as psychotherapy is paid for by medical funds, there will be many who believe it should be evaluated by the same quantitative measures.
>
> In fact, that is being done today in psychology, and as I wrote, that way of thinking is a disaster for our society. Truly, it is a disaster, but a disaster that fits perfectly with the political arrangements of our time and place. If psychopathology, as Jules Henry wrote, "is the final outcome of all that is wrong with a culture" (1963, p. 322), then how can therapy offer genuine help if it does not think contextually about the patient's suffering? Perhaps we could say that the way we conceive of and treat psychopathology, including the ways we pay for treatment, are indeed the outcome of what is wrong with our current society. Only a more historical/political understanding of therapy can adequately address this damaging situation.

It is with a heavy heart and much reluctance that I write this commentary, which requires me to comment on an exchange between Hoffman and Safran, two members of the psychoanalytic community whom I respect and have appreciated for many years. The issues they raise move me to examine the politics of our historical moment and face the increasingly precarious situation in which psychoanalysis/psychodynamic psychotherapy — in fact all of U.S. society — presently finds itself.

The Hoffman-Safran exchange features a disagreement about the evaluation of psychotherapy practices that is complex and rife with political (and personal) implications for the future. Importantly, their disagreement also opens up a more encompassing divide that reflects an ongoing struggle over the nature and meaning of psychotherapy and, by extension, the self, in our time. In this commentary I hope to explore these larger cultural-historical questions. It is disturbing to survey our current social world with these issues in mind, but of course, ultimately, we have no choice but to face them. They have been forced upon us by the politics of our time and place, and either our voices or our silence will be heard.

History and hermeneutics

Of course, this current dispute did not arise just last year, or last decade, and it includes not only Hoffman and Safran, but the intellectual traditions from which they speak. It is the product of the political and philosophical battles of the modern era, which was thought to have begun over 400 years ago. The modern era has been shaped in part by a philosophical framework outlined by Descartes. Cartesianism splits the world into opposing distinctions such as matter/spirit, body/mind, subjective/objective. It is this split that initially articulated the immense cultural shift that made possible the claims of objective knowledge about the natural world and, in time, about humans as well. Scientific objectivity, it was thought, could only be achieved by bracketing off the researcher's prejudgements, emotions, opinions, traditional knowledge, and folklore.

In the 20th century the intellectual movement known as the Interpretive Turn (see e.g., Hiley, Bohman, & Shusterman, 1991) emerged as a radical challenge to Cartesianism. Philosophical hermeneutics, one of the two main currents of the Interpretive Turn, draws on Martin Heidegger's (1962) discussion of historicity, engagement, and being. It maintains that humans are constituted by the cultural traditions into which we are thrown at birth and those that influence us over time, and that these traditions are "inescapably moral traditions" (Taylor, 1988). They frame our understanding of life — in fact, our most basic ability to perceive and make sense out of everyday experience.

Hermeneutics developed a profound appreciation for the constitutive nature of culture, which led to the idea that prejudgements cannot be bracketed off or erased when studying humans. Prejudgements, Hans-Georg Gadamer (1989) suggested, are the foundation of culture. It is because of our prejudgements that we can perceive and understand anything, relate to others, communicate, cooperate, make meaning, care for one another, pass on knowledge from generation to generation. Prejudgements, obviously, are necessarily limiting and also sometimes destructive (as in for instance racism or sexism); but they are also indispensable to being human. They are the way we divide the universe into comprehensible units and, as a result, things and events and ideas and identities show up for us, they take understandable shape and persuasive meaning.

This means that the claim to objectivity in scientific research, so remarkably successful in the physical sciences, becomes unhelpful and in fact profoundly misleading when studying what is meaningful to humans. It is simply not possible to study meaning if our meaning-making ability is somehow "bracketed off." The use of the physical science model and the claim of objectivity to answer all questions about human being is referred to as scientism. Hermeneutics, among other things, is an extended argument against scientism. The job of human living and learning, Gadamer argued, is not to try to erase or ignore prejudgements, but to sort through our prejudgements and those of others and determine which are worthy and which are not.

Therefore, hermeneuticists conclude that when researchers claim to bracket off their prejudgements, they only succeed in disguising them. For this reason, critics of scientism have called it "a view from nowhere" — meaning that its values and commitments are nowhere to be seen. Our only hope, hermeneuticists such as Heidegger argued, is to develop ways of thinking about human being that understand that people are on-going events, not static things that can be known, controlled, and repaired through the use of technicist, instrumental methods. Without such understanding, we are continually involved in a self-deception about the content and limits of human knowledge. Historically, some of our most damaging social problems can be traced to beliefs and actions justified by the warrant of objectivity.

For all of these reasons, I must disagree with Safran about several points. I am reluctant to do so because it is obvious that he is trying to meet hermeneutics half way, trying to be reasonable and open to Hoffman's concerns and yet still be (1) committed to the psychotherapy research agenda that has been a central aspect of his professional life; and (2) cognizant of and realistic about our current economic reality and thus the demands and coercions under which psychotherapists (and teachers and students and patients and citizens) chafe.

But the problem is that years ago I became convinced that the hermeneutic perspective made sense, and that perspective is a radical perspective. So, in ways I can't avoid, I do disagree with Safran. I want to join forces with the researchers who believe they are saving psychoanalysis from extinction by beating scientism at its own game. But I can't. At the heart of this issue are my most valued commitments — they cannot be forgotten or brushed aside. So I apologize to Jeremy and all those psychoanalytically oriented quantitative researchers out there. I want to be cooperative, but I can't agree to an exclusionary ideology that relegates case studies and interpretive research to second-class citizenship. It is not that I want you to stop conducting the kind of research you value — I just don't want you to claim that your research delivers the one truth and should exclusively determine how therapists practice.

My fear, and I think the fear of many of us, is that by "playing the science game," as Hans Strupp famously said, the game will come to play you. Gadamer wrote about culture as a kind of game structured through rules; language comes to speak us, and the rules of a particular cultural game, when we participate in it, come to play us. The danger is that by thinking you can use quantification to save psychoanalysis, you begin to believe scientism's extreme and exclusionary claims to truth.

This is because, in the process of enacting social practices, humans come to embody the moral understandings that have brought those practices to light. For instance, by working in a paradigm that believes the only path to truth is to decontaminate research through the bracketing off of the social realm, researchers — even psychoanalytically-oriented researchers — run the risk of destroying some of the most important understandings of relational psychoanalysis. Especially vulnerable are the relational movement's focus on the social realm, its belief that there is more than one truth in the text, its interest in emergent process, and its moral commitments to self-reflection and critical thought. To the degree that this happens is the degree to which researchers may well be committing an error similar to that which the United States made in Vietnam: "In order to save the village," an unnamed officer told reporter Peter Arnett in 1968, "we had to destroy it." By trying to prove psychoanalytic "effectiveness" quantitatively, they run the risk of destroying its most valuable and important qualities.

In order to unpack the above epistemological issues, there are several detailed questions I had hoped to address, but the limitations of space prevent them. Instead, I turn to a broader subject: why there is so much at stake in the Hoffman-Safran disagreement and what it can tell us about American society at this crucial time in the country's history. In order to do so I will keep in mind the four-part cultural history approach I previously introduced and have drawn from over the last 20 years (e.g., Cushman, 1990, 1995, 2009; Cushman & Gilford, 1999, 2000). This approach concerns itself with identifying and interpreting the predominant ways of being of a particular era (what cultural anthropologists call the self), and what those ways of being can tell us about the understandings of health, illness, and the good within that society, including the identity of its healers and the political consequences their healing practices. By doing so I hope to better understand our current disagreements over health care, our society as a whole, and our ever-worrisome future.

A brief historical background

The last 40 years have witnessed the emergence of two complementary if not interlocking forces: an expansion of economic deregulation and an explosion of electronic computer technology. Together these two forces, in combination with a neoconservative militarism, the terrorist attack on the Twin Towers in 2001, widespread financial corruption, and the economic disaster of 2007–2008, contributed to what is appearing to be an important shift in American society, one characterized by a dangerous economic stratification and changes in how the self of our time comes to light. These changes have reflected and contributed to much economic suffering, moral confusion, fragmentation of familial and communal relationships, disruption of the nation's political life, profound changes in the news and communications media, and on an individual level painful psychological distress — in other words, a significant shift in predominant ways of being of the emerging historical era. Predictably, these events have created opportunities for various strident ideological voices, voices that insistently promise truth, certainty, solutions, safety, peace of mind, power, ecstasy, revenge.

These conditions have added to the pressures experienced by American institutions, including systems of American health care. Many times over the last 400 years in Western society, formidable social disruptions have often been met with allegiances to either hyper-rational or romantic/ antinomian solutions. Both tendencies can be seen today in various spiritual and psychological movements, religious and political fundamentalisms, a glorification of military might, and nationalistic and racial jingoism, which draw from romantic ideology on the one hand, and the overreaching and sometimes arrogant social engineering of scientistic technicism, on the other. Currently, corporations and governmental agencies seem to be in the thrall of the hyper-rational, scientistic mode — given credence no doubt by the strides made in computer technology as applied to military, business, and entertainment industries.

We see the consequences of a reliance on modern-era, quantitative science in the professions of psychotherapy (e.g., randomized clinical trials, outcome studies, and process research) and education (e.g., academic competencies and standardized testing), where the budgets for care and learning increasingly are controlled through the industrialization of labor as measured by quantitative approaches to highly concrete and over-simplified behavioral goals. Often the major opposition to scientism in psychology has been a modified form of romanticism, as seen in some forms of humanistic psychology (see e.g., Bugental, 1987; Schneider, 1998), psychoanalysis (e.g., Kohut, 1977; Winnicott 1965) or more recently transpersonal and ecological psychology.

Due to mainstream psychology's historical claim to an empirical warrant and the poverty of its philosophical thought, psychologists often seem to believe that scientism and romanticism are the only two alternatives available. However, from my point of view the most philosophically sound form of opposition to scientism is philosophical hermeneutics (see, e.g., Fowers, 2010; Gadamer, 1989; Heidegger, 1962; Richardson, Fowers, & Guignon, 1999; Slife, Williams, & Barlow, 2001), even though it is generally neither well known nor well understood. It is, however, increasingly recognized and drawn upon by some recent theorizing in relational psychoanalysis (see e.g., Stern, 1997, 2010; Hoffman, 1998, 2009; Orange, 2009; Orange & Frie, 2009; Stolorow, Atwood, & Orange, 2002). I would, for instance, characterize many of Hoffman's concerns with scientism in the "Doublethinking" article as hermeneutic.

As a result of many influences and economic pressures, quantitative measures and the scientistic ideologies that justify them have become highly influential — perhaps hegemonic — in corporate decisions about which and how much health care workers get paid. In the near future it may be that the form and amount of psychotherapy — in fact the very existence of particular psychotherapy practices — will be determined by those quantitative measures. Hoffman's article and Safran's critique must be understood within this larger context.

The rock that won't read

Years ago, when asked why a physical-science model of research is not fitting for psychological research, some hermeneutically inclined philosophers of science would tell this story: When a practitioner of the physical sciences wants to understand more about a rock, the scientist will go out into the field, locate a suitable rock, transport it back to the laboratory, perform certain procedures on the rock, record the results, and write up the findings in an article, which eventually will be published. And the rock will not read the article. "Molecules," Alasdair MacIntyre pointed out, "do not read chemistry textbooks" and "articles about viruses ... are never rewritten ... in language that viruses can understand (1995, p. 898).

But of course humans do read articles about themselves, and in our psychological society we avidly read and are influenced especially by psychological articles. Charles Taylor (1985) has called humans "self-interpreting beings." When studying humans, our observations, interventions, and conclusions are not simply, unproblematically descriptive — because they influence our self-interpretations in profound ways, they are necessarily prescriptive. The study of humans, then, cannot be an activity made neutral by putatively objective procedures. It cannot be removed from the messy world of interpretations, meanings, and power relations. Human science is always already part of a moral discourse that has political and economic consequences.

Cultural studies is indebted to the Interpretive Turn, and especially Gadamer's concept of dialogue. Gadamer's philosophy builds from his disagreement with romantic-era hermeneutics, especially the belief that truth is buried deep within a person or a text, and therefore the only way to find that secret truth is to plumb the subject's depths, enter and discover its inner secrets. Gadamer rejected this approach to truth and the Cartesian framework on which it depends. Instead he argued that we cannot know a text or another person by "feeling into" them. What we can learn about, Gadamer suggested, is the social world that brings texts and persons to light. That can tell us a great deal about our subject. And, in time, it can also tell researchers a great deal about themselves.

Hermeneuticists also disagree with the modern-era, hyper-rationalist belief that a person's behavior is determined solely through some sort of conscious, deliberate, rational choice. Similarly, a determination about the best psychotherapy theory or evaluative practice cannot be decided solely or perhaps even primarily through the exercise of disengaged logic. Long before a therapist or a health care researcher comes to believe that a decision should be made about what kind of activity psychotherapy is or which kind of therapy is the correct therapy to use in a particular clinical moment, therapists or researchers will have so embodied the moral understandings of their specific cultural terrain that in some important way their decisions will have already been made. The decision as to what therapy is and how its value is best determined will be made long before these decisions and their justifications appear as research result. Instead, the treatment of choice will seem to have appeared as an objective "finding" delivered by the proper employment of research procedure. It will feel absolutely right, like it is the only logical, scientific, objective position to take. In other words, it will be experienced — and lived out — as a disguised moral imperative.[1]

Situating the current self

The hermeneutic perspective suggests that questions pertaining to psychotherapy evaluation are not determined solely through disengaged reason unproblematically applied to research data. They are also decided by the particular configuration of the self (and thus understandings about the good) of those involved in the debate. For instance, opinions about what is a proper datum, how it is correctly gathered and manipulated are themselves artifacts of the cultural terrain — they fit hand-in-glove with understandings about the proper way of being human and being a psychotherapy researcher. If we want to understand the disagreement between Hoffman and Safran — in fact, the larger dispute between hermeneuticists and objectivists — we have to understand what moral understandings each side embodies. And in order to accomplish that, we have to develop a sense of the kind of social world that would bring their two different responses, their two different understandings of human being — and thus their two different understandings of psychotherapy — to light.

That is a tall order, especially for this short commentary. It seems to me that over the course of the last thirty or so years a prominent understanding of human being has been changing.[2] When I finished writing "Why the Self Is Empty" in 1990 we had witnessed the last decades of a 400-year process that developed the modern-era, Western self — the bounded, masterful self. The late 20th century was the culmination of a historical process in which the self came to be understood as composed of a deep, mysterious, and primarily empty interior. Whatever was employed to temporarily fill that emptiness — be it particular types of consumer items or important persons in one's life — had to be brought into one's interior, either physically or psychologically. Change, in other words, was a matter of locating, consuming, and metabolizing the proper items or ideas, which would then lead to an "internal" transformation. Needless to say, this was an understanding of human being that fit hand-in-glove with late 20th century consumer capitalism. That is the way social life always is: the prominent self as it is understood in a specific cultural terrain must fit with the overall configuration of the social world.

But by the end of the 20th century, a new configuration of the self seemed to be emerging. At that time Peter Gilford and I made initial efforts to interpret it (Cushman & Gilford, 1999, 2000); by now it has become more recognizable. Peter and I tentatively called the new configuration the multiple self, a self that was less deep and interior. It was a self that seemed to have various identities that were clustered around the person, ready to be presented according to the needs of the moment.

Transformation now appears less an interior process dependent on ingesting and psychologically metabolizing consumables and more an exterior process comprised of figuring out what kind of person the immediate social environment requires and delivering it in a pleasing and seamless manner. The goal of the multiple self ceases to be living in a genuine, true, or authentic manner and instead becomes getting along in life and especially escaping the experience of being trapped in uncomfortable or dangerous situations. It is still a matter of purchasing the proper consumer items, but those items now seem to constitute or decorate or assist identities that appear to cluster around the exterior of the individual. Transformation itself, we might say, has been transformed into a kind of switching or morphing process. The major task of those identities, it seems, is both to fend off danger and facilitate being entertained. Recently, Orange (2009) has noticed the same type of non-deep, non-interiorized self, which she referred to as a "flattened self."[3]

Two different responses to the new terrain

The disagreement between Hoffman and Safran, then, might be reflective of two differing responses to this significant shift in the cultural terrain. The growing consensus in psychology that favors measurable behavioral evidence for therapeutic outcomes, manualized approaches to therapy, or academic competencies in graduate education seem reflective of a modern-era scientific tradition in sync with current understandings about what it means to be human in our particular society at this particular historical moment. Similarly, the relational psychoanalytic emphasis on interpretation, relationality, egalitarianism, emergent processes, and fallibility seems reflective of a self that embodies a different moral response to the changing historical era. Objectivist approaches to the conduct, evaluation, or teaching of therapy seem to be in step with mainstream sociopolitical trends toward a multiple or flattened self. Hoffman's hermeneutic/constructivist approach, on the other hand, seems to represent a kind of political force, complete with intimations of moral understandings, that opposes the emerging configuration.

The less deep the self is, the less self-reflective it is, the less capable of initiative, awareness, critical thought, strongly-held preferences, decisions, commitments, and beliefs. The flatter the self, the more dependent it is on a particular model of compliance: one that relies on rules, procedures, decision trees, and manualization. The less people are capable of self-reflection and moral discourse, the more confused, ungrounded, vulnerable, and potentially dangerous they seem to be — hence, the putative need for imposed, all-encompassing, authoritarian controls.

This interpretation of the Hoffman-Safran dispute might at least help us understand why there is such emotional heat generated in these discussions. Discourse about moral understandings is indispensible to humans. As Heidegger explained, humans are the animals who care about their comportment: we are moral beings. Although quantitative researchers think they have bracketed off their moral prejudgements and are only evaluating an issue based on scientific merit, hermeneuticists suggest that the very belief in bracketing is itself a reflection of a set of moral understandings. To modern era scientism, prejudgements are inaccurate or dangerous superstitions or evil prejudices that will twist or derail the quest for scientific truth. The good is understood to be the one, pure truth, devoid of prejudgements, untouched by interpretations, and therefore uncontaminated by the social realm. Scientistic research is inevitably, from the beginning, committed to a moral position about the right way to be human — in this case, the right way to be a therapist, researcher, or even patient. Scientism did not succeed in freeing itself from moral understandings, it only succeeded in disguising them.

If the correct way of evaluating a course of psychotherapy is comparing processes or outcomes with a preexisting list of processes and outcomes identified with "positive" change, what does that reveal about the understanding of the self that is reflected therein? In fact, what does the pressure to evaluate a course of psychotherapy according to a static, predetermined, ahistorical standard tell us about the self and its ills in the first place? What does this insistence upon externally determined "accountability" mean about our current understanding of the therapist? What does it mean about our understanding of a therapist if we believe the therapist's job can be properly conducted by following a procedural script, a script that even prescribes certain personal emotions or activities, such as having empathy for or allying with the patient? What does it mean about our understanding of the self that we think a proper course of therapy can — or must — be mapped prior to its initiation? What does it mean about our understanding of therapeutic processes if we believe that therapists can know themselves, their actions, and their patients so well that they can know exactly what their interventions will convey and how they will be interpreted by and will alter their patients?[4]

What is being reflected in consumer satisfaction inventories and quantitative outcome and process studies seems to be the understanding of a self that we could interpret as a rational, straightforward, uncomplex, predictable, non-deep self. It is a self that simply wants to conform to current understandings about what it should be like. It wants to purchase a procedure that will correct what is wrong with its behavior, or repair emotions, or achieve "closure" in order to rapidly get on with working, consuming, and the business of living.

Evidently, due to the compliance with which patients greet and in fact take-for-granted the suitability of consumer satisfaction measures that are completed after sessions, they are perfectly happy to be treated as consumers. In fact, they think of themselves that way long before they ever enter therapy. They are not, for instance, insulted by the implication that talking in an honest and intimate way is a process properly evaluated in ways similar to, for instance, buying a refrigerator or a pair of shoes or a pet hamster. Therapy, it seems, is now understood as a consumer activity and therefore is properly evaluated through consumer satisfaction measures.

To the degree that this is the case, it might explain why the whole concept of psychotherapy has been changing into a logic-driven (i.e., cognitive) process, the results of which are manifested in concrete (i.e., behavioral) markers that can be tracked and evaluated based on a pre-existing diagnostic framework determined by a highly procedural script. How different is this from how we think an automobile gets serviced, a television gets diagnosed and repaired, an artery unclogged through consuming the proper medication, or a type of software automatically upgraded?

This is not to say that Hoffman's perspective is an old-fashioned 20th century version of the self. Anyone who has read the relational literature of the last 30 years would have a difficult time believing that. Instead, let me suggest that what we are witnessing in Hoffman's article is an attempt to fight against the emerging dominant cultural configuration, including the multiple or flattened self, through psychotherapeutic means. Hoffman's position is, I believe, reflective of the broader moral understandings of the relational movement that draws from the values of various streams of American culture. These influences include the intellectual ideas of the Interpretive Turn (i.e., postmodernism and hermeneutics); the artistry of jazz and American blues; anti-war and civil rights commitments of the Left; feminism's critical interrogation of gender; traditional American values that uphold equality, freedom, and justice; Jewish values related to playful textual interpretation and Yiddishist-socialist traditions of political resistance; multiculturalism's emphasis on culture, communitarian values, and respect for difference; and in general the impetus of critique in psychoanalysis that existed from its inception.

How fitting is this cultural-historical interpretation? Can we find in our mainstream social world evidence that we are thinking these days in instrumental ways that conceive of humans as multiple or flattened selves? Even in 1999 Gilford and I found many instances of that phenomenon. Is there evidence in our society today that indicates we are conceiving of humans as machines, and healing as a purely technicist endeavor? Indeed, currently there is an abundance of evidence.

We think of ourselves as machines, but not machines from the industrial age; today we are 21st century electronic machines. Recall the number of popular films that feature humans who have undergone procedures that have substituted machine parts for living tissue. Our pop culture heroes, for instance, no longer require something like the 1962 bite of a radioactive spider that turned Peter Parker into someone with superhuman strength. Now science does the trick for the likes of the Terminator, the replicants in the film Blade Runner, and more recently Jake Sully, the disabled Marine in the film Avatar. Think back to a recent conversation that you engaged in or overheard that included someone referring to memorizing as "downloading," reading as "scanning," writing as "printing out," or modifying a memory or mental image as "photoshopping." For decades cognitivists have claimed that the human brain is simply a type of complex computer. And remember that today communicating is thought to be electronic "facebooking" and relational meeting has been reduced to electronic "friending."

Think about how we understand medical treatment today: most of us no longer expect a physician to have personal knowledge of a patient as an individual; perhaps many of us don't even think it appropriate – distance makes for objectivity and thus interpersonal safety. DSM checklists and decision trees, for instance, are designed to be impersonal in order to be maximally efficient — that's the whole point. Many of us are so acclimated to filling out forms online or to responding to automated telephone decision-trees that we get flustered if our call is answered by a person instead of a recording.

Procedural living

At the heart of these examples and activities are carefully crafted sets of procedures. We are now living in a social world that is based increasingly on procedures, procedures about even the most intimate or interpersonal aspects of our lives. It is a taken-for-granted understanding that life is composed of discrete tasks that can be broken down into a series of procedural steps leading to specific goals. When the behavioral steps are properly followed, the objective is attained.

In our world today, humans — especially humans in positions of power or authority — are generally assumed to be untrustworthy, even potentially dangerous. We seem to be suspicious or afraid of one another and acutely aware of the utter vulnerability of being human. Think of the power of anti-government, anti-incumbency movements, the plethora of horror movies, the extreme popularity of vampire flicks, and color-coded terrorist alerts — danger appears to be right around the next corner. Given this situation, the way to guarantee a marginal safety from the crime, corruption, and violence perpetrated by one's fellow humans is to control them. And the only way to control them in a democratic society is to expect everyone to follow a putatively objective list of behavioral procedures when undertaking a particular activity. If we all comply with the objective procedures, it is thought that appropriate or efficient or ethical behavior will be guaranteed, and thus everyone who associates with us can be reasonably assured that they will be safe from arbitrary happenings or malicious attack.

Perhaps this is what the overused term "accountability" means — we are all to some degree corrupt or dangerous until proven otherwise, and the way we prove our momentary benignity is by demonstrating that we have followed the accepted procedures (by counting our compliance). The last thing people want others to do is deviate from objectively established practices. Creativity, critical thought, spontaneity, surprise — especially in a relationship — means the loss of control. Deviation and difference mean danger.

Above all, let us remember that a computer — cognitive psychology's model for the human brain — is all procedure. It can't deviate because it is a machine; its speed and efficiency are produced precisely by its inability to deviate from the rule-based dictates programmed into it. Should we now say that about ourselves, as well? Hoffman's article fights against that cultural frame. Quantitative psychotherapy research, on the other hand, is its latest expression.

In the world we are living in today, proceduralism dominates. And so of course our social practices, including our psychotherapy practices, will inevitably reflect that world and its understandings. In his critique of Hoffman's paper, Safran in effect asked what harm will it do to go along with the health care administrators and quantitative researchers who are in control of funding sources and the general public who want straight talk about "what works," if basically we agree with their objectivist viewpoint anyway, just to a lesser degree.

But hermeneuticists encourage us to realize that social practices are not neutral "tools" that can be used for any purpose. When we use them they affect us, and if they are used enough, they come to constitute us. So treating humans as if they are things, rather than Heideggarian events, and procedures such as diagnostic decision trees, manualized treatments, and academic competencies as if they are the one way to ensure good therapy and meaningful learning, could have serious political consequences. The manuals and procedures insisted on by managed care organizations and the protocols of quantitative research practices are not simply neutral accessories that allow therapists to do their work in an efficient manner. They claim to be powerful social weapons, equipment that ensures competence, in the words of an APA committee (Kaslow et al., 2007[5]) on academic competencies. Inevitably, proceduralism and technicism will profoundly shape our understandings of therapists and patients, psychotherapy processes and psychotherapy evaluation. They will shape our understanding of learning, teaching, and therefore the success or failure of graduate education in our field. Most of all, they will shape our way of being and our understanding of ourselves and others far more effectively than we would like to think.

The prescriptive nature of putatively descriptive social science research, hermeneuticists teach, inevitably leads to a valorization of the researcher's preferred way of being (see e.g., Richardson & Fowers, 1998). Similarly, the frame of accountability inevitably leads to a valorization of an accounting way of being. In the case of psychotherapy, when therapists treat themselves and their patients as if they are machines, both will come to believe it. If patients believe they are machines, they will come to believe that they should be treated like machines, they will come to treat others as if they are machines, and they will become confused and suspicious if they are treated otherwise. "The good" will be understood to be good mechanics.[6] Therapy will be understood to be a technical process, the application of the proper mechanical technique to the problematic part of the computer. Running poorly? Get a tune up; it will take 45 minutes. Depression? Get the right medication. Need adjustment? Six sessions will get your thoughts straight.

Joel Kovel (1980) once suggested that the reification and medicalization characteristic of the early 20th century mental hygiene movement banalized psychoanalysis and objectified emotional conditions, thereby allowing "for an *exchange-value* to be placed on states of mind" (1980, p. 82, italics in original). That same tactic currently is alive and well and has been vastly refined. The same central concern, how to translate psychotherapy into terms that will allow it to fit within the capitalist marketplace, has resulted in the current Hoffman-Safran disagreement.

There is a television commercial that aired during football telecasts in Fall, 2010 about a new mobile phone, called, importantly, a "Droid," which if you remember Star Wars, is a human-like mechanical robot (e.g., R2D2). In the commercial, we see a well-dressed young man bored at his work station and preoccupied with the football game he hasn't been able to watch. Surreptitiously, he reaches for his new phone, which features a glowing red circle set on a black screen. The circle is composed of circles within circles that give off an aperture-like appearance. The voice-over explains that the new Droid "will change how you do football. ... [After watching games on the new screen] the way you see them will never be the same." The game then appears on screen, which we see over his shoulder, but then the camera swings around until it is aimed behind the phone so that we view his eye watching the phone. Quickly, his eye begins to change: his iris begins to resemble a series of gears — no, some sort of digital contraption, complete with smooth, mechanical whirring and clicking sounds. And then a metallic ball drops into his pupil, moves quickly to sync with the gears, and glows red, pulsating in an eerie, atomic-like way. Before our eyes, his eye becomes transformed into a digital receptor, a camera aperture: he is being turned into an electronic viewing machine. And it is happening because he is using a remarkably efficient new phone. As the commercial ends, we see again the phone in repose, only the strange, mechanical, electronic aperture quietly whirring and glowing red — watching. The panopticism of this scene seems inescapable: just who is watching and controlling whom?

In a second Droid commercial, the young man is in a business meeting, populated by several well-dressed people, all sitting around a large oblong table. He takes out his Droid and begins to search for information or calculate some problem or key-in some data. The calculation gets increasingly detailed, and his fingers punch in information at an ever-faster rate, almost as if the phone itself has taken over the action. And then, as his fingers work faster still, they begin turning into a robot's fingers, and then his hands and then wrists and arms all turn into metal parts of a machine. The voice-over states that the Droid, in order to hook "you up to everything you need to do," will turn "you into an instrument of efficiency." The man's fingers are now almost a blur, racing at superhuman speed. By using the Droid, the young man has been turned into a droid.

It is remarkable, is it not, that advertising executives seem to know more about the constitutive process of social practices than psychologists do? They know what we don't want to know: social practices constitute us. In 1997, Stern reminded us about how Sullivan characterized selective inattention: "One simply does not notice what one does not wish to know. And if one does notice, the implications of what is noticed cannot be drawn" (1997, p. 59). Perhaps we do not want to face what psychology's continuing elevation of quantification — our "flight to objectivity" (Bordo, 1987) — is doing to our psychotherapy practices, our way of being, and thus to us as a people.

Above all, the two Droid commercials seem to provide a helpful response to Safran's implicit question to Hoffman and to us all: aren't there ways we could be less extreme, pull together and make common cause with the new psychoanalytic researchers — after all, the alternatives are so much worse. In response, let us notice that the Droid commercials illustrate the hermeneutic warning Heidegger delivered about technology (1977). The tools we use initiate certain practices, and these practices carry with them a cultural framework that includes moral understandings about what it means to be human. We come to embody those understandings, live them out, and thus, inevitably, the self we relationally initiate others into we ourselves will become.

Reducing human living to procedures might appear to be the only hope for a self that cannot draw from its moral traditions, virtues, character, intuition, and experience — its relationality — and trust itself to make good decisions in the moment. In our current social world, the multiple, flattened self seems to believe it must comply with a scientifically determined set of behavioral rules. Due to the shape of our current cultural terrain, authoritarian proceduralism in psychology often comes to light as the only salvation from professional mediocrity, malpractice, confusion, even social chaos. But it is the moral limitations and political demands of our social world — not a putatively unassailable research finding — that asserts that claim. Do we really, even in the name of science, or even (secretly) in the name of financial wellbeing, want to be responsible for assenting to — in fact reproducing — that brave new world?

Notes

1 Importantly, none of this should be construed to mean that people cannot change; one way that change happens, Gadamer thought, is through an encounter with difference and with the moral questioning that can be the product of a response to difference. That is what he meant by dialogue, and the elaboration of that idea is what saves hermeneutics from becoming a historical determinism.
2 This cultural history approach is much indebted to Erich Fromm and his concept of the Marketing Personality (e.g., 1955).
3 It is true that there are relational analysts who write about multiplicity and accord the concept of multiple self states an important place in their work (e.g., Bromberg, 1993, 1996; Davies & Frawley, 1992, 1994; Stern, 2010). But these writers are not valorizing the kind of flatness demonstrated in contemporary pop culture. Their theories, like all theories, have their good and problematic aspects. Psychoanalytic multiplicity reflects the hermeneutic belief that there is more than one truth in a text or an issue, and in that way it

reinforces egalitarianism. Psychoanalytic multiplicity also supports the idea that individuals are composed of various desires, values, ideals, commitments, and emotional patterns, and therefore the standard should not be that humans can be reduced to one unified, unproblematic self. In this way multiple self theories are in opposition to the unitary, singular Victorian self — they valorize conflict, variation, and difference. However, although psychoanalytic multiplicity is certainly different from the pop cultural multiple self, both seem to be a reflection of the same social world. Because of that, of course psychoanalytic theorists need to be mindful of the pitfalls of multiplicity and vigilant in historically situating therapeutic theory and practice and guard against uncritically accepting all aspects of multiplicity. The worth of a society is determined finally by how cultural characteristics are used and to what purposes they are put.

4 See e.g., Stern (1997, p. 111) for a discussion about why this is not possible.
5 The word "ensure" (that is, to make something certain) is found sixteen times in the eight pages of text, one or more listings in each page.
6 See Fowers (2010) for a study about instrumentalism in psychology.

Chapter 11

Your cheatin' heart
From scientism to medicalization to an unethical psychotherapy[1]
(2013 APA Annual Convention)

Historical Introduction

I wrote this presentation, "Your Cheatin' Heart," for an interdivisional symposium titled "The DSM-5 and the Future of Mental Health Diagnosis: Critical Responses" at the 2013 APA convention. But it's not a talk about a romance gone wrong, like the story told by the country and western song[2] from which this title was taken (Williams, 1952). No, it is about a profession gone wrong.

This paper was an attempt to use current post traumatic stress disorder (PTSD) and peripartum depression (PPD) treatment philosophies to illustrate one way the fit between economic pressures and the mainstream asocial paradigm in psychology functions to silence the moral concerns and political insights of psychologists in clinical practice (see e.g., Ludlam, 2007; Lord, 2014; Pape, 2014). I was aware that this was the most politically explicit and confrontive talk I'd ever written for an APA convention. The program was scheduled for a large meeting room that held 500 people; even so people were jammed in the walkways and aisles. But instead of pitchforks and torches, the crowd was unusually attentive, and when I finished they gave my talk a standing ovation, a rare occurrence at APA conventions. I was shocked by the outpouring of support for what was a straightforward political challenge to the status quo.

So it turns out the song seems to be right after all. No matter how loudly mainstream psychologists, APA accredited graduate programs, and ambitious clinicians proclaim their loyalty to scientism, in the still of the night we can't escape the grieving of our own hearts: we know something is wrong. Whether, given the political forces arrayed against us, we can do something about it is another question, to which no one knows the answer. Yet. But during that program in 2013, the response to the talk indicated that perhaps many everyday psychologists know in their hearts that a major realignment of the profession's philosophy of science is desperately needed.

The title of this paper is my attempt to honor and give voice to the many therapists and doctoral students who have approached me over the years struggling with the conflict between needing to make a living by complying with the mandates of scientism and the demands of a neoliberal marketplace, and yet knowing in their hearts that something is wrong with the whole framework. We can pretend, we can claim that objective science is our only guide and the only legitimate arbiter of psychological questions. We can dutifully write slick advertising copy promoting our practices, evasively fill out insurance forms, and apply for research grants that privilege behavioral, instrumental language and swear we are telling the truth, but when darkness falls, and we are face to face with our own doubts and fears, we know we are not telling the whole truth. "Your cheatin' heart," Hank Williams sang,

> Will make you weep,
> You'll cry and cry,
> And try to sleep,
> But sleep won't come,
> The whole night through,
> Your cheatin' heart, will tell on you...

There is a good deal wrong with the predominant ways we conceive of and practice psychotherapy, including especially the ways we use this panel's topic, the DSM-5. There is much to be concerned about, much to criticize, from the DSM-5's content to its secretive deliberations to its collusion with Big Pharma to the extravagant promise that future DSMs will be grounded in neuroscientific research. But in this paper I want to address a different and more encompassing problem embodied by the DSM-5: the premise that emotional suffering and psychological difference can be identified and understood as asocial, discrete, intrapsychic medical disorders. This encourages treatment through the use of a medical model that deploys technicist interventions in an instrumental manner.

Under various cultural influences and sociopolitical pressures, psychotherapists increasingly have complied with corporate demands to become ever more behavioral, medicalized, and manualized. DSM III and following are good examples of that kind of compliance. Psychotherapy has become progressively less able to adequately consider sociopolitical issues that bear upon clinical matters or consider contexts outside of the nuclear family or sometimes even the therapeutic dyad, except in constrained and simplistic ways.

I have adopted a hermeneutic perspective that starts from a different premise: when human meaning is involved, it is not possible to follow physical science method and "bracket off" prejudgements. When we attempt that, we succeed not in bracketing off prejudgements, but only in disguising them. To illustrate this point, I introduce two examples of how a disguised political perspective has unknowingly influenced diagnostic categories in the DSM: PTSD, the category used since the introduction of the DSM III in 1980 to describe wartime trauma, and the more recent category Peripartum Depression (PPD). I do so by drawing on Donnel Stern's contemporary relational psychoanalytic theory about dissociative enactment and Peter Marin's 1981 study of Vietnam vets and his contention that PTSD is an expression of "moral pain" exacerbated by political betrayal.

In this paper I argue the scientism that permeates the descriptions and explanations in DSM III, IV, and 5 facilitates only a token approach to the social realm. Surprisingly, I believe this is true even about diagnostic categories such as PTSD and PPD, which initially were designed to take environmental factors into consideration. PTSD has been a brave attempt to recognize the pathogenic qualities of trauma, and therapists drawing from it have attenuated the suffering of many. To their credit, over the years practitioners working from within the paradigm have also altered it in attempts to make it less reductionist; I write this paper not to overlook or diminish their worthwhile accomplishments. Rather, my concern is that by utilizing only a limited understanding of the social realm, the DSM category PTSD, (especially when applied to returning soldiers), and PPD contribute to the ongoing history of psychology that mystify the link between individual and collective suffering. That act thereby makes difficult a more comprehensive understanding and meaningful treatment of wartime trauma, birthing and parental fears, and the society that brings them about. Currently in our profession a limited understanding of the social creates an intellectual tokenism that works hand-in-glove with state and corporate interests in health care. The result is a technicist psychotherapy that medicalizes, and thereby depoliticizes, political suffering.

A more comprehensive understanding of moral pain

Marin's work with Vietnam vets moved him to conclude in 1981 that they were struggling desperately to find a way to understand their actions and forgive themselves. Their pain was an expression of their moral conflicts.

But Marin also had something more troubling to say about the extreme and sometimes bizarre symptoms of returning vets, something that mainstream psychology has difficulty facing, because to face it would necessitate an uncomfortable excursion into the realm of history, politics, and morality. He believed the vets were confused, furious, and grieving over what the war meant about the country that sent them to such a corrupt, immoral errand. Marin became convinced that the newly returned vets were appalled by what they began to sense about the American society they returned to: they fell into despair over the general population's disinterest about, and avoidance and denial of the horrific realities of late 20th century warfare. They were shocked by the inability of civilians to face what the country had forced them into doing, living through, and being silent about.

Taking Marin's conclusions seriously would have necessitated challenging psychotherapy's century-long struggle to situate itself as a physical science that treats decontextual ills through the technical application of medical-style practices. His findings would have led psychology into the realm of history and culture. But psychologists are not well equipped to venture into that realm; we have been enculturated into a view of our field that believes the social is simply one among many influences at work on the free-standing, naturally constituted, self-contained individual. Most training programs do not recognize the profound ways that the social constitutes humans, and thereby psychologists have a difficult time adequately identifying the phenomena it is our responsibility to understand.

The most excruciating aspect of the vets' moral pain, Marin argued, was their realization that most of their families and friends and religious and political leaders couldn't or didn't want to notice the political aspects of the vets' suffering, and didn't want the vets themselves to realize or give voice to it. This knowledge — about the brutality and destructiveness of war and the profound economic inequalities and stratifications in the world — was too much for the vets to bear in solitude. The enforced silence imposed by a nation that did not want to know the truth of the war, a prison sealed by a narrow, medicalized therapeutic model, left most vets without the moral or political language needed to make sense of their experiences, just a vague, unarticulated sense of betrayal.

The meaning of dissociative symptoms in war stress injuries

In response, Marin thought, the vets did what all of us do when confronted with an event or knowledge that is too painful to face or face alone: they dissociated from it. Stern (1997, 2010) and other relational psychoanalysts have written extensively about these everyday psychological processes. He drew from philosophical hermeneutics to explain the unconscious in an unusual way: he thought that traumatic experiences or awarenesses are not stored fully formed in a sort of underground archeological vault, the way Freud conceived of it. Instead, they are kept "unformulated," that is, not able to be noticed or reflected upon, because they are not fully articulated in the first place. However, Stern argued that what is left unformulated is too important to be erased. It is kept psychologically close, unformulated but somehow partially available though disguised in phenomena such as dreams, fugue states, and especially dissociative enactments.

Some PTSD symptoms of returning Vietnam vets, for instance, could have been interpreted as expressions of unformulated thoughts and feelings that were then lived through by experiencing them in the moment — in other words, by enacting them. Part of what was being left unformulated and then enacted was the profound betrayal vets experienced because of our country's avoidance of what we made them do and witness and endure.

Of course, neither most of the Vietnam vets nor those of Iraq and Afghanistan have been able to fully articulate these ideas. The awarenesses of the moral betrayal perpetrated by their country by ordering them into war and then being unwilling to listen to them and face the horrific destructiveness of current warfare, learn from it, and reverse what Andrew Bacevich has called the new American militarism (2005), remain primarily unformulated by them. And yet these awarenesses appear, dimly and in disguised form, in nightmares, flashbacks, crazy talk, bloody and gruesome fantasies, alcohol and drug-induced accusations, random aggression, family violence, and suicide.

Their symptoms, now routinely identified as PTSD symptoms, are acted out in a dissociative haze. Some of these experiences could be interpreted as unconscious enactments that allow the expression of their unformulated or secret realizations but without the complication of directly realizing the source of their pain: the military-industrial-educational complex, the institutions and authorities that avoid noticing the profound flaws in U.S. foreign policy and the powerful arms and munitions industry that drives it, and tragically the family, friends, doctors, and therapists of the vets, who subtly dissuade them from putting words to that which they could realize, if given the chance.

In these cases the real enemy of the vets are those of us who just want our returning soldiers to be patched up enough to be shipped out in their next deployment, receive promotions and perhaps medals, and then retire and seamlessly carry on a quiet, apolitical family life. In a way, we are the people who are really plotting against, threatening, and attacking the vets. So, when returned soldiers, walking down a quiet street in their home town late at night, hear a loud noise and suddenly experience it as sniper fire, or are surprised by strangers and immediately think they are enemy soldiers, or have the eerie feeling that a loved one is plotting to kill them, sometimes they are not re-experiencing war scenes from their past life by projecting them onto their present circumstances (as PTSD theory maintains). Instead, sometimes they are experiencing their present experiences through the vernacular of war scenes from their past. It is the genius of psychological defenses such as unconscious enactments that allow suffering — in this case political suffering — to be experienced, and self-defenses enacted, without having to face up to the political and personal consequences that would result from a conscious naming of those who cause their suffering. And it is the genius of the DSM that depoliticized the Vietnam vets' "moral repugnance at the war ... [and] transformed ... [it] into a psychiatric symptom." Then, as now, historian Patrick Hagopian wrote, "dissidence became pathology" (Hagopian, 2013, p. 77).

This is one of the great tragedies of our time. The tremendous physical and emotional toll produced by 21st century combat is often decontextualized, individualized, and thereby diluted if not erased from public view. And there are times that psychotherapy contributes to this tragedy by refusing to fully contextualize our soldiers' suffering. When therapists are unable or unwilling to address and allow the vets to address the larger political and moral issues raised by America's now perpetual wars of occupation, we are significantly limited in how we respond to the suffering we are responsible for treating. We create ever-new technicist treatments, we test them in ways that provide putative proof of their effectiveness in so-called evidence-based practices; some of us even make the claim that we can inoculate soldiers before they are deployed by strengthening their "resilience." We patch them up in order to send them out again, and convey to them in many subtle but effective ways what they are not permitted to say. And thereby we prepare our country for initiating the next war because we cannot learn the lessons of the current war. By treating PTSD as a decontextualized, anomalous disorder, we depoliticize the main issue, which is war itself. And so we make invisible our continuing complicity in the ongoing corruption at the heart of our society.

By medicalizing and depoliticizing the wounds of war, we allow all of us, civilians and soldiers, doctors and patients, to avoid facing what our country is doing to our young soldiers, to combatants from other countries, to those we hold captive and torture, to civilian populations trapped in war zones, to our political strategies and alliances throughout the world, and especially to our moral culture and domestic budgets at home. And then, self-righteously, scientistic therapists bemoan wartime trauma, are proud of their efforts to treat and subdue it, and are pleased to accept new contracts with the V.A., CIA, DoD, and university grants funded by the NIMH.

The moral pain of mothering

In 2012 Maura Sheehy, a Brooklyn psychotherapist and writer, wrote about a woman who was pregnant and asked for an appointment because she was bothered by "floaters,"

> bits of protein floating around in her eye fluid that can be caused by pregnancy ... [and] are terribly annoying. ... [The patient reported that] "this is making me really anxious. I thought I should talk to someone so I can get over it and go on to have a great birth and a beautiful baby and be a happy mother."
>
> (p. 99)

There is something at once touching, disturbing, even heartbreaking about this statement. We sense immediately her naiveté, her vulnerability, her fears lurking just below the surface. We sense the pressures at work on her to handle motherhood perfectly. She knows, Sheehy contended, exactly how we expect — no, demand — her to act.

> [W]e don't want to hear doubt and fear and lack of knowledge and the threat of unhappiness ... from a mother. ... She "knows" she [is supposed to] ... be serene, confident, happy, nondesiring, not anxious. ... [I]f she continues down this road ... unwanted emotions may surface that could [cause ... a] difficult birth ... [and] an ugly, bad baby. ... We all know that all of these things are not only possible, or even likely, but guaranteed.
>
> (p. 100)

That is a shockingly bold and frightening statement. And there is so much more that we could add about a pregnant woman's fears, including the unavoidable fact that the birth will unrelentingly and forever change her body and her age, her identity, her consciousness, her every waking moment, her life itself. It is not only the mother's emotional ambivalence and psychological conflicts that "float" into consciousness and are confusing and frightening. So many young and inexperienced mothers are separated geographically or emotionally from their families of origin (especially their extended families), their communities and old friends, and thus from the help and advice that experienced loved ones could offer, right at the time they need it the most. But it is not only the anticipation and experience of birth that is frightening and unavoidably painful for the mother, and it is not only the difficulty U.S. culture has with recognizing and living with extreme and conflicting feelings (especially those of women). There is much more that exists in her social context that could well cause her to despair. For instance, according to Slate. com's crowd sourced data, as of July 28, 2013, 19,500 people have been killed by guns in the U.S. since the shootings of children at Sandy Hook Elementary School on December 14, 2012. The news carries daily reports of child abductions, violence against women, racist policies in America, suicide bombings and brutal counter-insurgency campaigns in Iraq and Afghanistan, and bloody civil war in Syria. We see film of tornadoes, flooding, wildfires, auto and airline crashes, and the continuing threat that the economic downturn of 2007 could return. The economic pressures on working class and middle class mothers to work and yet be perfect mothers, hard-driving careerists and simultaneously warm, all-knowing, self-sacrificing mothers seem impossible to reconcile.

Children are vulnerable, and our world is dangerous. I think it fair to say that becoming a parent requires a good deal of denial — perhaps, a series of delusions. Between the effects of baby pheromones, parental hormones, and psychological necessity, we come to believe that our babies will be safe, secure, smart, good looking, well-adjusted, happy, popular, and successful — contingent only on the mother's ability to perform properly. And as Sheehy has pointed out, it is not only the mother who come to believe this fantasy, but the mother's partner, extended family, and friends as well, in fact everyone who comes into contact with the mother, including doctors and therapists and clergy. To one degree or another, nobody likes to think about how difficult parenting is, how dangerous is our social world, how painful it is to watch a child get involved with and marked by the larger society in indelible and significant ways. And then of course there is always — always — the matter of death, ours and our children's, that we give them by bringing them into the world.

Birth visits upon our babies a myriad of hurts, unfairnesses, uncertainties, and tragedies, uncountable insults, pains, and worst of all those we cannot imagine, let alone anticipate or prevent. Birthing and raising a child are frightening tasks for which probably no one is fully prepared and educated.

Americans, especially middle class Americans, do not do well with the dark side of life. "Life, liberty, and the pursuit of happiness," that's what life is properly thought to consist of. Experience anything less and it is thought that you have failed. What we especially do not notice are the ways in which our bourgeois, consumerist social world has made mothering ever more difficult: such as the loss of family, community, and tradition, the inevitable and unending insecurity of life in a capitalist society, the emptiness and frustrations of living in a highly competitive, relativistic, rigidly gendered, economically stratified, and increasingly undemocratic society.

We don't like to be aware of all that. Pregnant women, inexperienced mothers, experienced mothers, young mothers, old mothers — all mothers — potentially remind us of all that we are trying to avoid. We don't want to hear about a mother's anxiety, depression, despair. It would remind us too much of our own. We want mothers, in the words of Sheehy's patient, to "get over it and go on to have a great birth and a beautiful baby and be a happy mother" (p. 99) so we can get over it and have a great adulthood and a beautiful and happy life.

Ah, but there are floaters, and they intrude. Anxiety and worry float into consciousness the way a fetus floats in the womb. The new mother's floaters potentially draw attention to the unformulated dangers or inequalities or injustices or absences in our social world, arrangements that we might address if only we could see them. What happens when a new mother starts to see her floaters? What do they embody? What does she start to see about herself and about us that we don't want her to see? What is lost from sight if we think they are just a bothersome psychiatric symptom that can be extinguished or controlled through a surgical, CBT, laser-like strike? What if her floaters are our floaters, but only she can see them?

Like the returning Vietnam War vets, mothers are betrayed by those of us who refuse to face up to the structural absences and oppressions that leave new mothers with impossible expectations, little communal support, and realistic personal danger. It is the disappointment about and sense of isolation from her loved ones — their inability or unwillingness to face the difficulties of mothering in our social world — that are important elements in the new mother's despair, and the DSM-5 doesn't adequately take those contextual factors into consideration. Without examining — I mean really examining — the sociopolitical context of mothers, their suffering will always be reduced to an individual dysfunction such as hormonal disregulation or mistaken ideas and thought of as an anomaly in an otherwise calm sea of normality. Without a critical perspective we cannot see the context, we cannot properly value it and study it and thereby develop more complex — and political — understandings about the suffering of our patients.

Psychologist as public intellectual and community activist

This is how a mainstream psychotherapy carves out and maintains a place for itself at the banquet table of health care payments in the early 21st century.

I am not discussing this issue because I think we should simply propose new elements for the DSM-5 descriptions of PTSD and PPD and the protocols linked to its manualized treatments. I am raising it in order to suggest that we cannot escape the moral and political nature of psychotherapy, no matter how strongly we maintain that our scientistic methods guarantee the putative objectivity of our practices. The DSM-5, like all practices under the influence of scientism, is a disguised moral discourse that reflects the political and moral status quo and has profound political consequences.

There is a familiar debate in psychology about whether our clinical emphasis should be placed on prevention or treatment. But I am saying something more than that: the very mode of mainstream treatment makes prevention more difficult. The prevention of the wounds of war and motherhood are our responsibility every bit as much as their healing. The suffering of young men and women around the world deserves no less from us.

Given how much our profession is in the thrall of scientism, I am sure this sounds preposterous (or at least unworkable) to many psychologists today. And indeed it is, if our goal is to continue down the well-trodden historical path of psychology, seeking desperately for ways to fit into consumer capitalism, to position our activities as a technicized, medicalized practice, as a scientized, sanitized, apolitical set of expert procedures that treat narrowly defined asocial, cognitive, and biochemical anomalies. "The petite bourgeois ideal," Harry Stack Sullivan once wrote,

> is all right for the psychiatrists who are correctly defined as doctors who have failed in the practice of medicine. They have found for themselves a useful function in sheltering society from those whom it has destroyed.
>
> (Sullivan, 1946, p. 81)

But if we conduct ourselves in that way, we betray our moral responsibilities to our patients, because we have betrayed our moral responsibilities to the nation. Ultimately, a decontextualized psychotherapy becomes an unethical psychotherapy by reproducing the very conditions that create the ills we are responsible for treating. And in times of war and mothering those ills are heartbreakingly tragic. If we make war palatable and legitimate by disconnecting wartime trauma from the larger questions about war itself we make the conduct of war permissible and thereby wartime trauma inevitable. There is only one effective way to prevent the effects of wartime trauma on our youth, and that is either to create political arrangements that remove the reasons and justifications for war or, failing that, to execute effectively political resistance that prevents them from going to war in the first place. Similarly, if we make our current political arrangements palatable and legitimate by disconnecting the causes of the mother's pregnancy, birth, and parenting fears from the social world into which her baby is born, we relocate the cause of her suffering to herself alone, excuse the status quo, and make political reform impossible.

When seduced by the siren song of bourgeois respectability, the putative certainty of scientistic proceduralism, and the iron-clad proscriptions against thinking historically and politically, psychologists are rendered ineffective in any sort of long-term preventive activity and thus effectively silenced politically. Due to our rigid allegiance to scientism and the ways the study of the humanities has been excluded from APA accredited psychology graduate programs, social roles such as the psychologist as public intellectual have disappeared from our field. Because of this situation, our patients — and the larger community — suffer.

We have more to say about the consequences of contemporary forces such as institutional racism, classism, misogyny, homophobia, and militarism than our narrowly proscribed roles permit. If we would allow ourselves to speak out in wise and learned ways about the crushing problems of our time, we could make a difference. When we march meekly into compliance with managed care or remain silent about psychologists active in military torture or are unable to make the connections between the long-term effects of childhood hunger or violence against women and the larger ideologies and social practices that cause them, we have effectively abandoned our ethical responsibilities.

This is what keeps us awake at night. Our cheatin' hearts know something is wrong — our dissociation and confusion is every bit as powerful as that of the returning soldiers and haunted mothers-to-be — and so our sleep won't come, the whole night through, because our cheatin' hearts will tell on us. It would be good if we would listen.

Notes

1 This paper is dedicated to Dr. Jules Burstein, colleague and good friend, who read and commented extensively (and argumentatively) on every paper I wrote from 1986 to 2012, until death tragically took him from us. He would have liked this talk.
2 "Your Cheatin' Heart" was written by Hank Williams in 1952. It is considered to be a standard, perhaps even the anthem, of country and western music.

Chapter 12

Horror, escape, and the struggle with Jewish identity

A review of *Contemporary Psychoanalysis and the Legacy of the Third Reich*

(2015 *Contemporary Psychoanalysis*, 51, 176–184)

Historical introduction

I was pleased to write a review article about Emily Kuriloff's new book, titled *Contemporary Psychoanalysis and the Legacy of the Third Reich*, although at first I had no idea what I would say. But soon I had a familiar feeling: usually I don't know what I am going to write, but I can tell something is there, anxious to be put into words. And indeed, when I sat down to write, some unexpected ideas poured out.

By the second half of 2014, the country was preparing for the forthcoming presidential election campaign. It appeared that the race would be the Democrat Hillary Clinton (a qualified candidate but not a great campaigner) vs. a group of undistinguished, boring Republican white men — in other words, a relatively unexciting campaign. But then something completely unanticipated happened: a hockey game broke out — that is, a brawl ensued. Donald Trump insulted, ridiculed, and finally slaughtered his Republican foes, captured the nomination, unbelievably won the national election, and immediately began creating chaos, divisiveness, and dispensed a type of nativist, xenophobic militarism that encouraged a shocking amount of proto-Nazi sentiment and behavior among a segment of the population.

When I started writing the review, I could not have anticipated the depth of racism and misogyny that would be unleashed by the far right's capture of the Republican Party. But I must have had a semi-conscious inkling of what was to come, because in this review I found myself warning about the combined forces of fundamentalism, authoritarianism, and racism, not only in relation to the past but pertinent to that pre-election moment. I didn't fully know then why I was writing what I wrote; some colleagues thought it overly dramatic and alarmist, others thought it puzzling that I was focusing on Jewish oppression, Jewish identity confusion, and advocating for the fit between Jewish traditions and Lefty politics.

In retrospect, I guess I knew something I didn't know I knew. It was true that I had been writing about the dangers of the alliance between the religious and political right since the 2000 election and the assent of George W. Bush's arrogant, far-right administration of militarists and free-market ideologues. But Kuriloff's book helped me make connections between my fears as an American and my fears as a Jew. After writing my review article, I came to realize that the studying and writing I had done (e.g., 2007, 2010) about the political meanings of Jewish biblical commentary (i.e., *midrash*) as an anti-fundamentalist, anti-authoritarian practice and its relationship to psychotherapy was preparation for what I sensed was to come. What started out as an attempt to better understand and then combat Republican agendas such as colonial wars of occupation, domestic repression, corrupt campaign funding laws, voter suppression activities, and heartbreakingly, Far Right government in Israel became — through the lens of Kuriloff's book — the realization that something more menacing was emerging. I began to understand that the events of the Bush years were reflections of a larger cultural groundswell of crudeness and anti-intellectualism that had been building for decades and reached a new level of intensity during the election campaign of 2015–2016.

If the history of the Jewish people teaches us anything, it is that when oppression and inequality of the poor and working classes are unremedied, and instead are anesthetized by spectacle and extreme authoritarian ideology, a despised Other is located or manufactured and then attacked. In what follows, terrible deeds abound. The only remedy is for those identified as Other to know well and be proud of their moral traditions, make their alliances with other oppressed groups, and stand strong and politically active together.

The 2016 election ushered into power the beginning of just such a hateful political dynamic, the type of regime history books about Weimer Germany describe. What at first seemed to be hysterical hand-wringing, by late 2017 has day-by-day become more compelling and realistic. How can we draw from accounts like Kuriloff's in order to recognize danger and work together to combat it? That seems to be our current task in a world increasingly reminiscent of the dark world that initially framed Kuriloff's subjects. The guidance that in the last page of my review I imagined in the dream workshop remains underdeveloped for us today, but it is not yet an impossibility; it continues to await our ability to bring it to life.

Emily Kuriloff has written a book that no one will want to read and that everyone must read. It is a book that is painful and soothing, terrifying and hopeful. At times it describes the most destructive of dead-ends, at others it opens a way into the light. Her interviews with psychoanalysts who are survivors and children of survivors expose souls who have stumbled in the darkness, who cobble together memory and forgetting in ways impossible to predict or fully understand. They do what they can to shape a life out of the human wreckage wrought by a time so saturated with hatred and evil that in truth it can have neither name nor explanation. At the same time, it also reveals these broken souls to be brave and hardy souls who honor the word "survivor," not because they emerge unscarred, but because they limp and know they limp, know something of what they have been through and choose to live on in the face of it all. They have children, continue as analysts or become analysts, struggle with their own demons, treat patients, train students, write articles and books, serve others, live a life of the mind.

Kuriloff studies, interviews, listens, thinks, questions herself. And by doing so she brings new understandings not only to the historical study of the Holocaust, not only to the clinical study of memory and trauma, and not only to the clinical study of survivor and bystander, analyst and layman, Jew and non-Jew, European and American, parent and child.

She also brings new understandings to the critical study of psychoanalytic theory, historical theory, theory itself. Kuriloff draws from Jewish tradition, postmodern and hermeneutic theory, and interpersonal and relational psychoanalysis to interpret old psychoanalytic theory in new ways — and then, to her credit, gently critiques her interpretive theories by historically situating them. This, in turn, leads to new questions that bring with them new possibilities. She accomplishes all this with careful scholarship and personal respect. She examines herself and others with a direct honesty that does not avoid difficult truths and, remarkably, does not slide away from the necessary — and alarming — ambiguities of her topic into the self-indulgent comfort of psychic splitting and the development of easy answers. She pursues her craft with a relentless integrity that allows her to live out her scholarly and psychoanalytic commitments in a way that is a model to all of us who aspire to write contextual relationally informed cultural history.

Perhaps the most riveting conclusion that leaps out of the pages of this thoughtful excursion through post-World War II psychoanalytic theory is how profound is the influence cast by the shadow of the Holocaust on the very theory of psychoanalysis, and especially on American psychoanalytic theory. By this, I do not point only to discussions about psychoanalytic theory on the nature of human aggression and conflict, the life and death instincts, or the origins of psychopathology. No, I mean something broader and more encompassing than any one of these issues. Kuriloff's book brings us face to face with a detailed awareness of how the Holocaust experiences of European Jewish psychoanalysts and their psychological defenses against those experiences had a profound influence on their clinical theories and practices.

This is important because throughout much of the 20th century, psychoanalysis, either explicitly or implicitly, treated theory as if it were the product of an ahistorical, pure body of scientific data, removed from the social realm and the personal struggles and limitations of its originators. There are, obviously, several historical/political reasons for this stance, as cultural historians have noted. For many contemporary analysts, especially those interpersonalists and relationalists influenced by the interpretive turn (see, e.g., Hiley, Bohman, & Shusterman, 1991), this is not a surprise. But when seen in the light of Kuriloff's detailed interviews and interpretations, the extent and depth of the ways Holocaust experiences directly shaped theory — especially the ways avoidance and dissociation altered foundational aspects of theory and dictated clinical practice and institutional rules — force the realization that the meaning and scientific privilege of putatively objective theory must be fundamentally reevaluated.

The presentation of analytic theory through a kind of asocial, intellectual history approach will seem infinitely more difficult — and rightly so — after Kuriloff. The hermeneutic argument that psychotherapy is a social artifact and in fact a type of moral discourse (see Cushman, 1995; Richardson, Fowers, & Guignon, 1999) will now become more understandable. This in no way is meant to imply that theory is unimportant or clinical work a hoax; it simply means that when it comes to matters of the heart, the reductionism of physical science methodology ("scientism") does not, cannot, fit. Things that matter, issues pertaining to what is meaningful in human life, what brings pain, what soothes, what ultimately brings strength and well-being will continue be the purview of psychotherapy. But the claims that practitioners make must be tempered by the growing awareness that our understandings are always historical products, and thus are necessarily uncertain and incomplete. If we can't live with that knowledge we will continue to make claims that are unsustainable over time and unintentionally but inevitably oppressive to others.

Where did the Jews go — and whither are they bound?

It is a testament to Kuriloff's evocative writing and the overall generativity of her topic that her book raises many important issues about the future of trauma studies, political theory, psychoanalysis and psychotherapy, the Jewish people, suffering, and oppressed populations everywhere. However, there is one topic in particular that her interviews bring to mind. Thinking back to those years in Europe before and during World War II, images of *streimal, pais,* and *babushka*-wearing Jews appear. The political promises of the Enlightenment, and the subsequent Haskalah movement in Western European Jewish communities, encouraged — and also coerced — Jews as culturally untethered individuals to join the exciting new scientific modern-era world of religious skepticism, political freedom, and egalitarianism. But even in those communities, for the most part, Jews still identified themselves as Jews and were still readily identified as such. For instance, Shakespeare was translated into Yiddish, the Hebrew Bible into English and German, and the Orthodox prayer service into German and English and subsequently radically redesigned by the Reform movement. Freud and some of his followers tended to think of the concept of the Jewish God as a superstitious self-deceitful fantasy, although many of them continued to identify as Jews and hold Jewish values. Some Jews, like Melanie Klein, tried to escape the fate of being Jewish altogether by baptizing their children and keeping their ethnicity a secret.

Thinking back to those pre-World War II days, one might well wonder where the Jews are today. Especially when thinking about how European Jewish communities were structured and organized, we could ask where are the multitude of religious teachers, folk healers, storytellers, and community leaders of today? Kuriloff's book quietly works its way toward this question. In an understated way she introduced the hermeneutic concept of the "cultural clearing" into her textual analysis. That concept imagines the social terrain to be like a room with no windows and only indirect lighting.

Given the particular shape of the outline of the cultural room, when the lights are on certain things, ideas, customs, roles, and identities come to light, and others are not visible. Given especially Kuriloff's probing interviews, we could ask how Jews come to light in our American Jewish communities today, and how the knowledge and lack of knowledge of the Holocaust affect our experiences of the present and our visions of the future. Yes, there are some Jews who do indeed continue to look and act like pre-World War II Jews, but those populations are few and far between, and for most of us impossible to join. For the most part, Jews are visually, linguistically, and increasingly ideologically indistinguishable from other Americans. And although no one much talks about this, most psychoanalysts, and especially relationalists, continue to be Jews — psychoanalysis remains "the Jewish Science," something about which Freud had many political and strategic qualms.

But perhaps this is not a problem, perhaps this is our way of trying to make sense of human consciousness and human frailty in this terribly complicated and difficult modern world. Perhaps psychoanalysis is one way of drawing together thousands of years of premodern-era, non-Western Judaic wisdom and hard-won contemporary scientific and political insights. Perhaps it is our way of giving to the world.

So how do Jews come to light in our world today? How do we understand ourselves as Jews, how do we appear to others, how do we live out our identity as Jews? Will Judaism survive and thrive, now that the threat of daily violence and destruction has abated, at least for the moment? It is a perplexing question, one many of us under the influence of a modern-era, Western cultural frame are uncomfortable thinking about, and of which some of us might well be resentful. Should one's Jewishness be a matter of public knowledge? Is it even a matter of personal knowledge? These are questions that only come to light in a modern-era clearing; 100 years ago, perhaps even 75 years ago, these questions would make no sense. But they do today.

How and where do Jews — especially the healers, scholars, teachers, and storytellers of previous centuries — come to light? In our highly secular, sophisticated, skeptical, cynical 21st-century social world, where do Jewish healing, learning, teaching, and storytelling take place? Where are the social sites in which these activities and relationships come to light? As I have written in previous articles (e.g., Cushman, 2007, 2015), I believe one of the sites in which Jewish intellectual and moral values —

usually unacknowledged — are being lived out is in the practices of relational psychoanalysis.

However, one inescapable impression gleaned from Kuriloff's interviews is that neither psychoanalysis nor Judaism will be able to survive unless a much more honest and knowledgeable encounter with the multidimensional legacy of the violent 20th century is developed. As we learn from Kuriloff's probing of psychoanalytic theory, American psychoanalytic theory — certainly many American Jewish analysts, and undoubtedly many American Jews — are still deeply disabled by and entrenched in the denial and avoidance of most things *Shoah*. In a way, American Jews, especially those of us born into the post-World War II Baby Boom cohort, are a bit like the "hidden children" of the Holocaust. We have been protected, hidden away from the hideousness of the last 1,000 years of violent anti-Semitism. There is much that we don't know, much that we don't want to know, but much that we must know, if we are to develop a future of some integrity and viability. We have been spared most of the violence and oppression of Christian Europe's anti-Semitism, but by being so protected we have been deprived of knowing a fuller truth about our people's history and the reality of our precarious position in Western society and the illegitimacy of Western superiority and U.S. exceptionalism. This in turn could lead to new creative meanings of our communal identity and the genuine solidarity we have with other oppressed people, all of which we might better understand, if we could break through our lack of knowledge of history and our avoidance of a critical political vision.

A true encounter with the legacy of the Third Reich could liberate therapeutic practice to delve deeply into the memories and meanings of historical and political happenings that remain unformulated — or at least clinically unexamined — in so many contemporary psychotherapy treatments. It would also free analytic theory to continue and deepen relational theory's focus on culture, history, gender, race, sexuality, and critical thought.

But would it really be helpful to dig up a past that Kuriloff has shown us we have spent the better part of 70 years avoiding? A past so horrific it might lead to depression, paralysis, ethnocentricity, even an embittered, paranoid mistrust of all others? That might be a fear many of us harbor secretly, perhaps unconsciously. Kuriloff's interviews demonstrate beyond question that the pain and terror of remembering and studying can lead not only to despair and suffering but also, ultimately, to a deeper, more meaningful, fuller embrace of life and cherishing of others.

I am reminded of a story Eli Wiesel once told. I was a young graduate rabbinic student in Los Angeles in the year 1968, and Wiesel — at that time a mostly unknown journalist and beginning novelist, was brought to town to speak. My teachers encouraged me to attend, and that night I witnessed one of the most memorable experiences of my life. One of many stories Wiesel told that night was a story about a grammatical convention in biblical Hebrew referred to as the *"vov* conversive" — and I have remembered it to this day. When a sentence contains two verbs in a row separated by the letter *vov*, and the two verbs are in different tenses, the second verb takes on the tense of the first verb. In biblical Hebrew, there are only two tenses, the perfect tense for an action that has been completed (what in English we might call the past tense), and the imperfect tense for an action that began in the past and is not yet completed (what in English we might call the future tense).

The *vov*, Wiesel went on, is a small but brave letter. It stands tall and straight, and its job is to unite words or phrases or thoughts: to connect, to bring together while honoring separateness. The *vov* conversive is a special letter, a magical letter, important especially for Jews after the Holocaust. As Jews, we must remember what happened, we must struggle with how to make meaning from it, we must not shrink from knowing, from facing the past, nor must we forget that we can exercise honesty and learning in order to build the future. And our commitment must always be to the future, to make meaning and exercise compassion not only for ourselves, but especially for those who come after us, for our people and for people everywhere.

So the *vov* conversive helps us see that the past is linked to the future through the brave little *vov*, the letter that says "and," not "but" — it links, it does not contradict. And the *vov* conversive shows us that by committing to the future, by using, for instance, the imperfect tense of the verb "to study" as the first verb, a *vov* conversive will help us change the second verb, something that looks like a completed event from the past (e.g., the verb "lived") "into an ongoing event in the future ("live" or "thrive"). The *vov* helps us draw from the past in order to serve, to enrich, to make a future for ourselves and our loved ones and for all people. The little *vov* shows us the way: the past may look like something inert and ended, but through human care and commitment, the past can be transformed into a living, meaningful, ongoing event that can enrich our relationships and heal our communities.

If today those of us who are therapists serve others and our communities in ways and for purposes that we really don't realize, if to some extent we are our era's teachers and storytellers and spiritual healers in a time that has precious little of such activities, then how do we do what our communities need us to do? This is indeed a perplexing question. But let us remember that as Jews we have over 2,000 years of guidance about such things: learned scholars have been studying and writing *midrash* (biblical commentary in the form of critical textual analysis and storytelling) since the beginning of the Common Era. As a people we have come to develop a deep, abiding appreciation for interpretation, intertextuality, relationality, the dialectic of absence and presence, and the indispensable importance of fighting fundamentalism and authoritarianism in all their guises (see Cushman, 2007, 2015). We can (and sometimes do now, more than we realize) draw from these traditions to teach, witness, and aid in healing. And let us notice, as Kuriloff demonstrates, that it is not only trauma that is transmitted intergenerationally. There is much that is contained in culture and mirrored in social practices that transmit caring, compassion, hope, tenacity. We learn how to listen and respect and reach out as well as to fear and suffer. Let us remember the *vov* conversive: committing ourselves to others transforms the past into help for the future. We may not always know how to help and how to shift Judaism into the 21st century, but change can happen — we are events, not things, and history, as Martin Luther King once said, "is an arc that bends toward justice."

The night after the Division 39 Spring Meeting this year, after returning home and sleeping in my bed for the first time in a week, I had a dream. I dreamt that the meeting was continuing, and I had signed up for what sounded like a wonderful workshop about how to recognize and utilize the similarities and complementarities between relational psychoanalysis and Jewish values and better serve the needs of contemporary American communities of all types. I woke up and, still in a dream-like state, feeling so hopeful, I realized that I was back home, and I'd better get moving if I was going to fly back to New York and attend that wonderful sounding workshop, something we all needed to learn about. And then, slowly, I realized there was no workshop like that. The convention was over, and I still didn't know what to do.

Somehow, I guess, some way, we need to let that workshop live in us, in our work and our lives. Somewhere it exists, I bet, in what Gerson (2009) called the "space between the scream and the silence" (p. 1342). "We would seem to need such a space," Kuriloff tells us. "Can the door to the psychoanalytic consulting room ... open to another sort of sanctified space that can capture, and transcend, the terrible historical moment that altered psychoanalysis forever?" (pp. 156–157). Perhaps, given the absence of my dream workshop, the *vov* can show us a way to find, or perhaps create anew, that sacred liminal space we so desperately need. It is located in the space between: between past and present, memory and forgetting, between one generation and another, one ethnic group and another, one therapist and one patient, and perhaps one therapist and another. It contains both despair and hope. It must come, as Donnel Stern (1990) has taught us, unbidden. But come it must.

Chapter 13

Relational psychoanalysis as political resistance

(2015 *Contemporary Psychoanalysis, 51*, 423–459)

Historical introduction

I am writing this historical introduction to "Relational Psychoanalysis as Political Resistance" in 2017, two years after the article was published. A lot has happened politically in those two years. The events of the 2016 presidential campaign and the first 100 days of the Trump administration have been even more maddening and frightening than most Progressives imagined, and in a way that demonstrates the salience of the type of resistance relational psychoanalysis helps develop and our country desperately needs.

It was gratifying to be able to write about relational ideas through a different lens, a spatial, hermeneutic lens, about an intellectual movement not usually identified with political activity. Yet once I could put my thoughts into those words, new possibilities opened up. I could then get a sense of how moral influence could be exercised without conscious, overt political action, how one's place in the social terrain could be interpreted in new ways that defy old labels and former disavowals. What if, despite mainstream psychotherapy's long-standing denial of political impact, a certain process is indeed at work that can be broadly conceived of as political. How then do we understand ourselves and the practices to which we have dedicated our professional lives?

The analysts who have contributed to the relational movement are some of the best minds of our time and I respect and admire them greatly. My work and especially my life have been enriched by their contributions many times over, and I feel much gratitude for them. They have quietly and without fanfare given something precious to us all, and I hope their ideas will grow, and their spirit continue to make a difference in our personal and our political lives.

Social theory — especially feminist, critical, postmodern, and hermeneutic theories — have had a noticeable influence on American psychotherapy. This is true especially in psychoanalysis, where some philosophical and sociological concepts have been integrated into what is now called relational psychoanalysis. Relational theory appeals to therapists of many stripes, not only because of its intellectual force but also because, like any popular theory, it fits well with the overall spirit of the times. We live in a social world characterized by preoccupations with — and the valorization of — communication, social interaction, and interpersonal relationship: preoccupations linked ironically to their vicissitudes and absences. It is not a coincidence that these activities are at the center of contemporary relational psychoanalytic theory and practice.

In this article, I argue that relational psychoanalysis is not only a psychological healing practice; it is also a social phenomenon, a site in the social terrain in which — strange though it may seem — an implicit (and perhaps unintentional) political resistance shows up. I draw heavily on the intellectual movement called the interpretative turn (e.g., Hiley, Bohman, & Shusterman, 1991) to examine such an unusual idea. The interpretative turn is constituted by two traditions: postmodern theories and hermeneutics. Whereas various postmodernisms such as deconstructionism and poststructuralism are focused on identifying and exposing the covert exercise of power in texts, hermeneuticists are focused on the significance of historical traditions and the moral understandings that they believe frame all aspects of a culture, including the exercise of power (Orange, 2010; Richardson, Fowers, & Guignon, 1999). From an interpretive perspective (e.g., Derrida, 1974; Foucault, 1975/1977; Gadamer, 1989; Heidegger, 1977), healing practices such as psychotherapy inevitably have political effects, and these effects usually reinforce the political status quo (Cushman, 1995; Mednick, 1989; Portuges, 2009; Samuels, 2001). What is unusual about relational psychoanalysis is that some of its practices function not to support, but to resist, the moral and political structures of its time and place.

By referring to the shape of political resistance I mean two things: First, there is a subtle way in which relational psychoanalysis could be interpreted as preparation, or, in its better moments a school, for resistance. This is because its practices can enable a way of being that is honest, self-reflective, critical, humble, curious, compassionate, and respectful of and willing to learn from difference. It is true that these personal qualities can be produced by the practices of different therapeutic schools, but the commitments relationalists make to honest interpersonal engagement and the clinical practices that bring it about (see e.g., Aron, 1991; Ehrenberg, 1974; Levenson, 1991b; Maroda, 1999; Stern, 2010) seem intended specifically to develop these traits. Further, they are usually justified not because they are in line with an inflexible theory or have been putatively "proven" to be the one effective practice for a specific therapeutic moment, but because they are thought by relationalists to be a good way to live. "Implicit theory," Stern (2012) explained, "is the expression of value positions that we often have not reflected on. It is our positions about what is good in life ... that underlie our theories of technique" (p. 33). The relationalists' commitments to what philosophers call the good (even though often implicit) oppose the dominant way of being of our time and could lead to direct political activity. Whether or in what ways activism would result, however, is an open question.[1]

But there is also a second meaning of resistance at play here. Hermeneuticists suggest that each social terrain is like a room that is lit only by indirect lighting. The shape of the room is determined by the particular language, customs, beliefs, moral understandings, means of production, institutions, science, art, and laws — the overall cultural effects of a society. Due to the particular contour of a terrain, various things, people, and activities are illuminated and will show up in certain ways. For instance, in every social terrain there will be sites in which politics of a certain type will be available, and within this space, various acts, allegiances, and commitments that fit with that culture will be able to be lived out. The presence of political alternatives, on the other hand, are often harder to detect, and their activities and influence more difficult to recognize. This is particularly true in the first decades of the 21st century, where the profusion of consumer items, such as smart phones and designer shoes, tend to obscure from view the moral confusion and economic suffering that are also significant features of the terrain. With such elusive and seemingly unconnected social effects, it is difficult to see the links between glitz and suffering, know what to fight against, and how to do so. Thus, political resistance sometimes appears in surprising shapes and locations.

The last 400 years of Western society have been marked by an undermining of the public commons (i.e., both the specific social sites in which meanings are debated and negotiated and a more general sense of the collective — the public realm). This has been accomplished by an ongoing weakening of the historical traditions and communal values that support the commons and keep it vital (see, e.g., Bellah, Madsen, Sullivan, & Swidler, 1985; Habermas, 1991; Sennett, 1988; Taylor, 1989). In the last 35 years, conservative and neoliberal rule in the United States has imposed a regime of privatization and commercialization that has further shrunk the commons. As a result, in our current social world, opportunities for effective political activism from the Left have narrowed (e.g., Bauman, 1999; Gitlin, 1995). It is fortunate that progressive motivations and commitments have not been destroyed (e.g., Botticelli, 2004), although explicit opportunities to live them out are increasingly limited. Thus, the possibility of carrying out some sort of politically meaningful Left-oriented activity is often available through roles and identities that sometimes appear benign or apolitical, even to those who live them out. I mean to suggest that relational psychoanalysis is one of those spaces in which resistance can quietly, subtly, even unintentionally, show up.

In order to examine relational psychoanalysis' political effects, I utilize the hermeneutic concept of the self (i.e., embodied cultural understandings about the correct ways to be human). I first identify the emergence of a recent and problematic way of being that has become increasingly prominent in the United States: a flattened, multiple self (Cushman & Gilford, 1999,2000; Jacobson, 1997; Orange, 2009). This is a way of being that has diverged sharply from the emphasis on interiority and the valorization of "authenticity" of the modern era. Thus it emerges as a self that is thin or superficial and valorizes flexibility and shape shifting. This new self is preoccupied with consuming for the sake of creating and presenting identities in order to fend off danger or attract others. Although an interest in multiplicity is shared by both the flattened, multiple self and psychoanalytic theory about multiple self states (e.g., Bromberg, 1993, 1996, 1998; Davies, 1998; Davies & Frawley, 1994) they are two different phenomena (see endnote 2 and the "Is Multiplicity Reflection or Resistance?" section).

I especially want to examine the flattened, multiple self's connection to two of the more serious — and entangled — political problems of our time. They are (1) the neoliberal proceduralization of American society (Binkley, 2011; Layton, 2010; Rose, 2007), leading especially to the overreliance of procedural concepts such as competencies in education and health care (Botticelli, 2006; Hoffman, 2009) — what is referred to as the industrialization of those fields; and (2) a significant increase in either a political indifference or a rigid political fundamentalism among the general population. Finally, I indicate how relational psychoanalysis is a site that sometimes opposes a neoliberal way of being, the political arrangements that it serves, and the psychological attitudes that enable it.

I do not mean to suggest that relationality, as a thing in and of itself, is an unproblematic natural force for good. A concept like relationality is a cultural artifact — as such, its moral and political meanings are contingent on how they function in a particular society. For that reason, relational theory and practice cannot be exempt from ideology and culture critique. Their worth can only be understood through interpretation that situates theory and practice within their sociohistorical context. A predominant way of being in any one historical era, and the social practices that fit with it, usually have both good and bad aspects. What matters is how successfully their good qualities can be used to attenuate their more destructive tendencies.

For instance, the concept of relationality — i.e., the attention to and valorization of the many forms, activities, and meanings of relational life — does not only show up in psychotherapy (see e.g., Gergen, 2009; Sampson, 1993). At the present time, a focus on relationship is pervasive in American popular culture; for instance, relationships are considered the bedrock of family life, and are used to sell consumer products, influence political opinion, and recruit for military organizations. A television commercial depicted computer competition as an ongoing conversation between two people, one named "Mac" and the other "PC"; commercials for medications almost always feature people interacting with friends or loved ones; politically oriented right-wing radio talk shows consciously create a personal connection with the host that includes nicknames, in-group jargon, and the cultivation of group identity; in recruitment commercials, the Army is often referred to as "a band of brothers." Relationality, in other words, can be used for diverse, even incompatible, purposes.

Due to the conservative political traditions from which this flattened, multiple self and its political arrangements emerge, it stands to reason that the forces that oppose them will come from the political Left. But let us remember that potential political resistance exists within a larger cultural terrain that includes both problems and their alternatives. If political resistance cannot speak the language of its time and place, it cannot be persuasive. So it should not be surprising that problematic aspects of the era (e.g., the flattened, multiple self) and social practices that sometimes oppose these aspects (e.g., relational psychoanalysis) also have things in common.[2]

A brief historical overview

As many historians have noted (e.g., Lears, 1983; Susman, 1984), by the last decade of the 19th century American ideas about the essential qualities of the self began to focus on impressing and attracting others rather than on deeply felt Victorian commitments to living out a traditional moral code. Several aspects of Western, and especially American, history have reflected and contributed to that shift. Over the course of the 20th century, the economy moved from a focus on production to one of consumption and from an emphasis on physical labor to one of salesmanship; important personality characteristics shifted from Victorian "character" to Roaring Twenties "personality" and more recently to communicative (i.e., relational) expertise; psychopathology turned from hysteria and neurasthenia to what are sometimes called disorders of the self, that is, to psychological processes identified with narcissism and more recently dissociation (Guralnik & Simeon, 2010); and psychotherapy practices moved from an authoritarian style about intrapsychic events to a collaborative style about interpersonal or intersubjective events. All of these more recent phenomena are featured in current relational theory.

Above all, relational psychoanalysis is a combination of some of the most important intellectual movements of our time: it includes aspects of the interpretative turn, feminism, critical theory, and anti-racism in political theory, and interpersonal, object relations, and self psychology in psychoanalytic theory (Seligman, 2005). But relational psychoanalysis is not simply an isolated intellectual or scientific theory. It is also a cultural product, and as such, it inevitably and powerfully reflects and affects moral understandings and exerts subtle political influence.

Of course, it is not by chance that, even in psychoanalysis, some sort of left-oriented political potential would show up during the late 20th century. First, soon after mid-century, interpersonal analysts carried on the social vision of Sullivan, Horney, and Fromm, and then young analysts from the post-World War II Baby Boom cohort carried on the idealistic, rebellious, liberationist, socially oriented spirit of the 1960s in their work, even though in the form of a technical healing practice. Some of these early relationalists were left-leaning civil rights and peace activists in their younger days. They turned to psychotherapy for various personal, political, and financial reasons in the last quarter of the 20th century, when the war in Vietnam ended, the Left began to unravel, and intellectual jobs, especially with a social change component, became increasingly scarce.

As their psychoanalytic careers developed, the Baby Boom analysts quietly, but determinedly, questioned authority and lived out new and creative practices. With a style that fit with their times, they were optimistic, integrative, colorful, sometimes brilliant. They coined a new term — "relational" — for the embrace of the newer, nonorthodox, post-ego psychology theories that appealed to them, synthesized them under a new philosophical framework,[3] and challenged the old guard. It is not surprising that their new practices featured a less formal, less depriving, more expressive, egalitarian, emotional, mutual, cooperative exchange between analyst and patient. These qualities — although obviously reflections of contemporary popular and intellectual culture — were contained in theoretical moves carefully buttressed by textual support from earlier psychoanalytic literature (Seligman, 2003). Thus, this young cohort fought for a place within the psychoanalytic establishment.

Today, in response to increasingly powerful neoliberal corporate forces insisting on medicalizing therapeutic practices, quantifying outcomes, and controlling labor — what is referred to as the industrialization of health care — many schools of psychotherapy have capitulated by relying increasingly on a medical model of care. This model is highly technicist and behavioral, using cognitivist language and a physical science methodology that ignores social context and interactive process; it privileges quantified outcomes research that produces what is called "evidence-based practices." All of this has led to an authoritarian management of the labor force (i.e., therapists) by means of a hierarchical administrative structure featuring a rigid bureaucratic proceduralism. Unlike most schools of psychotherapy, psychoanalysis has been less willing to comply with those pressures. However, recently the neoliberal ethic has made inroads even there (Botticelli, 2006; Walls, 2007, 2012).

Pockets of resistance in psychoanalysis do remain, and in my opinion, the most explicit and philosophically sound is currently being produced by the relationalists. Some (e.g., Cushman, 2013b; Hoffman, 2009; Stern, 2013; Tolleson, 2009; Walls, 2012; Warren, 2010) have publicly argued against the technicism and instrumentalism that frame the industrialization of psychotherapy. These writers have intentionally drawn from the interpretative turn, especially feminist postmodernism and philosophical hermeneutics, to make the case for valorizing a nonmanualized, nonscientistic, more interpretive, collaborative, emergent practice of psychotherapy.

This resistance opposes a way of being that is increasingly dominant in our time. It is sad that in the United States as a whole, opposition to the hegemony of neoliberalism, of which the industrialization of psychotherapy is but one manifestation, is difficult to locate today. This is partly true because any resistance against such a subtle nuanced political phenomenon must necessarily be equally subtle and nuanced. And U.S. society, currently, is not exactly known for those qualities.

By making the observation that relational psychoanalysis is a site of resistance, I am not claiming that it is the best, most effective, or strongest form of resistance the Left could develop — not at all. I am simply interpreting its ideas and practices as expressing and living out certain moral understandings about the potential limitations, worthy possibilities, and proper comportment of humans that oppose the emerging technicist, instrumentalist tendencies of the flattened self and the political arrangements, procedures, and institutions it serves.

This political claim would undoubtedly make most analysts, even many relational analysts, extremely uncomfortable. I do not mean that relational psychoanalysis is a conscious, strategic, calculated effort to deceive or subvert. But I do think relational psychoanalysis functions in ways that have social effects, effects that reach into the realm of moral and political meaning, far beyond the limitations that U.S. society popularly ascribes to healing practices.

In fact, Botticelli (2004) argued that important characteristics of relational practices — such as egalitarianism, feminism, antiracism, and the questioning of authority — that might ordinarily lead to more explicit political expression are curiously limited to events and relationships within the analytic hour. He believed that they represent an attempt to live out a circumscribed political vision in a world closed off from other more explicit political activity, a "replacement" for a more direct and explicit politics.

The commitments that animate this article arise not from a disagreement with Botticelli but rather with a sharing of his concerns and an interpretation of the puzzle from a slightly different perspective. Perhaps we need not only a "rediscovery" of the political, but an understanding of the political as it does show up in our world. That could lead to a sense of what lasting political change requires: the capacity for recognition of and respect and care for the other, and the realization that psychological relatedness in that spirit must necessarily lead to concrete political action.

What kinds of resistance?

Resistance appears to be coming to light in relational psychoanalysis in three ways. First, relational theory and practice are founded on, and have been elaborating, a philosophical foundation that directly challenges a modern-era Cartesianism (e.g., Fairfield, Layton, & Stack, 2002; Frie, 1997, 2011; Levenson, 1972, 1983; Mitchell, 1988; Stern, 1991, 2012; Stolorow, Atwood, & Orange, 2002). This is an important development, because much of what is destructive about current political arrangements (e.g., Bauman, 1999, 2006; Sennett, 1988) initially rested on the Cartesian split between matter and spirit, mind and body, and the further political splits that followed (see e.g., Bernstein, 1983; Bordo, 1987; Flax, 1992; Stolorow et al., 2002).

Second, the consequences of relational psychoanalysis' non-Cartesian foundation are beginning to bear more explicit forms of progressive political fruit in therapeutic theory (e.g., Layton, Hollander, & Gutwill, 2006). There are subtle signs that the connections among philosophical theory, clinical practice, and progressive political activity are becoming more visible. For instance, one can see the effects of postmodern thought and Gadamer's philosophical hermeneutics in Irwin Hoffman's 2009 article "Doublethinking Our Way to Scientific Legitimacy," an article that forcefully opposes the industrialization of psychotherapy. One can also see the influence of the interpretative turn in the defense of Hoffman found in articles by Cushman (2013a), Stern (2013), Walls (2012), and Warren (2010). The explicit use of Gadamer in contemporary relational theory was first initiated by Stern in his groundbreaking work in 1989, 1990, and 1991. In a recent article, Stern (2012) applied Gadamer's philosophy by discussing the implicit moral understandings that frame current psychotherapy theories. By doing so, he demonstrated his long-held awareness that therapy is a moral discourse — not a technical, procedural practice, but a moral practice with political consequences.

Also, a cultural history approach to psychoanalysis, used by Harry Stack Sullivan (e.g., 1964) and Erich Fromm (e.g., 1955), has been drawn upon by clinicians such as Neil Altman (2005), Rachel Peltz (2005), Susie Orbach (2008), Lynne Layton (e.g., 2009, 2010), Orna Guralnik and Daphne Simeon (2010), Steven Botticelli (2012), and Roger Frie (2014). It is just such a cultural history approach, I argued in 1994, that if properly developed can lead to a more explicit, philosophically sound, self-aware political consciousness (Cushman, 1994). In fact, the earlier philosophical foundation has made possible the relational leap from a one-person to a two-person psychology (Levenson, 1991a), and still more so from a two-person to a more explicit cultural and political (i.e., three-person) psychology (Altman, 1995a; Benjamin, 2009; Cushman, 1995).

Third, the last two decades have witnessed relationalists engaged in more explicit ventures in political analysis and activity. For instance, feminists, multiculturalists, queer theorists, hermeneuticists, and post-modernists such as Altman (1995a, 2000, 2006), Aronson (2007), Botticelli (2004, 2006, 2012), Cheuvront (2010, 2013), Cushman (2000, 2002, 2014), Dimen (1991, 2011), Goldner (1991), Gump (2000, 2010), Guralnik (2011), Haaken (1998), Harris (1991, 2000a), Harris and Botticelli (2010), Hartman (2005), Hollander (1997), Layton (1998, 2008, 2009, 2010, 2014), Leary (1995, 2000, 2007, 2012), Orbach (2006, 2008), and Scholom (2013) are addressing issues related to gender, militarism, class, race, ethnicity, and sexual orientation; Levenasian therapists such as Goodman (in press), Goodman and Freeman (2015), Huett and Goodman (2012), and Rozmarin (2007, 2011) have critiqued the consequences of war, scientism, and managed care in the treatment of the poor and dispossessed; Gerber (1990) has described attending to explicit political issues in clinical work; and Division 39 political activists (e.g., Altman, Hollander, Reisner, Soldz) continue to play a role in the fight to oppose the role of psychologists in the Bush — and now Obama — administrations' torture practices.[4]

I know it seems questionable to suggest that the practices of Western-style psychotherapy could be involved in political resistance, given that therapy is often criticized as the purveyor of a decontextualized individualism that encourages a noncommunal, if not narcissistic and certainly politically disengaged, way of being. In fact, viewed from the perspective of some forms of social theory (Foucault, 1975/1977; Kovel, 1980; Rose, 2007), psychotherapy has often been the instrument of a compliant, regressive, conservative politics.

However, by suggesting other possibilities, I do not mean to imply that relational psychoanalysis is the only current site of political resistance. In fact, I believe that political criticisms of relational practice — for instance, that it does not adequately attend to the world outside the consulting room, treat an economically diverse population, and make the leap from the interpersonal to the explicitly political — are, generally speaking, well-founded. But I have come to believe that it is indeed functioning as a quiet, somewhat unintended site of Left-oriented resistance and, in fact, potentially an important site, if therapists could better understand their place in the history of Western society as it relates to this particular political moment. It would take unusually perceptive and skilled therapists to understand and live out the kind of relational practice in the detailed political terms that embrace and extend generalized political resistance into a more overt activism without violating their therapeutic commitments. But I believe that extension is possible, in fact plausible, if therapists could draw more robustly and intentionally from the interpretative turn.

Our historical moment: consumerism, electronics, and technicism

There are many disturbing events and institutions in our current social world that warrant immediate attention; they call out to us as citizens to oppose certain policies, redesign specific political structures, institute new processes and do away with others. In this article I only discuss one, which is intimately related to issues that touch on psychoanalysis in the United States.

Consumerism continues unabated and in fact has deepened in the last 30 years due in part to the now overwhelming presence of computers, electronic gadgets, communications systems, social media, and the software that controls them. This has had a negative effect on the political awareness and activism of the population as a whole and the youth in particular (e.g., Carr, 2010; Lanier, 2010). These devices and platforms have brought about important transformations in everyday life through their computational speed, research capacity, and communicative possibilities, but they have multiplied the burdens of middle-class employment by providing recent reductions of the workforce and worker benefits with a putatively rational justification. This technological explosion has also caused a kind of social isolation among the young by retarding social-skill development, delegitimizing the humanities in the schools, and negatively affecting brain development (Carr, 2010).

This electronic revolution, in concert with the powerful entertainment and sports industries, has produced and reflected the growing technicism and instrumentalism[5] of American society. When combined with an omnipresent American racism, homophobia, and misogyny, and an increasing neoliberal competitiveness that is the product of the economic and emotional insecurity characteristic of late capitalist societies, instrumentalism has exacerbated American militarism to a frightening degree. And the continuing wounds to a putatively American exceptionalism produced by the war in Vietnam, the attacks of 9/11, and ongoing failures of colonial adventures in the Middle East serve only to escalate these protofascist tendencies. The immense popularity of U.S.-style football and electronic war games reflect this worrisome dynamic.

Escape from the real world of face-to-face relationships has become ever more possible and seductive with each passing year. The purchase and consumption of goods and the search for evermore stimulating, outrageous, and crass entertainment has overtaken much of American life and especially much of how Americans think of and understand themselves. Bill Moyers and Michael Winship (2013) have written that self-deceit and intellectual laziness are destroying the ability to participate meaningfully in a democratic society. "Ideology and self-interest trump the facts or even caring about the facts.... The ground is all too fertile for those who will only believe whatever best fits their resentment or particular brand of paranoia. ... [The greatest danger] is ... 'the self-deception that believes the lie.'"

Along with the increasing violence, anti-intellectualism, and militarism in popular culture, and the continuing erosion of historical traditions and community involvement, has come an increased suspicion and fear of others. Judging from the introduction of various rigid and self-righteous ethical codes in business and education, it appears that there is a growing consensus that the only protection against the aggression, greed, and violence of others is the installation of detailed, step-wise procedural practices such as the installation of an overwhelming number of

Relational psychoanalysis as political resistance 187

HIPAA regulations in health-care settings. Procedures are commonly thought of as the only means of controlling the otherwise unpredictable and dangerous other.

Above all, there is little organized disagreement with, let alone rebellion against, this state of affairs. The vast majority of citizens go about their lives either struggling to survive and gain a small amount of security for themselves and their families, or so immersed in the electronic consumer and entertainment culture that they do not seem to care about much beyond their next purchase, incoming tweet, or participation in a multiple online role-playing game such as *Second Life, Farmville, Siege Online, Stormfall: Age of War*, or *Criminal Syndicate*. In these games, participants electronically join a team of other users and invent, design, name, and direct an avatar. Games continue on indefinitely even though individual participants sign off. Virtual money is earned and spent, virtual crops are grown, sold, and consumed, and battles are waged. In the process, avatars can even contract PTSD and attend virtual trauma therapy sessions, which must be completed before returning to battle.

Until we can intelligently and self-reflectively think, study, and cooperate with others in order to organize against the forces that have created our current political arrangements, it is difficult to imagine how any effective resistance will be able to succeed. The absence of the ability to effectively engage in those activities, alongside the great political necessity of doing so, is of course not a random coincidence. Research such as that conducted by Carr (2010), Turkle (2011), and Watkins (2009) indicates that the effectiveness of the strategy that the Roman poet Juvenal (1918) long ago (late first century, CE) called "bread and circuses" is today exacerbated many fold by advances in electronic computational and communications technology. All eyes are on the screen. The intellectual, political, and interpersonal characteristics of the flattened, multiple self will need to be shifted if we as a people can become capable of making the important changes that are needed. The current practices of relational psychoanalysis seem to be one of the practices that could be well suited to shifting the limitations of that self.

From emptiness to multiplicity

It seems imperative that we explore the puzzling way Americans are manifesting the kind of political paralysis, disinterest, and self-deceit described above. But instead of interpreting it through the Marxist concept of false consciousness, let us learn about it hermeneutically by studying the way of being that brings it about in order to interpret the social context that brings it to light. In 1999 and 2000, Peter Gilford and I suggested that the United States is witnessing a shift in the early 21st-century way of being, from the last 100 years of an increasingly empty self (see e.g., Cushman, 1990, 1995) to a newly emerging multiple self.

The empty self experienced a deep interior emptiness that needed to be filled up through the taking in of consumer items, charismatic leaders, or therapists. But recently there has been a shift, graphically reflected in popular culture, from an empty self to a shallower, flatter self, suffering less from being empty of meaning and initiative than anxious about the dangers of social interaction and searching, always, for opportunities to be entertained. It is a self populated with a multitude of identities developed over time by avoiding and controlling aversive social interactions and purchasing various consumer products that contribute to that avoidance. These multiple identities cluster around the outside of the person, waiting to be called to center stage, depending on the social needs of the moment.

A 1998 television commercial opened with a young man racing an expensive sports car through the deep curves of a rural coastal road. He was dressed in an unkempt, grungy manner, played hard rock music on the radio, and wore an insolent, somewhat arrogant look on his face. A sour-faced, middle-aged motorcycle cop was hiding behind a billboard. He became instantly furious at the young man, turned on his siren, and took out after him.

The driver spied the cop in his rear view mirror and smiled knowingly. Before the cop could catch up and pull him over, the kid quickly pulled on a tweedy conservative sport coat, scholarly glasses, switched to a classical music station, and took out a portable electric razor and shaved. By the time the cop appeared at the driver's side window, the young man's appearance had radically changed. The cop looked astonished, completely taken by surprise, confused and disoriented. He stumbled away, muttering to himself, unable to follow through with an arrest or any kind of punishment.

The young guy watched in the rear-view mirror as the cop weaved back to his motorcycle. A small, quiet, self-satisfied smile played on his lips. He had used various consumer products to change his appearance, and by doing so he presented to the world a different identity. This new identity allowed him to escape a dangerous unreasoning authority — something he could not have accomplished otherwise. It was a shift in his outward appearance that saved him, a new identity, not an inward transformation of his private true self.

I believe this shift from an empty to a flattened multiple self has become more entrenched in the last 15 years. I discussed the relationship between electronic living such as online computer use and participation in multiple online role-playing games, on the one hand, and the ongoing undermining of historical traditions, communal experiences, and the public commons on the other (Cushman, 2011a). The flattened, multiple self is also reflected in the fascination with psychological theory that describes human thinking as the product of information processing equipment (not thoughtful self-reflection), pop culture that depicts superheroes as cyborgs, and television commercials that portray humans as poorly functioning computers that need an infusion of electronic or metal components in order to succeed.

Noticing these changes in cultural images that prescribe ways of being human can help us understand why there is little resistance against the beliefs that brains are organic computers; that sociobiology and neuroscience hold the keys to understanding (and by extension normalizing) human behavior; and that the secret to creating a safe, law-abiding society is to develop and enforce the correct set of procedural rules. Computers do not possess deep interiors with the capacity for thoughtfulness and creativity. They work because they follow simple orders, encoded in their software — they are procedural all the way down. Our social world is increasingly characterizing humans in the same way.

Think about all the digitized procedural forms one must fill out or procedural rules with which one must comply during an average day. From medical forms to insurance forms to tax forms to the procedural menu provided by an outgoing recorded phone message, an increasing amount of our daily lives is given over to the restricted choices of procedural living. In higher education, the concept of academic competencies (defined by hyperconcrete behavioral results) determines what teachers teach and students learn. In psychotherapy, therapists are being pressured to follow manualized treatments and encouraged to administer post-session consumer satisfaction surveys to patients in order to ascertain how well the therapist is complying with what quantitative research has determined to be proper therapeutic procedures. It seems humans are becoming thought of as poorly functioning electronic machines that simply need to become more robot-like, i.e., better at following the orders of manuals, procedures, and decision trees.

A young man is in a business meeting, populated by several well-dressed people, all sitting around a large conference table. He takes out his new smart phone called, it is important to note, a "Droid," which technically is a human-like mechanical robot (e.g., R2D2 from the *Star Wars* movies). He begins to search for information or calculate some problem or key-in some data. The calculation gets increasingly detailed, and his fingers move at an ever-faster rate, almost as if the phone itself has taken over his actions. And then, as his fingers work faster still, they begin turning into a robot's fingers, and his hands and then his wrists and arms all turn into metal parts of a machine. The voice-over states that the Droid, in order to hook "you up to everything you need to do," will turn "you into an instrument of efficiency." The man's fingers are now almost a blur, racing at superhuman speed. His Droid has turned him into an android.

This commercial illustrates a self that is machine-like and controlled through obedience to various official behavioral procedures that demand strict compliance. But of course Americans, who pride themselves on being highly individualistic and autonomous, would never tolerate being described as robots. So the description is disguised with pseudo-scientific technical terms and the inflated claims of a physical-science method applied to human problems (i.e., scientism). This disguise is made especially effective by the ethic of consumerism, enacted today through a multitude of social practices that help us live out the embodied understanding that persons are consumers. Consumers live in a social terrain that resembles a giant supermarket: everything is available to them as long as they have the money (or the credit). Autonomy and intelligence are important to consumers primarily because they need to make micro-decisions about what to buy, supposedly unencumbered by moral or political constraints and the opinions of others. Autonomy is valuable primarily because it allows for unencumbered purchasing, intelligence because it enables the correct choice of competing consumer items. When efficiency becomes the most prominent element of success, and success the most prominent producer of purchasing power, we don't notice that humans are thought of as robotic, because efficient performance facilitates consumption.

In the world of the supermarket, consumer items are thought to be important to the degree that they match the momentary wishes of the consumer. Items such as clothing, breakfast cereals, computer accessories, home furnishings, and automotive accessories are available in any number of combinations — what matters is that they are sufficiently compatible so that they can be mixed and matched at the consumer's whim. Things increasingly come to light in this world as discrete, simple, individual components readily available to be combined and used.

In the realm of psychotherapy, this way of being comes to light in the more recent *DSM*s through Axis I diagnostic categories, in which persons are thought to be composed of simple hyperconcrete behaviors that can be mixed and matched according to specific symptom descriptions — a kind of Lego-like picture of human being. This view is reflected in various advertising and marketing practices, such as the recent television commercial for a computer notepad called The Surface. It is a sunny day, and there are many good-looking young people of many shapes, genders, and colors in the picture, but they do not seem to be interacting. One young man takes out his notepad, turns it around, and attaches a flat keypad to it with a loud, satisfying "click." Others immediately notice, and one by one they begin clicking their notepads in unison, and then in time to a rhythm, then in time to a loud upbeat song. They sing and dance, handing off their notepads, exchanging keypads and screens of different colors, and the clicking is intoxicating. The notepads and keypads fly from one person to another, exciting, engaging, uniting everyone in a joyous dance. The equipment seems to have a life of its own, flying and spinning through the air in time to the music, unifying and inspiring everyone.

The commercial is like a dance celebrating interchangeability, compatibility, and plasticity — all different colors and shapes and functions cooperating and enjoying one another's easily accessible (i.e., "surface") parts. Consumer items — and by implication, humans — are therefore thought to be composed of simple components that can be cobbled together in various shapes and designs, limited only by the desires of the individual consumer, the effectiveness of the latest technology, or in psychology the putative accuracy of the most recent assessment tool. The revolutionary change that *DSM-III* (American Psychiatric Association, 1980) introduced was the shift from large complex configurations of personality to the conceptual simples of the behavioristic Axis I. Gone is the concept of the *DSM-II* (American Psychiatric Association, 1968) neurosis, for instance, and in its place are various combinations of behavioral signs of anxiety and depression.

If consumer desire is too extreme or unrealistic for everyday fantasies, which more and more appears to be the case, there is a consumer solution for that as well. Electronic games can transport us to a world in which one's avatars are famous, possess superhuman qualities, or live a life free from the restrictions of ordinary laws or rules. This relation with alternative selves is graphically portrayed in the film *Avatar*. Jake Sully's life as a career soldier at the beginning of the movie was crass, superficial, cruel. He had been marked, in fact disabled, by it: he could no longer walk. But then, through futuristic science, his avatar was transported to a radically different physical and social world, one that was beautiful, spiritual, proud, authentic. He comes to be influenced by these new values and tries to convince those in control of his old world that the destructive and cruel path they were on was wrong, but to no avail. By the end of the film (no surprise here), he chooses to remain permanently in his avatar and live forever after in this new world. It is a kind of sci-fi version of the previously described television commercial about the young man, the sports car, and the old, sour-faced motorcycle cop. Escape, by shifting into a new identity, was the only option.[6]

We might say that this film portrays a new kind of a healing technology: a virtual, behavioral therapeutic for a flattened, multiple, self. Purchase the proper product, such as an expensive pair of basketball shoes, an ultra-stylish purse, a luxury car, an exciting video game or DVD, and you will be delivered into a new world — and a reconfigured self — that previously you could only imagine. Multiplicity, and the morphing it enables, saves the day.

A relational alternative

Many political observers have commented on the increase in working- and middle-class Americans who oscillate between political disinterest or right-wing fundamentalist politics. This is a trend developed successfully in Richard Nixon's 1968 presidential campaign, his so-called "Southern Strategy" that attracted Southern Democrats to the Republican Party. It was carried further by Ronald Reagan's highly successful pursuit of blue-collar Democratic voters, dubbed "Reagan Democrats," in the presidential campaign of 1980 (see, e.g., Berman, 2012). This trend is currently reflected in the political climate's discernible shift to the right.

Rather than interpreting this phenomenon by using the idea that the working- and middle-classes are victims of a false consciousness, I prefer a hermeneutic approach. This perspective suggests that, in fact, their consciousness is true to the way of being of their time and place. We live out a flattened multiple self. We are constituted as consumers, and in fact, a particular kind of consumer — one who focuses on purchasing and consuming items or experiences in order to (1) avoid or escape potentially dangerous interpersonal situations through shape-shifting; (2) impress others and become a minor celebrity on social media; and (3) be entertained. Americans are isolated individualists who usually don't organize against bad communal or national policies because they don't really see them or consider them important. All too often, those who do organize do so on behalf of anti-intellectual hate-mongering leaders who offer one-dimensional solutions to complex moral and political dilemmas. The need and motivation for political resistance rarely or episodically come to light or sometimes come to light in racist and misogynist shapes because of the way the self is currently configured. By living out a flattened, multiple self, Americans are busily preoccupied with visions of the good, different from those valued by postmodern or Left-leaning academics — visions best thought of as different, perhaps wrong, but not false.

Thus, from a hermeneutic perspective, any political resistance movement from the Left would have to develop ideas about how to help shift that configuration of the self and the understandings of the good that it serves. Viewed from this perspective, relational psychoanalysis seems to be engaged in just such a process, although implicitly, not exactly consciously, and for the most part through individual, not societal, change. This is a tall order indeed, and one limited by an important flaw: At some point, psychological change must lead to political activity if it is to effect political change (see e.g., Botticelli, 2004; Tolleson, 2009).

Still, relational efforts inspire hope and do imply, as Botticelli (2004) suggested, expanded political meanings. Relational theory began emerging explicitly in the early 1980s. In 1983, Jay Greenberg and Stephen Mitchell (see also Mitchell, 1988) began a remarkable synthesis of interpersonal, object relations, self psychology, and attachment theory, drawing heavily on the interpersonal tradition of Sullivan, Fromm, Levenson, Ghent, Racker, and Ehrenberg, among others, and called it "relational psychoanalysis." Mitchell argued that a new therapeutic paradigm was emerging, one that was exquisitely attuned to the powerful omnipresent reality and meaningfulness of relationship. Infants grew, friendships arose, psychopathology developed, lovers loved, therapists treated, all in the context of relationship. By riding the cultural trends of the day, Mitchell called classical and ego psychoanalysis into question because of their reliance on a Cartesian framework, a one-person psychology, and scientific tendencies. He challenged analytic concepts, such as the analyst as blank screen, as the only "healthy" member of the dyad, and as the unquestioned arbiter of reality.

Susie Orbach (2008) recently suggested that usually when relational writers offer brief historical sketches of the relational movement in psychoanalysis, they do not properly recognize the influence of social movements such as the New Left, radical therapy and radical psychiatry, and especially feminism. However, in 1982 Orbach and Luise Eichenbaum, aware of the political perspectives that these movements brought to psychotherapy, consciously applied such perspectives to their work at The Women's Therapy Centre of that era (e.g., Eichenbaum & Orbach, 1982). Orbach mentioned that an emphasis on "the actual" affected most psychoanalytic schools in the 1970s and 1980s, including the attachment literature and the infant research conducted by Beatrice Beebe and colleagues. Of course, humanistic psychology (e.g., Grogan, 2013) was also influenced by this orientation. It is not difficult to see how an emphasis on the political arrangements of gender, race, class, and sexual orientation led to a more focused clinical awareness of lived experience and its effect on psychological patterning. Practices such as women's consciousness raising groups and self-help groups for mental patients and Vietnam veterans were at that time thought to reflect what Eichenbaum and Orbach referred to as "social object relations theory" or "feminist object relations." Orbach (2008) eventually accepted Mitchell's term, "relational," and added to it an emphasis on the democratic nature of the movement's practices.

Meanwhile, in 1983, Donnel Stern published a treatment of the unconscious from a non-Cartesian perspective. Stern reenvisioned the unconscious as dissociative experiences that remain "unformulated," not repressed and fully formed artifacts buried in a Freudian-style Cartesian archeological warehouse. This opened up a new approach to memory, awareness, and psychological change. Change, therefore, is built first of all on experiencing that which has been unformulated. This requires a different kind of therapeutic process that looks for gaps, absences, and puzzles; it calls forth interpretations that rely not simply on the past but also on present experiences, not on the unquestioned authority of the therapist who discovers an already existing singular truth and delivers it unilaterally, but on the collaborative interpretive relationship between therapist and patient. Mutual interpretative processes, Stern wrote, develop emergent and contingent truths.

Also in 1983, Irwin Hoffman, drawing on his research with collaborator Merton Gill, made an important addition to early theory with the article, "The Patient as the Interpreter of the Analyst's Experience." This was a radical attack on the blank-screen concept and those writers who claimed to agree with the attack but still held to the Cartesian frame — what Hoffman called the conservative critic. Hoffman showed how this was a major philosophical contradiction and encouraged the more robust radical critic who could reconceptualize (and thereby depathologize) transference–countertransference dynamics and directly challenge the Cartesianism of the one-person approach.

Jessica Benjamin published *The Bonds of Love* in 1988. This was a complex feminist study of human development, attachment, and Western arrangements of gender. Her work and the work of other feminists such as Muriel Dimen, Virginia Goldner, Adrienne Harris, and Lynne Layton have added a great deal to the meanings of gender and oppression. Over the years, Benjamin elaborated on her initial research, developing it into a sophisticated and nuanced (and implicit) project of moral development. Her discussion of the instrumentalism present in everyday forms of sadomasochism — what she refers to as the "doer–done to" relation — and her subsequent application of that concept from interpersonal to political venues (Benjamin, 2004), has been an important contribution to relational theory and practice. Recently her concept of "mutual recognition" — the opposite of "doer–done to" dynamics — has contributed to relational psychoanalysis's (partially disguised) vision of the good, and has been applied to both interpersonal and international politics. Drawing on that concept, Judith Butler (2009, p. 20) wrote that "loss makes a tenuous 'we' of us all," to explain the ongoing global difficulty with living through collaborative, respectful, peace-loving ways of being.

Stern's work — and by extension relational psychoanalytic theory — were greatly enhanced when he found Gadamer's philosophical work in the late 1980s. With Gadamer's help, Stern came to describe psychoanalysis as an emergent process. Its material is the moral understandings and cultural meanings that have been embodied by the patient and cannot be forced by some sort of scientistic proceduralism or simplistic manualized script into a previously designed mold. "Courting Surprise," published in 1990, is a poetic clinical application of Gadamer's insights into the mysteries of the creative unbidden, processes at the heart of art, literature, and psychotherapy. In 1991, Stern wrote the more theoretical "A Philosophy for the Embedded Analyst," a description of how hermeneutics could be applied to therapy. Stern drew on Gadamer in order to broaden psychotherapy by extending theory into a fuller appreciation of the mysteries of a non-Cartesian world, one in which a human being is both constituted and yet not fully determined by the historical era. Relationship is the water humans swim in and self-contained individualism is a wrong-headed ideology. Interpretation is not something specific, universal, and certain that the therapist has privileged access to, but rather something contingent, local, and questionable. The therapist, as well as the patient, brings his or her own limitations, foibles, and struggles to the therapy hour, and both are affected by the mutual influence of the dyad. In Stern's hands, Gadamer's concept of dialogue therefore becomes a way of describing the moments in which, through respectful listening and care, the therapeutic partners come to understand, educate, and influence one another and in the process experience meaningful therapeutic change.

In 1991, Lew Aron published "The Patient's Experience of the Analyst's Subjectivity." In this article, he expanded on and supplemented Hoffman's work with insights especially from Benjamin's work on intersubjectivity. He emphasized the mutual but asymmetrical nature of analysis, the importance of the analyst's emotional and psychological life becoming known to the patient, and the crucial need of the analyst to be able to tolerate being seen by and vulnerable to the patient. These efforts, taken together, developed a nonauthoritarian, anti-fundamentalist practice that stressed respect for the other.

RoseMarie Perez Foster's (1992) examination of bilingualism from a relational perspective explicitly brought race and ethnicity into the relational literature. This was soon followed by Altman's groundbreaking book *The Analyst in the Inner City* (1995a) and several articles on race (e.g., 2000, 2004, 2006), and Leary's (1995, 2000, 2007, 2012), Gump's

(2000, 2010), Suchet's (2004, 2007, 2010), Guralnik's (2011), and Lobban's (2011a, 2011b, 2011c, 2012) important work on racial issues and enactments in the clinical setting. These authors focus on the damaging effects of racism on all races and ethnicities in the United States, and especially the ways that shame is embodied in both the privileged and the oppressed. Altman (2006), in fact, noted that psychoanalysis, in order to appear more acceptable to American society, often distanced itself from people of color in various unconscious but subtle ways. The effects of economic class and sexual orientation (e.g., Botticelli, 2004; Cheuvront, 2013, 2014; Hartman, 2005; Layton, 2004) have also been acknowledged, but much work remains to be done.

In 2010, Stern, demonstrating his indebtedness to Philip Bromberg's influential contributions to trauma theory and the postmodern concept of multiplicity in psychoanalysis (e.g., Bromberg, 1998), published *Partners in Thought*. This book was dedicated to a description of how dissociative processes, both everyday selective inattention and extreme dissociation caused by trauma, force certain feelings, ideas, and events to remain unformulated. These form into multiple self states that are usually out of awareness and unknown to one another. They remain so, Stern wrote, until revealed by unintentional enactments during intense interactions with others. In this view, the analyst — sometimes the recipient of the process, sometimes the unintentional initiator — is caught up in the mutual misery of an enactment by virtue of his or her own vulnerabilities, limitations, and problems. Somehow, sometimes, through care and some combination of skillful noticing, wisdom, and luck, the therapeutic dyad pulls out of the enactment, is able to come to interpret the enacted drama, and ultimately the therapy is enriched. More of the patient's history is experienced, more self states are identified and therefore brought into conflict with one another and, as a result, more comes to light, and more becomes formulated, but it is mostly an unbidden process. It cannot be forced (although wisdom and a commitment to the other can help prepare for it): it just happens, and then the two can meet the moment and struggle through it.

Is multiplicity reflection or resistance?

A confusing aspect of the current social terrain is that at the same time relational psychoanalysis can be interpreted as a form of resistance to the flattened, multiple self, an important theme in current relational theory is the concept of multiplicity and especially multiple self states. Is this a contradiction, and if not, how can we understand the similarity between terms? First, there are important differences between the two concepts, as discussed briefly in endnote 2. Second, it seems obvious that a preoccupation with change — especially psychological change — is in the air. Do persons in therapy change because of electrical events in the brain, or insight and the resolution of conflict, or empathic resonance and the internalization of a good object, or a shift in perspective? Or, is it the very nature of the self that it is composed of multiple self states that alternate in prominence, thereby giving the appearance of change? And what does all this have to do with one's identity or identities? Throughout the history of psychoanalysis, and certainly today, how psychological change is theorized is the subject of intense interest.

However, a crucial hermeneutic insight about theory is that, whether we draw from Freud's tripartite model of conflict, unconscious object relations, or dissociation, enactment, and multiple self states in order to explain change, we will always do so by drawing from the era's cultural-historical traditions. From a political perspective, this is just fine, as long as we don't take the theory so seriously that we come to believe it transcends our time and place. If we do make that mistake, then the particular cultural frame of our era will be all we can see, and we will drown in it. We will think the moral understandings and political arrangements of our time — and the psychological ills they produce — are the only ones possible. In doing so, we will become blind to the political causes of our suffering, or we will explain them away by proclaiming them to be universal unchanging elements of human culture — permanent aspects of all human societies we can do nothing to prevent. We will simply be reproducing the status quo without realizing it. We will think we are being revolutionary, but we will be wrong. This is a mistake psychotherapy theorists have made repeatedly in psychology's relatively short history.

As long as relational theories of dissociation and multiple self states are held lightly, not treated as objective, universal, singular truths but recognized as historically situated, sometimes useful ways of organizing our current world, then those theories will be differentiated from the historical interpretation of the flattened, multiple self. Relational theories and the current self both draw on the concept of multiplicity, but they use it differently.

However, there is a problem if relational theories are thought to be the latest version of the one truth — if, to borrow the critique that Layton (1990) applied to Kohut, they see appearance and call it essence. Then the same problem arises for relational thinking that I (Cushman, 1995) have suggested arises for so many other theories of process and change in psychotherapy: The theories, originally devised to be avenues of liberation, instead become part of the enforcement of the political and moral status quo. Commitment to a point of view — in this case relational psychoanalysis — is perfectly consistent with hermeneutic inquiry. Commitment is not the problem, because commitment can and must be questioned. From a hermeneutic perspective, our job is to respect and learn well the traditions we were thrown into at birth and have constituted us, and then continuously and conscientiously critique them. "The problem arises," Stern recently observed,

> when commitment becomes unthinking belief. When this happens, ideas that were originally closely tailored to their contexts start to be treated as timeless truths. To whatever extent the mainstream psychoanalysis of decades ago continues to be defended by its adherents, it is being treated as just that kind of timeless truth. Relational psychoanalysis was devised, in part, as a corrective to that objectivism. Now the trick will be for the new ideas to avoid the same fate.
> (D.B. Stern, personal communication, February 25, 2014)

There is much more to relational psychoanalysis than the few contributions discussed above, but space does not allow for further elaboration. Even so, I hope the political ramifications of these relational concepts are by now obvious. We live in a Cartesian world that splits mind and body, rationality and emotion, male and female, individual and community, physical science and philosophy, objectivity and subjectivity, doctor and patient, heterosexuality and homosexuality and — most important — imputes to the first position in the split a privileged unquestioned right to dominate over the second. Many other relationalists, such as Hirsch (1997), Ghent (1989), Ogden (1986, 1997), Orange (2009, 2010), and Racker (1988), also contributed to articulating a philosophical foundation for the new theory that attacked Cartesianism and thereby critiqued the therapeutic practices predicated on it. By doing so, they

1   began describing a therapeutic process much less rigid, more egalitarian, more personal, and one far more fitting for the last third of the 20th century, when young Baby Boomer therapists were coming of age professionally;
2   initiated a tradition that over time has moved some analysts into explicit opposition to the scientism and technicism that is approaching hegemonic proportions in the profession of psychotherapy (for instance, Stern's 2012 effort that identified psychotherapy theories with implicit moral values directly challenged the objectivist scientistic claims of mainstream theory);
3   explored and extended the ramifications of relational theory into explicit practices that have important political uses. Stern's (1991) application of Gadamer's concept of dialogue, in combination with multiculturalism's concept of an encounter with difference (e.g., Cushman, 2005a, 2005b, 2009), can be thought of as a description of how one can come to listen to foreign experiences and opposing points of view, be open and nondefensive enough to learn from them, and have the flexibility and integrity to shift one's allegiances accordingly. This is in line with the therapeutic stance Orange (2009) called "contrite fallibilism," Cheuvront's (2013) description of diaspora experiences, and Frie's (2011) and Guignon's (2004) descriptions of Heidegger's concept of authenticity. In a similar vein, Benjamin's condemnation of "doer–done to" relations and her subsequent valorization of "mutual recognition," and Hoffman's (2009) jeremiad against "the desiccation of human experience" provide us with glimpses into an interpersonal and international morality of care, respect, and cooperation;
4   and built a philosophical foundation from which other relationalists could catapult relational practice into a far more explicit political discourse, such as fighting racism, voter suppression, misogyny, compulsory heterosexuality, war, torture, colonial occupations, and economic stratification.

What can be seen in all this work is a consistent interpretation, a particular moral vision, of relationality. It is a vision that focuses on the care of and engagement with the other, a recognition of the inevitable hurts and mistakes that happen with interpersonal involvement, the honest recognition of one's culpability, the awareness of one's imperfections and limitations, and the importance of attempting reparation. It is an attempt to resist the temptation to collude with an American status quo that demands that therapists comply with the predominant ideology of the moment by normalizing instead of encountering the other and pathologizing instead of contextualizing difference. There is an attempt to resist the status quo that privileges quantification, manualization, and physical science method over hermeneutic interpretation, emergent meaning, and the realization that transference–countertransference dynamics are common and nonpathological clinical experiences.

My aim in this article has not been to evangelize for relational psychoanalysis, but to notice a historical event: What is showing up in the site we call relational psychoanalysis is a description of processes that bring about change, change that can be applied to political as well as psychological life. In fact, I suppose we could say that getting better at what Stern (1990) called "courting surprise" (i.e., developing the facility for experiencing *psychological* change), which could well lead to getting better at courting *political* surprise (i.e., developing the facility for creating political change, finding political allies, and entering into collaborative political ventures with them; see, e.g., Layton, 2005b).

Participating in relational psychoanalysis either as a therapist or a patient might mean that one has begun preparing oneself for, or has enrolled in, a subtle school for political resistance. If, how, or to what degree all this gets extended by relational psychoanalysis into explicit political activity remains an open question. But perhaps, in some small way, through its activities, the bedrock of democratic citizenship in the 21st century might be strengthened. Because democracy in the United States is now seriously in doubt, various attempts to develop an engaged, knowledgeable, self-reflective, respectful, humble, and yes, relational citizenry — like the practices of relational psychoanalysis are essential elements in the reclaiming and rebuilding of democracy. The viability, the very survival, of a democratic peace-seeking Western society might well depend on the success or failure of those types of brave but uncertain ventures.

As mentioned earlier, Butler noted that "[l]oss has made a tenuous 'we' of us all" (Butler, 2009, p. 20). But realize that Butler's statement highlights both the heartbreaking limits and exquisite possibilities of human life: a tenuous "we" is far preferable to no "we" — and perhaps it is the most we can hope for or aspire to in our current historical moment, as we hurtle through the enormity of space on our little blue planet, trapped and liberated as we are — tragically, beautifully, always and forever east of Eden.

Notes

1 This is a continuing dilemma for political activism in psychology: How to shift from what Watzlawick, Weakland, and Fisch (1974, p. 10) called first-order change (from psychological change located in the individual, the dyad, or the family) to second-order change (to larger systemic, foundational change located in the political arrangements of a society)? Over the last 100 years, several schools of psychology, such as Reichian body work, interactionism in social psychology, radical psychiatry, and humanistic psychology have all failed to articulate and live out real-life solutions to that enormous problem. And of course some forms of ego psychology, object relations theory, and cognitive psychology were from their beginnings uninterested or functioned to directly oppose the connection between therapy and political activism (see Buss, 1979; Sampson, 1981). Could relational psychoanalysis, by drawing on the interpretative turn's emphasis on history, critique, and moral discourse, be able to find a way?
2 Relational analysts such as Bromberg (1993, 1996, 1998), Davies (1998), Davies and Frawley (1994), and Stern (2010) write about multiplicity and accord the concept of multiple self states an important place in their work. However, these writers are not valorizing the kind of flatness prevalent in contemporary pop culture. Psychoanalytic multiplicity reflects the hermeneutic belief that there is more than one truth in a text or an issue, and in that way it opposes fundamentalism and reinforces egalitarianism. Psychoanalytic multiplicity also supports the idea that individuals are constituted by various desires, values, ideals, commitments, cultural traditions, and emotional patterns. Thus, multiplicity opposes the belief that humans can and should be reduced to one unified unproblematic self. In this way, the concept opposes the unitary singular Victorian self; it valorizes conflict, variation, and difference. Of course, relational theories, like all theories, have their good and problematic aspects. Clinicians need to be mindful of the pitfalls as well as the advantages of multiplicity and be vigilant in historically situating therapeutic theory and guarding against uncritically accepting all aspects of any theory. See also "Is Multiplicity Reflection or Resistance?" in this article.
3 See Levenson (2006) for his concerns that this strategy obscures their meaningful differences.
4 I do not mean to suggest that relational theory either naturally leads to a left-oriented politics, or that a left-oriented politics inevitably leads to a relational orientation. Certainly there are relational psychoanalysts whose politics are not oriented to the left. Likewise, there have been writers who have attempted

an integration of psychoanalysis and Marxism but would not be considered relationalists (e.g., Erich Fromm, Norman O. Brown, Russell Jacoby, Joel Kovel, Herbert Marcuse). These writers have generated a number of ideas such as the importance of psychological freedom; a rejection of normalizing therapies through a privileging of the id; and the description of and opposition to consumer capitalism's creation of a "repressive desublimation," but none of these concepts were understood as being expressed through relational practices.

5 That is, the belief that others exist to be used in order to achieve one's personal ends and that technical advancements are the best means to that end.

6 The story line is reminiscent of the 1990 film *Dances With Wolves* (Costner, 1990), also drawn from the genre of the American frontier and the European encounter with the Plains Indian tribes. But in that encounter, we see a transformation in the deep self of a Victorian man. In *Avatar*, the hero's deep self does not seem to exist and therefore cannot be transformed. Instead, the change is accomplished primarily by transporting him into another identity: an avatar.

Chapter 14

The Golem must live, the Golem must die

(2015 APA Annual Convention)

Historical introduction

This article has a long history of becoming. Several strands of my personal development as a life-long student — in literature, Judaic studies, folklore and mythology, American history, psychology, and hermeneutics — helped me think about contemporary historical events and trends, and especially the connections between them. For instance, what might be the connections between a growing American militarism in foreign policy (including drone assassinations) and domestic policing, the American invasions of the Middle East, an ever-increasing rate of African American incarceration, the effects of computer use and social media, the recent increase in economic inequality, neoliberal subjectivity, managed mental health care, and the accompanying control of psychotherapy by quantified outcome studies, bureaucratic proceduralism, and manualization?

In particular, I came to notice that often the problematic actions of professions and countries originate in attempts to create or maintain their safety but then degenerate into motivations related to greed, revaunchism, prejudices, power-hunger. Eventually I began to apply Jewish folklore about the Golem, in combination with the central Jewish tradition's prohibition against idolatry and valorization of interpretation, in order to wonder about how or to what degree those trends and events were related to or entangled with one another or were mutually reinforcing in some way.

This chapter was first written as an APA invited address in 2014, during which time Division 24 honored me with the award for Distinguished Lifetime Contributions to Philosophical and Theoretical Psychology. It was my proudest moment as a psychologist. Then, in 2016, I gave another version of the paper at the Psychology and the Other conference in

> Cambridge, Massachusetts. I was accompanied that day by Joel Rosenberg, my best friend at Hebrew Union College, the graduate rabbinic seminary we both attended in the late 1960s. He wrote a commentary on the paper, and both papers appeared in *Memories and Monsters*, edited by Eric Severson and David Goodman, published by Routledge in 2017.

Throughout the history of modern-era Western psychology, psychologists have laid claim to the legitimacy accorded the physical sciences by presenting their practices as scientistic;[1] but alternative visions of psychology, while not warmly welcomed, were tolerated. As time went on, however, the profession has come to desire more and more: more legitimacy, more wealth, more influence, more power. As a result, APA now demands near total submission to scientistic ideology. These desires and the abuses they produce threaten to destroy us. As I explain below, they are our Golem.

Fortunately, there are also theories and values available that could offer an alternative vision for psychology. They are visions drawn from hermeneutics, historical study, relational theory, critical thought and, for me, also from a particular confluence of Jewish traditions. In my mind these traditions combine to encourage political resistance against the militarism, scientism, and proceduralism of our time. One way I attempt resistance, and encourage my students to attempt it, is through studying and writing the critical cultural history of psychology.

The *Aleph* and the Golem

In the late 1960s I first studied midrash, that is Jewish biblical commentary from late antiquity (starting approximately at the beginning of the Common Era), which are stories about stories. From midrash I learned about the importance of paradox and the value of playfulness, contextuality, intertextuality, and relationality in Jewish tradition. I learned about the presence-absence dialectic: out of the apparent absence of direct Divine intervention, the rabbis of long ago and their students created a new kind of presence: a relational presence, located in the space between study partners (see Aron, 2007; Cushman, 2007; Stern, D., 1996). I learned about the concept of the bringing on of the Messiah. I learned that, in the words of Rabbi Tarfon, "you are not required to complete the task [that is, the bringing on of the Messiah], but neither are you free to desist from it." "The struggle to survive," Elie Wiesel wrote in 1966,

> will begin here, in this room, where we are sitting. Whether or not the Messiah comes doesn't matter; we'll manage without him. It is because it is too late that we are commanded to hope. We shall be honest and humble and strong, and then he will come, he will come every day, thousands of times every day. He will have no face, because he will have a thousand faces. The Messiah isn't one man ... he's all men (*sic*). As long as there are men there will be a Messiah. One day you'll sing, and he will sing in you.
>
> (Wiesel, 1966, p. 225)

This interpretative, relational, anti-fundamentalist, story-telling stream of Jewish tradition demonstrates some of the moral understandings that can help us oppose contemporary trends in mainstream psychology and can be applied in order to offer alternative theory and practices.

The Immense *Aleph*

Once, sometime probably in the first centuries of the Common Era, the midrashic rabbis tried to decide what in the entire body of Judaic literature was the direct word of God and what was only human interpretation (Scholem, 1965, pp. 29–31). Many ideas, over many weeks, were offered and debated. They got close to agreement many times, only to be disappointed repeatedly. One rabbi suggested the entire Hebrew Bible, then another argued for the Five Books of Moses, then the first book (Genesis), then another the Ten Commandments, then the first commandment, then the first word of the first commandment, then the first letter of the first word of the first commandment. Finally, miraculously, everyone agreed with that. That letter is an *aleph*, and in this story it is referred to as the Immense *Aleph*, because the rabbis thought it was the only direct sound of God's voice. All of God's love and care and wisdom, all that he hoped to give to humans, is contained in that one letter. The sound of the Immense *Aleph*, awe-inspiring and terrible, pregnant with a meaning beyond human comprehension, must have been filled to the breaking point with the overwhelming intensity of the direct experience of God. All the rest, except for that one sound, is interpretation.

Now, that's amazing: midrash has been going on now for over 2,000 years and the main justification for it is that every word, letter and mark in the Hebrew Bible is meant by God to communicate something to humans, and it is our job to interpret them.

So if only one letter is the direct word of God, that is a remarkably paradoxical and playful statement. But there is more: the letter *aleph* is a silent letter. There is an immensity that the world offers, but it makes no sound until humans interpret it. Even God's voice was unhearable, the rabbis realized, until generations of poor, anonymous Jewish scholars in Mediterranean academies and later in tiny European *shtetls* put pen to paper and interpreted God's silences through their particular and quite varied languages and cultural understandings. It is only through our imaginative interpretive insights that God's voice speaks — an important aspect of the partnership, the covenant, between the Jews and God. And our insights, of course, are always imperfect: uncertain, as the hermeneuticists like to say, and incomplete. Not knowing, or not knowing perfectly, is not easy to tolerate, but we must in order to live a fully human life.

Life would be so much easier if there were only one truth and we could know it perfectly. The Immense *Aleph* is without end, pregnant with what is possible, but vulnerable to all the fears and flaws of the human heart. Interpretation — creative responses that draw from the wisdom of cultural traditions — is that important: it is all we have, and yet it is enough. But it is not easy.

The Golem

Let us now travel forward in time to 1580. In Prague, so the story goes, the Chief Rabbi Judah Loew was faced with rumors about a looming pogrom against the Jews, one in an endless history of violent, bloody attacks on defenseless minority Jewish communities throughout Europe and the Middle East over the last 1500 years (Margolis & Marx, 1973). Legally unable to mount an army, and denied legal protections in Feudal, Medieval Europe, Rabbi Loew tried to save his people by turning to mystical Jewish practices. Out of the clay of the Vlatava River he fashioned a giant, human-shaped figure, called the Golem (Idel, 1989). Through secret incantations, and by writing the word *emet*, meaning truth, on the forehead of the giant, he brought the Golem to life. The Golem's job was to protect the Jews from marauding anti-Semitic mobs, and he did so brilliantly over several months. The Golem would magically increase in size and strength in proportion to the strength of the enemy so that he could protect the Jews no matter how fierce the attack, and the threat was temporarily extinguished. Truth was his strength and his shield.

But the longer the Golem remained alive, the more he began to enjoy life. The legend tells us he came to love the sunsets over the river; he would sit and quietly watch the colors of twilight. He also loved to wander in the forest, a lonely, hulking figure at home with the woodland animals. But then trouble began: the enormous Golem frightened the townspeople, and indeed, due to his great strength, he did cause trouble from time to time, and the non-Jewish townspeople complained. Rabbi Loew came to realize the problem and face the truth: he had to act for the good of all, even those who had previously done his people harm. Although the Golem pleaded with the rabbi to let him live on, and although the Rabbi had grown fond of the giant, he could not allow the Golem to harm others. With much sadness, he erased from the giant's forehead the first letter of *emet*; the word then became *met*, which means death, and the Golem ceased living.

Now, the first letter of the word *emet* is *aleph*. So a few years ago it occurred to me that perhaps the letter that the rabbi erased was not just any old *aleph*, but was indeed the Immense *Aleph*. This makes sense, because it is precisely the capacity to interpret that makes us fully human. If the value of interpretation, symbolized by the *aleph*, is removed from us, then we just follow orders: we can't question, we can't think critically, we can only be robotic true believers, accepting the pronouncements of those in power, believing that there is only one truth in the text and those in control know what it is. In other words, without interpretation we become fundamentalists or mindless conformists, tools of authoritarian leaders and rigid ideologies. Or we become proponents of scientism, unwilling to see the value of nuanced philosophical thought about matters of the heart.

Erich Fromm (1966) thought that midrashic process could be understood as a fight against idolatry. Midrash can inspire us to develop a way of life that features intellectual honesty, flexibility, and an openness of difference always informed, necessarily, by the historical traditions that value and enable these qualities. It is a definition of the good in Jewish life. When texts, religious belief systems, leaders, or therapists lose sight of the simultaneous power and fragility of human interpretation, they lose touch with an essential aspect of humanity. When a text becomes an idol, God becomes a thing (visible, named, and therefore known), and human creativity and relatedness become deadened. Subservience follows idolatry and leads to apocalyptic visions and inflated fantasies. In our desperation, God is thought to be an intimate and immanent presence who stands ready to intervene whenever needed.

However, "to really understand the concept of the coming of the Messiah," a wise rabbi once told me, "you must realize he will never come" (William Cutter, personal communication, 1967). An important Jewish understanding is that, contrary to the Christian Bible (see John 1) the word is not made flesh. The word remains the word, and the word, as always, remains contingent, imperfect, incomplete. Words require interpretation and must be critically examined. "Midrash refuses," David Stern (1996) argued, "to make the identification between God and Torah literal" (pp. 29). Words are surrounded by gaps, puzzles, inconsistencies, contradictions. Readers, religious leaders, therapists, and patients fall into those textual gaps, engage with their interlocutors there, wrestle with God there. We live in those gaps; we are our best selves there.

The problem with Golems

Initially the Golem had to live in order to protect a small, despised minority. And although his presence brought security to the Jews, he had to cease living because his great strength had begun to cause harm to others. The rabbi realized that, although the power that the Golem brought to the community was greatly satisfying and brought a sense of security rarely experienced by Jews in what was then their 1,500 year diaspora, the Golem's power ultimately violated the rabbi's most deeply held moral principles.

Within the corporate structure of Medieval society, Jewish communities were allowed into a particular duchy or principality only when specifically invited in order to start or enhance the territory's capitalist economy. Jews were not granted rights and protections except under specific circumstances specified by particular rulers, protections that could be — and eventually always were — revoked for economic gain or political leverage. Jews, as resident aliens, usually were prohibited from farming or joining an artisan guild, only allowed to lend money or sometimes be involved in commerce, activities the Church declared sinful and prohibited Christian believers from engaging in. Jews were forced to live in geographically restricted areas, often in walled-in areas that came to be called ghettos. And they were routinely humiliated, for instance forced to wear identifying clothing such as a yellow star. Later, inevitably, they would be outrageously taxed or extorted, forcibly converted to Christianity or left to the mob, and either expelled or prevented from leaving, depending on the ruler's momentary financial and political situation. They were not allowed to establish their own state or organize a military. The Jews were a despised and defenseless minority, continually vulnerable to and tortured through specific laws (Marcus, 1983), religious Crusades, or semi-organized, vicious attacks on person and property called pogroms (Margolis & Marx, 1973; Sachar, 1979).

However, over time Jewish communities developed a creative response to their legal restrictions, a response Rabbi Loew embodied in his decisions about the Golem. Without the legal ability to protect their communities, Jews developed a culture based on values such as communalism, compassion, and pacifism. They developed religious customs and communal practices that required the protection of the stranger and the poor, aided widows and orphans, and justified those practices through complex textual interpretations attributed to God's commands. Of course, Medieval Jews weren't saints, they were entirely human, and with that comes the potential for hypocrisy, greed, cruelty, and the wish for revenge. Still, culture does constitute the self, and given the inescapable situation the Jews lived in for many centuries, it seems clear that they made a virtue out of a necessity. The values of nonviolence, compassion, textual study, critical historical interpretation, and relationality were central to Jewish communal life for the better part of the last 2,000 years (Cushman, 2007; Stern, D., 1996). The moral commitments that moved Rabbi Loew to end the Golem's life and the manner in which he did so put into action some of the central values of Jewish Medieval culture.

Today, corporate influences in health care and military power are indeed seductive, but ultimately the indiscriminate and unnecessary exercise of power are wrong and must be stopped, even if that means a community or a profession must live with less money and security. Great strength can cause harm even unintentionally, and sadly, especially when combined with current neoliberal instrumentalism (see Fowers, 2010; Sugarman, 2015) or what relational psychoanalyst Jessica Benjamin famously called a "doer and done to" relation (Benjamin, 1990), it tends to degenerate into the wish to dominate. Then we interpret all problems as military or financial problems and can conceive of only coercive solutions.

The wish to dominate, however, does not appear out of nowhere. It is the embodiment of the way of being of the modern era, writ large. The centrality of domination is what made the Cartesian split an important force in early modern-era Western imperialism (that is, the domination of non-Christians and people of color, labor, and women) (Cushman, 1995, pp. 30–33, 356–387). One way of explaining the current popularity of mean-spirited political domination is by drawing on recent theory about "social" narcissism, a concept not based on theory that focuses solely on psychological wounding from the early years of life. In this explanation a charismatic demagogue manifesting domination as a way of being is understood to be living in a narcissistic inflation, a defensive way of being meant to cover up unconscious guilt or shame from, among other things, racism or the increasing economic inequality in the U.S. Neoliberal theory about both the rightness and effectiveness of unrestricted capitalism serves to (1) justify oppression, (2) avoid the awareness of the complicity of the affluent and the privileged, and (3) cover over what precedes the wish to dominate, which is the wounding and self-blame experienced by all in a neoliberal, racist world. Similarly, supporters of such policies or leaders are drawn by the vicarious triumphalism and personal inflation engendered by neoliberal justifications and blame, even if its policies are ultimately politically and/or economically damaging to the same supporters. In such ways the doer and done to dynamic thrives and continues to be reproduced in both interpersonal interactions and larger social structures such as institutional racism or militaristic foreign policy.

When strength is combined with the wish to dominate, exploitation and abuse multiply; national defense shifts into aggression, borders are seen as colonial opportunities, and tragically, republics transmogrify into empires. Empires, inevitably, destroy democracy and degrade and defile their own citizens. Rabbi Loew had to remove life from the Golem not only to protect the non-Jews but also to maintain the moral integrity of his own people.

Critical cultural histories of psychology

Hasidism (a Jewish sect originating in the 18th century) has taught that in order to make a better world we must begin here, where we stand (Buber, 1958). If this is true, what are we to do today, here, where we stand, in universities and/or psychotherapy offices? From my point of view, it is our responsibility to interpret and critique our field, to put into question our most cherished theories, to notice and study and comment on the relationship our theories have to the larger cultural frame and the more detailed political arrangements of our time and place. It is not enough for us only to carry on philosophical and theoretical elaborations and debates as if philosophy and clinical theory are removed from the larger events and forces of the social world around us. It is our responsibility to make a better world by studying the connections between our professional practices and the politics of our world and offer alternative ways of thinking and practicing.

Hermeneutic contributions to this project have been extremely important. Martin Heidegger (1962), Hans-Georg Gadamer (1989), and Charles Taylor (1989) have explained why textual criticism is always, necessarily, a moral enterprise. This is because interpretations are framed by understandings of the good, whether acknowledged or disguised. As a result, hermeneutic cultural history cannot claim that it is an objective practice — all research in the human sciences, all research into what matters to humans, is necessarily a type of moral discourse. Critical cultural historians cannot claim what is called "a view from nowhere"; they are responsible for describing the moral commitments that motivate and frame their work.

For that reason, I have featured the *Aleph* and Golem stories; my commitments are grounded in a combination of Jewish interpretive traditions, philosophical hermeneutics, and critical theory. This might seem like an unlikely combination, but to me it makes sense. Jewish midrashic tradition embodies qualities such as the importance of interpretive processes over objectivist claims, contextualization as a way of study, intertextuality as a way of understanding human literature, and compassionate relationality as a way of being (Cushman, 2007; Orange, 2009, 2010). Altogether, these four qualities could be thought of as comprising important elements of resistance to a fundamentalist and idolatrous way of being, and the development of a respectful, engaged, diverse democratic way of life. These qualities are fundamental to philosophical hermeneutics.

Critical and postmodern theories could be interpreted as an attempt to apply Heidegger's focus on historicity in order to research the disguised exercise of power in cultural products (including the humanities and social sciences). But unfortunately, they are often absent Gadamer's and Taylor's awareness of the inescapably moral nature of historical traditions, and therefore need Gadamer's concept of dialogue in order to contribute constructively to our current dilemmas (Cushman, 2005; Richardson, Fowers, & Guignon, 1999). So this combination of midrashic, hermeneutic, and critical traditions gives me a way of interpreting historical events, a way of understanding their larger political contexts, a motivation for undertaking and enduring the difficulties of textual study, and then a commitment to communicating its results, including ideas about creative alternatives.

Starting in 1990, I wrote about the empty self and its fit with the politics of the post-World War II era (Cushman, 1990, 1995, pp. 34–90). These days we are confronted with a new configuration of the self, new arrangements of power and privilege, new ways our clinical theories fit with the political status quo. So now we need new cultural histories of our field, new research that identifies how our practices either resist or collude with the destructive elements of our time and place, and how to develop alternative practices that could shape a different social world.

Early 21st century America: virtual worlds, multiple selves

I believe the predominant self of our time is now reflected and produced in part by the growing hegemony of electronic machines, gadgets, activities, games, and communication processes; the overall frame of consumerism; and a socioeconomic climate and psychological way of being created by neoliberal theory and practice. It began to shift from an empty self to what Peter Gilford and I (Cushman, 2015; Cushman & Gilford, 1999, 2000) now call a shallower, multiple self. This new self suffers less from being empty of meaning and initiative than from anxiety about interpersonal relations, a psychological reaction caused by an ongoing traumatizing social world, an edgy, competitive desire to dominate and exploit, and a compulsion to search, always, for opportunities to consume and be entertained. It is a self populated with a multitude of identities developed over time by living in an electronic, computerized world, identities that focus on avoiding and controlling aversive social interactions and purchasing various consumer products. These multiple identities cluster around the outside of the person, waiting to be called to center stage, depending on the social needs of the moment.

At present I am particularly concerned with the connection between two kinds of phenomena in our contemporary social world. One is the way the flattened, multiple self functions, for instance how people live, interact, and especially perform or use identity when on Facebook, online dating services, and massively multiplayer online role playing games (MMORPGs) like Second Life, Farmville, or Piercing Blow. The second is the iron grip that behavioral tools such as quantitative outcome studies (Hoffman, 2009; Stern, 2013; Walls, 2012), manualized psychotherapy treatments (Lord, 2014), and academic competencies in graduate education in psychology (Cushman, 2012) currently have on the profession, including the shape and spirit of the APA code of ethics.

In other words, the cultural terrain of our contemporary social world is one that brings to light both an obsession with electronic communication and entertainment, and an ever-growing, increasingly taken-for-granted reliance on a quantifiable, bureaucratic proceduralism. It seems counterintuitive that these two seemingly opposite types of phenomena are linked. But I believe they have certain qualities and functions in common. We either make electronic Golems to aid and protect us, or we try to turn ourselves into Golems: non-interpretive, intellectually deadened, fundamentalist worker bees or heroic war machines.

Electronic living and the multiple self

There is a type of popular film that portrays the idea that Golem-like machines are simply better versions of humans, or that humans need to become more effective by being infused with machine parts. For instance, there is a television commercial in which a young man is in a business meeting, populated by several well-dressed people, all sitting around a large conference table. He takes out a new smart phone, called a Droid, and begins to search for information or calculate some problem or key-in some data. The calculation gets increasingly detailed, and his fingers punch in information at an ever-faster rate, almost as if the phone itself has taken over his actions. And then, as his fingers work faster still, they begin turning into a robot's fingers, and then his hands and wrists and arms all turn into metal parts of a machine. The voice-over states that the Droid, in order to hook "you up to everything you need to do," will turn "you into an instrument of efficiency." The man's fingers are now almost a blur, racing at superhuman speed. His Droid has turned him into an android.

What happens to the self and our understandings of the good when our model is an information processing machine? When humans become just another electronic image, a virtual persona, then what is to stop us not only from inventing and living through avatars but also from thinking of ourselves as avatars? A person comes to light now as a multiple self, composed of a cluster of images — perhaps some of them virtual images — from which one chooses at any one time, depending on who one needs to impress or attract or sell something to or protect oneself from. These various images might well be attractive, flashy, even beautiful, but they are flattened: they have little substance or depth, no reason for being except to perform a specific purpose in a larger, fictive game — they are entirely instrumental.

This relation between alternative selves and our current social world is portrayed artistically in the 2009 film *Avatar* (Cameron, 2009). Jake Sully's life before being scientifically transformed into an avatar was crass, superficial, cruel. He had been marked, in fact disabled, by it. But through scientific advances he was transformed into an avatar, and then the avatar was transported to a radically different physical and social world, one that was beautiful, spiritual, proud. Jake came to embody new values, and tried to convince those in control of his old world that the path they were on was wrong, but to no avail. By the end of the film (no surprise here), he chose to remain permanently in his avatar and live in that new world. His only hope was to leave his old self and escape into his avatar and the world to which his avatar belonged — escape is the only option. In the new, electronic world of today we seem to be developing a new kind of a healing technology: a virtual therapeutic for a multiple, flattened self.

Electronic living and managed care

There are obvious reasons related to the accumulation of capital and the exercise of political control that bureaucratic forms, actuarial tables, and financial calculations are prominent in the decision-making processes and public relations campaigns of the corporations and federal agencies that now control health care. In turn, those in control have come to insist that therapists submit scientized, behavioral conceptualizations and evaluations of therapy in order for their practices to be reimbursed. Complying with those procedures has effected profound changes in the ways therapists now define and evaluate mental ills, their therapeutic practices, their own roles, capacities, and limits, and thus the ways they conceive of, enact, and teach therapeutic theory and practice.

For instance, one hundred percent of evidence-supported treatments for trauma are manualized (Lord, 2014). In a second example, on July 21, 2014, Magellan Health Inc. announced that it "will soon offer expanded computerized cognitive behavioral treatment programs." It will do so in order to "address common concerns in the behavioral health community ... [such as] a lack of access to clinicians..." (Magellan, 2014, p. 2). Evidently the way to address the shortage of therapists is to do away with them entirely. Here we see proceduralism, in the form of manuals and computer programming, as substitutes for human meeting, for those precious moments when, together, we make presence and meaning out of absence and grief. If quantitative measures determine outcome, then only practices that can be reduced to numbers — and thus rendered countable — will be thought of as proper data that could be used to determine worthwhile outcomes. Similarly, only those ills that can be reduced to numbers and countable problems, those identified in Axis I of DSMs III and IV, will come to be understood as proper — and reimbursable — diagnoses.

Often contemporary psychological explanations of the human mind such as cognitive theory are modeled on computer processes. In our time human mentation is described in computer language, the distinction between machines and humans narrows (and in some pop culture venues becomes nonexistent), and the superiority of war machinery such as cyborgs or Terminators is often taken for granted. When U.S. society's criteria for what is valuable are based primarily on efficiency, computational speed, and physical strength, computers and war machines will of course be superior to slower, weaker, vulnerable humans.

In the shadow of managed care and in sync with the larger electronic and neoliberal consumer culture, psychologists have been influenced by and in turn have given voice to increasingly quantified and cognitivist understandings of human being. As a result, we have quietly and perhaps even willingly acceded to a hyperconcrete, mechanistic, instrumental understanding of psychotherapy practices and then have structured graduate degree programs accordingly. It is a structure based on market values and a semi-magical belief in the effectiveness of pre-established behavioral procedures for every interpersonal interaction, psychotherapy event, and academic learning situation. Michael Sandel (Sandel, 1984) once described the U.S. as a procedural republic, but now it seems increasingly clear that the U.S. isn't really a republic anymore. We are an empire now, a procedural empire.

Electronic living, proceduralism, and psychotherapy

Computers and scientistic therapeutics may seem to be radically different phenomena, but in fact their origins and functions are similar: they both depend on quantification and procedural rules. A computer is a machine that simply follows orders, orders programmed into it through what is called a procedure code. So computers, in a way, are all procedure — they do not, cannot, interpret. Heidegger (1977) argued that modern-era technology is not a neutral tool, it is a frame of reference that affects every aspect of social life. In that framework, most everything shows up as either a resource to be used (what he called "standing reserve") or the machine that uses it. The modern, technological world, in combination with neoliberal political ideology, brings to light all interactions, including human relating, into "doer and done to" relations.

What happens to psychotherapy theories and practices when the profession is shaped by these 21st century influences? When psychotherapy adopts the language of machine-like processes and thinks of the self as a kind of computer, it will have a hand not only in reflecting but also reproducing that same kind of self — a self that is multiple, flattened, superficial, robotic. In our consumerized economy, this self searches for flashing images, glitzy products, and self-improvement strategies that increase one's aggressive, competitive edge. It is hungry for stimulation and entertainment, such as celebrity scandals, violent circuses, catchy slogans, simple questions and easy answers.

It is a self, above all, that requires procedures in order to function properly, and it requires others to follow procedures in order to feel safe from them. This is because a doer-done-to landscape is a frightening, dangerous place, and humans within that landscape lose confidence in or a capacity for engaging in moral discourse in order to enrich their lives, protect themselves, and improve their society. In such a world, it is thought that only proceduralism — the willingness to follow scientistically produced orders — can save us from one another. When a person aspires to be a robot, programmed rules become the only path to peaceful coexistence.

The technical reflection of a multiple, robotic self is Axis I of DSMs III and IV. Humans are thought of as a collection of specific, concrete behaviors (i.e., signs and symptoms) that have been reduced to their simplest, uncontestable, ahistorical elements — a kind of Lego approach to human psychology. Treatment then becomes understood as the execution of a specific intervention designed for that particular symptom. When the symptom has been properly isolated and broken down to its smallest behavioral denominator, treatment is then thought to be simply a matter of locating and administering the symptom's matching therapeutic intervention: the specific key that turns the particular diagnostic lock for which it has been designed. In this vision, therapy has a predetermined quality: mechanical, unilateral, and surgical in its precision. For every problem there is thought to be a quick, direct, decontextualized solution, if only the therapist adheres precisely to the script.

It follows from these technical innovations that, in sync with good modern-era thinking, everything psychological can be readily — and clearly — understood. Increasingly, student clinics and community agencies are encouraged to administer a consumer satisfaction survey-like instrument at the end of a session. It is thought the results will indicate whether the patient has been properly understood, empathized with, and symptoms disappeared; whether the predesigned therapy plan has been followed, the previous behavioral goals met, the therapeutic alliance properly maintained, and any new goals effectively set. Psychotherapy, then, takes on the cast of a straightforward consumer transaction, like buying a hamster or shopping for a new refrigerator. The relational psychoanalytic value of disagreement and conflict, and the importance of understanding through interpretive processes their causes and meanings (e.g., Stern, 2010) are lost when the patient is thought of as a "consumer" — and the therapist a "provider" — of therapy.

All this is a relatively new way of conceiving of therapy, although an entirely necessary one, if the profession is to fit smoothly into the scientized world of neoliberal managed care. Once the technological frame has been set, the only problems that come to light are those that can be reduced to the kinds of solutions that procedures and electronic machines can solve. Depression becomes a chemical imbalance or a mistaken way of thinking that can be fixed by the administration of the proper medication and the correct rational thought. Then the patient is quickly returned to the roles of worker and consumer. Depression, anxiety, and dissociation as expressions of moral confusion (Sheehy, 2011), economic insecurity (Bauman, 1999), or political despair (Marin, 1981) rarely come to light in such a world.

The degree to which our psychotherapy theories reduce human being to this kind of vision is the degree to which our practices support the economic and political forces that created and continue to maintain a world of extreme economic stratification, a militarized police force and racist system of imprisonment, colonial wars of occupation, and spinning electronic circuses. It is these circuses, of course, that make learning and thinking and self-reflection uninteresting, bothersome, and finally unattainable. Increasingly, it seems that we strive to portray ourselves as minor celebrities — we glamorize ourselves online, display our activities, and exaggerate (and invent) our happiest moments — we are our own paparazzi. We are becoming the kind of persons who are uninterested in, increasingly incapable of, political nuance and creativity, independent interpretive thinking, tolerating difference, or dwelling in a social world of uncertainty.

Scientism brings with it an ever-expanding inability to think philosophically about these important issues and engage with others about the moral understandings these behaviors reflect. Without a better way to engage in discourse, we run the risk of creating the automatic closure of what Gadamer (1989) called "dialogue" (that is, a meaningful encounter with difference). The absence of dialogue in turn will result in an increase in normalizing practices, mainstream values, and the political status quo — all produced through putatively scientific practices. Different cultural beliefs, philosophical questioning, and political critique could soon be in danger of being considered symptoms of what managed care companies call "non-compliance." Whether applied to ever-narrowing APA requirements for graduate school accreditation or clinical prescriptions in evidence-supported manualized treatments, scientific procedures are likely to interpret difference, disagreement, or opposition as unprofessional, inappropriate, perhaps even unethical. This will result in the rejection of an accreditation application, a therapy claim, or perhaps before long the cancellation of a community agency's or private practice's liability insurance.

In other words, governmental agencies and big business develop various rules and practices that suit their financial and political needs, and professional associations like APA adapt to, justify, and then enforce those rules and practices as their own. These institutions shape a series of interlocking procedures that control the practice of psychology in many ways. The ideology that initiates this vicious cycle and the procedures that police it form a panoptic, self-sealing structure. In managed care, Leyerle wrote in 1994, "providers as well as patients are placed under surveillance by utilization review agencies" (p. 187). It may be that "the major goal never has been to cut health care costs but to institutionalize the surveillance and control mechanisms themselves" (p. 190). Kaslow et al. (2007), the APA task force on assessing academic competencies in doctoral education, predicted that in the future, through the strict use of academic competencies, a psychology curriculum could "ensure" that graduates would be competent and ethical. In a startling expression of overconfidence, the authors of the eight-page article used the word "ensure" 16 times. The committee was proud to predict that there will be a time when practicing psychologists will be evaluated by a competency system throughout their working lives. Proceduralism will be in complete control; interpretation will be dead.

It is ironic indeed that it is this same Nadine Kaslow, President of the APA in 2014, who recently wrote to APA members responding to reports about the APA's collaboration with the Department of Defense's program of torture. In her letter she expresses surprise and is appalled by the degree and nature of the APA's involvement in the protection and defense of the psychologists who planned and carried them out, and the subsequent cover-up of its own complicity. But any of us who followed critically the progression of events as they occurred had a strong sense of what was happening. None of us can claim surprise, anymore than could Captain Renault in the movie "Casablanca" who was "shocked, shocked" that there was gambling in Rick's Café Americain.

However, it is likely that there will be no comprehensive reevaluation of APA ethics nor the way it is taught in APA accredited graduate programs. There will just be greater vigilance in policing behavior and coercing compliance. At least in its present form, APA seems unable to question the larger scientific foundations of its vision. It is unlikely we will see a hermeneutic redesign of and education about the Ethics Code based on the understanding that psychotherapy is a moral discourse. It seems doubtful that mainstream psychology will be able to realize the bankruptcy of its approach and the absolute necessity of a different perspective built on a more solid philosophical framework. No, there will only be the promise of a more procedural scientism. So probably — sadly — APA's solution will simply be more of the same. Repetition will compound tragedy.

Conclusion

Psychologists have a responsibility to resist this convergence of historical forces, to educate ourselves and alert the public. We must tell them that what in the name of consumer protection and the elimination of budgetary waste, in the guise of the march of progressive science and responsible economic policy, is in fact the exercise of power meant to control therapists and researchers in order to increase compliance and conformity in our citizenry. If therapists and graduate students weren't controlled by all these panoptic rules and procedures and protocols, we might be freer to draw from different historical and human science traditions that would enable us to think in ways more contextual, moral, political, relational. Critical cultural history is a good vehicle for studying and interpreting complex matters like the fit between a cultural/political terrain and the healing technologies that are embedded in that terrain. It can help us realize that to the degree that our practices reproduce the status quo, we are contributing to some of the very suffering we are supposed to be healing.

Being implicated in the ills we are responsible for healing is no way to bring on the Messiah. The way to make the world a better place is to look beyond the triumphalism that neoliberalism guarantees and the safety that militarism and corporate proceduralism putatively "ensures," and to fight against the violence and financial exploitation that Golem-like organizations eventually bring. At times in the life of a people or a nation it is no doubt helpful to be militarily strong enough to maintain safety, or in the case of a profession like psychology influential enough to be respected and financially viable. But too much power, combined with a neoliberal subjectivity, turns strength and the pursuit of status or money into domination and destructiveness. Critique, especially hermeneutic, historical critique framed in an explicit moral stance that leads to alternative social arrangements is vital to a just and good society.

It is not domination and control that save us from fear and despair — in fact, they cause great suffering, create bitter enemies, and bring on the very dangers they set out to avoid. Instead, what saves us from despair and works to help us imagine and actively strive for a more just political world are the moments of care and concern that make meaning in the mutual space between us and can move us to organize in order to fight for larger institutional political change. It is those moments that make life worthwhile, that help us live interpretively and self-reflectively and draw on historical and religious traditions in order to resist the urge to comply with fundamentalisms. Those moments make it possible to tolerate disappointment and absence, become politically active, embrace and develop the beauty and meaning that does come to light, and thus create a different kind of presence. It is that kind of experience that relational psychoanalysis works to create (Cushman, 2015). In this paper I suggest that critical cultural history can have a hand in improving our social world by demonstrating what is missing in our current terrain and what is needed in order to reshape it. It is good that the Golem exists, for a while. But then it must die, for the good of all.

Note

1 Scientism is the belief that only a physical science model of research can determine the truth about all human concerns, including those related to what in the 1830s Tocqueville called "habits of the heart," that is moral understandings related to human meaning, relationship, and engagement in public life.

Chapter 15

The earthquake that is the Hoffman Report on torture

Toward a re-moralization of psychology

(2016 APA Annual Convention)

Historical introduction

The Hoffman Report was commissioned by APA to investigate accusations of collusion between the APA and the Department of Defense regarding the activities of psychologists in what the Bush administration called the military's "enhanced interrogation" program. This paper was begun as a series of notes I developed as a member of a Division 24 task force tasked with developing a divisional response to the meanings of the Hoffman Report for the profession. As I learned more about the subject, the notes grew into a paper. In 2016 I delivered the paper as an invited address at the APA annual convention, and soon after I submitted it to *American Psychologist*. Sadly, it was turned down under puzzling circumstances and I was not allowed to revise and resubmit. I was not surprised: the paper concluded that the way mainstream psychology and APA in particular shapes and teaches ethics leads practitioners to be confused and vulnerable to ethically ambiguous situations.

One *AP* reviewer complained that the topic was too focused for *AP* and suggested I send it to a more specifically philosophically-oriented journal. I then sent it to *Psychoanalytic Dialogues*, which rejected it; one reviewer at *Dialogues* stated it was too broad a topic for the journal and suggested I send it to *American Psychologist*, which seemed like the appropriate venue. And so it goes, business as usual for an author trying to get an article published. But the third submission worked out well. *Psychoanalysis, Self, and Context*, an international journal, readily accepted it, and in fact built a special journal around it.

I am pleased because the special issue will keep the topic in the public eye. I am writing this introduction in the summer of 2017, and in September psychologists James Mitchell and John Bruce Jessen were about to be tried in a Spokane Washington court under the Alien Tort Statue for their roles in developing and promoting the CIA's post-9/11 interrogation

> program — they settled out of court. They are the two psychologists responsible for creating and administering aspects of the interrogation program they claim drew from Martin Seligman's social psychology theory "Learned Helplessness." Their program developed techniques used during the Bush administration's wars in Afghanistan and Iraq, including the practices used in the infamous detention centers and prisons in Abu Ghraib, Iraq and Guantanamo, Cuba. Concurrently, the Trump administration's bizarre antics have captured the attention of the news media, threatening to crowd out important questions related to the morality of torture and who was responsible for executing it.
>
> But equally important as legal culpability is the issue I raise in this paper: the many ways mainstream psychology shapes its ethics and educates practitioners about the politics of psychological practice. My interpretation of the Hoffman Report is that APA-accredited doctoral programs do not adequately prepare students to meet the ethical issues that will confront them in their professional work. Without in-depth training in history, philosophy, and relational theory, practicing psychologists will be vulnerable to the various and inevitable seductions present in psychological work, work always saturated with ethical challenges.

The Hoffman Report (Hoffman, Carter, Lopez et al., 2015) was commissioned by the American Psychological Association (APA) in order to investigate whether some APA leaders colluded with the United States Department of Defense (DoD) in order to misrepresent the DoD's practice of torture and shape APA's public stance on the ethics of torture. Doing so would have facilitated and legitimized the active participation of psychologists in those practices. Could such a betrayal be true? If true, how could it have been accomplished? And if accomplished, what philosophy of science, sociohistorical forces, and political maneuverings brought it about and how can similar actions be prevented in the future?

Although the Hoffman Report addressed only the internal activities of the APA regarding the interrogation practices of the DoD, the larger concerns raised by those actions do not pertain solely to psychology as a specific academic discipline. Psychiatrists, psychoanalysts, and social workers as clinicians, researchers, theorists, and instructors have been and/or are employed by the DoD and the CIA, and the same with some behavioral and social scientists such as sociologists, economists, and anthropologists. Also, the difficulty rank-and-file psychologists had in recognizing and condemning unethical behavior in interrogation practices in all likelihood was also present to some degree in practitioners from other psychologically related disciplines. Writers such as McAvoy (2014) and Rose (1985, 1990) have referred to these related disciplines as the psy disciplines, because they focus on the processes, functions, and behavioral expressions of the mind in the broad sense of the term. When it is fitting, I also use that term.

However, because the Hoffman Report is focused on the APA's actions, sometimes the article's focus necessitates that the language used addresses psychologists. But please keep in mind that the ethical issues at play, including the effects of historical forces and ideologies such as individualism, consumer capitalism, neoliberalism, and scientism, affect all psy disciplines, although to differing degrees. (For instance, the American Psychiatric Association and the American Psychoanalytic Association mostly avoided colluding with the DoD in the post 9/11 years, and social work has traditionally been more aware of and respectful of historical/political context in theory and practice than psychologists.

The Hoffman Report found that, indeed, some senior APA leaders worked secretly with the DoD to fit with and advance the abusive interrogation policies of the Bush administration. Unfortunately, other APA leaders trusted and relied on the opinions and guidance of the leaders who were in collusion with the DoD. Finally, the overall membership of APA and non-affiliated practitioners either (1) ignored the entanglements of the APA, ethics, and torture, (2) saw nothing wrong with APA's position, or (3) couldn't effectively organize in order to stop it. The result was a continuing obfuscation of the definition and ethics of torture and the delay of many years in what should have been accomplished years sooner, which is the prevention of psychologists from engaging in the planning, facilitating, justifying, and carrying out of torture under the protection of APA ethics. The success of the collusion between the DoD and the APA aided the Bush administration's aggressive war policies, enabled psychology as a guild to further ingratiate itself with the Pentagon, made a few psychologists wealthy, and effectively neutralized the voice of what by 2008 had become a majority of APA members.

The Report's discoveries and conclusions are like an earthquake that reveals a deep fault line. What is public knowledge but assiduously ignored — the brokenness beneath the taken-for-granted solidity of the earth's crust — becomes visible only after a cataclysmic event. Earthquakes reveal a profoundly unsettling — but undeniable — truth about the precarious nature of the ground upon which we stand. For psychology, the Hoffman Report was such an event; it shook the moral ground and professional identity of psychologists. But painful as it is to think about, I believe it has revealed something crucial about the profession of psychology and in general all the psy disciplines. It has exposed an important flaw in the foundation of psychology's dominant philosophy of science and in the training and professional practices that emerge from it. Practitioners need to address and remedy this, or else new moral disasters not yet anticipated may well be generated (Pope, 2011; Soldz, 2006).

However, addressing the above flaw will be difficult to accomplish because there are both historical forces and the predominant personality type of our era arrayed against that change. As I hope to illustrate, the way of being (i.e., the self) of many psy practitioners in the United States is a reflection of the predominant way of being in the country as a whole. The current self, Peter Gilford and I (1999, 2000) have suggested, is shifting from the post-World War II empty self (see Cushman, 1990, 1995) to what might be called a flattened, multiple self. This new, 21st century way of being is a remarkable combination of early 21st century consumerism, electronic communication experiences, and neoliberal political culture (e.g., Cushman, 2015, 2017b; Sugarman, 2015). Currently, the entrepreneurial opportunities that appear to be available in our neoliberal society to the flattened, multiple self are often too great for most of us in any walk of life to resist. And, as will be argued, today the ways we train and advise psy practitioners makes moral discourse difficult for us to exercise effectively. This is especially true given the extreme pressures we face from managed care, research funding organizations, and neoliberal college and university budget strategies.

The Hoffman Report found that the misdeeds of a few APA leaders have been egregious indeed. But it was not just the few who caused this debacle to unfold. The limitations of the many — the avoidance, political naivete, and lack of moral clarity — must not be overlooked because of the wrongdoing of the few. The deficiencies of the many are easy to overlook because they are so much in sync with mainstream psy disciplines in the U.S. and even more so with recent and powerful cultural and political trends in mainstream America. In truth, for many years Americans avoided or overlooked the deceits and abuses of the Bush administration's policies. But if we can honestly face our deficiencies we can restructure graduate educational practices in order to address them, and by doing so shape more ethical and politically progressive ways of practicing.

Ultimately, the failings that led to APA's entanglements in torture are less the product of personal, individual failures and more the outgrowth of psychology's unique place in American culture and the philosophical foundations of APA's understanding of psychology. APA's vision is anchored in a scientistic warrant and an ahistorical and technicist perspective on psychology's practices, which first in the late 19th and early 20th centuries initiated and then later maintained a mutually beneficial relationship with the capitalist marketplace. Most recently, APA's stance has slid comfortably into neoliberal, technicist, and militaristic trends in the larger society, a situation that has further legitimized and enabled psychology's fit with the consumer economy and also employment and research funding opportunities located in the U.S. military and the national security state. These forces led to a form of guild pragmatism that has driven APA's capitulation to the corporations controlling managed care, its privileging of behavioral, cognitivist, and manualized treatments, its coercive control of graduate school education, its shaping of a mechanized professional ethics, and its subsequent normalization of the employment of psychologists in the military's interrogation practices.

The Hoffman Report illuminated some of the consequences of APA's continuing and unquestioning embrace of the modern-era's conception of the natural sciences and psychology's membership in that sphere. The Report also demonstrated APA's considerable power to define psychology's philosophical perspective and social role in American society. All of this has resulted in an ethics vulnerable to strategic maneuvers that distort the profession in ways that are usually too subtle to be noticed by most, until a serious ethical breech has occurred.

In order to make sense of the activities and consequences of contemporary institutions such as the psy disciplines I have drawn from interdisciplinary approaches such as hermeneutics and cultural history. Thirty-five years ago I began trying to situate psychologically-oriented theories and practices in a historical context. This approach has helped me interpret and develop understandings about their social roles, moral positions, and political consequences. In 1979 Paul Ricoeur described this type of approach as one that "rises to the level of a hermeneutics of culture. ... It makes interpretation into a moment of culture; it changes the world by interpreting it" (Ricoeur, 1979, p. 3).

Of course, hermeneutic interpretation always invites controversy. I expect this chapter will encourage various reactions as well, and I welcome them; critiques aid in refining hermeneutic research and thus the ways we all think about this important topic.

What happened?

The Hoffman Report concluded that in the immediate post-9/11 years some senior leaders of the APA were secretly engaged in justifying the participation of psychologists in the planning and execution of torture perpetrated by the U.S. military and intelligence agencies on imprisoned Middle Eastern combatants and bystanders. In particular, the leaders worked within the parameters created by post-9/11 legal memos created by the Bush administration. The memos argued that certain torture practices were not torture but were simply "enhanced interrogation," which were then declared both legal and ethical.

The administration's ongoing war strategy attempted to legally justify torture practices by ignoring and reinterpreting international law (such as the U.N. Convention Against Torture) through a series of secret in-house memos such as the Gonzales memo of January, 2002, the Yoo memo of February 7, 2002 and the Bybee memo of August 1, 2002 (Cohen, 2012). Fortunately, over time these memos became public knowledge and were then declassified in June, 2004 (Priest & Smith, 2004). Although the memos were described as policy "clarifications" and "reservations," in fact they instituted significant changes in the U.S. definition of torture, which gave legal cover to what are now recognized as serious policy violations perpetrated in Abu Ghraib prison in Iraq, the so-called "black sites" throughout the world (Mayer, 2008, 2011), and the U.S. prison at Guantanamo Bay, Cuba (Falkoff, 2011).

The Hoffman Report documented how some senior APA leaders, including the then Director of Ethics, in secret concert with the DoD, crafted APA's policy about the definition of interrogation and torture. By doing so they were then able to manipulate well-meaning but naïve APA leaders and members of the Council of Representatives in order to legitimize the participation of psychologists in the planning and carrying out of torture. They claimed that the presence of psychologists in interrogations was indispensible because it would protect prisoners by monitoring their mental status in order to detect and halt any damaging techniques done by their interrogators. Therefore, the administration argued, any interrogation in which psychologists were present would by definition be considered ethical (Soldz, 2011). As events have shown, this belief was manifestly incorrect. The Council of Representatives' decision that this contention was believable demonstrated how historically unfamiliar and/or politically naïve those well-meaning psychologists were to make the policy decisions with which they were entrusted.[1] The deceitful actions of the few and the limitations and confusions of the many during the torture deliberations constitute a shameful stain on the history of American psychology.

The senior APA leaders collaborating with the DoD stretched and manipulated the meaning of the official ethical imperative "Do No Harm" far beyond its breaking point. And then, once traces and signs of the involvement became apparent, many psychologists of various stripes — APA leaders, APA members, and non-members — found it difficult to recognize what was happening, face the truth, effectively challenge the offending policies, and stop them in a timely manner.

Fortunately, there were ongoing, good-faith attempts to alter the APA's official stance from both outside and inside APA (Bush, 2015; Olson, Soldz, & Davis, 2008), especially by activist members motivated by what they had discovered through careful study. The 2015 Council of Representative Resolution 23B was a recent and successful attempt, generated and crafted by APA members in consultation with legal counsel. It was part of a tenacious, ongoing but until then mostly unsuccessful attempt by activists to impact the ethics committee's stance on psychologists in military interrogations. The Council's 2006, 2007, 2008, and 2013 resolutions attempted to stop psychologists from engaging in any form of torture, but for many years the activists were prevented from succeeding by the disguised legal and rhetorical manipulations developed by the few and by the activists' unintentional legal missteps.

The Bush administration's Understandings and Reservations to the UN Convention Against Torture (based on the 2002 Yoo & Bybee memos) found ways to subtly craft the definition of torture and its applicability to military prisoners in order to introduce and continue its torture practices. The Council of Representatives made several political mistakes, such as trusting the Bush administration's terms and definitions, which caused the good-faith efforts of the anti-torture activists to fail. In 2015, however, the activists finally corrected all the excessive caution, legal loopholes, and political mistakes found in the earlier resolutions, and Resolution 23B was passed. However even now there is ongoing resistance generated against and attempts to undermine or subvert 23B by challenging the Hoffman Report's conclusions and undoing 23B's call to change the Ethics Code (see e.g., *PsychCoalition*, 2016). Most recently, some psychologists identified and criticized in the Report filed suit against the APA and the legal firm that produced the Report. The battle over the definition and morality of torture continues.

What does it mean?

It is the contention of this article that the greater significance of the APA torture fiasco, like the earthquake and its suddenly visible fault line, lies in what it reveals about what is below the surface of psychology and the psy professions. In particular, it reveals the disjunction between the dominant philosophy of science in psychological practice and the ways the conception, development, and teaching of psychological ethics should be carried out. The involvement of psychologists in the justification for and design of torture has graphically demonstrated this problem. The significance of the fault line is reflected in the ways clinicians, researchers, and teachers locate our work in the larger social terrain: how we claim a warrant for our work and justify our profession to the public and to the corporations and federal organizations that regulate health policy, manage the economics and politics of mental health care, interpret ethics, and control research funding both in the public sector and in the national security state.

A most genuine and critical soul-searching is in order, conducted not just by us as individuals but especially by us as a profession. How did we allow this series of betrayals, humiliations, and sadistic acts to be thought of as a subject of legal debate, instead of recognizing it as an ethical scandal? Torture is an utterly reprehensible act, unjustifiable both ethically and practically. It is a betrayal that wounds the very soul of the prisoner (Apuzzo, Fink, & Risen, 2016), degrades the perpetrator, and undermines the moral integrity of the society that is responsible for it. It starkly illuminates what must be considered the most egregious of human mistakes: treating fellow humans as things to be used, not precious lives to be cherished and honored. It enacts the opposite of Aristotle's description of a virtuous way of life (see e.g., Fowers, 2015), because it is a graphic performance of an instrumental relationship, one that strikes at the very core of human social existence by its objectification of the other and its denial of the limits of one's own understandings. The worship of a leader or the state that leads to the debasement of one's fellow humans is in part what the Hebrew prophets meant by idolatry (see Fromm, 1955, 1966). It is the process by which humans first uncritically admire and worship inanimate and human-made creations such as wealth, automobiles, social status, national emblems, revanchist fantasies, or demagogic behavior, and by so doing are themselves turned into things.

On a more mundane note, it has long been acknowledged that torture is an inefficient and counterproductive way of extracting information (e.g., Cohen, 2011; Greenberg, 2005; Luban, 2014). A popular justification for torture — the so-called "ticking time bomb" scenario — has been shown to be ridiculously impractical and unrealistic (e.g., Kruglanski, 2015, Luban, 2014, pp. 45–66), "built on a set of assumptions that amount to intellectual fraud" (Luban, 2014, p. 45).

Because torture is so unreliable and costly in terms of time, money, and personnel, we might ask whether it might be motivated unconsciously not only by a quest for information (its public justification), but by revenge and the wish to dominate or the desperate attempt to hold together a disintegrating sense of self. Torture serves to enact power not only by terrifying the enemy but also by influencing the home population, both military personnel and civilians. Torture establishes a frame in which, ultimately, no one is safe; compliance and passivity are all that matter. So it functions to keep home populations under control by radiating strength, generating popularity, and smothering dissent (not unlike the social narcissistic dynamic mentioned above). And because most citizens in one way or another know and remain silent about the torture that is perpetuated in their name, they become implicated in it. In other words, torture degrades and abuses everyone: enemies, allies, and the home population alike (Luban, 2014, p. 73). Torture undermines a society; it destroys its moral traditions, its pride, its relational life, its youth, and thereby, inevitably, its hopes for the future. It is utterly destructive.

Why then, when so much information about the evil of torture is available, was it so difficult for psychologists to understand the political and ethical issues involved, consult the APA Ethics Code, and act accordingly? I offer three interrelated answers to this question: philosophical inexperience, historical and political naiveté, and the allure of financial gain and increased guild influence.

The 2007 Council of Representatives vote

An event at the 2007 APA convention illustrates all three of the forces and their interrelatedness to one another. Division 24 (Theoretical and Philosophical Psychology) was advised that at the upcoming meeting of the Council of Representatives an amendment — stating it would not be ethical for psychologists to have a direct role in military and intelligence interrogations — would be discussed and voted on (Olson, Soldz, & Davis, 2008, p. 2). A similar amendment had been proposed and defeated in 2006. The 2006 Council did support a general statement against torture, although the Hoffman Report found that it was worded in such a way as to fall prey to the strategies of those dedicated to the military's interrogation practices at Guantanamo and elsewhere.

Later that evening the Division 24 representative returned from the Council meeting and reported the results of its deliberations. The representatives had endured a complex discussion and in the end, as in 2006, they adopted a generic anti-torture statement. However, they neglected to prohibit psychologists from being present in interrogation sessions in the future, provided they not engage in "certain abusive techniques" (Soldz, 2011, p. 189). This provided a crucial aspect of the interrelated loopholes that were crafted and used repeatedly after 9/11 to provide the appearance of ethical behavior while in actuality mystifying the issues and justifying the Bush administrations torture practices (D. Aalbers, personal communication, 2015, 2017; S. Soldz, personal communication, 2016). These strategies manipulated politically naïve psychologists on the Council into unwittingly supporting policy directives that allowed for continuing abuses with no ethical or legal consequences (Soldz, 2011). In fact, APA policy and the participation of psychologists in interrogations "became critical components of a before-the-fact amnesty for future investigations" (Soldz, 2011, p. 179).

Some of us in Division 24 were shocked by the Council's decision and asked the representative why the 2007 statement was so limited. He explained that during the discussion military psychologists presented a united front bolstered by the Bush administration's legal arguments about the definition of torture and the certainty that as psychologists they were indispensible to protecting the lives and well being of the prisoners. They also impressed on the representatives that if a stronger statement were to be passed (for example absolutely prohibiting psychologists from being present during interrogations), psychologists would either lose their jobs or suffer a serious curtailment of job descriptions and responsibilities. As a result, the Council decided they couldn't make a decision that would have such a detrimental effect on their colleagues' employment (J. Christopher, personal communication, August, 2007) and quite possibly disrupt the relationship between the APA and the military (and thereby the income generating grants and budget lines that relationship generates or indirectly facilitates).

The pursuit of sociopolitical status and financial gain in psychology's history

The propensity to favor financial gain or social status over a nebulous or poorly understood ethics has been a theme found many times in the history of modern-era psychology. The absence of philosophically learned moral discourse in the profession leads to a thin, easily manipulated relationship with ethics. In the course of the history of psychology, when ethics is ignored or finessed in service of questionable theories or activities, the combination of financial gain/social status enhancement and the scientific justification for those activities usually go hand in hand.

In fact, in psychology there is a sizable history of researchers using putatively objective findings in order to justify the pursuit of questionable theories and acts. Critical historians of psychology have described many instances of the misrepresentations or distortions of previous theory, such as Tichener's misuse of Wundt's theory of experimentation (see Danziger, 1979); the embrace of racism in the pseudoscience of race (see Guthrie, 1998 on eugenics in psychology); overreaching claims of behaviorism (see Danziger, 1990 on Watson's contention that he was developing the universal laws that could predict and control human behavior); the creation and continued deployment of inaccurate origin myths (see Harris, 1979 on Watson's Baby Albert experiments or Gillespie, 1988 on the Hawthorne Experiments of the 1920s); the exploitation of wartime policies (see Samelson, 1979 on Yerkes and Terman's strategy of inserting early intelligence testing in the selection and placement of new recruits in order to norm the test); the indications of racism, misogyny, and homophobia in research and theory (see Bayer, 1988; Drinka, 1984; Guthrie, 1998; Lewin, 1984; Mednick, 1989) — all in service of advancing questionable or destructive ideologies, individual financial gain, or guild interests, clothed in the protective coloration of a putative science.

Throughout the Cold War and continuing to this day, there have been ongoing allegations that there were psychologists who cooperated with and worked for the CIA and DoD during the Korean Conflict and the war in Indochina (see e.g., McCoy, 2011) and in the teaching and training of Central and South American dictatorships in the practices of torture, counter-insurgency, and assassination at the notorious School of the Americas, now renamed the Western Hemisphere Institute for Security Cooperation (e.g., Karlin, 2012; Priest, 1996; Quigley, 2011). After the 9/11 terrorist attack, psychological theories such as learned helplessness (Seligman, 1972) have been used by psychologists in the employ of the CIA and the DoD to design new psychologically-oriented interrogation techniques.

Recently the APA, under various economic and political pressures, proclaimed psychology to be a STEM (Science, Technology, Engineering, and Math) discipline (APA Board of Directors, 2011, p. 121) and created the concept of evidence-supported practices. This is a phrase that implies practices not based on a quantitative, severely limited definition of evidence are ineffective, perhaps even unethical. After studying the APA Resolution on Advocacy for Psychology as a STEM Discipline (APA, 2011), Churchill (2012) argued that the strong implication of the resolution is that "any forms of psychology that do not contribute to the perception of psychology as a natural science are to be eradicated" (p. 222). The previous list of historical examples of scientific fallacies — perhaps well-intentioned, but fallacies none-the-less — were justified through appeals to a similar natural science warrant.

Professional organizations have often considered one of their primary responsibilities to be the creation of job opportunities for their members. This is a worthy objective for APA given psychology's potential for reducing human suffering and an understandable one given the financial pressures of a capitalist economy. However, often many of psychology's organizations and institutions have been unable or unwilling to conduct an ongoing critical history and intellectually solid moral discourse that could question and effectively resist the ethical pitfalls and financial seductions of the marketplace.

During this current historical moment the entrepreneurial opportunities in the DoD's interrogation settings blurred and overwhelmed ethical concerns. A number of political and legal justifications were put forth to explain the decisions made, and in truth there are many complexities involved. But ultimately there is no end to the power and persuasiveness of what Hales (1985) called the self-image management motive to muddy the ethical waters and intensify self-deception, especially in service of gaining power and affluence.

Sadly, the APA's secret involvement with the DoD, and the $80 million in contracts obtained by the two psychologists who helped develop, instruct, and carry out torture, are simply two in a history of incidents of poorly developed moral choices in the profession. A brief cultural history exploration of some of the sociohistorical and philosophical factors that create the conditions for this most recent collusion and the subsequent ineptitude, ineffectiveness, or silence of the profession is offered in the sections that follow.

Scientism and its consequences

What has become an important question in the aftermath of the Hoffman Report is whether there is something in the foundation of the psy disciplines that has contributed to the devious and destructive acts of the few, and the selective inattention, philosophical limitations, historical and political naiveté, or fearful silence of the many. This is a most uncomfortable question but one we must seriously consider. In this article I suggest that scientism has been an important element of psychology's inability to meet the moral challenges presented by the Bush administration's policy of torture. Scientism is the philosophy of science that claims "science, modeled on the natural sciences, is the only source of true knowledge" (Hutchinson, 2011), even about topics directly related to morality and meaning (see also e.g., Sorell, 1991; Zammito, 2004; Hughes, 2016). This approach brings many financial rewards in a modern capitalist society but is hindered in its ability to address moral dilemmas.

Scientism is the belief that all human problems — including moral and political issues and activities that Tocqueville in the 1830s called "habits of the heart" — can only be solved by the application of a certain framework of thinking and its attendant method associated with the physical or natural sciences. Scientism is "an exaggerated trust in the efficacy of the methods of natural science applied to all areas of investigation (as in philosophy, the social sciences, and the humanities)" (Ryder, 2005). The modern-era empirical sciences have been an integral part of the cultural terrain that evolved during the last 400 years in Western society, and of course they have brought amazing discoveries and inventions that have transformed the social terrain. They are anchored by a deep belief in a disengaged rationality (as articulated by Rene Descartes) in combination with modern-era positivism.

At the same time, especially in the last few years, mainstream psychology has often ignored or disputed different philosophies of science, including the intellectual movement referred to as the Interpretive Turn (Hiley, Bohman, & Shusterman, 1991). But the Turn can help us understand that psychologists have tried to build a human science at the point of contact between two tectonic plates — the demands of scientism and the development of and instruction about a meaningful ethics code — that conflict with one another in ways that are impossible to prevent and sometimes result in ethical confusion and unethical acts.

The Interpretive Turn can be understood as composed of two intellectual traditions, postmodernism and hermeneutics. Derrida (1976), Harvey (1990), Foucault (1977), Lyotard (1984), and Zizek (2009) are thought to be important postmodern and poststructuralist thinkers; they search for traces of the exercise of power (which they believe are always present but disguised) in literary, artistic, religious, legal, social science, and medical texts. The hermeneutic tradition, following Heidegger (1962) and Gadamer (1989), can be characterized as a historical/cultural/moral understanding of human being (Dreyfus, 1991; Guignon, 1983; Hahn, 1997; Richardson, Fowers, & Guignon, 1999). In this understanding, Cartesian distinctions do not make sense. For instance, mind is not separate from body, it *is* the body; science is not opposed to culture, it is *an expression* of culture; the individual is not thought to oppose society, the individual is *constituted* by society. Further, there is a reflexiveness to these domains; mind, science, and individuals in turn also shape the body, culture, and society.

Modern-era Western science is often focused on the march of progressive truth, and scientism can be understood as its extreme and dogmatic version when applied to human meaning. One interpretation of scientism in psychology is that there are true, independent, indisputable brute "facts" out there, and over time they can be discovered and collected. This discovery and collection is thought to be achieved through the correct use of the one method that guarantees objectivity, and deliver results that are cumulative. In this way the basic laws of human nature are thought to be discovered and then refined, approaching ever more closely a correspondence to the inert, independent world of nature. Parenthetically, this rigid version of natural science method is not followed nearly as dogmatically in the natural sciences as it is in psychology.

In the philosophy of inductive science that gives rise to what Gadamer (1989) called "method," prejudgements are thought to contaminate the putative objectivity of the scientific method. They must be bracketed off in order for the proper method to be enacted. Obviously, however, cultural expressions such as language, historical traditions, philosophical beliefs, and moral understandings are all composed of prejudgements and therefore cannot be bracketed off. Because the modern-era empirical sciences generally take for granted Cartesian divisions such as between science and culture, cultural expressions are not considered legitimate contributors to pure science. So when psychology claims a scientistic warrant, it is in the unenviable position of trying to determine good ways for humans to live by using a method that claims it has bracketed off all ideas about good ways to live. That contradiction lies at the heart of mainstream scientized psychology.

That contradiction, hermeneuticists argue, is the reason why researchers who attempt to bracket off prejudgements succeed only in disguising them (e.g., Richardson, Fowers, & Guignon, 1999; MacIntyre, 1995; Slife & Williams, 1995). And in fact, as critical historians of psychology have demonstrated, this is often what happens. When one's prejudgements get disguised, the political status quo, such as the ideology of self-contained individualism (e.g., Heller, Sosna, & Wellbery, 1986; Richardson, Fowers, & Guignon, 1999; Sampson, 1981, 1988) or current arrangements of gender, class, sexual orientation, and race (Guthrie, 1998; Lewin, 1984), get reproduced unintentionally in the findings of scientistic research. The current claims of evidence-supported practices, which often fall prey to the research flaw of "circularity" (see e.g., Smedslund, 1985), reinforce in psychotherapy outcome studies what some believe is the predominant way of being of our current digital era, the flattened, multiple self (Cushman & Gilford, 1999, 2000; Jacobson, 1997; Orange, 2009) and the behavioral, cognitivist, and manualized treatments that fit with that self.

But psychologists who practice scientism do not see the fundamental contradiction they perpetuate. Under the influence of more extreme forms of scientism, the APA designers and evaluators of graduate psychology curricula evidently decided there is little need for history. This is probably the case because it is believed that science, in a continual state of progressive refinement, will in time deliver the one truth. Past understandings, in other words, are not necessary because inevitably they will be transcended by more current findings. Philosophy is not needed because it is simply composed of nonscientific prejudgements. Likewise, political studies, literary criticism, feminism, and religion are all thought to be unnecessary or peripheral at best, but more likely non-verifiable subjectivism. All that is needed to move in the proper direction is the exercise of the proper method.

Practitioners of the Interpretive Turn, especially hermeneuticists (e.g., Bernstein, 1983; Rabinow & Sullivan, 1979; Taylor, 1985a & b, 1989) critique modern-era scientism. In psychoanalysis, writers from the interpersonal, self psychology, intersubjective, relational, and contextual traditions have developed critiques of scientism and offered alternatives. The contention that scientistic method, when applied to questions about moral values, is itself a historical/cultural product of Western, rationalist traditions (e.g., Cushman, 2013a), seems invisible to mainstream scientistic psychologists. They do not understand that the findings they believe are the product of objective method are framed by disguised moral understandings and inevitably result in subtle but important political consequences. Hermeneuticists believe that scientism cannot produce thoughtful moral understandings and then a workable code of ethics. Only philosophically sound moral discourse — albeit messy, complicated, sometimes ambiguous, always uncertain and incomplete — can work toward that goal. The results of natural science practices might be able to contribute to addressing human problems if utilized thoughtfully and with reservations and skepticism about its absolute claims, but it cannot substitute for moral discourse.

Even in psychoanalysis, as Irwin Hoffman (2012) suggested, the tendency to claim a scientistic warrant is still present in the literature, in both systematic empirical research and in positivist case studies. In 1983, he wrote about the tokenism that inhered in what he called the conservative (as opposed to the radical social) critique of the blank screen concept in psychoanalysis. In 2009 he drew from the Interpretive Turn in order to expand his original critique of conservative psychoanalytic thinking by focusing on new trends in the management and research of care in psychotherapy.

Among other points, Hoffman argued against the privileging of systematic quantitative research on process and outcome and for in-depth case studies. Other issues were opened up as the article proceeded, including managed care, randomized clinical trials (RCT), the hegemony of the *Diagnostic and Statistical Manual* (American Psychiatric Association, 2013) (DSM), and the relatively new *Psychodynamic Diagnostic Manuel* (PDM Task Force, 2006). A project, Hoffman argued, that falls prey to problems similar to those that plague the DSM. Hoffman's 2009 article was thought to be so pivotal to the field that the journal *Psychoanalytic Dialogues* devoted parts of three issues to its explication. Jeremy Safran (2012) was asked to write a commentary on the article, to which Hoffman (2012) responded. Peter Fonagy (2013), Donnel Stern (2013), Carlo Strenger (2013), and I (2013a) were also invited to comment on the exchange, and finally Hoffman wrote responses to both Fonagy and Strenger in 2013. In my response I noted that many ask

> aren't there ways we could be less extreme, pull together and make common cause with the new psychoanalytic researchers — after all, the alternatives are so much worse[?]. ... [But no, because] the tools we use initiate certain practices, and these practices carry with them a cultural framework that includes moral understandings about what it means to be human. ... Due to the shape of our current cultural terrain, authoritarian proceduralism in psychology often comes to light as the only salvation from professional mediocrity ... [or] malpractice. But it is the moral limitations and political demands of our social world — not a putatively unassailable research finding — that asserts that claim. Do we really, even in the name of science, or ... financial well being, want to be responsible for assenting to — in fact reproducing — that brave new world?
>
> (Cushman, 2013a, p. 222)

These issues are complicated and difficult to sort through, especially when financial and social pressures are considered. But ultimately, I suggested that compliance with scientific dictates about psychotherapy outcomes or the system of graduate school competencies naively but effectively reinforces the political status quo.

Especially when psychologists present psychology as a STEM discipline (APA Board of Directors, 2011), the need for moral guidance and a vibrant professional code of ethics becomes crucial (Churchill, 2012). But because mainstream scientism in psychology believes it has divorced itself from the opportunity to develop and be guided by moral understandings, the official ethics it develops must, by definition, be unequal to the task. A method that excludes moral philosophy from its deliberations cannot develop a moral vision of the profession's end goals — a *telos* — which would then lead to a fitting ethical code (Pope, 2011), one that is open to a continuing process of engaged dialogue and worthy of voluntary (Soldz, Arrigo, & Olson, 2016), deeply felt emotional commitments (see Nussbaum, 2013).

A vicious cycle

The point here is not to claim some evil conspiracy, but to suggest that we might be involved with sociohistorical forces, a cultural system, and thus a predominant self that are as powerful as they are subtle and diffuse. Ultimately, it is our job as psychologically-oriented practitioners to understand those forces as best we can because they affect us deeply, and as we are enculturated into the psy disciplines we come to embody them in particular — and powerful — ways. This is the issue that Peter Gilford and I (2000) raised in the article "Will Managed Care Change Our Way of Being?" If we are not conscious of the forces and practices we come to embody, and thereby cannot critique them politically, we are increasingly less able to realize how we as psy practitioners reproduce the very ills we are responsible for treating. Without that awareness it is difficult to meet the moral moment and thus fulfill our ethical obligations to society.

The incompatibility between mainstream psychology's modern-era scientism and learned moral discourse is manifested in how psychological ethics is usually taught in mainstream American psychology graduate programs. The lack of a solid grounding in critical historical, philosophical, and psychodynamic relational or intersubjective study results in a lessening of what Gadamer called practical wisdom. This absence, for instance, is currently reflected in the mainstream's radical turn to an increasingly disengaged, technicist, procedural psychotherapy. Many writers in the tradition of the Interpretive Turn (e.g., Goodman & Severson, 2016; Orange, 2010, 2011; Stolorow, Atwood, & Orange, 2002) suggest that mainstream psychotherapy tends to leave practitioners poorly prepared to treat current complex psychological maladies or make the ethical decisions that inhere in practitioners daily professional lives. Sadly, the lack of historical consciousness, philosophical sophistication, and relational/intersubjective sensibility can also be found in other branches of the psy disciplines.

The following sections describe the dynamic that perpetuates the interlocking procedures and rules of this vicious cycle: (1) scientism (and its fit with neoliberalism) leads to an increasing reliance on procedures; (2) a reliance on procedures contributes to a new way of being — proceduralism; (3) proceduralism leads to a type of current-day panopticism, an ever-present anxiety or guardedness about being seen and punished (see Dreyfus & Rabinow, 1982, pp. 184–204). Finally, the result of that anxiety leads to (4) ongoing but subtle attempts to avoid legal or guild punishment by memorizing and anxiously adhering to whichever set of ethical rules is dominant at the moment. In turn, (5) rigid adherence to mechanical rules requires a theory to justify rigid adherence, thus a further turn to scientism. (6) scientism reinforces proceduralism, and the cycle begins anew.

From scientism to proceduralism

Because prejudgements are integral to any language and culture, scientism in the social sciences becomes impossible without a great deal of creative sleight-of-hand. In fact, scientism's project necessitates a new language, constituted by a scientific idiom and shorn as much as possible of depth, ambiguity, poetry, and nuance. The goal is to make the most efficient use of words with as little room for paradox and uncertain meanings as possible. Because moral understandings are a kind of prejudgement, they must be mistrusted; they are thought to be subjective and unverifiable, not the product of true science.

So activities that provide opportunities for moral discourse, intellectual exploration, or artistic endeavor represent a danger to scientistic practices. For this reason highly delineated behaviorist and cognitivist procedures increasingly have become favored in psychological teaching, research, and therapy. Those procedures seem uncluttered, direct, and especially easily quantified, evaluated, measured. They claim to create little ambiguity and seemingly require little or no interpretation — they fit perfectly with the claims of scientism. Without the permission or under-developed ability to think philosophically in order to engage in moral discourse, it is thought that the only way to solve moral dilemmas and develop ethical standards is to reduce human being to quantifiable data points that can be manipulated in ways that putatively will how to live. In a scientific worldview, it is only quantification that can help us determine how to live, and only the strict adherence to procedures can save us from subjectivism and ultimately chaos.

The reliance on procedures in order to putatively ensure objectivity fits well with one of the predominant political/cultural ideologies of our time: neoliberalism (Brown, 2003; Harvey, 2003). Dominant ideologies shape a dominant way of being, and in our time a neoliberal subjectivity, sometimes referred to in cultural studies of psychology as the "enterprising character" (Hickinbottom-Brawn, 2013; Sugarman 2015) or a "flattened multiple self" (Cushman & Gilford, 2000) is increasingly prominent. These terms describe a way of being that exists in a neo-Hobbesian landscape of all against all. In general it is a way of being that is the product of the capitalist marketplace, but in the early 21st century it is a particular type of marketplace. Individuals regard themselves as highly changeable — and supremely instrumental — products that must be branded, marketed (especially electronically marketed), and continually sold and resold to one's target population. In psychotherapy, practitioners are under intense pressure to brand themselves on social media, advertise in inventive, alluring ways, and make easy to understand claims about their expertise that fit well with the technicist, medicalized social terrain of the moment (Binkley, 2011).

In other words, we are witnessing the growing power of a business ethic, determined through a behaviorist, cost-benefit calculus. It is an ethic that forces labor to comply with increasingly demanding requirements. In clinical settings this way of being is dominating over other forms of meaning: the least expenditure for the most gain. In such a social world, philosophy is thought to be a waste of time, history is irrelevant, critical self-reflection is an impediment to success, and moral discourse is sentimental tripe. The bureaucratic use of scientism, stripped of all unnecessary (intellectual and moral) baggage, is thought to deliver the most important information in the least amount of time. Scientism is thought to be valuable because it is efficient — in a neoliberal world the highest of compliments.

APA, feeling intense pressures to fit with the changing marketplace and continue to strengthen its influence on state and federal health care regulations, has shaped its accreditation criteria and flexed its muscle in order to stay competitive in an increasingly demanding economic terrain. In the race to achieve and maintain APA accreditation, graduate level programs have been subtly but powerfully forced to greatly reduce or completely squeeze out philosophy and history from their curricula. Sadly, in a neoliberal world, fewer and fewer Americans have a refined capacity to understand one another, recognize the other's point of view, or care deeply for one another. As a result, psychology's current lack of philosophical and historical expertise fits with a recently emerging and over-determined product of neoliberalism: the felt sense that other people are dangerous. In such a world human life exists in a stark terrain best characterized by Benjamin's (e.g., 2004) concept of a "doer and done to" world.

As a result, many of us in American society come to believe that our only hope for some semblance of safety is if everyone is required to follow certain specific, highly behavioral, clearly spelled out procedures for conducting business, interacting socially, and settling disputes. It forces us into a bloodless and mechanical way of relating, but it seems it is the only way in which safety can be imagined.

Proceduralism in psychology

Unfortunately, it then goes without saying that mainstream approaches to professional activities in psychology, such as teaching, research, and clinical treatment, will increasingly require strict adherence to behavioral rules — procedures — without deviation. One of the features of a significant increase in the use of procedures is that students and practicing psychologists come to embody those practices, and thus the moral understandings that frame those practices. These moral understandings will seem like second nature, commonsensical truths. A different understanding of the self — that is, ideas about what humans are capable of and what is good human behavior — has gotten developed.

Obviously, procedural language is the highest standard in the corporate world of health care (bent as it is on ever-increasing financial profit) and in the federal bureaucracy (beset as it is by an ever-shrinking budget). Health care is often controlled by corporate directives and governmental policies that demand cost-cutting measures and a superficial understanding of what the current idiom calls "accountability." Proceduralism provides the means that best fits a cost-benefit perspective, and thus science must be reduced to scientism, simply a tool for manipulation and control. In such a world, knowledge acquisition has only pragmatic value. Contrast that with non-scientistic forms of science, in which the pursuit of knowledge is what Aristotle called a constitutive good (Fowers, 2010) — a good in itself. A psychological science open to a more philosophically solid understanding of human being seems to be of little use to those who now control health care. In a non-scientistic psychotherapy, the therapist and patient cannot as easily be controlled, and therapy may venture into realms more financially costly or politically dangerous.

For all the above sociohistorical reasons, it has appeared commonsensical for psychology to adopt proceduralism as a way of being. Today it is psychology's primary means of activity and it threatens to constitute psychology's core identity. Proceduralism is in sync with the language of the day and the values of our historical era. It lends legitimacy to psychological practice and a gravitas to its results and thereby rewards mainstream psychology with a flow of money, recognition, and influence, the goods valued most by guild advocates. It then follows that the way to evaluate psychology students, teachers, researchers, and therapists is by employing a framework of predetermined procedural categories that are called "competencies." Competencies, in turn, are composed of a series of behavioral achievements determined by what are called "rubrics," which are detailed instructions for how certain evaluations are determined. In this way, all students are taught and evaluated by what is claimed to be the same objective, uniform manner: direct, understandable, and extremely efficient.

Similarly, it is thought that psychotherapy must be kept uniform, simple, highly concrete, easily evaluated. Imagine standards for doctoral-level learning that are reduced only to student products that are behavioral, that can apply only to one competency, and that have no complex and ambiguous intellectual content. What will come of the wild and beautiful experience of learning when it is reduced to a formulaic set of clichéd categories satisfied by a matching set of exclusively behavioral performances? The teaching of psychology will become something akin to an anti-intellectual practice that will drive much of the nuance, depth, and meaning out of its curricula.

The current standard, what mainstream psychology calls "evidence-supported" or "evidence-based practices," includes treatment practices that putatively have been determined to produce the best results that can be found using quantitative behavioral procedures.[2] Evidence-supported practices are thought to be distilled into step-by-step behavioral actions and codified into treatment manuals. The hegemony — and fallacy — of proceduralism is demonstrated by the realization that 100% of the evidence-supported treatments for psychological trauma are now only in the form of manuals (Lord, 2014). This unilateral, technicist, preplanned approach to therapy is, for instance, the opposite of relational psychoanalysis' practices of mutuality, self-reflection, nuance, and relentless honesty.

From proceduralism to panopticism

However, it will not be easy for the institutions of mainstream psychology to make students and psychologists follow the prescribed procedures. So faculty, funding agencies, federal policies, and managed care organizations must find ways to carefully monitor and control their workers. In a way, proceduralism is all about surveillance — it is surveillance made concrete in everyday activities. Student records are now framed by electronic forms that track students' bureaucratic, academic, and psychological performances. In the future, an APA committee (Kaslow et al., 2007) proudly announced, competencies will be used to evaluate therapists, teachers, and researchers throughout the entirety of their working lives. The promise that competencies will "ensure" an ethically competent profession (the word was used 16 times in the text's 8 pages) appears ironic indeed, given what we now know about APA's difficulties recognizing and then stopping its collusion with the DoD, including 2014, the year the chair of that committee, Dr. Kaslow, served as president of APA.

Michel Foucault (1977) argued that surveillance is emblematic of the modern era in Western society. Foucault named this phenomenon after a 19th century prison design called "the Panopticon" (the "all-seeing" prison), and indeed many prisons since that time have been structured architecturally in a similar manner. In a panoptic prison the guards are able to observe the prisoners without the prisoners knowing if or when they are being observed. Prisoners will be punished if they are caught breaking the rules and rewarded if they follow the rules. But they never know when they are being surveilled, so the structure is designed to force them to learn to surveil themselves at all times. Indeed, it appears as though Foucault were prescient: today we live in an electronic panoptic environment, in psychology graduate school or professional work environments no less than elsewhere.

In this current-day panopticism, anxiety (or at least guardedness) flourishes. We teach our doctoral students how to surveil others by administering various personality inventories that will be used in court proceedings such as competency hearings, divorce and child custody determinations, and criminal trials. Besides step-by-step instruction on how to administer and interpret evaluative tools, we also teach our students to watch others by how we watch them: they become surveillers through the process of themselves being surveilled.

Ongoing panoptic living causes many of the psychology students I have met, taught, and conversed with these last 30 years to live in a degree of low-level suspicion and guardedness that marks their everyday existence. Among other things it instills in them a way of being that is characterized by an avoidance of risk and the necessity of knowing the rules and automatically conforming to them. Too often, memorization is substituted for learning, automatic compliance for thoughtfully choosing, calculation for thinking.

Recently, a veteran instructor of continuing education courses in ethics noted that he receives lower evaluations about his ethics workshops when he presents historical background, philosophical dilemmas, and political binds related to the difficult situations in which therapists currently find themselves. For the most part, workshop attendees are focused on how to keep from getting sued or surrendering their licenses. Philosophical issues seem to them besides the point — it is their anxiety that preoccupies them. They just want to be told what to do in order to be safe.

When memorization substitutes for learning and compliance for thoughtful, reasoned choice, and when suspicion and guardedness are present in the everyday moments of one's work life, moral issues really can't be grappled with effectively. Professional ethics requires engaged study, flexibility, and self-reflectiveness in order for practitioners to be able to resist automatic compliance to rigid procedures, questionable policies, or veiled threats from or seductions by authority. But if the only process known is the strict following of procedures, then a learned and creative working through of moral challenges is difficult to imagine, let alone accomplish. When one does not know how to reason through an ethical dilemma, and has not had the experience of and guidance in doing so, fear and confusion increase. At that point, the impulse to conform, comply, or create loopholes becomes increasingly difficult to resist. It seems reasonable to wonder if this dynamic was at work on the APA leaders and military and civilian psychologists who colluded with the DoD.

This vicious cycle explains some aspects of APA's torture debacle. How otherwise could thousands of members of the largest guild of mental health in the world, who were required to undergo years of certification for membership, have largely ignored or been ignorant of activities that perfected ways of driving other humans insane? The problem isn't solely what the few perpetrated, the problem is why so many of us were considerably unaware, naïve, uninvolved, or ineffective in stopping it.

An alternative: historical consciousness, moral dialogue, and relationality

However, just because the above cycle is vicious doesn't mean it is inescapable. As hermeneuticists such as Gadamer have suggested, the sociohistorical constitutes us but it does not determine us. Human being is historical, and it is also being — that is, humans are events, and deeply engaged with others. The social world is a powerful influence in our lives, and yet it is constituted by many forces, traditions, everyday social practices, moral understandings. Each of us is a point of intersecting traditions. We are continually tacking between the moral understandings and embodied actions acquired from our traditions and the traditions of others, attempting to determine the right thing to do and to discern the meaning and significance of our lives, whether or not we are consciously aware of it. We are more in flux and dependent on others than we realize and more than we want to realize.

Figuring out how to learn from our nature as moral, ever-evolving, and relational beings makes it possible to shift slightly from the predominant ways of being found in a particular society. An encounter with difference, what Gadamer called "dialogue," either directly with another person or with a text, can help us think and act a bit differently than before. All of this can contribute to more solid and helpful forms of relationally- or intersubjectively-oriented psychotherapy and progressive political resistance (Cushman, 2015). In hermeneutic practice these activities are what prevent an appreciation of the power of history from becoming a historical determinism.

An alternative to the vicious cycle discussed above is training in historical consciousness, moral discourse, and psychodynamic relational or intersubjective theory, but in our current social terrain that type of training is difficult to locate. There is little time for them in a scientized APA-accredited curriculum, there is no methodological reason to include them, and in any event, due to their decreasing presence in the curriculum, in the near future most young faculty members won't know how to engage in them, let alone teach them.

The teaching of a critical cultural history — both the broad sweep of American history (including minority and labor histories) as well as the more specific history of Western psychology — would enhance the capacity of students to engage in moral discourse (Cushman, 2017a) and aid in breaking the vicious cycle that leads to politically and morally reprehensible actions (Cushman, 2017b). The teaching of psychology's history — not as a kind of intellectual tokenism, nor as a ceremonial history, nor as a repetition and celebration of origin myths (Furumoto, 1988) — would help students historically situate psychology in Western society and the U.S. in particular. Then psy practitioners of all kinds would be better able to notice and understand how and why previous generations of psychologists made unsupportable claims or chose paths that led to money, influence, and fame but at the expense of honesty and intellectual integrity. The profession's professed ideals such as gender and racial equality, the protection of the oppressed, and the pledge to do no harm would have a context that would better allow psy practitioners to put such values into practice.

Without an understanding of that type of critical history, practitioners will have difficulty understanding why past psychologists have fallen prey to the seductive opportunities that inevitably came their way, or in the future why we ourselves, our colleagues, or our organizations may do so. As Franz Samelson wrote in 1974, "a science without memory is at the mercy of the forces of the day" (p. 229). When better equipped with a critical perspective, psy practitioners will be better able to recognize our own avoidances and self-deceptions in order to better escape threats or evade temptations.

However, critical history, philosophy, and psychodynamic relational, intersubjective, or contextual practice, with precious few exceptions, are not taught in our doctoral programs, nor is the overall *telos* of psychology adequately explored and developed. As a result, ethics is considered to be a set of behavioral rules imposed from the outside that one must follow. There is no vehicle for simply and quickly understanding the reasons for and nuances of the ethics code of one's particular profession, nor for developing the capacity to respond to the myriad ethical dilemmas that arise with learned, creative interpretations and responses. These are the product of years of philosophical study, historical consciousness, and relationally engaged practice — Gadamer's practical wisdom. Instead, in our time there is mostly an automatic but simplistic adherence to rules, fueled by fear and vulnerable to circumstances that might bring personal advantage, if only a scientistic justification or bending of the rules can be found.

If the only motivation is to avoid a direct violation of the specifics of an ethics code, despite its spirit, the bending of the rules is fair game. Without a more learned and sophisticated vision of and relationship to ethics, and a more nuanced awareness of history and politics, there is little to stop enterprising clinicians and researchers from finding loopholes and legal fictions that justify ambitious purposes. In our contemporary neoliberal world (see e.g., Binkley, 2011; Hickinbottom-Brawn, 2013; Sugarman, 2015), business is war, and all's fair in war, so long as you don't get caught. Or, as a popular saying among players in the great American pop cultural spectacle of our time — the NFL — goes, "if you're not cheating, you're not trying." When winning is the supreme value, ethics is reduced to an obstacle to be avoided, or ideally a tool to be creatively used, in service of victory.

Helping students develop a keener historical consciousness would aid them in better understanding the need to learn and apply philosophical concepts to psychological practices such as psychotherapy and research interviewing. A hermeneutic perspective on the history of psychology can easily move into an appreciation of hermeneutic philosophers such as Heidegger, Gadamer, Emanuel Levinas (1987), Charles Taylor (1989),

Richard Bernstein (1983), and Charles Guignon (1983), and then psychodynamic theory and practice. The connections between a hermeneutically-informed history, philosophy, and relationality then become obvious — and indispensible to an ethical psychology.

The moments of silence, self-reflection, interpersonal honesty, and self-awareness — qualities developed through a psychodynamically-oriented psychotherapy — are in direct opposition to the fast-paced, quick-fix demands of daily life in early 21st century neoliberal society and the cognitive behavioral therapies preferred by managed care corporations. Far from the accusations that psychoanalytic theory is an ineffective fossil from a previous historical era, contemporary relational/intersubjective psychoanalytic psychotherapy is one of the few social practices that offer an alternative way of being to the pathogenic, empty multiplicity and manic consumerism of our time and place. Its emphasis on relationality and intersubjectivity fits well with hermeneutic, contextual understandings about history, politics, and morality. This combination of approaches will help students realize, for instance, that psychotherapy, research interviewing, and policy decision-making are all forms of moral discourse (e.g., Cushman, 1995; Gerber, 1990, in press; Stern, 2012); thus the necessity of learning how to engage meaningfully in them.

Hermeneuticists have been writing about this for decades now. Gadamer's concept of dialogue might be thought of as a way of conceiving of an encounter with difference or what multiculturalists call a difficult conversation. Fowers (2005, 2010, 2015) has applied Aristotle to psychological theory and practice. In particular he has shown how a commitment to constitutive goods militates against instrumentalism, including psychological instrumentalism. These philosophical and historical sources explain how essential Gadamerian dialogue is to human relationships and thus to psychological practice (Cushman, 1995, 2005, 2015; Richardson, Fowers, & Guignon, 1999). Psychoanalysts such as Coburn (2011), Frie (2011, 2014), Orange (2009), Stern (e.g., 1991, 1997, 2010, 2015), and Stolorow (2007) have elaborated on and applied some of these philosophical and relational/intersubjective concepts at length and to good effect. And relationalists are drawing on the Interpretive Turn to better understand the relationship between psychotherapy and social critique (e.g., Harris, 1991; Layton, 2004a, 2014), thereby applying relational concepts to current political issues (Altman, 1995a, 2005),

Botticelli (2004, 2007), Brothers (2012, 2014), Gerber (1990, in press), Gerson (2012), Harris & Botticelli, 202010), Hartman (2007), Hollander (1997), Layton (2002, 2006), Layton, Hollander, & Gutwill (2006), Peltz (2005), Tolleson (2009), and Walls (2006).

The re-moralization of psychology

By drawing from the creative vision of what we might call the North American psychological interpretation of hermeneutics (Cushman, 2017a; Faulconer & Williams, 1985; Frie, 2011; Martin, Sugarman, & Hickinbottom-Brawn, 2013; Orange, 2009, 2016; Richardson, Fowers, & Guignon (1999); Slife, Williams, & Barlow, 2001; Stern, 2012; Sugarman, 2015; Taylor, 1989), psy discipline graduate departments could develop improved ways of preparing students for living a life conducive to moral discourse. Discovering and refining understandings about what one values, knowing where those values come from, and critiquing and practicing those values makes it possible to engage with others about these vital topics. Knowing where one stands and also having the capacity to put into question where one stands is a necessity in moral discourse — it is what makes respect for the other, honest interaction, and psychological change possible. It is one of the qualities that distinguish moral discourse from moralism (Cushman, 2016). When dialogue is practiced moral issues become clearer and an ethical framework becomes more understandable, more involving, and hopefully more achievable for practitioners.

In other words, learning, critiquing, and practicing the values of one's historical traditions, being open to encounters with difference, developing a critical historical consciousness, and living a psychodynamically-informed relational or intersubjective life facilitate moral decision-making and ethical living. That is a way of drawing simultaneously from both streams of the Interpretive Turn: critical postmodern and hermeneutic traditions. These qualities are the antithesis of a scientistic, neoliberal, disengaged, procedural way of life. They demonstrate how a psychological practice that relies on the contemporary formula of memorization, guardedness, manualization, and submission makes for a profoundly weak and ineffective ethical framework. Under such mainstream influences, it is inevitable that psychologists occasionally violate the ethics code, sometimes in small ways, sometimes in shocking and highly destructive ways.

An ethics weakly connected to the process of moral discourse, forced on practitioners by the threat of punishment and with practitioners having little or no involvement in the process of creating and shaping an ethical code, is likely to fail. It will be unable to withstand the manipulations of capitalism, the military, and the pressures and seductions constantly emerging in an early 21st century American consumer culture.

In order to create a truly engaged, understandable, and effective ethical practice we must become better at teaching history, philosophy, and psychodynamic relationally- or intersubjectively-oriented practices to our students in order to deemphasize scientism in psychological science. That will take a supreme effort of soul-searching and education in both graduate and continuing education programs, but this goal — the re-moralization of psychology — is indispensible to the psy disciplines now and in the years to come. It will not be easy, it will require much critical study and soul-searching, but it is the right thing to do.

Notes

1 This was not the first time psychologists made political decisions of great import that, due to an interest in financial gain and a lack of historical background and political experience, ultimately were bad for psychology as a profession and the country as a whole. For instance, Sarason (1981) reported on similar mistakes made during the famous Boulder Conference of 1949, mistakes that had widespread political consequences felt to this day (see Cushman & Gilford, 2000).
2 When regarding psychotherapy, the persuasiveness of the argument for evidence-supported treatments depends on whether quantitative date is considered the only acceptable evidence. When this is the case, evidence-supported treatments exemplify the dangers of research circularity (see e.g., Hoffman, 2009; Cushman, 2013; Stern, 2013).

Chapter 16

Living in the politics of uncertainty

Cultural history as generative hermeneutics

(2017 APA Division 24 MidWinter Meeting)

Historical introduction

I was asked to write a paper about the fundamentals of cultural history as a hermeneutic practice for the 2017 MidWinter meeting of Division 24 (Theoretical and Philosophic Psychology). I was glad to do so because it gave me the opportunity to think hermeneutically about the unusual — perhaps bizarre — historical moment we as a country were living through and baffled by.

The symposium — "The Crisis in the Humanities and Social Sciences" — was scheduled for March 12, less than two months after Donald Trump's inauguration as the 45th President, four months and eight days after the election of November 8, 2016. So between the long, ugly election campaign and the first few months of the new administration, there was much by which to be puzzled, frightened, and enraged. I wanted to write about it so I could find out more of my thoughts about the election and its aftermath and more about what I could learn about us as a country. I especially wanted to try to put into words what I sensed but found difficult to articulate: the connections between consumer capitalism, our evolving digital life, racism, and the strange pronouncements and chaotic right wing actions of the new president. Finally, I wanted to suggest a way for young psychologists in Division 24 to get a better fundamental understanding of the value of cultural history and hopefully a stronger motivation to practice meaningful, politically critical, and above all generative hermeneutic work — something that could build as well as criticize. For that reason in particular, I had hoped to write something inspiring. I thought at the time it might be the last talk I ever give at an APA event, and I wanted it to be a good one.

To study the history of humans is to be struck by the profound, unending fragility of the human psyche, especially our vulnerability to political demagoguery, scapegoating, and mob hysteria. The fragility I refer to is not simply a question about an individual's sanity but instead about the overwhelming, indispensible human need for culture: for a mental framework about reality, that is about what is, and for a moral framework about what is good.

It is astonishing to study human groups throughout history and witness the extraordinary variety of cultural visions about what is real or illusion, good or bad, ethical or corrupt, and correspondingly what kind of creatures humans are, what actions we are capable of, what activities we should and shouldn't perform, what we should strive for and avoid, where we fit in the array of gods, animals, and plants. These visions are colorful, majestic, ridiculous, inspiring, disgusting. Because humans are constituted by a particular cultural vision, our stories and understandings seem to us the only reality that is possible. It doesn't matter how outlandish those ideas might appear to others, the images, narratives, and proscriptions we live by are inscribed in and on our bodies: humans are constituted by them.

One way to get a sense of how powerfully individuals are wedded to a particular cultural worldview is to notice what happens when our worldview is challenged by events that contradict or threaten fundamental aspects of our worldview. Often those events or opinions are ignored, explained away, attacked, banished, destroyed.

Another way to notice how important culture is to humans is to witness what happens when a cultural tradition slowly becomes significantly undermined by political events or historical forces to the degree that, over time, that way of being becomes deprived of a vibrant, meaningful worldview. Watch how eagerly group members search for a new worldview, assimilate it, use it, and thereby come to protect it, swear by it, even proselytize it to others.

This is true not only for broad, generalized worldviews but also smaller, more circumscribed belief systems, such as adherence to a political party or loyalty to a charismatic leader. The need for a cultural framework in desperate times is palatable, and the hunger for a belief system or group belonging creates an intense susceptibility to easy answers, superficial solutions, scapegoating ideologies, charismatic leadership.

Human fragility and hermeneutic theory

We are psychologically fragile beings; we are not capable of generating solely within ourselves the governing mechanisms or tools necessary to live and survive. We need a cultural framework to complete us; without one we cannot be human. Now, Division 24 members will recognize this as a hermeneutic argument. I draw upon it in order to discuss the topic of this panel and especially the topic of my paper, because I think it is a valuable approach to questions about what it is to be human, what it means to live a good life, and in conjunction with those two aspirations, how and why to write history.

Martin Heidegger's (1962) concept of the cultural clearing gives us a way to grapple with the broad questions mentioned above, questions about what is real, what is the good, and what humans are capable of. While witnessing Heidegger's political corruption resulting from his anti-Semitism and political ambition, Heidegger's onetime student Hans-Georg Gadamer (1989) gave us a way of thinking about relationality and psychological change — what he called dialogue — that helped hermeneutics avoid being a historical determinism. Michel Foucault (1979), Richard Bernstein (1976, 1983), and Charles Taylor (1989) demonstrated the genius of Heidegger's historical focus by applying a critical historicity, thereby demonstrating the power of historical and cultural traditions. Most recently, what we might call the North American psychological interpretation of hermeneutics, led by Division 24 members Blaine Fowers, Charlie Guignon, Jack Martin, Frank Richardson, Louie Sass, Brent Slife, and Jeff Sugarman, has drawn from earlier scholars in order to apply hermeneutic ideas to our current philosophical struggles with locating a way of living beyond the false dilemma of objectivism or relativism.

The topic of this panel, the crisis in the humanities and social sciences, is a reflection of that struggle, one recognizable throughout Western society. Starting in the late-Middle Ages, under the growing influence of various sociopolitical forces and ideologies such as individualism, capitalism, urbanization, and secularism, the modern era witnessed an unraveling of the Medieval world view. It was a time marked by disorientation, fear, and insecurity. The dominance of the Church declined and over time the new empirical science and the philosophies that fit with it appeared and grew in influence. This emergent cultural terrain valorized control (over both the natural world and one's own emotions), technical rationality, and instrumentalism. Physical science method, marked by a belief in the rejection of folkways and traditions, filled the gap left by the loss of certainty in the corporate structure of medieval society.

Among other things, European global exploration (and imperialism) brought with it an awareness of cultural differences that was shocking and disorienting to early moderns and then the Victorians. That awareness confronted Western cultures with the necessity of explaining the variety of non-Western cultures while still maintaining an overriding belief in Christian and white supremacy. By the Victorian era a variety of approaches were utilized, including the empirical sciences, antinomian or esoteric spiritualism, and a putatively scientific framework based on class and race theory.

In the late 20th century, under the influence of many sociopolitical forces, mainstream intellectual explanations of identity and difference were challenged. In the discipline of history, for instance, starting in the 1950s, Marxism and culture theory began to emerge and are now prominent. In the humanities and social sciences, postmodern approaches such as constructivism and deconstructionism emerged, sometimes in combination with or opposition to hermeneutics. What most of these intellectual movements have in common is the rejection of a naïve realism and its scientific partner, objectivism.

However heady and *au currant* the rejection of naïve realism and objectivism was, it also brought with it a difficult dilemma: how to justify one's morality and politics without recourse to some all-encompassing certainty. If all one can do is critique and tear down, life gets increasingly dispirited and empty, there is little secure ground upon which to stand, and political activity becomes increasingly difficult to justify. A sense of solidness dissolves and opposition to objectivism or scientism loses traction. Especially problematic is an ability to make moral judgments, a characteristic that opens the door to the demagoguery of far right political and religious ideologies.

The crisis

And so here we arrive at the crisis: without recourse to the one perfect truth, how is it possible to hold strong opinions about the good, take principled stands, and convince others to join with us? In psychology, scientism — bolstered by managed care directives and the growing influence of neoliberal politics — has gained in strength and is now thought to be hegemonic in clinical work and research.

Postmodernism and Marxism (and even some particularly elegant combinations of the two), despite many important contributions, have not adequately responded to the crisis. Culture theory holds the possibility for a better approach, but I believe only if used in combination with two of the philosophical originators of culture theory, Heidegger and Gadamer.

Marxism, for instance, has failed to adequately explain and recover from its failure to recruit the proletariat. Nixon's law and order strategy, Reagan Democrats, and most recently Trump's "America First" theme are examples of the Left's failure to solve this puzzle. The concept of false consciousness was salient indeed to the intelligentsia, but not surprisingly it never made enough headway with those who were implicitly considered too ignorant to make choices in their own best interest.

A better alternative for this important puzzle is my proposal for today: cultural history — when it combines critical culture theory and hermeneutics — provides us an opportunity to think about, study, and discuss current events in psychology and the larger society in ways that can be both politically aware and generative. It combines a focus on culture with a respect for collective memory that is indispensible to a democracy. Hermeneutic cultural history gives us a *way* to write history and a *reason* to write it. It gives us a way to critique the past and present so as to see ways into a better future. It gives us a way to be less afraid to speak about moral understandings and willing to use power ethically if we can attain it. It helps us be capable of both resisting the status quo and building a better world. In our social world of today, that is a tall order indeed, but if we can't do that, all else will fail.

The beauty and the terror of the clearing

Heidegger's concept of the cultural clearing is a remarkable idea. It gives us a way of thinking about human being that makes possible a different way of writing history, one that recognizes both the power and the limits of culture, and demonstrates how contemporary cultural artifacts such as movies, cell phones, and psychotherapy theories both reflect and reproduce the political status quo. It also demonstrates how the horizon of a clearing is not only powerful but also changeable — it is both of those things because it is perspectival. It looks like a thing, it functions like a thing, but it is not a thing. It is a process. Horizons move, and thus by their very nature they can be influenced by a change in perspective, by an encounter with difference, by a new text, by tolerating critical thought even about a cherished theory or basic tenet in a belief system.

The hermeneutic concept of the self consists of what is thought to be the proper way of thinking and acting in a particular clearing. The self emerges, comes to light, as a result of the specific boundaries of the clearing. How that comes to be, nobody knows; it is a mystery. It is amazing, it is beautiful, it is beyond understanding. How a particular clearing comes to produce the various social practices that make up a culture is accomplished through remarkably subtle, implicit, unseen ways. How those practices come to be translated into a language, everyday acts, moral understandings, religious beliefs, a way of being, is a remarkable mystery. But somehow, some way, all the varied social products come together to form a whole.

Even though in inexplicable ways, the clearing does bring all those things to light. The study of what does come to light and how it functions socially and politically in a historical era is what cultural history hopes to bring about. This is what was hinted at in the second half of the 20th century by what was then called the history of material culture, or the Annales school of history (i.e., history from the bottom up). The task of a critical, hermeneutic, cultural history is to grasp the remarkable interrelatedness of a culture — to sense for an instant how the disparate pieces of the social fabric are woven into the whole. To get a sense of how they politically reinforce, reproduce, collude with, resist and reshape one another, to understand the innocence, the cynicism, the terror, and the brave fiction of it all — that is the challenge of a critical, hermeneutic cultural history.

An example: memories, lies, and the image

We are living through a profoundly confusing political moment, one that might well threaten the very existence of American democracy. It presents us with an opportunity to conduct the practice of what Foucault called "genealogy." He suggested that the encounter with a bizarre or puzzling phenomenon from the past can initiate a study of the social world that brought that puzzlement to light. Difference is not something to be avoided or corrected, but rather a window into a different social world and thus a different way of being human. In 2017 the free press is under attack from the most powerful person and the most powerful political institution in the world: President Donald Trump and his administration. Many fear that he is either delusional or a serial and strategic liar. Further, he seems unable to tolerate being disagreed with or proven wrong. These are troubling traits in anyone, but in the leader of a democracy it is potentially disastrous. He attacks the news media directly, fires long-term government employees who question his policies, and holds huge, emotionally-drenched public rallies in front of supporters in which he announces and repeats obvious falsehoods and hurls unfounded accusations and blame in order to defame opponents and scapegoat minorities.

This behavior from a leader of a powerful country is disturbing in itself. But even more troubling is the undeniable fact that a significant percentage of the population voted for him and still supports him even with continuing news reports about his chaotic and mean-spirited first months in office. How can we understand this political series of events and be able to respond creatively and effectively to them?

In 1972 Hannah Arendt wrote about the crucial importance of truthfulness in the public realm. It was, she thought, what made for the nobility of democratic institutions and raised them above the coercions and corruptions of dictatorships. Without collective memory about past untruthfulness, she suggested, the public commons cannot adequately function. Of course, lying has been and will continue to be an aspect of political processes. But Arendt argued that political lying in the U.S. changed during the Vietnam War; the nature of that change has meaning for us in our current predicament.

During the beginning of the war, Arendt argued that lying was done in service of strategic U.S. military objectives. However, the nature or function of lying changed as the war progressed; slowly, lying began functioning not to achieve specific objectives but to bolster the image of the U.S. internationally and President Lyndon Johnson domestically. The development and protection of "the image" replaced military or diplomatic goals. The image of American military might became omnipresent in strategy meetings and undoubtedly led to Johnson's seeming inability to develop an exit strategy. Ultimately, the tangle of lies resulted in a moral and public relations disaster from which consecutive generations of military leaders have striven to rehabilitate. It has been this attempt to resuscitate the military's reputation, Andrew Bacevich (e.g., 2005) argued, that in part has led to so many counter-productive, even catastrophic, foreign and domestic policy decisions in the years since Vietnam.

We could argue that in the armed conflicts that followed Vietnam, lying — and especially lying in order to produce or polish an image — has been the overarching common theme of presidential explanations and justifications. Think of Reagan's Grenada adventure, G.H.W. Bush's excursion into Panama, Clinton's military intervention in Serbia, and of course more recently G.H. Bush's disastrous wars in Iraq and Afghanistan and Obama's costly misadventure in Libya.

The question for a critical, hermeneutic cultural history must be: how could such lying be effective in an open, democratic society that claims to have a fully functioning free press? What kind of cultural clearing would prepare the population for and in fact encourage the onslaught of deceitfulness, and the continuing attacks on the truth, that the American public has endured for so long and for such nefarious and fatal policies?

The answer to that question can help us better understand the decades-long slide into the corrupt, dishonest political landscape from which we suffer today. How have our shared understandings about what is real, what are facts, what is important, and what constitutes ethical argumentation descended to such a pathetic standard? It seems as though questions about what is important in life have devolved into a state of such subjectivity — and thus so contingent upon the personal needs of individuals to prop up their endangered way of being — that it is difficult for many to care and be vigilant about some common understandings about what constitutes reality, truthfulness, honesty. What seems to matter increasingly is what is called winning, and to that end common agreements over the most basic of issues are contingent on supporting at all costs the image one projects to the world. In service of the image, most all acts are permissible if they can be explained away through various claims, assertions, or scapegoating. Reality, it seems now, is dependent on what rules or commonly held agreements can be effectively violated in order to enhance the image. Remember a saying common among players in the great pop cultural spectacle of our time, the NFL: "if you're not cheating, you're not trying."

How has this orientation to reality and morality come about? Several forces come to mind, including the philosophical frame of the Cartesian split, which forces a choice between a naïve objectivism or an acultural, interiorized subjectivism. In our current historical moment this split is especially powerful when it converges with the political ideology of neoliberalism and the hegemony of digital, electronic living. Several writers (e.g., Binkley, 2011; Harvey, 2007; Hickinbottom-Brawn, 2013; Sugarman, 2015) have discussed the ideology of neoliberalism and how it is reflected in everyday practices. Governmental restrictions on business should be undone to allow for the unfettered genius of the free market. An individual is properly understood to be an entrepreneurial self that needs to be branded, marketed, and sold on the open market. The capitalist marketplace is the reigning frame of reference in neoliberalism, and humans must therefore take a highly instrumental orientation to their lives. Selves are best thought of as consumer images that can be enhanced by purchasing the proper accouterments or experiences or equipment. This applies regardless of what the individual is attempting to achieve, including getting a job, purchasing a wardrobe or a car, starting a psychotherapy private practice, or attracting a romantic partner. The reduction of human relationality to the strategies of the marketplace is obvious and tragic.

Electronics and the self

The influence of electronic devices, which fits in many ways with aspects of neoliberal life, is the other main influence on the distinctions between truth and falsehood or reality and illusion. The electronic image has been of increasing importance in the U.S. starting in the 1950s with the advent and then increasing popularity of television. But the suspension of disbelief necessary to enjoy a play in the theater or a drama on television has taken a huge leap with the invention and now omnipresence of digital electronics. The impact of electronic movies, games, social media, personal websites, blogs, and most recently virtual reality headsets must be taken into consideration when examining what human interaction and reality orientation mean to Americans.

In 1999 and 2000 Peter Gilford and I suggested that the predominant understanding of the American self was undergoing an important change. We characterized the change as one from an empty self (Cushman, 1990) to the multiple self. In the world of the empty self, when individuals were distressed in ways characteristic of the second half of the 20th century, they would experience emptiness and a wish to be filled up with or made cohesive by purchasing consumer goods or the personality or ideology of a charismatic leader. But beginning in the last few years of the 20th century, rather than emptiness individuals were experiencing a generalized anxiety and a fear that important others — especially unreasoning authority — would overlook, reject, or hurt them, that others were inherently dangerous, and that the way to protect oneself was to shift from one identity to another, depending on the requirements of the moment.

Behavioral symptoms such as social anxiety and the concept of psychological trauma became elevated to diagnostic categories and entered everyday vocabulary. Their content and causes became unquestioned, taken-for-granted understandings about everyday life. With the growing omnipresence of anxiety and trauma-based reactions, the recognition and then terror of vulnerability necessitated making the wish for escape a commonplace event. And the quickest means of escape would be either into an electronic fantasy world or into an entirely different — and more powerful, perhaps invulnerable — self.

This shifting would be accomplished by purchasing consumer items that would help the individual appear to be a different person — or even a nonperson such as a cyborg or android — thereby escaping the dangers posed by the initial social situation. Electronic escape — readily available through the strategic staging and managing of pictures on one's Facebook page or website, the use of visually brilliant gaming software available for all sorts of electronic devices, or the experience of submersion into magical films that feature life-like robots superior physically and cognitively to humans — has become an everyday, unremarkable aspect of our social terrain. Aptly named virtual reality devices played in headsets or goggles are really just the most recent and extreme example of this flight from everyday social reality; they are devices that deliver an all-encompassing all-sensory experience of a different world. When running an electronic game or fantasy experience, the substitution of one world for another is complete — what an ad for a Google headset describes as "A world of your own." It is the ultimate escape.

I use this example to illustrate a main goal of a cultural history approach: to attempt to sketch out a description of aspects of the cultural clearing that brings to light the self of a particular era, its moral understandings and political functions. Rather than describing the unique personality of a king, queen, or politician, or the false consciousness of an economic class, the hermeneutic historian explores the social world that brings a particular way of being to light. This is done in hopes of describing aspects of the clearing that shape a particular self, because individuals constituted by that clearing unconsciously live out the moral understandings and political commitments of that particular kind of consciousness.

Reagan Democrats, for instance, were not being false to their hopes and ideals, they were being true to hopes and ideals that had been ignored and prejudices that had been left unchallenged by centrist or liberal elites. Currently, Progressives are shocked that former working class voters would think that Trump represents working class interests, because they don't understand those interests. Trump supporters are expressing a different embodied understanding of the good then that of the elites. They are furious for being left behind by an economy that is delivering untold wealth to a relative few and ignoring the disappointment, degradation, and suffering of the working classes and the dispossessed.

Trump supporters are not disturbed by Trump's untruths because they now live in a social world that has a different understanding of truth and reality, honesty and deception. They are used to being lied to, but unlike the moderate Democrats who appear to ignore their plight, Trump publicly recognizes it, and the response from his blue collar supporters is a euphoric outpouring of hope and loyalty. Whether Trump will help his followers is another story. But the cultural history point is that they think he will, and they think he will because their social world has brought a particular shape of the self to light, and that shape fits well with Trump's claims and promises, with his own way of being.

The euphoria of Trump's supporters will move them to escape into a fantasied world in which the elites will be defeated and they will be delivered back to a time of safety and security, when according to the understandings of their clearing, America was "great."

Playing to this fantasy, Trump scapegoats minorities of all types; he isolates them and blames them for a myriad of social problems. His supporters join with him, made gleeful by the fantasy of a world split only into good guys and bad guys, which is promised magically to be cleansed from those they fear or despise. It is a fantasy world that returns them to their rightful place as the only "true" Americans; those in a make-believe world that once before made, and in the future will once again make, America great. The racism here is just barely below the surface. The similarities to Hitler's vision of a *Judenfrei* Germany in control of all of Europe appear inescapable.

Trump supporters don't care that he contradicts himself or misspeaks or repeats facts that are untrue. When they are under pressure or get desperate to find some comfort or safe group with which to identify, they also will ignore inconvenient facts or discover "alternative facts" that support what they desperately want to believe — just as he does. Trump lives in a different reality, and they want to live there also. Yes, he might be twisting the truth, but in this digital world what is the truth, really? It is what you want it to be. Besides, for once someone is twisting the truth in a way that promises to help them or a way that appeals to their hopes and self-righteous rage. Yes, the simple-mindedness and fairy-tale nature of current political discourse sounds all too much like the alternative realities generated by today's electronic software — and for good reason: it is exactly that software that both reflects and reproduces our contemporary social world.

The provenance of our current political splitness is not difficult to find: it is beamed to the population in an avalanche of mainstream crime shows or in scapegoating, hate-filled venues on television and online websites that create their own facts to suit their political and financial purposes and lie with impunity in order to justify placing blame on their designated targets and prove their ideological message. The vindication Trump supporters feel when viewing these venues is difficult to overstate. Their grief and rage finally make sense to them, their envy and hatred are suddenly justified, and they don't have to engage in time-consuming and challenging study in history, politics, and the humanities. That is especially convenient because such research might move them to question deeply held commitments about long-held American values, such as the transcendent truths of capitalism, personal competitiveness, white supremacy, and American exceptionalism.

Of course, every subculture has good and bad aspects, as do those of the white working classes that support Trump. In relation to some of their grievances and anger, their frustrations are certainly understandable. On the other hand, some of those frustrations are fed by an unacknowledged envy of intellectuals and elites, which then gets turned into a scapegoating of learnedness and a disavowal of the value and goodness of knowledge and its acquisition. Their anger is also exacerbated by an avoidance of facing the more accurate causes of the systemic exploitation from which they suffer. For some members of this class, avoidance is abetted by a barely disguised but intense racism, anti-Semitism, misogyny, and homophobia. And there is nothing quite as effective at scapegoating traditionally despised minorities (and thus avoiding the fundamental causes of the exploitation) as charismatic demagoguery from the right. But let us remember that white working class subcultures hold no monopoly on racism and xenophobia — to one degree or another all white U.S. subcultures are implicated in those belief and practices.

So where does this brief cultural interpretive example lead? It could lead to a deepening respect for difference, in this case class differences that can shed light on, among other things, the serious economic disparities in the country and the blindness of some intellectuals and progressives to those disparities and to their relative socioeconomic privilege. Those are awarenesses that must be faced before a more accurate and compassionate understanding of and stronger alliance with the working classes can be forged. It could lead to an awareness of structural socioeconomic oppressions that must be directly addressed. It could lead to a condemnation of the severe economic inequities and stratifications in the society that have increased under administrations that instituted tax cuts for the rich, a rollback of federal regulations in finance, industry and the environment, all under the justification of trickledown economic theory. It could lead to a rigorous effort of political education, bereft of shaming, focused on the destructiveness of scapegoating and institutional racism. It could lead to an examination of the many factors that have led to the insecurities and fears especially of the young, that move them to crave escape and at-a-distance, electronic relating. And it could lead to new generative conversations that could help reconstitute learned and meaningful moral discourse.

Uncertainty: the most frightening obstacle

In other words, hermeneutic cultural history keeps our focus on the social world, not dark secrets located in the putatively interiorized psychological processes of uniquely individualized historical actors. In this chapter I have attempted to encourage others to research and write critical, hermeneutic cultural history. However, there is an important disadvantage to employing this approach. It introduces a difficult personal challenge: by experiencing history in this way we will be forced to develop an understanding of the mystical, precariously constituted foundation upon which human social life is built. Realizing that our most cherished beliefs and institutions are social artifacts and not the one, true reality itself is potentially too disorienting for us often to tolerate. Historians who use a cultural history approach and their readers will inevitably find themselves at the edge of an awe-inspiring abyss. This is an abyss similar to what critical hermeneutic therapists live through while practicing and yet rejecting the mainstream psychotherapy theories popular at any given time. Living a critical practice is a precarious, frightening, and yet deeply moral, endeavor. An old Bloom County cartoon (Breathed, 1985, pp. 97, 107) comes to mind.

Oliver Wendell Jones, the prepubescent scientist-computer genius, is sitting on the roof of his family home, gazing at the heavens through his powerful telescope. But even though he is a genius, he is still only a child, and after a short time he is overcome by the terrible complexity and vastness of space and the insignificance of human life. He drops the telescope, runs into his room, dives into bed, and pulls the covers over his head for comfort. For a while he just shakes. Later he staggers to the kitchen to wallow "in the welcome mundanity of a chocolate chip cookie." The reality of it all is just too much for Oliver; but he does see the majesty of it, if only for a moment.

So then, why do it? Why write a critical, hermeneutic cultural history? Well, because it is the best response to the crisis in the social sciences and humanities that anyone has yet come up with. Because it is the best hope we have to influence others about the political and moral issues that matter the most to us. Because it is the best hope we have to understand our lives and those of others, to study our ennobling and our shameful moments, and resist the status quo in effective yet moral ways. Because by writing hermeneutic cultural history we can not only critique but also create — we are motivated to write because of our moral understandings, and we can draw from those understandings in order to imagine a better world and better ways to bring about that world.

Life for the hermeneutic cultural historian is a life of dialogue. Whether we are encountering difference in a text we are studying or a person we are engaging with, we are always trying to better understand the other's actions, opinions, beliefs, and commitments by better understanding the cultural clearing that brought them to light. And in that process we will find, when we are lucky, that we will get a better understanding of, and thus a slightly different perspective on, the clearing that brought our actions, opinions, beliefs, and commitments to light. By doing so we will be better at critiquing our cherished theories and traditions, deciding what is good about what we believe and commit to, and what is good about what others believe and commit to, and thus what we must shift or change about ourselves.

We continue to write history, we persevere even in dark times, because we believe it is the best, most loving gift we can give to others. In this world, where so many turn to authoritarianism and to leaders who scapegoat others, who refuse to consider other points of view, who are so shaken by disappointment, hurt, or fear that they cannot tolerate compassion or uncertainty, we must write history. We have to keep critical, hermeneutic thought alive by keeping collective memory alive. As Cathy Caruth (2013) suggested, it is crucially important to make the decision to witness — to witness while living in the world of the lie. To remember, and help others remember, and by doing so assert the values of honesty, courage, and compassion. By doing so we affirm the importance of striving for a better world. By practicing a hermeneutic cultural history we learn more about the past and especially what matters — what is good — from the past, affirm the importance of collective memory, discover ways of drawing from memory, and realize the responsibility to reach out to others who are different. By doing so we learn more about our own clearing, the goodness that lies in those who are different, and the goodness that lies in us. That, more than anything else, will help us build a different, better, future.

References

Aeschylus. (1953). *Oresteia* (R. Lattimore, Trans.). Chicago: University of Chicago Press. (Original work produced 457 BC).
Allport, G. (1954). *The nature of prejudice*. Reading, MA: Addison-Wesley.
Altman, N. (1995a). *The analyst in the inner city: Race, class, and culture through a psychoanalytic lens*. Hillsdale, NJ: The Analytic Press.
Altman, N. (1995b). Theoretical integration and personal committment: Commentary on Seligman and Shanok. *Psychoanalytic Dialogues, 5*, 595–604.
Altman, N. (2000). Black and white thinking: A psychoanalyst reconsiders race. *Psychoanalytic Dialogues, 10*, 589–605.
Altman, N. (2004). Whiteness uncovered: Commentary on papers by Melanie Suchet and Gillian Straker. *Psychoanalytic Dialogues, 14*, 439–446.
Altman, N. (2005). Manic society: Toward the depressive position. *Psychoanalytic Dialogues, 15*, 321–346.
Altman, N. (2006). How psychoanalysis became white in the United States, and how that might change. *Psychoanalytic Perspectives, 3*, 65–72. [Taylor & Francis Online].
American Psychiatric Association (1987). *Diagnostic and statistical manual of mental disorders* (rev. ed.). Washington, D.C.: American Psychiatric Association.
American Psychiatric Association (1994). *Diagnostic and statistical manual of mental disorders* (4th edition). Washington, D.C.: American Psychiatric Association.
American Psychiatric Association (2013). *Diagnostic and statistical manual of mental disorders* (5th edition). Washington, D.C.: American Psychiatric Association.
American Psychiatric Institute (1968). *Diagnostic and statistical manual of mental disorders* (2nd ed.). Washington, DC: American Psychiatric Association.
American Psychiatric Institute (1980). *Diagnostic and statistical manual of mental disorders* (3rd ed.). Washington, DC: American Psychiatric Association.
Apuzzo, M., Fink, S., & Risen, J. (Oct. 8, 2016). How U.S. torture left a legacy of damaged minds. *The New York Times*.

Arendt, H. (1972). *Crises of the republic.* New York: Harcourt Brace.
Aron, L. (1991). The patient's experience of the analyst's subjectivity. *Psychoanalytic Dialogues, 1,* 29–51. [Taylor & Francis Online].
Aron, L. (2007). Black fire on white fire, resting on the knee of the holy and blessed one. *Contemporary Psychoanalysis, 43,* 89–111.
Aron, L. (2007). Black fire on white fire, resting on the knee of the holy and blessed one. *Contemporary Psychoanalysis, 43,* 89–111.
Aronson, S. (2007). Symposium on sameness and difference in the consulting room: I am everyday people. *Contemporary Psychoanalysis, 43,* 449–450. [Taylor & Francis Online], [Web of Science ®].
Artz, l. & Murphy, B.O. (2000). *Cultural hegemony in the United States.* Thousand Oaks, CA: Sage.
Ash, M. (1983). The self-presentation of a discipline: History of psychology in the United States between pedagogy and scholarship. In L. Graham, W. Lepinies, & P. Weingart (Eds.), *Functions and uses of disciplinary histories* (pp. 143–189). Boston, MA: Reidel.
Atwood, E., & Stolorow, R. (1984). *Structures of subjectivity: Explorations in psychoanalytic phenomenology.* Hillsdale, NJ: Analytic Press.
Augustine. (1986). *Confessions* (R.S. Pine-Coffin, Trans.). New York: Dorset Press. (Original work produced 397 BC). Hillsdale, NJ: Analytic Press.
Austad, C.S., and Berman, W. (Eds.). (1991). *Psychotherapy in managed health care: The optimal use of time and resources.* Washington, DC: American Psychological Association.
Bacevich, A. (2005). *The new American militarism: How Americans are seduced by war.* Oxford, UK: Oxford University Press.
Barratt, B.B. (1995a). Review essay: *Madness and Modernism* by Louis Sass. *Psychoanalytic Dialogues, 5,* 113–121.
Barratt, B.B. (1995b). Reply to Louis Sass. *Psychoanalytic Dialogues, 5,* 137–143.
Bauman, Z, (1999). *In search of politics.* Stanford, CA: Stanford University Press.
Bauman, Z. (2006). *Liquid fear.* Cambridge, UK: Wiley.
Baumeister, R. (1986). *Identity: Cultural change and the struggle for self.* New York: Oxford University Press.
Baumeister, R. (1987). How the self became a problem: A psychological review of historical research. *Journal of Personality and Social Psychology, 52,* 163–176.
Bayer, R. (1988). *Homosexuality and American psychiatry: The politics of diagnosis.* Princeton, NJ: Princeton University Press.
Bennett, M.J. (1989). The catalytic function in psychotherapy. *Psychiatry, 52,* 351–364.
Bellah, R.N., Madsen, R., Sullivan, W.M., Swidler, A. & Tipton, S.M. (1985). *Habits of the heart: Individualism and commitment in American life.* Berkeley, CA: University of California Press.

Benjamin, J. (1988). *The bonds of love: Psychoanalysis, feminism, and the problem of domination.* New York: Pantheon Books.

Benjamin, J. (1999). An outline of intersubjectivity: The development of recognition. *Psychoanalytic Psychology, 75,* 33–46.

Benjamin, J. (2004). Beyond doer and done to: An intersubjective view of thirdness. *Psychoanalytic Quarterly, 73,* 5–46. [CrossRef], [PubMed], [Web of Science ®].

Benjamin, J. (2009). A relational psychoanalysis perspective on the necessity of acknowledging failure in order to restore the facilitating and containing features of the intersubjective relationship (the shared third). *International Journal of Psychoanalysis, 90,* 441–450. [CrossRef], [PubMed], [Web of Science ®].

Bergin, A.E., & Garfield, S.L. (1994). *Handbook of psychotherapy and behavior change* (4th ed.). New York: Wiley.

Berman, A. (2012, February 27). Who will "Reagan Democrats" support in 2012? *The Nation.* Retrieved from www.thenation.com/article/who-will-reagan-democrats-support-2012/.

Bernheimer, C., & Kahane, C. (Eds.). (1985). *In Dora's case: Freud-hysteria-feminism.* New York: Columbia University Press.

Bernstein, R.J. (1976). *The restructuring of social and political theory.* New York: Harcourt Brace Jovanovich.

Bernstein, R.J. (1983). *Beyond objectivism and relativism: Science, hermeneutics, and praxis.* Philadelphia, PA: University of Pennsylvania Press.

Bernstein, R.J. (1991). *The new constellation: The ethical-political horizons of modernity/postmodernity.* Cambridge, MA: MIT Press.

Beutler, L.E., Machado, P.P.P., & Neufeldt, S.A. (1994). Therapist variables. In A.E. Bergin & S.L. Garfield (Eds.), *Handbook of psychotherapy and behavior change* (4th ed., pp. 229–269). New York: Wiley.

Biale, D., Galchinsky, M. & Heschel, S. (1998). *Insider/Outsider: American Jews and multiculturalism.* Berkeley and Los Angeles: University of California Press.

Binder, J.L. (1977). Modes of focusing in psychoanalytic short-term therapy. *Psychotherapy: Research and Practice, 14,* 232–241.

Binkley, S. (2011). Psychological life as enterprise: social practice and the government of neo-liberal interiority. *History of the Human Sciences, 24,* 83–102.

Blum, J., Morgan, E., Rose, W., Schlesinger, A., Stampp, K., & Woodward, C. (1973). *The national experience: A history of the United States* (3rd ad.). New York: Harcourt Brace Jovanovich.

Bollas, C. (1987). *The shadower of the object: Psychoanalysis of the unthought known.* New York: Columbia University Press.

Bollas, C., & Sundelson, D. (1995). *The new informants.* Northvale, NJ: Jason Aronson.

Bordo, S. (1987). *The flight to objectivity: Essays on Cartesianism and culture.* Albany, NY: State University of New York Press.

Bordo, S. (1988). Anorexia nervosa: Psychopathology as the crystallization of culture. In 1. Diamond & L. Quinby (Eds.), *Feminism and Foucault: Reflections on resistance* (pp. 87–117). Boston, MA: Northeastern University Press.

Boskin, J. (1968). *Urban racial violence in the Twentieth Century.* Westerville, OH: Glencoe.

Boss, M. (1982). *Psychoanalysis and daseinanalysis.* Jersey City, NJ: Da Capo. (Original work published 1963).

Botticelli, S. (2004). The politics of relational psychoanalysis. *Psychoanalytic Dialogues, 14*, 635–651.

Botticelli, S. (2006). Globalization, psychoanalysis, and the provision of care: Roundtable on global woman. *Studies in Gender & Sexuality, 7*, 71–80. [Taylor & Francis Online].

Botticelli, S. (2007). Return of the repressed: Class in psychoanalytic process. In M. Suchet, A. Harris, & L. Aron (Eds.) *Relational psychoanalysis: New voices* (pp. 121–134). New York: Routledge.

Botticelli, S. (2012). Weak ties, slight claims: The psychotherapy relationship in an era of reduced expectations. *Contemporary Psychoanalysis, 48*, 394–407. [Taylor & Francis Online], [Web of Science ®].

Bouhoutsos, J., Holroyd, J., Lerman, H., Forer, B., & Greenberg, M. (1983). Sexual intimacy between psychotherapists and patients. *Professional Psychology: Research and Practice, 14*. 185–196.

Boulette, T., & Anderson, S. (1986). "Mind control" and the battering of women. *The Celtic Studies Journal, 3*, 25–35.

Brammel, D., & Friend, R. (1981). Hawthorne, the myth of the docile worker, and class bias in psychology. *American Psychologist, 36*, 867–878.

Brandell, G. (1979). *Freud: A man of his century.* Atlantic Heights, NJ: Harvester Press.

Breathed, B. (1985). *Penguin dreams and stranger things.* Boston, MA: Little, Brown and Co.

Brodkin, K. (1998). *How Jews became white folks and what that says about race in America.* New Brunswick, NJ: Rutgers University Press.

Bromberg, P.M. (1993). Shadow and substance: A relational perspective on clinical process. *Psychoanalytic Psychology, 10*, 147–168.

Bromberg, P.M. (1996). Standing in the spaces: The multiplicity of self and the psychoanalytic relationship. *Contemporary Psychoanalysis, 32*, 509–535.

Bromberg, P.M. (1998). *Standing in the spaces: Essays on clinical process, trauma, and dissociation.* New York: Routledge.

Brothers, D. (2012). Trauma, gender, and the dark side of twinship. *International Journal of Psychoanalytic Self Psychology, 7*, 391–405.

Brothers, D. (2014). War, peace, and promise-making: Becoming a late-life activist. *Psychoanalytic Inquiry, 34*, 766–775.

Buber, M. (1958). *Hasidism and modern man* (Ed. & Trans. M. Friedman). New York: Harper & Row.

Budman, S.H., & Gurman, A.S. (1988). *The theory and practice of brief therapy*. New York: Guilford Press.

Budman, S.H., & Gurman, A.S. (1992). A time-sensitive model of brief therapy: The I-D-E approach. In S.H. Budman, M.F. Hoyt, & S. Friedman (Eds.), *The first session in brief therapy* (pp. 111–134). New York: Guilford Press.

Bush, R. (2015, Sept. 11). Q&A: UD's Scott Churchill on preventing psychologists from aiding in torture. Dallas Morning News. Retrieved from http://DoD.dallasnews.com/opinion/commentary/2015/09/11/qa-ud-s-dr.-scott-.

Buss, A.R. (Ed.). (1979). *Psychology in social context*. New York: Wiley.

Butler, J. (2009). *Precarious life: The powers of mourning and violence*. New York: Verso.

Cameron, J. (Director). (2009). *Avatar* [Motion picture]. United States: Twentieth Century Fox.

Carr, N. (2010). *The shallows: What the internet is doing to our brains*. New York: Norton.

Cheuvront, J.P. (2010). Life-long coupled relationships and psychoanalysis: Reconsidering developmental milestones and measures of normality in clinical theory. International Journal of Psychoanalytic Self Psychology, 5, 37–58. [Taylor & Francis Online].

Cheuvront, J.P. (2013, April). The experiences of diaspora: Directions for psychoanalysis from the intersections of culture. Paper presented at APA Division 39 conference, Boston, MA.

Caruth, C. (2013). *Literature in the ashes of history*. Baltimore: Johns Hopkins University Press.

Chessick, R. (1986). Heidegger for psychotherapists. *American Journal of Psychotherapy, 40*, 83–95.

Churchill, S.D. (2012). Humanistic psychology and STEM disciplines: Strange bedfellows? *The Humanistic Psychologist, 40*, 221–223.

Clark, J. (1983). On the further study of destructive cultism. In D.A. Halperin (Ed.), *Psychodynamic perspectives on religion, sect, and cult* (pp. 363–368). Boston, MA: John Wright PSG Ltd.

Coburn, W.J. (2011). Recontextualizing individuality and therapeutic action in psychoanalysis and psychotherapy. In R. Frie & W.J. Coburn (Eds.) *Persons in context: The challenge of individuality in theory and practice* (pp. 121–142). New York: Routledge.

Cohen, A. (2012). The torture memos, 10 years later. *The Atlantic*, February 6, p. 2. Retrieved at http://DoD.theatlantic.com/national/archieve/2012/02/the-torture-memos-10-years-later/252439/.

Cohen, M. (2011) (Ed.). *The United States and torture: Interrogation, incarceration, and abuse*. New York: New York University Press.

Coleman, J.C. (1964). *Abnormal psychology and modern life* (3rd edition). Glenville, IL: Scott, Foresman.

Costner, K. (Director). (1990). *Dances with wolves* [Motion picture]. United States: Orion Pictures.

Crawford, R. (1999). Transgression for what? A response to Simon Williams. *Health, 3*, 355–366.

Cummings, N.A., & Sayama, M. (1995). *Focused psychotherapy: A casebook of brief intermittent psychotherapy throughout the life cycle.* New York: Brunner/Mazel.

Curtis-Bowles, H. (1997). *The application of psychoanalytic theory and practice to African Americans.* Unpublished manuscript.

Cushman, P. (1984). The politics of vulnerability: Youth in religious cults. *Psychohistory Review, 12*, 5–17.

Cushman, P. (1986). The self besieged: Recruitment-indoctrination processes in restrictive groups. *Journal for the Theory of Social Behavior, 16*, 1–32.

Cushman, P. (1987). History, psychology, and the abyss: A constructionist-Kohutian proposal. *Psychohistory Review, 15*, 29–45.

Cushman, P (1989). Iron fists/velvet gloves: A study of a mass marathon psychology training. *Psychotherapy: Theory, Research, Practice, & Training 26*, 23–39.

Cushman, P. (1990). Why the self is empty: Toward a historically situated psychology. *American Psychologist, 45*, 599–611.

Cushman, P. (1991). Ideology obscured: Political uses of the self in Daniel Stern's infant. *American Psychologist, 46*, 206–219.

Cushman, P. (1994). Confronting Sullivan's spider: Hermeneutics and the politics of therapy. *Contemporary Psychoanalysis, 30*, 800–844. [Taylor & Francis Online], [Web of Science ®].

Cushman, P. (1995). *Constructing the self, constructing America: A cultural history of psychotherapy.* New York: Da Capo.

Cushman, P. (1996a). Review essay: *Psychoanalytic Dialogues, 6*, 859–874.

Cushman, P. (1996b). Locating dialogue: Reply to Flax. *Psychoanalytic Dialogues, 6*, 883–894.

Cushman, P. (1997, November 8). Beyond a postmodern "multiple self" and identity politics: Toward a moral and political psychoanalysis. Paper delivered at the William Alanson White conference Building New Bridges: Clinical Psychoanalysis Across Disciplines, New York.

Cushman, P. (2000). White guilt, political activity, and the analyst: Commentary on paper by Neil Altman, *Psychoanalytic Dialogues, 10*, 607–618. [Taylor & Francis Online], [Web of Science ®].

Cushman, P. (2001). *Multiculturalism and the problem of privelege. History as transformative practice.* The Mary Whiton Calkins Lecture presented at the annual meeting of the American Psychological Association, San Francisco, CA.

Cushman, P. (2002). How psychology erodes personhood. *Journal of Theoretical and Philosophical Psychology, 22*, 103–113. [CrossRef].

Cushman, P. (2005a). Between arrogance and a dead-end: Psychoanalysis and the Heidegger-Foucault dilemma. *Contemporary Psychoanalysis, 41*, 399–417.

Cushman, P. (2005b). Clinical applications: A reply to Layton. *Contemporary Psychoanalysis, 41*, 431–446. [Taylor & Francis Online], [Web of Science ®].

Cushman, P. (2007). A burning world, an absent God: Midrash, hermeneutics, and relational psychoanalysis. *Contemporary Psychoanalysis, 43*, 47–88.

Cushman, P. (2009). Empathy — What one hand giveth, the other taketh away: Commentary on paper by Lynne Layton. *Psychoanalytic Dialogues, 19*, 121–137.

Cushman, P. (2011a). *Multiple selves, virtual worlds, and the procedural empire*. Presented at the annual meeting of the American Association of Psychoanalytic Clinical Social Workers, Los Angeles, CA.

Cushman, P. (2011b). The danger of cure, the value of healing: Toward a midrashic way of being. In W. Cutter (Ed.), *Midrash & medicine: Healing body and soul in the Jewish interpretive tradition* (pp. 211–233). Woodstock, VT: Jewish Lights.

Cushman, P. (2012). Defenseless in the face of the status quo: Psychology without a critical humanities. *The Humanistic Psychologist, 40*, 262–269.

Cushman, P. (2013a). Because the rock will not read the article: A Discussion of Jeremy D. Safran's critique of Irwin Z. Hoffman's "Doublethinking our way to 'scientific' legitimacy." *Psychoanalytic Dialogues, 23*, 211–224.

Cushman, P. (2013b). *"Your cheatin' heart": From scientism to medicalization to an unethical psychotherapy*. Paper presented at the American Psychological Association, Honolulu, Hawaii.

Cushman, P. (2014, August). *The golem must live, the golem must die: On the importance of writing critical cultural histories of psychology*. Presented at the American Psychological Association Division 24 (Theoretical and Philosophical), American Psychological Association Annual Convention, Washington, DC.

Cushman, P. (2015). Relational psychoanalysis as political resistance. *Contemporary Psychoanalysis, 51*, 423–459.

Cushman, P. (2016). Abelove's historical vision: Gentle warnings against moralism, colonialism, and an apolitical identity politics. *Studies in Gender & Sexuality, 17*, 86–94.

Cushman, P. (2017a). *Living in the politics of uncertainty: Cultural history as generative hermeneutics*. Paper presented at the Theoretical and Philosophical division of the American Psychological Association, mid-winter meeting, Richmond, VA.

Cushman, P. (2017b). The golem must live, the golem must die. In E.R. Severson & D.M. Goodman (Eds.), *Memories and monsters: Psychology, trauma, and narrative*. New York: Routledge.

Cushman, P. & Gilford, P. (1999). From emptiness to multiplicity: The self at the year 2000. *Psychohistory Review, 27*, 15–31.

Cushman, P. & Gilford, P. (2000). Will managed care changing our way of being? *American Psychologist, 55*, 985–996.

Danziger, K. (1979). The social origins of modern psychology. In A.R. Buss ((Ed.), *Psychology in social context* (pp. 27–45). New York: Irvington.

Danziger, K. (1990). *Constructing the subject: Historical origins of psychological research*. Cambridge, UK: Cambridge University Press.

Davies, J.M. (1998). The multiple aspects of multiplicity: Symposium on clinical choices in psychoanalysis. *Psychoanalytic Dialogues, 8*, 195–206.

Davies, J.M., & Frawley, M.G. (1992). Dissociative processes and transference-countertransference paradigms in the psychoanalytically oriented treatment of adult survivors of childhood sexual abuse. *Psychoanalytic Dialogues, 2*, 5–36.

Davies, J.M., & Frawley, M.G. (1994). *Treating the adult survivor of childhood sexual abuse*. New York: Basic Books.

Derrida, J. (1976). *Of grammatology*. Trans. G. Spivak. Baltimore: John UP.

Derrida, J. (1974). White mythology: Metaphor in the text of philosophy. *New Literary History, 6*, 5–74. [CrossRef].

Dimen, M. (1991). Deconstructing difference: Gender, splitting, and transitional space. *Psychoanalytic Dialogues, 1*, 335–352. [Taylor & Francis Online].

Dimen, M. (Ed.). (2011). *With culture in mind: Psychoanalytic stories*. New York: Routledge.

Doherty, W. (1994). Bridging psychotherapy and moral responsibility. *Responsive Community, 4*, 41–52.

Downing, J.N. (2000). *Between conviction and uncertainty: Philosophical guidelines for the practing therapist*. Albany, NY: State University of New York Press.

Dreyfus, H.L. (1991). *Being-in-the-world: A commentary on Heidegger's Being and Time*. Cambridge, MA: MIT Press.

Dreyfus, H.L. & Rabinow, P. (1982). *Michel Foucault: Beyond structuralism and hermeneutics*. Chicago, Il: University of Chicago Press.

Dreyfus, H., & Rubin, J. (1987, November). *Augustine of Hippo*. Paper presented at the workshop Inventing the modern self. Berkeley, CA.

Dreyfus, H., & Wakefield, J. (1988). From depth psychology to breadth psychology: A phenomenological approach to psychopathology. In S. Messer, L. Sass, & R. Woolfolk (Eds.), *Hermeneutics and psychological theory: Interpretive perspectives on personality, psychotherapy, and psychopathology* (pp. 272–288). New Brunswick, NJ: Rutgers University Press.

Drinka, G. (1984). *The birth of neurosis: Myth, malady, and the Victorians*. New York: Simon & Schuster.

DuBois, W.E.B. (1961). *The souls of Black Folk*. New York: Signet. (Original work published 1903).

Dyer, R (1993). *Images*. New York: Routledge.

Ehrenberg, D. (1974). The intimate edge in therapeutic relatedness. *Contemporary Psychoanalysis, 10*, 423–437. [Taylor & Francis Online], [Web of Science ®].

Ehrlich, R. (1985). The social dimension of Heinz Kohut's psychology of the self. *Psychoanalysis and Contemporary Thought, 8*, 333–354.

Eichenbaum, L., & Orbach, S. (1982). *Outside in ... inside out: Women's psychology. A feminist psychoanalytic approach*. New York: Pelican.

Eliot, T.S. (1971). The hollow men. In *T. S. Eliot. The complete poems and plays, 1909–1950*. New York: Harcourt Brace Jovanovich. (Original work published 1925).

Ewen, S. (1989). Advertising and the development of consumer society. In 1. Angus & S. Jhally (Eds.), *Cultural politics in contemporary America* (pp. 82–95). New York: Routledge.

Fairfield, S., Layton, L., & Stack, C. (Eds.) (2002). *Bringing the plague: Toward a postmodern psychoanalysis*. New York: Other Press.

Falkoff, M.D. (2011). This is to whom it may concern: A Guantanamo narrative. In M. Cohen (Ed.) *The United States and torture: Interrogation, incarceration, and abuse* (pp. 161–175). New York: New York University Press.

Faulconer, J., & Williams, R. (1985). Temporality in human action: An alternative to positivism and historicism. *American Psychologist, 40*, 1179–1188.

Flax, J. (1992). *Thinking fragments: Psychoanalysis, feminism, and postmodernism in the contemporary West*. Berkeley: University of California Press.

Flax, J. (1996a). Review essay. *Psychoanalytic Dialogues, 6*, 847–857.

Flax, J. (1996b). With no way home: Reply to Cushman. *Psychoanalytic Dialogues, 6*, 875–881.

Flexner, E. (1959). *Century of struggle*. Cambridge, MA: Harvard University Press.

Fonagy, P. (2013). There is room for even more doublethink: The perilous status of psychoanalytic research. *Psychoanalytic Dialogues, 23*, 116–122.

Foster, R.P. (1992). Psychoanalysis and the bilingual patient: Some observations on the influence of language choice on the transference. *Psychoanalytic Psychology, 9*, 61–76. [CrossRef].

Foucault, M. (1970). *The order of things: An archeology of the human sciences*. New York: Random House.

Foucault, M. (1979). *Discipline and punishment: The birth of the prison*. New York: Vintage/Random House.

Foucault, M. (1980a). *The history of sexuality. Volume 1: An introduction.* New York: Random House.

Foucault, M. (1980b). Truth and power. In C. Gordon (Ed.), *Power-knowledge: Selected interviews and other writings by Michel Foucault* (pp. 109–133). New York: Random House.

Foucault, M. (1985). *The history of sexuality, vol. 2: The uses of pleasure.* (R. Hurley, Trans.). New York: Random House.

Foucault, M. (1986). *The history of sexuality, vol. 3: The care of the self.* (R. Hurley, Trans.). New York: Random House.

Foucault, M. (1987). Technologies of the self. In L. Martin, H. Gutman, & P. Hutton (Eds.), *Technologies of the self: A seminar with Michel Foucault* (pp. 16–49). Amherst: University of Massachusetts Press.

Fowers, B.J. (2010). Instrumentalism and psychology: Beyond using and being used. *Theory & Psychology, 20,* 102–124.

Fowers, B.J. (2015). *The evolution of ethics: Human sociality and the emergence of ethical mindedness.* New York: Palgrave Macmillan.

Fowers, B.J., & Richardson, F.C. (1996). Why is multiculturalism good? *American Psychologist, 51,* 609–621.

Fox, R., & Lears, T. (Eds.). (1983). *The culture of consumption: Critical essays in American history, 1880–1980.* New York: Pantheon Books.

Freud, S. (1953). Three essays on the theory of sexuality. In J. Strachey (Ed. & Trans.), *The standard edition of the complete psychological works of Sigmund Freud* (Vol. 7, pp. 231–243). London: Hogarth Press. (Original work published 1905).

Freud, S. (1961). *Civilization and its discontents* (J. Strachey, Trans.). New York: Nonon. (Original work published 1930).

Frie, R. (1997). *Subjectivity and intersubjectivity in modern philosophy and psychoanalysis.* Lanham, MD: Rowman & Littlefield.

Frie, R. (2011). Culture and context: From individualism to situated experience. In R. Frie & W.J. Coburn (Eds.) *Persons in context: The challenge of individuality in theory and practice* (pp. 3–19). New York: Routledge.

Frie, R. (2014). What is cultural psychoanalysis? Psychoanalytic anthropology and the interpersonal tradition. *Contemporary Psychoanalysis, 50,* 371–394.

Friedman, B. (1988). *Day of reckoning The consequences of American economic policy under Reagan and after.* New York: Random House.

Fromm, E. (1955). *The sane society.* New York: Holt, Rinehart, & Winston.

Fromm, E. (1966). *You shall be as gods: a radical interpretation of the Old Testament and its tradition.* New York: Henry Holt.

Furumoto, L. (1988). The new history of psychology. In I.S. Cohen (Ed.) *The G. Stanley Hall Lecture Series* (pp. 9–16). Washington, D.C.: American Psychological Association.

Gadamer, H.-G. (1975). *Truth and method.* New York: Crossroads.

Gadamer, H.-G. (1979). The problem of historical consciousness. In P. Rabinow & W. Sullivan (Eds.), *Interpretive social science: A reader* (pp. 103–160). Berkeley: University of California Press.

Gadamer, H.-G. (1989). *Truth and method* (D. Marshall & J. Weinsheimer, Trans.). New York: Crossroads. (Original work published 1960).

Gadlin, H. & Rubin, S. (1979. Interactionism: A nonresolution of the person-situation controversy. In A.R. Buss (Ed.) *Psychology in social context,* (pp. 213–238). New York: Irvington.

Gaines, S.O. & Reed, E.S. (1996). Prejudice: From Allport to DuBois. *American Psychologist, 50,* 96–103.

Gantt, E.E. (1996). Social constructionism and the ethics of hedonism. *Journal of Theoretical and Philosophical Psychology, 16,* 125–140.

Garfield, S.L. (1992). Major issues in psychotherapy research. In D. Freedheim & H. Freudenberger (Eds.), *History of psychotherapy: A century of change* (pp. 335–359). Washington, DC: American Psychological Association.

Geertz, C. (1973). *The interpretation of cultures.* New York: Basic Books.

Geha, R.E. (1993a). Transferred fictions. *Psychoanalytic Dialogues, 3,* 209–243.

Geha, R.E. (1993a). On the "mere" fictions of psychoanalysis. Reply to Sass. *Psychoanalytic Dialogues, 3,* 255–266.

Gendlin, E. (1987). A philosophical critique of the concept of narcissism: The significance of the awareness movement. In D. Levin (Ed.), *Pathologies of the modern self: Postmodern studies on narcissism, schizophrenia. and depression* (pp. 251–304). New York: New York University Press.

Gerber, L. (1990). Integrating political-societal concerns in psychotherapy. *American Journal of Psychotherapy, 44,* 471–483.

Gerber, L. (1992). Intimate politics: Connectedness and the social-political self. *Psychotherapy: Theory/Research/Practice/Training, 29,* 626–630.

Gerber, L. (1996). The road not taken: A case study. *Psychohistory Review, 24,* 53–60.

Gerber, L. (in press). Hidden injuries: Stories of social class, politics, and the face of The Other. *Psychoanalysis, Self, and Context.*

Gergen, K. (1973). Social psychology as history. *Journal of Personality and Social Psychology, 26,* 309–320.

Gergen, K. (1985). The social constructionist movement in modern psychology. *American Psychologist, 40,* 266–275.

Gergen, K. (1988). If persons are texts. In S. Messer, L. Sass, & R. Woolfolk (Eds.), *Hermeneutics and psychological theory: Interpretive perspectives on personality, psychotherapy, and psychopathology* (pp. 28–51). New Brunswick, NJ: Rutgers University Press.

Gergen, K.J. (2009). *Relational being: Beyond self and community.* New York: Oxford University Press.

Gerson, S. (2009). When the third is dead: Memory, mourning, and witnessing in the aftermath of the Holocaust. *International Journal of Psychoanalysis, 90*, 1341–1357.

Gerson, S. (2012). When the third is dead: Memory, mourning, and witnessing in the aftermath of the holocaust. In L. Aron & A. Harris (Eds.) *Relational Psychoanalysis: Expansion of Theory* (pp. 347–366). New York: Routledge.

Ghent, E. (1989). Credo: The dialectics of one-person and two-person psychologies. *Contemporary Psychoanalysis, 25*, 169–211. [Taylor & Francis Online], [Web of Science ®].

Gilford, P. (1997, February). Managing a technical self. Paper presented at the 17th Annual Meeting of Division 39, Psychoanalysis, American Psychological Association, Denver, CO.

Gilford, P. (1999). The normalizing effects of managed care on psychotherapy. In K. Weigerber (Ed.) (pp. 199–216). *The traumatic bond between the psychotherapist and managed care.* Norvale, NJ: Jason Aronson.

Gilford, P. (2000). *The self in managed mental health care: A hermeneutic inquiry.* Doctoral dissertation, California School of Professional Psychology, Alameda, CA.

Gillespie, R. (1988). The Hawthorn experiments and the politics of experimentation. In J. Morawski (Ed.), *The rise of experimentation in American psychology* (pp. 114- 137). New Haven, CT: Yale University Press.

Gilman, S.L. (1993). *Freud, race, and gender.* Princeton, NJ: Princeton University Press.

Ginsberg, B. (1986). *The captive public: How mass opinion promotes state power.* New York: Basic Books.

Giorgi, A. (1970). *Psychology as a human science.* New York: Harper & Row.

Gitlin, T. (1995). *The twilight of common dreams: Why America is wracked by culture wars.* New York: Holt.

Goldner, V. (1991). Toward a critical relational theory of gender. *Psychoanalytic Dialogues, 1*, 249–272.

Goldman, E. (1960). *The crucial decade — and after: America, 1945–1960.* New York: Vintage Books.

Goodman, D. (2016). McDonaldization of psychotherapy: Processed foods, processed therapies, and economic class. *Theory and Psychology, 26*, 77–95.

Goodman, D., & Freeman, M. (Eds.). (2015). *Psychology and the other.* New York: Oxford University Press.

Goodman, M., Brown, J.A., & Deitz, P.M. (1996). *Managing managed care II: A handbook for mental health professionals* (2nd ed.). Washington, DC: American Psychiatric Press.

Goodman, D.M. & Severson, E.R. (Eds.) (2016). *The ethical turn: Otherness and subjectivity in contemporary psychoanalysis.* New York: Routledge.

Gould, R.L. (1996). The use of computers in therapy. In T. Trabin (Ed.), The computerization of behavioral healthcare (pp. 39–62). San Francisco: Jossey-Bass.

Gramsci, A. (1947). *Selections from the prison notebooks*, (Q. Howe & G.N. Smith, Trans.). New York: International Publishes.

Greenberg, J.R., & Mitchell, S.A. (1983). Object relations in psychoanalytic theory. Cambridge, MA: Harvard University Press.

Greenberg, K. (2005). *The torture debate in America*. Cambridge, UK: Cambridge University Press.

Greenblatt, S. (1980). *Renaissance self-fashioning*. Chicago: University of Chicago Press.

Greifinger, J. (1995). Therapeutic discourse as moral conversation: Psychoanalysis, modernity, and the ideal of authenticity. *Communication Review, 1*, 53–81.

Grogan, J. (2013). *Encountering America: Humanistic psychology, sixties culture, and the shaping of the modern self*. New York: HarperCollins.

Guignon, C.B. (1983). *Heidegger and the problem of knowledge*. Indianapolis, IN: Hackett.

Guignon, C.B. (1993). Authenticity, moral values, and psychotherapy. In C.B. Guignon (Ed.) *Cambridge Companion to Heidegger* (pp. 215–239). Cambridge, UK: Cambridge University Press.

Guignon, C. (2004). *On being authentic*. New York: Routledge.

Gump, J.P. (2000). A white therapist, an African American patient: Shame in the therapeutic dyad. Commentary on paper by Neil Altman. *Psychoanalytic Dialogues, 10*, 619–632. [Taylor & Francis Online], [Web of Science ®].

Gump, J.P. (2010). Reality matters: The shadow of trauma on African American subjectivity. *Psychoanalytic Psychology, 27*, 42–54. [CrossRef], [Web of Science ®].

Guralnik, O. (2011). Ede: Race, the law, and I. *Studies in Gender & Sexuality, 12*, 22–26. [Taylor & Francis Online].

Guralnik, O., & Simeon, D. (2010). Depersonalization: Standing in the spaces between recognition and interpellation. *Psychoanalytic Dialogues, 20*, 400–416. [Taylor & Francis Online], [Web of Science ®].

Guthrie, R.V. (1998). *Even the rat was white: A historical view of psychology*. Boston: Allyn and Bacon.

Haaken, J. (1998). *Pillar of salt: Gender, memory, and the perils of looking back*. New Brunswick, NJ: Rutgers University Press.

Haaken, J., & Adams, R. (1983). Pathology as "personal growth": A participant observation study of Lifespring training. *Psychiatry, 46*, 270–280.

Habermas, J. (1991). *The philosophical discourse of modernity*. Cambridge, MA: MIT Press.

Hahn, L.E. (Ed.) (1997). The *philosophy of Hans-Georg Gadamer*. Peru, IL: Open Court.

Hales, S. (1985). The inadvertent rediscovery of self in social psychology. *Journal for the Theory of Social Behaviour, 15*, 237–280.

Hales, S. (1986). Epilogue: Rethinking the business of psychology. *Journal for the Theory of Social Behavior, 16*, 57–76.

Harre, R. (1984). *Personal being: A theory for individual psychology*. Cambridge. MA: Harvard University Press.

Harre, R. (Ed.). (1986a). *The social construction of emotions*. Oxford: Basil Blackwell.

Harre, R. (1986b). Social sources of mental content and order. In J. Margolis, R Manicas, R. Harre, & P. Secord (Eds.), *Psychology: Designing the discipline*. Oxford, UK: Basil Blackwell.

Harris, A. (1991). Symposium on gender: Introduction, *Psychoanalytic Dialogues, 1*, 243–248.

Harris, A. (1998). Envy, aggression, and ambition, the circulating tensions in female psychic life. *Gender and Psychoanalysis, 2*, 289–325.

Harris, A. (2000a). Gender as soft assembly: Tomboy's stories. *Studies in Gender and Sexuality*, 1, 223–250. [Taylor & Francis Online].

Harris, A. (2000b). Haunted talk, healing action: Commentary on paper by Kimberlyn Leary. *Psychoanalytic Dialogues, 10*, 655–662.

Harris, A. & Botticelli, S. (2010). *First do no harm: The paradoxical encounters of psychoanalysis, warmaking, and resistance*. New York: Routledge.

Hagopian, P. (2013). *American immunity, war crimes, and the limits of International law*. Amherst, MA: University of Massachusetts Press.

Harris, B. (1979). Whatever happened to Little Albert? *American Psychologist, 34*, 151- 160.

Hartman, S. (2005). Class unconscious: From dialectical materialism to relational material. *Psychoanalysis, Culture, & Society, 10*, 121–137. [CrossRef].

Hartman, S. (2007). Class unconscious: From dialectical materialism to relational material. In M. Suchet, A. Harris, L. Aron (Eds.) *Relational Psychoanalysis: New Voices* (pp. 209–225).

Harvey, D. (1990). *The condition of postmodernity*. Oxford: Blackwell.

Heelas, P. & Lock, A. (1981). *Indigenous psychologies: The anthropology of the self*. New York: Academic Press.

Heidegger, M. (1962). *Being and time* (J. Macquarrie & E. Robinson, Trans.). New York: Crossroads. (Original work published 1927).

Heidegger, M. (1977). *The question concerning technology and other essays* (W. Lovitt, Trans.). New York: Harper & Row.

Heller, T.C., Sosna, M., & Wellbery, D.E. (Eds.) (1986). *Reconstructing individualism: autonomy, individuality, and the self in Western thought*. Stanford, CA: Stanford University Press.

Henry, J. (1963). *Culture against man.* New York: Random House.

Hertz, J.H. (1945). *Sayings of the fathers.* New York: Behrman House.

Hickinbottom-Brawn, S. (2013). Brand "you": The emergence of social anxiety disorder in the age of enterprise. *Theory & Psychology, 23,* 732–751.

Hiley, D.R., Bohman, J.G., & Shusterman, R. (Eds.) (1991). *The interpretive turn: Philosophy, science, culture.* Ithica, NY: Cornell University Press.

Hirsch, I. (1997). The widening of the concept of dissociation. *Journal of the American Academy of Psychoanalysis, 25,* 603–615. [PubMed].

Hochman, J. (1984). Iatrognic symptoms associated with a therapy cult: Examination of an extinct "new psychotherapy" with respect to psychiatric deterioration and "brainwashing." *Psychiatry. 47,* 366–377.

Hoffman, D.H., Carter, D.J., Lopez, C.R.V., Benzmiller, H.L., Guo, A.X., Latifi, S.Y., & Craig, D.C. (2015). Report to the Special Committee of the Board of Directors of the American Psychological Association: Independent review relating to APA Ethics Guidelines, national security interrogations, and torture. Chicago, IL, USA: Sidley Austin LLP. Retrieved from http://DoD.apa.org/independent-review/APA-FINAL-Report-7.2.15.pdf.

Hoffman, I.Z. (1983). The patient as the interpreter of the analyst's experience. *Contemporary Psychoanalysis, 19,* 389–422.

Hoffman, I.Z. (1998)). *Ritual and spontaneity in the psychoanalytic processes: A dialectical-constructivist view.* Hillsdale, NJ: The Analytic Press.

Hoffman, I.Z. (2009). Doublethinking our way to "scientific" legitimacy: The desiccation of human experience. *Journal of the American Psychoanalytic Association, 57,* 1043–1069.

Hoffman, I.Z. (2012). Response to Safran: The development of critical psychoanalytic sensibility, *Psychoanalytic Dialogues, 22,* 721–731.

Hoffman, I.Z. (2013a). Response to Fonagy. *Psychoanalytic Dialogues, 23,* 123–127.

Hoffman, I.Z. (2013b). Response to Strenger. *Psychoanalytic Dialogues, 23,* 225–229.

Hollander, N.C. (1997). *Love in a time of hate: Liberation psychology in Latin America.* New Brunswick, NJ: Rutgers University Press.

Holroyd, J., & Brodsky, A. (1977). Psychologists' attitudes and practices regarding erotic and nonerotic physical contact with patients. *American Psychologist, 32,* 843–849.

Horner, A. (1984). *Object relations and the developing ego in therapy.* New York: Jason Aronson.

Hoy, D.C. (1978). *The critical circle: Literature, history, and philosophical hermeneutics.* Berkeley & Los Angeles, CA: University of California Press.

Hoyt, M.F. (1995). *Brief therapy and managed care.* San Francisco: Jossey-Bass.

Huett, S.D., & Goodman, D.M. (2012). Levinas on managed care: The (a)proximal, faceless third-party and the psychotherapeutic dyad. *Journal of Theoretical & Philosophical Psychology, 32,* 86–102. [CrossRef].

Hughes, A.L. (2016). The folly of scientism. *The New Atlantis.* Retrieved from www.thenewatlantis.com/publications/article_detail.asp?id=684&css=print.

Hutchinson, T. (2011). *Monopolizing knowledge.* Belmont, MA: Fias.

Hutton, P. (1988). Foucault, Freud, and the technologies of the self. In L. Martin, H. Gutman, & P. Hutton (Eds.), *Technologies of the self: A seminar with Michel Foucault* (pp. 120–144). Amherst, MA: University of Massachusetts Press.

Idel, G. (1989). *Golem.* NY: SUNY Press.

Ignatiev, N. (1995). *How the Irish became White.* New York: Routledge.

Institute of Medicine. (1997). *Managing managed care: Quality improvement in behavioral health.* Washington, DC: National Academy Press.

Jay, M. (1986). In the empire of the gaze: Foucault and the denigration of vision in twentieth-century French thought. In D.C. Hoy (Ed.) *Foucault: A critical reader* (pp. 175–204). Oxford, UK: Basil Blackwell.

Jacobson, L. (1997). The soul of psychoanalysis in the modern world: Reflections on the work of Christopher Bollas. *Psychoanalytic Dialogues, 7*, 81–115.

Johnson, L.D. (1995). *Psychotherapy in the age of accountability.* New York: Norton.

Juvenal. (1918). Satires (G.G. Ramsay, Trans.) Bloomington: University of Indiana Press.

Karlin, M. (2012). The United States has been enabling torture for decades. *Truthout.* Retrieved from http://DoD.truth-out.org/opinion/item/7273:the-united-states-has-been-enabling-torture-for-decades

Kaslow, N.J., Rubin, N.J., Bebeau, M.J., Leigh, W., Lictenberg, J.W., Nelson, P.D., Portnoy, S.M., Rubin, N.J., & Smith, I.L. (2007). Guiding principles and recommendations for the assessment of competence. *Professional Psychology: Research and Practice, 38, 1441–451.*

Kates, R. (1990). Jews into Frenchmen: Nationality and representation in revolutionary France. In F. Feher (Ed.), *The French revolution and the birth of modernity.* Berkeley & Los Angeles: University of California Press.

Kirk, S.A., & Kutchins, H. (1992). *The selling of DSM: The rhetoric of science in psychiatry.* New York: Aldine de Gruyter.

Kernberg, O. (1975). *Borderline conditions and pathological narcissism.* New York: Aronson.

Kessen, W. (1979). The American child and other cultural inventions. *American Psychologist, 34.* 815–820.

Kisch, J. (1991). The need for psychopharmacological collaboration in managed mental health care. In C.S. Austad & W.H. Berman (Eds.), *Psychotherapy in managed health care: The optimal use of time and resources* (pp. 81–85). Washington, DC: American Psychological Association.

Kobrin, E (1978). The fall in household size and the rise of tbe primary individual in the United States. In M. Gordon (Ed.), *The American family in social-historical perspective* (pp. 69–81). New York: St. Martin's Press.

Kohut, H. (1971). *The analysis of the self.* New York: International Universities Press.

Kohut, H. (1977). *The restoration of the self.* New York: International Universities Press.

Kohut, H. (1984). *How does analysis cure?* Chicago: University of Chicago Press.

Kovel, J. (1970). *White racism: A psychohistory.* New York: Pantheon.

Kovel, J. (1980). The American mental health industry. In D. Inglesby (Ed.), *Critical psychiatry: The politics of mental health* (pp. 72–101). New York: Random House.

Kovel, J. (2000). Reflections on white racism. *Psychoanalytic Dialogues, 10*, 579–587.

Kritzman, L.D. (Ed.) (1988). *Michel Foucault: Politics, philosophy, culture.* New York: Routledge.

Kruglanski, A. (2015). The ticking time bomb: How effective is torture? *The National Interest: Foreign Policy Experts Roundtable.* Retrieved from Nationalinterest.org/featurestheticking-time-bomb-dilemma-how-effective-torture-11950.

Lambert, M.J., & Bergin, A.E. (1994). The effectiveness of psychotherapy. In A.E. Bergin & S.L. Garfield (Eds.), *Handbook of psychotherapy and behavior change* (4th ed., pp. 143–189). New York: Wiley.

Lanier, J. (2010). You are not a gadget. New York: Vintage Books.

Lasch, C. (1978). *The culture of narcissism: American life in an age of diminishing expectations.* New York: W.W. Norton.

Lasch, C. (1984). *The minimal self: Psychic survival in troubled times.* New York: Norton.

Layton, L. (1990). A deconstruction of Kohut's concept of the self. *Contemporary Psychoanalysis, 26*, 420–429. [Taylor & Francis Online], [Web of Science ®].

Layton, L. (1998). *Who's that girl? Who's that boy? Clinical practice meets postmodern gender theory.* New York: Routledge.

Layton, L. (2002). Cultural hierarchies, splitting, and the heterosexist unconscious. In S. Fairfield, L. Layton, & C. Stack (Eds.) *Bringing the plague: Toward a postmodern psychoanalysis,* (pp. 195–223). New York: Other Press.

Layton, L. (2004a). A fork in the royal road: On defining the unconscious and its stakes for social theory. *Psychoanalysis, Culture, & Society, 9*, 33–51.

Layton, L. (2004b). That place gives me the heebie-jeebies. *International Journal of Critical Psychology, 10*, 36–50.

Layton, L. (2005a). Commentary on roundtable: "Is politics the last taboo in psychoanalysis?" *Psychoanalytic Perspectives, 2*, 3–8. [Taylor & Francis Online].

Layton, L. (2005b). Notes toward a nonconformist clinical practice: Response to Philip Cushman's "Between arrogance and a dead-end: Psychoanalysis and the Heidegger-Foucault dilemma. *Contemporary Psychoanalysis, 41*, 419–429.

Layton, L. (2006). Racial identities, racial enactments, and normative unconscious processes. *Psychoanalytic Quarterly, LXXV*, 237–269.

Layton, L. (2008). Relational thinking: from culture to couch and couch to culture. In S. Clarke, H. Hahn, & P. Hoggett, (Eds.), *Object relations and social relations: The implications of the relational turn in psychoanalysis* (pp. 1–28). London: Studio Publishing Services.

Layton, L. (2009). Who's responsible? Our mutual implication in each other's suffering. *Psychoanalytic Dialogues, 19*, 105–120. [Taylor & Francis Online], [Web of Science ®].

Layton, L. (2010). Irrational exuberance: Neoliberal subjectivity and the perversion of truth. *Subjectivity, 3*, 303–322. [CrossRef].

Layton, L. (2013). Psychoanalysis and politics: Historicising subjectivity. *Mens Sana Monogr, 11*, 68–81. [CrossRef].

Layton, L. (2014). Grandiosity, neoliberalism, and neoconservativism. *Psychoanalytic Inquiry, 34*, 463–474.

Layton, L., Hollander, N.C., & Gutwill, S. (Eds.) (2006). *Psychoanalysis, class, & politics: Encounters in the clinical setting.* New York: Routledge.

Leahey, T.H. (1987). *A history of psychology: Main currents in psychological thought.* Englewood Clifts, New Jersey: Prentice Hall.

Lears, T.J. (1981). *No place of grace: Antimodernism and the transformation of American culture, 1880–1920.* New York: Pantheon.

Lears, T.J. (1983). From salvation to self-realization: Advertising and the therapeutic roots of the consumer culture, 1880–1930. In R. Fox & J. Lears (Eds.), *The culture of consumption: Critical essays in American history, 1880–1980* (pp. 3–38). New York: Pantheon Books.

Leary, K. (1995). Interpreting in the dark: Race and ethnicity in psychoanalytic psychotherapy. *Psychoanalytic Quarterly, 66*, 639–653.

Leary, K. (1997). Race, self-disclosure, and "forbidden talk": Race and ethnicity in contemporary clinical practice. *Psychoanalytic Quarterly, 66*, 163–189.

Leary, K. (2000). Racial enactment in dynamic treatment. *Psychoanalytic Dialogues, 10*, 639–653.

Leary, K. (2007). Racial insult and repair. *Psychoanalytic Dialogues, 17*, 539–549. [Taylor & Francis Online], [Web of Science ®].

Leary, K. (2012). Race as an adaptive challenge: Working with diversity in the clinical consulting room. *Psychoanalytic Psychology, 29*, 279–291. [CrossRef], [Web of Science ®].

Lesser, R.C. & Schoenberg, E. (Eds.) (1999). *The obscure object of desire: Freud's female homosexual revisited.* New York: Routledge.

Levenson, E.A. (1972). *The fallacy of understanding and the ambiguity of change.* Hillsdale, NJ: Analytic Press.

Levenson, E.A. (1983). *The ambiguity of change: An inquiry into the nature of psychoanalytic reality.* New York: Basic Books.

Levenson, E.A. (1991a). Standoffs, impasses and stalemates. *Contemporary Psychoanalysis, 27*, 511–517. [Taylor & Francis Online], [Web of Science ®].

Levenson, E.A. (1991b). Whatever happened to the cat? In The purloined self: *Interpersonal perspectives in psychoanalysis* (pp. 225–237). New York: William Alanson White Institute.

Levenson, E.A. (2006). Fifty years of evolving interpersonal psychoanalysis. *Contemporary Psychoanalysis, 42*(4), 557–564. [Taylor & Francis Online], [Web of Science ®].

Levin, D. (1987a). Clinical stories: A modem self in the fury of being. In D. Levin (Ed.), *Pathologies of the modern self: Postmodern studies on narcissism, schizophrenia, and depression* (pp. 479–537). New York: New York University Press.

Levin, D. (Ed.). (1987b). *Pathologies of the modern self: Postmodern studies on narcissism, schizophrenia, and depression.* New York: New York University Press.

Levin, D. (1987c). Psychopathology in the epoch of nihilism. In D. Levin (Ed.), *Pathologies of the modern self: Postmodern studies on narcissism, schizophrenia, and depression* (pp. 21–83). New York: New York University Press.

Levinas, E. (1987). *Time and the other* (R. Cohen, Trans.). Pittsburgh, PA: Duquesne University Press.

Lewin, M. (1984). *In the shadow of the past: Psychology portrays the sexes.* New York: Columbia University Press.

Leyerle, B. (1994). *The private regulation of American health care.* Armonk, NY: Sharpe.

Lifton, R. (1968). Protean man. *Partisan Review, 35*, 13–27.

Lobban, G. (2011a). Glenys: White or not. In M. Dimen (Ed.), *With culture in mind: Psychoanalytic stories* (pp. 81–86). New York: Routledge.

Lobban, G. (2011b). Li-an: Wounded by war. In M. Dimen (Ed.), *With culture in mind: Psychoanalytic stories* (pp. 25–30). New York: Routledge. [Taylor & Francis Online].

Lobban, G. (2011c). Martha: Resignification road. In M. Dimen (Ed.), *With culture in mind: Psychoanalytic stories* (pp. 155–161). New York: Routledge.

Lobban, G. (2012). Troubling whiteness: Commentary on Harris's "The house of difference." *Studies in Gender & Sexuality, 13*, 224–230. [Taylor & Francis Online].

Logan, R. (1987). Historical change in prevailing sense of self. In K. Yardley & T. Honess (Eds.), *Self and identity: Psychosocial perspectives* (pp. 13–26). Chichester, UK: Wiley.

Lord, S.P. (2014). *Ways of being in trauma-based society: Discovering the politics and moral culture of the trauma industry through hermeneutic interpretation of evidence-supported PTSD treatment manuals.* (Unpublished doctoral dissertation). Antioch University Seattle.

Loring, M., & Powell, B. (1988). Gender, race. and DSM-III: A study of the objectivity of psychiatric diagnostic behavior. *Journal of Health and Social Behavior, 29*, 1- 22.

Lourie, I., Howe, S., & Roebuck, L. (1996). Lessons learned from two behavioral managed care approaches with special implications for children, adolescents, and their families. In R.W. Manderscheid & M.A. Sonnenschein (Eds.), *Mental health, United States, 1996* (DHHS Publication No. SMA 96–3098, 7th ed., pp. 27–44). Washington, DC: U.S. Government Printing Office.

Lowe, D. (1982). *History of bourgeois perception.* Chicago: University of Chicago Press.

Lowe, D. (1988). *Capitalism and the body.* Unpublished manuscript.

Luban, D. (2014). *Torture, power, and law.* Cambridge, England: Cambridge University Press.

Ludlam, J.G. (2007). *The double-edged sword of posttraumatic stress disorder: A historical analysis of trauma diagnoses.* (Unpublished doctoral dissertation). California School of Professional Psychology.

Lyotard, J.F. (1984). *The postmodern condition.* Trans. Bennington and Massumi. Minneapolis, MN: University of Minnesota Press.

MacIntyre, A. (1995). How psychology makes itself true — or false. In S. Koch & D.E. Leary (Eds.), *A century of psychology as science* (pp. 897–903). Washington, DC: American Psychological Association.

Macey, D. (1993). *The lives of Michel Foucault: A biography.* New York: Pantheon.

Magellan Health, Business Wire Press Release (2014). Magellan Health to offer expanded computerized cognitive behavioral therapy services. Retrieved July 27, 2014.

Malabre, A. (1987). *Beyond our means: How reckless borrowing now threatens to overwhelm us.* New York: Vintage Books.

Marchand, R. (1985). *Advertising the American dream: Making way for modernity, 1920–1940.* Berkeley: University of California Press.

Marcus, J.R. (1983). *The Jew in the medieval world: A source book, 315–1791.* New York: Atheneum.

Marecek, J. & Gillham, J. (2006). Is three a crowd? Clients, clinicians, and managed care. *American Journal of Orthopsychiatry, 76*, 251–259.

Margolis, M.I. & Marx, A. (1973). *A history of the Jewish people.* New York: Atheneum.

Marin, P. (1979, February). Spiritual obedience. *Harper's Magazine*, (pp. 43–88).

Marin, P. (1981*).* Living with moral pain. *Psychology Today, 15*, 68–80.

Martin, J. & Sugarman, J. (1999). *The psychology of human possibility and constraint.* Albany, NY: State University of New York Press.

Maroda, K.J. (1999). *Seduction, surrender, and transformation: Emotional engagement in the analytic process.* Hillsdale, NJ: Analytic Press.

McAvoy, J. (2014). Psy disciplines. In T. Teo (Ed.) *Encyclopedia of critical psychology* (pp. 1527–1529). New York: Springer.

Masterson, J.E (1981). *The narcissistic and borderline disorders: An integrated developmental approach.* New York: Bruner/Mazel.

Mayer, J. (2008). *The dark side: The inside story of how the war on terror turned into a war on American ideals.* New York: Doubleday.

Mayer, J. (2011). Outsourcing torture: The secret history of America's 'Extraordinary Rendition' program. In M. Cohen (Ed.), *The United States and torture: Interrogation, incarceration, and abuse* (pp. 137–160). New York: New York University Press.

Mayo, E. (1933). *The human problems of an industrial civilization.* New York: Macmillan.

McCoy, A.W. (2011). Mind maze: The CIA's pursuit of psychological torture. In M. Cohen (Ed.) *The United States and torture: Interrogation, incarceration, and abuse* (pp. 161–175). New York: New York University Press.

Mednick, M.T. (1989). On the politics of psychological constructs: Stop the bandwagon, I want to get off. *American Psychologist, 44,* 1118–1123.

Messer, S., Sass, L., & Woolfolk, R. (Eds.). (1988). *Herrneneutics and psychological theory: Interpretive perspectives on personality, psychotherapy, and psychopathology.* New Brunswick, NJ: Rutgers University Press.

Messer, S.B. & Woolfolk, R.L. (1998). Philosophical issues in psychotherapy. *Clinical Psychology: Science and Practice, 5,* 251–263.

Meyer, D. (1980). *Positive thinkers: Religion as pop psychology from Mary Baker Eddy to Oral Roberts* (2nd ed.). New York: Pantheon Books.

Meyer, J. (1986). Myths of socialization and of personality. In T. Heller, M. Sosna, & D. Wellbery (Eds.), *Reconstructing individualism: Autonomy, individuality, and the self in Western thought* (pp. 208–221). Stanford CA: Stanford University Press.

Miller, A. (1981). *Prisoners of childhood: How narcissistic parents form and deform the emotional lives of their gifted children.* New York: Basic Books.

Miller, I.J. (1994). *What managed care is doing to outpatient mental health: A look behind the veil of secrecy.* Boulder. CO: Boulder Psychotherapists' Press.

Miller, I.J. (1996). Managed care is harmful to outpatient mental health services: A call for accountability. *Professional Psychology: Research and Practice, 22.* 26–35.

Mitchell, S.A. (1988). *Relational concepts in psychoanalysis: An integration.* Cambridge, MA: Harvard University Press.

Modleski, I. (1986). *Studies in entertainment: Critical approaches to mass culture.* Indianapolis: Indiana University Press.

Morawski, J. (1984). Historiography as a metatheoretical text for social psychology. In K. Gergen & M. Gergen (Eds.), *Historical social psychology* (pp. 37–60). Hillsdale, NJ: Erlbaum.

Morawski, J. (1988). Impossible experiments and practical constructions: The social basis of psychologists' work. In J. Morawski (Ed.), *The rise of experimentation in American psychology* (pp. 37–60). New Haven, CT: Yale University Press.

Morris, C. (1972). *The discovery of the individual, 1050–1200.* London: Camelot Press.

Moyers, B., & Winship, M. (2013, October 27). *The lies that will kill America.* Retrieved from www.truth-out.org/opinion/item/19645-the-lies-that-will-kill-america.

Nussbaum, M.C. (2013). *Political emotions: Why love matters for justice.* Cambridge, MA: Harvard University Press.

Ofshe, R., & Singer, M. (1986). Attacks on peripheral versus central elements of self and the impact of thought reforming techniques. *Celtic Studies Journal, 3,* 3–24.

Ogden, T.H. (1986). *The matrix of the mind: Object relations and the psychoanalytic dialogue.* Northvale, NJ: Jason Aronson.

Ogden, T.H. (1994). *Subjects of analysis.* Northvale, NJ: Jason Aronson.

Olson, A.M. (1994). *Heidegger and Jaspers.* Philadelphia, PA: Temple University Press.

Olson, B., Soldz, S., & Davis, M. (2008). The ethics of interrogation and the American Psychological Association: A critique of policy and process. Retrieved from www.ncbi.nlm.nih.gov/pmc/articles/PMC2248202/.

Orange, D. (2009). Toward the art of the living dialogue: Between constructivism and hermeneutics in psychoanalytic thinking. In D. Orange & R. Frie (Eds.), *Beyond postmodernism: new dimensions in clinical theory and practice* (pp. 117–142). New York: Routledge.

Orange, D., & Frie, R. (Eds.) (2009). *Beyond postmodernism: New dimensions in clinical theory and practice.* New York: Routledge.

Orange, D. (2010). *Thinking for clinicians: Philosophical resources for contemporary psychoanalysis and the humanistic psychotherapies.* New York: Routledge.

Orange, D.M. (2011). *The suffering stranger: Hermeneutics for everyday clinical practice.* New York: Routledge.

Orange, D. (2016). *Climate crisis, psychoanalysis, and radical ethics.* New York: Routledge.

Orbach, S. (2006). *Fat as a feminist issue.* London: Random House.

Orbach, S. (2008). Democratizing psychoanalysis. In S. Clarke, H. Hahn, & P. Hoggett (Eds.), *Object relations and social relations: The implications of the relational turn in psychoanalysis* (pp. 25–43). London: Studio Publishing Services.

Orlinsky, D.E., & Howard, K.I. (1986). Process and outcome in psychotherapy. In S. L, Garfield & A.E. Bergin (Eds.), *Handbook of psychotherapy and behavior change* (3rd ed., pp. 311–381). New York: Wiley.

Pape, K.M. (2014). *Mothering and the functional self: A hermeneutic exploration of texts on perinatal mood and anxiety disorders.* (Unpublished doctoral dissertation). Antioch University Seattle.

PDM Task Force (2006). *Psychodynamic Diagnostic Manual.* Silver Spring, MD: Alliance of Psychoanalytic Organizations.

Peltz, R. (2005). The manic society. *Psychoanalytic Dialogues, 15,* 409–414.

Persons, J.B., & Silberschatz, G. (1998). Are results of randomized controlled trials useful to psychotherapists? *Journal of Consulting and Clinical Psychology, 66,* 126–135.

Pigott, H.E. (1997). Computer decision-support as a clinician's tool. In R. Schreter, S. Sharfstein, & C. Schreter (Eds.), *Managing care, not dollars: The continuum of mental health services* (pp. 245–263). Washington DC: American Psychiatric Press.

Pope, K.S. (2011). Psychologists and detainee interrogations: Key decisions, opportunities lost, and lessons learned. *Annual Review of Clinical Psychology, 7,* 459–481. Retrieved from www.anualreviews.org/doi/abs/10.1146/annurev-clinpsy-032210-104612.

Portuges, S. (2009). The politics of psychoanalytic neutrality. *International Journal of Applied Psychoanalytic Studies, 6,* 61–73. [CrossRef].

Priest, D. (1996). U.S. instructed Latins on executions, torture: Manuals used 1982- 1991, Pentagon reveals. *Washington Post,* Sept. 21, 1996.

Priest, D. & Smith, R.J. (2004). Memo offered justification for use of torture, *Washington Post,* June 8, 2004, p. A01.

Prilleltensky, 1. (1989). Psychology and the status quo. *American Psychologist, 44,* 795–802.

PsychCoalition (2016). Retrieved from http://psychcoalition.org/index.html on June 26, 2016.

Quigley, B. (2011). Torture and human rights abuses at the School of Americas-WHINSEC. In M. Cohen (Ed.) *The United States and torture: Interrogation, incarceration, and abuse* (pp. 161–175). New York: New York University Press.

Rabinow, P. & Sullivan, W.M. (Eds.) (1979). *Interpretive social science: A reader.* Berkeley, CA. University of California.

Rabinow, P., & Sullivan, W. (1987). The interpretive turn. In P. Rabinow & W. Sullivan (Eds.), *Interpretive social science: A second look* (pp. 1–30). Berkeley, CA: University of California Press.

Racker, H. (1988). Transference and countertransference. In D. Tuckett (Ed.), *The International Psycho-Analytic Library* (Vol. 73, pp. 1–196). London: Hogarth Press & the Institute of Psycho-Analysis.

Ricoeur, P. (1979). Psychoanalysis and the movement of contemporary culture. In P. Rabinow & W.M. Sullivan (Eds.) *Interpretive Social Science* (pp. 301–339). Berkeley, CA: University of California Press.

Richardson, F.C., & Fowers, B.J. (1998). Interpretive social science: An overview. *American Behavioral Scientist, 41*, 465–495.

Richardson, F.C., Fowers, B.J., & Guignon, C. (1999). *Re-envisioning psychology: Moral dimensions of theory and practice.* San Francisco, CA: Jossey-Bass.

Richardson, F.C., Rogers, A. & McCarroll, J. (1998). Toward a dialogical self. *American Behavioral Scientist, 41*, 196–215.

Richardson, L.M., & Austad, C.S. (1991). Realities of mental health practice in managed-care settings. *Professional Psychology: Research and Practice, 22*, 52–59.

Riebel, L. (1979). Falsifiability, self-sealing doctrines, and humanistic psychology. *Humanistic Psychology Institute Review, 2*, 41–59.

Rieff, P. (1966). *The triumph of the therapeutic: Uses of faith after Freud.* Chicago: University of Chicago Press.

Riesman, D., Glazer, N., & Denny, R. (1953). *The lonely crowd: A study of the changing American character.* Garden City, NY: Doubleday.

Risser, J. (1997). *Hermeneutics and the voice of the other: Re-reading Gadamer's philosophical hermeneutics.* Albany, NY: State University of New York Press.

Ritzer, G. (1993). *The McDonaldization of society.* Thousand Oaks, CA: Pine Forge Press.

Rockmore, T. (1997). *On Heidegger's narcissism and philosophy.* Berkeley & Los Angeles: University of California Press.

Rose, N. (1985). *The psychological complex: Psychology, politics, & society in England, 1869–1939.* London: Routledge.

Rose, N. (1989). *Governing the soul: The shaping of the private self.* London: Free Association Press.

Rose, N. (1990). *Governing the soul: The shaping of the private self.* London: Routledge.

Rose, N. (2007). *The politics of life itself: Biomedicine, power, and subjectivity in the 21st century.* Princeton, NJ: Princeton University Press. [CrossRef].

Rozmarin, E. (2007). An other in psychoanalysis: Emmanuel Levinas's critique of knowledge and analytic sense. *Contemporary Psychoanalysis, 43*, 327–360. [Taylor & Francis Online], [Web of Science ®].

Rozmarin, E. (2011). To be is to betray: On the place of collective history and freedom in psychoanalysis. *Psychoanalytic Dialogues, 21*, 320–345. [Taylor & Francis Online], [Web of Science ®].

Rudavsky, D. (1967). *Emancipation and adjustment.* New York: Behrman House.
Ryan, W. (1971). *Blaming the victim.* New York: Vintage.
Ryder, M. (2005). "Scientism." *Encyclopedia of science, technology, and ethics, 3rd edition.* Detroit: MacMillian.
Sachar, A.L. (1979). *A history of the Jews.* New York: Knopf.
Safran, J.D. (2012). Doublethinking or dialectical thinking: A critical appreciation of Hoffman's doublethinking critique. *Psychoanalytic Dialogues, 22,* 710–720.
Safran, J.D., & Segal, Z.V. (1990). *Interpersonal process in cognitive therapy.* New York: Basic Books.
Salinger, J.D. (1962). *Nine Stories.* New York: Signet.
Samelson, F. (1974). History, origin myth and ideology: Comte's "discovery" of social psychology. *Journal for the Theory of Social Behaviour, 4,* 217–231.
Samelson, F. (1979). Putting psychology on the map: Ideology and intelligence testing. In A.R. Buss (Ed.), *Psychology in social context* (pp. 103–168). New York: Irvington.
Sampson, E.E. (1977). Psychology and the American ideal. *Journal of Personality and Social Psychology, 32,* 309–320.
Sampson, E.E. (1981). Cognitive psychology as ideology. *American Psychologist, 36,* 730–743.
Sampson, E.E. (1983). *Justice and the critique of pure psychology.* New York: Plenum.
Sampson, E.E. (1985). The decentralization of identity: Towards a revised concept of personal and social order. *American Psychologist, 40,* 1203–1211.
Sampson, E.E. (1988). The debate on individualism: Indigenous psychologies of the individual and their role in personal and societal functioning. *American Psychologist, 43,* 15–22.
Sampson, E.E. (1993). *Celebrating the other: A dialogic account of human nature.* Boulder, CO: Westview Press.
Samuels, A. (1993). *The political psyche.* New York: Routledge.
Samuels, A. (2001). *Politics on the couch.* London: Profile Books.
Sandel, M.J. (1984). The procedural republic and the unencumbered self. *Political Theory, 12,* 81–95.
Sandel, M.J. (1996). *Democracy's discontent: America in search of a public philosophy.* Cambridge, MA: Belknap/Harvard.
Sarason, S. (1981). An asocial psychology and a misdirected clinical psychotherapy. *American Psychologist, 36,* 827–836.
Sass, L. (1987). Schreber's panopticism: Psychosis and the modern soul. *Social Research, 54,* 101–145.
Sass, L. (1988a). Humanism, hermeneutics, and the concept of the human subject. In S. Messer, L. Sass, & R. Woolfolk (Eds.), *Hermeneutics and*

psychological theory: Interpretive perspectives on personality, psychotherapy, and psychopathology (pp. 222–271). New Brunswick, NJ: Rutgers University Press.

Sass, L. (1988b). The self and its vicissitudes: An archeological study of the psychoanalytic avant-garde. *Social Research, 55*, 551–607.

Sass, L.A. (1993). Psychoanalysis as "conversation" and as "fiction": Commentary on Charles Spezzano's "Relational model of inquiry and truth" and Richard Geha's "Transferred fictions." *Psychoanalytic Dialogues, 3*, 245–253.

Sass, L.A. (1995a). Review essay: Psychoanalysis and the postmodern impulse by Barnaby Barrett. *Psychoanalytic Dialogues, 5*, 123–136.

Sass, L.A. (1995b). Reply to Barnaby Barratt. *Psychoanalytic Dialogues, 5*, 145–149.

Scheibe, K. (1988). Metamorphoses in the psychologist's advantage. In J. Morawski (Ed.), *The rise of experimentalism in American psychology* (pp. 53–71). New Haven, CT: Yale University Press.

Scheibler, I. (2000). *Gadamer: Between Heidegger and Habermas.* Lanham, MD: Rowman & Littlefield.

Schiebinger, L. (1987). Skeletons in the closet: The first illustrations of the female skeleton in eighteenth century anatomy. In C. Gallagher & T. Laqueur (Eds.), The making of the modern body: Sexuality and society in the nineteenth century (pp. 42–82). Berkeley, CA: University of California Press.

Schneider, K.J. (1998). Toward a science of the heart: Romanticism and the revival of psychology. *American Psychologist, 53*, 277–289.

Scholem, G. (1965). On the Kabballah and its symbolism. New York: Schoken.

Scholom, A. (2013, Spring). Challenging the system: American fantasies and resistance to real reform in American Association for Psychoanalysis. Clinical Social Work Newsletter, pp. 4–9, 18–25.

Scull, A. (1993). *The most solitary of afflictions: Madness and society in Britain, 1700- 1900.* New Haven, CT: Yale University Press.

Seligman, M.E. (1972). Learned helplessness. *Annual Review of Medicine, 23*, 407- 412.

Seligman, M.E.P., Walker, E.F., & Rosenhans, D.L. (Eds.) (2001). *Abnormal psychology* (4th edition). New York: W.W. Norton.

Seligman, S. (2003). The developmental perspective in relational psychoanalysis. *Contemporary Psychoanalysis, 39*, 477–508. [Taylor & Francis Online], [Web of Science ®].

Seligman, S. (2005). Dynamic systems theories as a metaframework for psychoanalysis. *Psychoanalytic Dialogues, 15*, 285–319. [Taylor & Francis Online], [Web of Science ®].

Sennett, R. (1988). *The fall of public man*. New York: Random House.

Sennett, R. & Cobb, J. (1993). *The hidden injuries of class*. New York: Norton.

Severson, E.R., & Goodman, D.M. (Eds.) (2017). *Memories and monsters: Psychology, trauma, & narrative*. New York: Routledge.

Sheehy, M. (2013). Anonymous: Floaters. In M. Dimen (Ed.), *With culture in mind: Psychoanalytic Stories (pp. 99–105)*. New York: Routledge.

Singer, M. (1979, January). Coming out of the cults. *Psychology Today*, pp. 72, 75–76, 79–80. 82.

Singer, M. (1981, November). A brief history of therapeutic common sense. Paper presented at the workshop, The Active Therapist, University of California Extension, Berkeley, CA.

Slife, B.D., & Williams, R.N. (1995). *What's behind the research? Discovering hidden assumptions in the behavioral sciences*. Thousand Oaks, CA: Sage.

Slife, B.D., Williams, R.N., & Barlow, S.H. (Eds.). (2001). *Critical thinking about psychotherapy: Translating new ideas into practice*. Thousand Oaks, CA: Sage.

Sluga, H. (1993). *Heidegger's crisis: Philosophy and politics in Nazi Germany*. Cambridge, MA: Harvard University Press.

Smedslund, J. (1985). Necessarily true cultural psychologies. In K. Gergen & K. Davis (Eds.), *The social construction of the person* (pp. 73–87). New York: Springer-Verlag.

Smith-Rosenberg, C. (1981). The use and abuse of illness in the James family circle: A view of neurasthenia as a social phenomenon. In R. Brugger (Ed.), *Our selves/our past: Psychological approaches to American history* (pp. 205–227). Baltimore, MD: Johns Hopkins University Press.

Soldz, S. (2006). Psychologists, Guantanamo, and torture: A profession struggles to save its soul. Retrieved Aug. 20, 2006, from http://DoD. Dissidentvoice.org.

Soldz, S. (2011). Psychologists, torture, and civil society: Complicity, institutional failure, and the struggle for professional transformation. In M. Cohen (Ed.), *The United States and torture* (pp. 177–202). New York: New York University Press.

Soldz, S., Arrigo, J.M., & Olson, B. (2016). The ethics of operational psychology workshop: Report on process, findings, and ethical conundrums, September 15–17, 2015. Coalition For an Ethical Psychology, Working Paper Number 2, July, 2016.

Sorell, T. (1991). *Scientism: Philosophy and the infatuation with science*. New York: Routledge.

Spezzano, C. (1993a). A relational model of inquiry and truth: The place of psychoanalysis in the human conversation. *Psychoanalytic Dialogues, 3*, 177–208.

Spezzano, C. (1993b). Illusions of candor: Reply to Sass. *Psychoanalytic Dialogues, 3, 267–278*.

Stancombe, J., & White, S. (1998). Psychotherapy without foundations? Hermeneutics, discourse, and the end of certainty. *Theory & Psychology, 8*. 579–599.

Stern, D. (1996). *Midrash and theory*. Evanston, IL: Northwestern University Press.

Stern, D.B. (1983). Unformulated experience: From familiar chaos to creative disorder. *Contemporary Psychoanalysis, 19*, 71–99. [Taylor & Francis Online], [Web of Science ®].

Stern, D.B. (1989). The analyst's unformulated experience of the patient. *Contemporary Psychoanalysis, 25*, 1–33. [Taylor & Francis Online], [Web of Science ®].

Stern, D.B. (1990). Courting surprise: Unbidden perceptions in clinical practice. *Contemporary Psychoanalysis, 26*, 452–478. [Taylor & Francis Online], [Web of Science ®].

Stern, D.B. (1991). A philosophy for the embedded analyst: Gadamer's hermeneutics and the social paradigm of psychoanalysis. *Contemporary Psychoanalysis, 27*, 51–80.

Stern, D.B. (1997). *Unformulated experience: From dissociation to imagination in psychoanalysis*. Hillsdale, NJ: The Analytic Press.

Stern, D.B. (2002). What you know first: Construction and deconstruction in relational psychoanalysis. In S. Fairfield, L. Layton, & C. Stack (Eds.) *Bringing the plague,: Toward a postmodern psychoanalysis* (pp. 167–194). New York: Other Press.

Stern, D.B. (2010). *Partners in thought*. New York: Routledge.

Stern, D.B. (2012). Implicit theories of technique and the values that inspire them. *Psychoanalytic Inquiry, 32*, 33–49. [Taylor & Francis Online], [Web of Science ®].

Stern, D.B. (2013). Psychotherapy is an emergent process: In favor of acknowledging hermeneutics and against the privileging of systematic empirical research. *Psychoanalytic Dialogues, 23*, 102–115. [Taylor & Francis Online], [Web of Science ®].

Stern, D.N. (1985). *The interpersonal world of the infant: A view from psychoanalysis and developmental psychology*. New York Basic Books.

Stigliano, A. (1989). Hermeneutical practice. *Saybrook Review, 7*, 47–70.

Stiles, W.B., & Shapiro, D.A. (1989). Abuse of the drug metaphor in psychotherapy process-outcome research. *Clinical Psychology Review, 9*. 521–543.

Stolorow, R.D. (2007). *Trauma and human existence: Autobiographical, psychoanalytic, and philosophical reflections*. New York: Routledge.

Stolorow, R.D., Atwood, G.E., & Orange, D.M. (2002). *Worlds of experience: Interweaving philosophical and clinical dimensions in psychoanalysis*. New York: Basic Books.

Strenger, C. (2013). Why psychoanalysis must not discard science and human nature. *Psychoanalytic Dialogues, 23*, 197–210.

Strozier, C. (1978). Heinz Kohut and the historical imagination. *Psychohistory Review, 7*, 36–39.

Strupp, H.H. (1996). The tripartite model and the Consumer Reports study. *American Psychologist, 51*, 1017–1024.

Strupp, H.H., & Howard, K.I. (1992). A brief history of psychotherapy research. In D.K. Freedheim, H.J. Freudenberger, J.W. Kessler, S.B. Messer, D.R. Peterson, H.H. Strupp, & P.L. Wachtel (Eds.), *History of psychotherapy: A century of change* (pp. 309–334). Washington DC: American Psychological Association.

Suchet, M. (2004). A relational encounter with race. *Psychoanalytic Dialogues, 14*, 423–438. [Taylor & Francis Online], [Web of Science ®].

Suchet, M. (2007). Unraveling whiteness. *Psychoanalytic Dialogues, 17*, 867–886. [Taylor & Francis Online], [Web of Science ®].

Suchet, M. (2010). Searching for the ethical: Reply to commentaries. *Psychoanalytic Dialogues, 20*, 191–195. [Taylor & Francis Online], [Web of Science ®].

Sue, D.W., & Sue, D. (1999). *Counseling the culturally different: Theory and practice* (3rd ed.). New York: Wiley.

Sugarman, J. (2015). Neoliberalism and psychological ethics. *Journal of Theoretical and Philosophical Psychology, 23*, 102–115.

Sullivan, H.S. (1946). The illusion of personal individuality. In H.S. Perry (Ed.), *The fusion of psychiatry and social science* (pp. 198–226). New York: Norton.

Sullivan, H.S. (1964). *The collected works of Harry Stack Sullivan, M.D.* New York: Norton.

Susman, W.I. (1973/1984). *Culture as history: The transformation of American society in the twentieth century.* New York: Pantheon.

Taylor, C. (1985a). *Human agency and language: Philosophical papers 1.* New York: Cambridge University Press.

Taylor, C. (1985b). Interpretation and the sciences of man. In *Philosophy and the human sciences* (pp. 15–57). Cambridge, UK: Cambridge University Press.

Taylor, C. (1985c). *Philosophy and the human sciences: Philosophical papers 2.* Cambridge, UK: Cambridge University Press.

Taylor, C. (1986). Foucault on freedom and truth. In D.C. Hoy (Ed.), *Foucault: A critical reader* (pp. 69–102). Oxford, UK: Basil Blackwell.

Taylor, C. (1988). The moral topography of the self. In S.B. Messer, L.A. Sass, & R.L. Woolfolk (Eds.), *Hermeneutics and psychological theory: Interpretive perspectives on personality, psychotherapy, and psychpathology* (pp. 298–320). New Brunswick, NJ: Rutgers University Press.

Taylor, C. (1989). *Sources of the self: The making of the modern identity.* Cambridge, MA: Harvard University Press.

Taylor, C. (1991). *The ethics of authenticity.* Cambridge, MA: Harvard University Press.

Temerlin, M., & Temerlin, J. (1982). Psychotherapy cults: An iatrogenic perversion. *Psychotherapy: Therapy, Research, and Practice, 19*, 131–141.

Thandeka (1999). The cost of whiteness. *Tikkun, 14*, 33–38.

The song of Roland (W. Merwin, Trans.). (1963). In *Medieval epics* (pp. 86–203). New York: Random House.

Tolleson, J. (2009). Saving the world one patient at a time: Psychoanalysis and social critique. *Psychotherapeutic Politics International, 7*, 190–205.

Tompkins, M.A. (1997). Case formulation in cognitive-behavioral therapy. In R.L. Leahy (Ed.), *Practicing cognitive therapy: A guide to interventions* (pp. 37–59). Northvale, NJ: Jason Aronson.

Trigg, R. (1985). *Understanding social science: A philosophical introduction to the social sciences*. New York: Basil Blackwell.

Trilling, L. (1971). *Sincerity and authenticity*. Cambridge, MA: Harvard University Press.

Tuckfelt, S., Fink, J., & Warren, M.P. (1997). *The psychotherapists' guide to managed care in the 21st century: Surviving Big Brother and providing quality mental health services*. Northvale, NJ: Jason Aronson.

Turkle, S. (2011). *Alone together: Why we expect more from technology and less from each other*. New York: Basic Books.

Vallenstein, E.S. (1998). *Blaming the brain: The truth about drugs and mental health*. New York: Free Press.

Van den Berg, J. (1961). *The changing nature of man: Introduction to a historical psychology* New York: W.W. Norton.

Vonnegut, Jr., K. (1965). *God bless you, Mr. Rosewater*. New York: Dell.

Walls, G.B. (1994, November). Biological determinism, managed care and the new political right. Paper presented at the Annual Meeting of the Illinois Psychological Association, Chicago, IL.

Walls, G.B. (1999). The curious discrediting of psychoanalytic outcome research. *Psychologist/Psychoanalyst, 19*, 6–9.

Walls, G.B. (2004). Toward a critical global psychoanalysis. *Psychoanalytic Dialogues, 14*, 605–634.

Walls, G. (2006). The normative unconscious and the political contexts of change in psychotherapy. In L. Layton, N.C. Hollander, & S. Gutwill (Eds.), *Psychoanalysis, class, & politics: Encounters in the clinical setting* (pp. 118–128). New York: Routledge.

Walls, G. (2007, April). Diagnosis, epistemology, and politics: The PDM paradigm. Presented at the American Psychological Association Division 39 (Psychoanalysis) Spring Meeting, Toronto, Canada.

Walls, G. (2012). Is systematic quantitative research scientifically rigorous? Methodological and statistical considerations. *Journal of the American Psychoanalytic Association, 60*, 145–152. [CrossRef], [PubMed], [Web of Science ®].

Warnke, G. (1987). *Gadamer: Hermeneutics, tradition, and reason:* Stanford, CA: Stanford University Press.

Warren, S. (2010). Comment on David Wolitsky's "Critique of Hoffman's paper." *International Association for Relational Psychoanalysis & Psychotherapy enews, 9* (2).

Watkins, S.C. (2009). *The young and the digital: What the migration to social-network sites, games, and anytime, anywhere media means for our future.* Boston, MA: Beacon Press.

Watzlawick, P., Weakland, J.H., & Fisch, R. (1974). *Change: Principles of problem formation and problem resolution.* New York: Norton.

Weisgerber, K. (Ed.). (1999). *The traumatic bond between the psychotherapist and managed care.* Northvale, NJ: Jason Aronson.

Welter, B. (1966). The cult of true womanhood. *American Quarterly, 16,* 151–174.

West, L., & Singer, M. (1980). Cults, quacks, and non-professional psychotherapies. In H. Kaplan, A. Freedman, & B. Sadock (Eds.), *Comprehensive textbook of psychiatry* (Vol. 3). Baltimore, MD: Williams & Williams.

Westerman, M.A. & Steen, E.M. (2007). Going beyond the internal-external dichotomy in clinical psychology: The theory of interpersonal defense as an example of a post-Cartesian, participatory approach. *Theory & Psychology, 17,* 323–351.

Whitehead, T. (1938). *The industrial worker* (2 vols.). Cambridge, MA: Harvard University Press.

Whittington, H.G. (1993). Mental health myths that hamper employer management of costs and quality. *Behavioral Healthcare Tomorrow, 2,* 26–29.

Wiesel, E. (1966/1996). *The Town Beyond the Wall.* New York: Holt, Rinehart, & Winston.

Wile, D. (1984). Kohut, Kernberg, and accusatory interpretations. *Psychotherapy: Theory Research, Practice, & Training, 22,* 353–364.

Williams, H. (1952). *Your cheatin' heart.* ISWC T-070.248.357–5.

Wilson, C. (1983). The rhetoric of consumption: Mass-market magazines and the demise of the gentle reader, 1880–1920. In R. Fox & T. Lears (Eds.), *The culture of consumption: Critical essays in American history, 1880–1980* (pp. 41–64). New York: Pantheon.

Winnicott, D.W. (1965). *The maturation process and the facilitating environment.* London: Hogarth Press.

Wolfe, A. (1989). *Whose keeper? Social science and moral obligation.* Berkeley & Los Angeles: University of California Press.

Wolin, R. (1990). *The politics of being: The political thought of Martin Heidegger.* New York: Columbia University Press.

Wolin, R. (1992). *The terms of cultural criticism: The Frankfurt school, existentialism, poststructuralism.* New York: Columbia University Press.

Woodruff, P. (2001). *Reverence: Renewing a forgotten virtue.* Oxford, UK: Oxford University Press.

Woods, D.R., & Cagney, T. (1993). Clinician update: The nuts and bolts of managing managed care. *Behavioral Healthcare Tomorrow, 20,* 38–39.

Zammito, J.H. (2004). *A nice derangements of epistemes: Post-positivism in the study of science from Quine to Latour.* Chicago: University of Chicago Press.

Zaretsky, E. (1976). *Capitalism, the family, and personal life.* New York: Harper & Row.

Zinn, H. (1973). *Postwar America: 1945–1971.* New York: Bobbs-Merrill.

Zizek, S. (2009). *The essential Zizek: The complete set.* New York: Verso.

Index

Aalbers, D. 232
absences 10, 20, 23, 27, 97, 101, 173–4, 176, 187, 195, 216, 219, 222, 233; of community tradition 10; of dialogue 219; of political resistance 49; social 10; structural 162
Abu Ghraib prison 224, 228
abuse 28–30, 69, 102, 205, 211, 226, 231; drug 20; medical 74; political 29; in psychotherapy 28
actions 32, 34–5, 40, 49, 51, 108, 111, 113, 115, 137, 145, 215, 224–5, 229; behavioral 245; deceitful 229; embodied 247; moral 90; planned 57; reprehensible 248; right wing 253; unconscious 40
activists 229–30; anti-torture 230; environmental 7; political 184
Acts and Regulations, *Affordable Care Act* 121
administrations 56, 184, 219, 228–9, 259, 265; adventurism in Central America 7; far-right 166; new 253
ads 16, 19, 23; cigarette 24; deodorant 24; substituting the concept of lifestyle 24
advertisements *see* ads
advertising 7, 10, 16–17, 23–6, 72, 81, 191; claims 55; copy 154; executives 25, 150; industry 16, 19, 25, 31; strategies (political) 10
Affordable Care Act 121

Afghanistan 157, 160, 224, 260
African Americans 36, 44–5; incarceration of 204; and Jewish American relations 44
agreements 65, 83, 98, 122, 206, 260; common 98, 260; false 98; patient's 67
alliances 17, 65–6, 159, 166, 265; collaborative 66; false 65; maintenance of teamwork 58; propitious 72; therapeutic 65–6, 218
Allport, G. 41–2
Altman, Neil 40–6, 184, 197, 250; ability to interpret and learn from his own countertransference about race 44; discussions on the origins of racism 42; groundbreaking book *The Analyst in the Inner City* 196; and his article "Black and White Thinking: A Psychoanalyst Reconsiders Race" 40; and white guilt 44
"America First" (Donald Trump theme) 257
American 16, 18–20, 80, 124, 158, 160, 234, 263; culture 129, 146, 227; Jewish communities 170–1; military 259; psychology 94, 122, 229
American Psychological Association 33, 121, 153, 164, 204–5, 220, 223–5, 227–30, 233–4, 243, 245; accredited doctoral programs 224;

Annual Convention 33, 153, 204, 223, 232; code of ethics 214; designers and evaluators of graduate psychology curricula 238; difficulties stopping its collusion with the Department of Defence 245; entanglements in torture 227; ethics 220, 225, 232; leaders 224–6, 228–9, 247; members 220, 225, 229; symposium titled "Does Psychology Erode Personhood?" 77; task force on assessing academic competencies in doctoral educatio n 220; torture fiasco 230
American Psychologist 6, 51, 223
The Analyst in the Inner City 196
analysts 39–50, 93, 134, 167, 175, 181–2, 194, 196–7, 200; being direct or authentic 44; increasing pressures on 134; white 49
anti-social diagnosis 87
anti-torture activists 230
APA *see* American Psychological Association
Arendt, Hannah 96, 259
Aronson, Jason 184
arrogance 83, 91–105; and affluence 83; of monoculturalism 94
articles 3, 141, 167, 170, 183, 196; "What is Enlightenment?" 101; "Why the Self Is Empty" 6; "Will Managed Care Change Our Way of Being?" 240
Austad, C.S. 58–9, 65–6
authenticity 92, 94, 96–8, 103, 108, 178, 200; Martin Heidegger's concept of 98, 103, 200; practice of 103; process of 97
avatars 122, 125–9, 187, 192, 215
Axis II disorders 60, 86
Bacevich, Andrew 157, 260
Baumeister, R. 14–15, 19
Beebe, Beatrice 194

behaviors 27, 45, 49, 56, 58–9, 64, 85, 111, 116, 119, 130, 132, 145, 165; common therapy-interfering 66; complex 84; concrete 57, 218; demagogic 231; discrete 85; ethical 147, 232; human 107, 189, 233; observable 85, 89; quantifiable 73; unethical 225
Benjamin, Jessica 184, 195, 211, 243
Berger, Peter 4
Berman, W. 59, 65–6, 193
Bernstein, Richard 70, 96, 98, 100, 183, 238, 250, 255
betrayals 4, 44, 46, 157, 224, 230; moral 157; political 155
"Between Arrogance and a Dead-End" 106
birth 97, 114, 120, 125, 136, 160–1, 164, 199; difficulty of 160; great 159, 162
Bollas, Christopher 29
Botticelli, Steven 178–9, 181–4, 193, 197, 251
Bromberg, Philip 178, 197
Buber, Martin 48, 212
Budman, S.H. 59
Bush, George W. 7, 39, 79, 92, 106, 166, 184, 229
Bush administration 92, 223, 225, 228, 233
Buss, Alan 37
Butler, Judith 195, 201

Calkins, Mary 36
care 26, 29, 31, 71–2, 75, 117, 136, 140, 181, 183, 196–7, 200; human 172; preventive medical 20; psychological 71, 73; in psychotherapy 239
Carr, N. 126–7, 185–7
Cartesian split between matter and spirit 110
Caruth, Cathy 267
celebrities 17–18, 24, 103, 126, 129

Cheuvront, J.P. 184, 197, 200
children 7, 21, 46, 88, 112, 160–1, 167, 169
churches 69, 71, 115, 210, 255
Churchill, Scott 234, 240
Civil War 39, 45, 107, 160
clients 55–6, 58, 114, 117
clinical psychology 81
Clinton, Bill 39–40; and the cancelation of crucial banking and investment regulations 39; and the oppression of Black America 39; and the Work-For-Welfare plan 39
cognitive therapy 64
Cohen, M. 228, 231
Cold War 80, 100, 234
commitment therapies 27
communal guilt 49
communities 10, 12–13, 19, 24, 27, 36, 49, 80, 84, 160–1, 169, 173, 199, 209–10; behavioral health 216; contemporary American 173; Jewish 45, 207–10; minority 49; psychoanalytic 135; rural 14; white 49
compassion 4–5, 99, 128, 172–3, 210, 212, 265, 267
competencies 178, 244–5; academic 121–3, 131, 140, 143, 148, 189, 214, 220; graduate school 240
compliance 8, 30, 53, 58–60, 66–7, 144–5, 148, 154, 164, 190, 219–21, 231, 240, 246–7; automatic 246–7; coercing 220; patient 58; strict 190
computers 122, 128, 131–3, 148–9, 185, 189, 216–17; complex 147; functioning 189; organic 189; poor 132; and scientist therapeutics 217
consumerism 7, 20, 109–10, 124–5, 185, 190, 213, 226, 250
consumers 24–5, 81, 83, 86, 130, 145, 190–3, 218–19; acquisitive 75; average 23; electronic 187; individual 191; middle-class 42

Contemporary Psychoanalysis and the Legacy of the Third Reich 91, 93, 106, 165, 175
control 10–11, 14–15, 20, 23, 40, 42, 52–4, 147–8, 215–16, 220, 222, 231, 233, 244–5; coercive 227; complete 220; of health care 216, 244; mechanisms 63, 220; political 67, 215; of psychotherapy 204; systematic 72; of therapists and researchers 221
Crawford, Rob 101
crisis 59, 253, 255–7, 266; developmental 59; narcissistic 30
Crow, Jim 39
cultural artifacts 2–3, 9, 13, 179
cultural conceptualizations and configurations of self 8
cultural expressions 237
cultural history 2, 7, 52, 138, 184, 212, 227, 253, 257–8, 260, 262, 265–7; approach to psychoanalysis 184; exploration of 235; fundamentals of 253; informed 167; value of 253
cultural understandings 99, 132, 207
culture 1–2, 9, 13, 97, 102, 135–6, 176–7, 228, 236–7, 257–8; and history 36; human 198; important 254; intellectual 181; moral 159; non-Western 256; political 226; popular 186, 188; and psychology 91; theory 33, 256–7; traditional 24
current self 10–11, 142, 198, 226; configuration of the 10; constructed as empty 11; political antecedents and consequences of the 11
Cushman, P 20, 30, 98–9, 111–12, 114, 168, 182–4, 188–9, 199–200, 210–14, 226, 238–9, 248, 250–1
Cutter, William 209

Danziger, K. 37, 233
Davies, J.M. 178
democracy 201, 211, 257–9

Department of Defense 159, 220, 223–5, 228–9, 234–5, 245, 247
depression 17, 161, 171, 192, 219; economic 17; peripartum 153
Descartes, Rene 11, 136, 236
despair 4, 25, 37, 156, 160–1, 172, 174, 222; and hopelessness 128; new mother's 162; political 219
diagnosis 56–7, 59, 62–3, 73, 81, 86, 88, 216; adult 88; anti-social 87; nonpejorative 65; popular 21; primary 60; psychiatric 56
Diagnostic and Statistical Manual of Mental Disorders 73, 77, 84, 88, 154–5, 158, 191, 239
dialogue 92, 94, 96–9, 103, 105, 109, 196, 200, 213, 219, 223, 248, 250–1, 255; absence of 219; and activism 103; engaged 72, 240; and Hans-Georg Gadamer's concept of 94, 103, 105, 109, 119, 141, 196, 200, 213, 250; misdirected 104; responsible 73
Dimen, Muriel 184
disorders 21, 28–9, 59, 81, 85–6, 125, 180; anomalous 159; eating 20; medical 154; mental 52, 73; posttraumatic stress 153
doctoral students 154, 246
doctors 158–9, 161, 163, 199; and clergy 161; and patients 159; and therapists 161
DoD *see* Department of Defense
DSM *see* Diagnostic and Statistical Manual
Dubois, W.E.B. 36, 41–3, 47

earthquakes 223, 225, 230
EBTs *see* Evidence Based Treatments
economic injustices 49
economic problems 17
electronic machines 132, 146, 213, 219; contemporary 129; poorly functioning 190; production of 122

emptiness 12, 19–21, 23, 81, 99, 123–5, 128, 142, 161, 187; avaricious 70; by building the self of the patient 21; deep interior 188; experiencing of 128, 262; and fragmentation 12, 21; and frustrations 161; individuals 262; to multiplicity 187; and personality 81; universal nature of 81
empty self 6–7, 10, 12, 19–23, 25–8, 31–2, 81–3, 86, 90, 123, 129–30, 188, 213, 261
entertainment industries 139
ethics 77–8, 223–5, 227–8, 230, 233, 238, 240, 242, 246, 249, 252; of authenticity 297; code 221, 230, 236, 238, 249, 251; psychological 77, 230, 240; and psychotherapy 77; of torture 224–5; workshops 246
Evidence Based Treatments 122–3, 130–2

families 12, 36, 45, 117, 125, 156, 158, 160–1, 187; extended 79, 160–1; and friends 156; new 19; particular 113; postwar 19; young middle-class 19
fantasy 24, 46, 161, 263; experience 262; self-deceitful 169; world 262–3
Fonagy, Peter 134, 239
forces 102–3, 116, 125, 137, 139, 179, 187, 227, 232, 240, 243, 246–7, 249, 260–1; combined 165; contemporary 164; corporate 181; dominant 54; historical 10, 221, 225–6, 254; intellectual 176; militarized police 219; moral 99; political 12, 92, 132, 144, 153, 219; primary 116; sociopolitical 60, 87, 255–6
Foucault, Michel 11–15, 43, 53, 59, 61, 69, 92–4, 99–104, 176, 185, 236, 245–6, 255, 258; genealogical

Foucault, Michel *continued*
  praxis 101; and the Heidegger-Foucault dilemma 91–105; and the reduction of moral discourse 94
Fowers, Blaine 48, 70, 72, 118, 124, 140, 168, 176, 210, 213, 231, 236–7, 244, 250–1
Fox-Genovese, Elizabeth 33
freedom 48, 146; paltry 67; political 67, 169
Frie, Roger 183, 200, 250, 251
friends 3–4, 6, 17, 125, 131, 156, 158, 161, 179; and families 156; old 160
Fromm, Erich 16, 18, 22, 180, 184, 193, 208, 231
functions 13, 15, 22, 26–7, 55, 59, 63, 131–2, 214, 217, 225, 231, 258–9; brain 131; economic 15; important 27; political 6, 124, 262
Furumoto, Laurel 31, 37, 248

Gadamer, Hans-Georg 34–5, 92, 97–8, 103, 106, 136–8, 140–1, 176, 183, 196, 212, 236–7, 240, 247–9; concepts compatible with early twenty-first century Western psychological culture 98; helps Stern describe psychoanalysis as an emergent process 196; and Martin Heidegger 255; philosophical hermeneutics of 183; philosophical work of 195
Gadlin, Howard 37
Gatsby, Jay 80
Geertz, Clifford 2, 12, 24, 108
gender 15, 40, 47, 108, 112, 125, 146, 171, 184, 191, 194–5, 237, 248; and political arrangements 194; prescriptions 60; and race 40; roles 15; scapegoating 52
Gerber, L. 63, 184, 250–1
Gergen, K. 9, 11–12, 179
Germany 95, 102–3, 166, 264

Gilford, Peter 54, 61, 72, 82, 87, 111, 138, 143, 146, 178, 213, 238, 242
goals 63, 65, 68, 70, 90, 94, 102, 107, 113, 119–20, 143, 147, 238, 240–1; of psychotherapy 90; and strategies 67; of treatment 67, 86
God 4, 20, 71, 115–16, 206–7, 209–10, 254; direct word of 206–7; interpreted 207
Goldman, E. 17–18
Golem 204–22
Goodman, David 59, 122, 184, 205
graduate students 51, 91, 133, 221
Gramsci, Antonio 106, 108–9
Great Depression 17, 124
Greenberg, Jay 30, 193, 231
groups 22, 43, 47, 50, 67, 69, 102, 115, 134, 165, 254; American immigrant minority 46, 88; cultural 9; ethnic 46, 50, 60, 95, 174; human 254; oppressed 46, 166; peer consultation 73; peripheral 102; restrictive 30; safe 264; self-help 194; women's consciousness raising 194
Guignon, Charles 48, 70, 72, 99, 118, 124, 140, 168, 176, 200, 213, 236–7, 250–1
guilt 45–7, 49–50; communal 49; experiences of 90; and shame of ethnic group and class 50; unconscious 211

Hare-Mustin, Rachel 37
Harris, Adrienne 184, 233, 250
healing 10, 12, 27, 53, 74, 115–16, 132–3, 146, 163, 173, 221; practices 2–3, 124, 139, 176, 181–2; processes 29; responses 27; technologies 52, 77, 132, 192, 215, 221
health care 70, 73, 139, 155, 179, 181, 210, 244; administrators 148; corporations 123; costs 63, 220; decisions 89; mental 52, 54, 63,

121, 230; payments 162; practices 71; researchers 141; systems 70–2, 74; workers 140
heart 8, 34, 38, 58, 137, 147, 153–64, 168, 196, 208, 236–7; human 207; of mainstream scientized psychology 237
Heidegger, Martin 8–9, 13, 34, 92–8, 100, 103–4, 107–8, 120, 136–7, 140, 144, 212, 255, 257; involvement with National Socialism 94–6; philosophy of 95–6, 107, 116
Henry, Jules 12, 135
hermeneutic conception of psychotherapy 72
hermeneutic practice 248, 253
hermeneuticists 4, 8, 89, 93–4, 107, 111–13, 137, 141–2, 144, 148–9, 176–7, 237–8, 247, 250
hermeneutics 2–4, 6, 8, 33, 91, 93, 106, 136–7, 204–5, 212–13, 227, 250–1, 255–8, 265–7
historical traditions 2, 47, 75, 124, 176, 178, 186, 189, 208, 213, 237, 251
History of Sexuality 101
Hoffman, Irwin Z. 134–7, 140, 142–3, 150, 179, 182–3, 195, 200, 214, 224, 238–9
Hoffman Report 223–52
Hollander, N.C. 183–4, 251
Holocaust 96, 167–8, 170–2
"homework noncompliance" 66–7
Hoy, David 98
human life *see* life
human nature 13–14, 53, 108, 237
human problems 190, 235
human sciences 42, 69, 99, 141, 212, 236
humanistic psychology 110, 140, 194
humanities 84, 91–2, 121, 164, 186, 209, 213, 236, 255–6, 264, 266; and social sciences 91–2, 213, 253, 255–6, 266

humans 13, 71–2, 107–8, 132–3, 136–8, 141, 144, 146–8, 189–91, 206–7, 214–15, 218, 247, 254–5; films featuring 146; history of 254; portraying 189; in positions of power 147; vulnerable 216

identities 82, 111, 116, 123, 125, 137, 139, 143, 170, 178, 188–9, 198, 214, 256; alternative 125, 128; communal 45–6, 171; conflicted 123; familial 97; group 179; insider 47; modern 297; multiple 188, 214; professional 226
ideology 10, 15, 25–6, 28–9, 31, 69, 108, 119, 129, 179, 220, 225, 255, 261–2; cognitive 129; conformist 108; cultural 201, 242; destructive 234; disguised 101; dominant 28, 99; exclusionary 138; extreme authoritarian 166; political 43, 201, 217, 242, 261; psychological 26; religious 256; romantic 139; scientistic 140, 205
indigenous psychologies 2, 9, 108
industrialization 10, 14, 140, 179, 181; postwar 18; of psychotherapy 182–3
industries 19, 265; cosmetics 19; digital 39; electronic 20; entertainment 139; self-improvement 16, 20, 31; sports 186
information 55, 150, 190, 214, 231; gathering of 126, 231; important 243; processing equipment 189; processing machines 215
injustices 48–9, 162
interpersonal 64, 69, 92–3, 96–7, 147, 167, 180, 185, 193, 195, 200, 238; analysts 180; characteristics 187; environment 28; honesty 250; interactions 93, 211, 217; involvement 200; psychiatry 108; relations 103, 213; relationships 176; traditions 193

interpretative turn 176, 180, 182–3, 185
"interpretative turn" (Hiley, Bohman & Shusterman) 41, 91–3, 106–7, 110, 136, 141, 146, 168, 176, 236, 238–9, 241, 250–1
interrogation 223, 228–9, 232–3; definition of 228; enhanced 228; extended 73; military 229; participation of psychologists in 228, 232; programs 223–4; sessions 232; and torture 228
interviews 56, 167–9; Emily Kuriloff's probing 170–1; and Michel Foucault 101
Iraq 157, 160, 224, 228, 260

Jacobson, Lawrence 123, 128, 178, 238
James, William 36, 77
Jaspers, Karl 96
Jay, Martin 100–1
Jewish 47, 169–70; communities 45, 207–10; identities 165–74; oppression 165; traditions 95–6, 165, 167, 205–6, 212
Jews 45, 47, 94–5, 102, 166–7, 169–70, 172–3, 207–10; American 171; Medieval 210; and the "place" inhabited in the European modern era 47; poor 45; pre-World, War II 170
Jim Crow era of repression 39

Kaslow, Nadine 148, 220, 245
King, Rodney 40
Klein, Melanie 169
knowledge 57, 69, 126, 136, 156–7, 160, 169–71, 235, 244, 264; acquisition of 244; expert 57; human 137; new 104; objective 136; personal 147, 170; public 170, 225, 228; scientific 71; traditional 136
Kohut, Heinz 12, 20–1, 23, 26, 28–30, 140, 199; method of treatment 21; self psychology of 21, 81

Kovel, Joel 37, 69, 74, 149, 185
Kuriloff, Emily 165–71, 173–4

Lasch, C. 18–21, 124
Layton, Lynne 106–9, 178, 183–4, 195, 197, 199, 201, 250–1
leaders 20, 208, 211, 225, 228, 231, 259, 267; anti-intellectual hate-mongering 193; APA 224–6, 228–9, 247; authoritarian 208; charismatic 188, 254, 262; military 260; political 20, 156; religious 87, 209; senior 228
Lears, T.J. 11, 15–16, 19–20, 23, 25, 180
Leary, K. 43, 45, 184, 196
legacy 165, 171; historical 41; multidimensional 171
Levenson, E.A. 177, 183–4, 193
Levin, D. 11–12, 18, 21, 70
Levinas, Emanuel 249
life 3–4, 24–5, 34–6, 112–13, 117, 127–9, 142–3, 160–1, 166–8, 172, 207–8, 211, 251, 266; American 20, 81, 186; daily 13, 250; digital 253; everyday 34, 38, 107, 110, 130, 185, 262; good 32, 82, 255; intersubjective 251; Jewish communal 208, 210; modern 24–5; political 139; problem-free 24; professional 137; psychological 56, 59, 196, 201; relational 127, 179, 231; style solutions 23–31
Lobban, G. 197
Lowe, D. 14–15, 17

machines 72, 126, 132–3, 146, 148–50, 190, 214–17; computing 131; war 18, 214, 216
MacIntyre, Alasdair 141
Malabre, A. 12, 18–19
managed care 51–4, 57–9, 61, 64–72, 74–5, 84, 164, 184, 215–16, 219–20, 226–7, 239–40;

arrangements 55, 68, 84; companies 59, 62–3; corporations 54, 134, 250; discourse 54–5, 62, 69, 71; effects of 63; environments 55, 61–2; ideologies 55; justification of psychotherapy in 55; organizations 40, 51, 53–5, 58–60, 63–4, 68, 86, 148, 245; patient in 59; practices 54–5, 68; and psychotherapy 70; systems 63; therapists 65
manualized treatments 122, 148, 162, 189, 219, 227, 238
Marecek, Jeanne 37
Marin, Peter 18, 156–7, 219
Martin, Jack 98, 251, 255
Marxism 256–7
Massively Multiplayer Online Role Playing Game 125, 127–9, 214
Masterson, J.E. 21–2
MCOs *see* managed care organizations
medication 64–5, 179; correct 146, 149, 219; psychotropic 54, 59
Medieval Jews 210
memories 147, 167, 171, 174, 194, 205, 248, 258, 267; collective 257, 259, 267; historical 4, 131
mental disorders 52, 73
mental patients 194
mental problems 25
Messer, S. 9
Messiah 205–6, 209, 221
midrash 166, 173, 205, 207–8
military 43, 129, 139, 210–11, 223, 227–8, 232–3, 247, 252; American 259; leaders 260; objectives 259; organizations 179; personnel 231; power 210; prisoners 229; prisons 92; torture 164
mistakes 3–4, 36, 38, 48, 125, 198, 200; Foucault's 104; fundamental 11; human 230; tragic 46; unforgiveable 38
Mitchell, Stephen 183, 193–4
MMORPGs *see* Massively Multiplayer Online Role Playing Game
modalities 68; psychotherapeutic 26; symptom-reduction 122
modern state 11, 14–15, 31
money 7, 11–12, 19, 89, 118, 190, 209–10, 221, 231, 244, 248
"the Money River" 47
moral discourse 70, 72, 90, 94, 117–18, 141, 144, 212, 218, 221, 238, 241–2, 248, 250–2
moral pain 155–6, 159
moral responsibilities 163
moral traditions 35, 100, 102, 104, 136, 151, 166, 231
moral understandings 100–2, 107, 109, 111, 116–18, 142, 144, 146, 176–7, 237–41, 243, 247, 257–8, 262–3
Moran, Bruce 78
Morawski, J. 8, 13
mothering 159, 161–3
mothers 118, 160–2
Moyers, Bill 186
multiculturalism 40, 200
multiple identities 188, 214
"multiple self" 61, 82–3, 86, 90, 123, 126, 130–1, 143, 178–80, 187, 189, 197–8, 213–15, 226; emerging 84, 188; flattened 189, 193, 242; states 178, 198
multiplicity 51, 80, 90, 93, 126, 178, 187, 192, 197–8; postmodern concept of 197; in psychoanalysis 197
mysteries 42, 71, 92, 99, 107–20, 196, 258

narcissism 10, 22, 70, 81, 125, 130, 180; a culture of 124; healthy 81; social 211
natural sciences 227, 234–7
Nazis and Nazism 38, 92, 94–7
neoliberalism 51, 121, 182, 221, 225, 241–3, 261

"new self" 17, 61, 82–4, 123, 178, 213; *see also* "multiple self"
Nixon, Richard 192
noncompliance (as used in documentation) 58, 67, 219
"Notes Toward a Nonconformist Clinical Practice" 106

Olson, A.M. 96, 229, 232, 240
opposition 7–8, 32, 140, 182, 219, 256; direct 250; encountering 41; explicit 200; to hermeneutics 256; to scientism in psychology 140
oppressed groups 46, 166
oppression 39, 41, 47, 102, 104, 106, 162, 166, 171, 195, 211; Jewish 165; ongoing 43; political 49; structural socioeconomic 265
Orange, Donna 128
Orbach, Susie 184, 194

Parker, Peter 146
Partners in Thought 197
patients 26–30, 48–9, 53–68, 73–4, 78, 86–8, 111–20, 133–5, 144–5, 147–9, 159, 162–4, 195–6, 218–20; adult 21; of color 40, 47–9; compliant 74; displaying independent thought 59; docile 59; and doctors 159; helping 109, 119; manipulative 66; mental 194; noncompliant 59; sick 66; and therapists 36, 118; tortured 112
Peltz, Rachel 184, 251
peripartum depression 153
personality disorders 85–6; anti-social 87–9; borderline 21; pejorative Axis II borderline 59
philosophical foundations 91, 93, 105, 184, 199–200, 227; of APA's understanding of psychology 227; of interpretive therapeutic ideology 94; that directly challenges a modern-era Cartesianism 183

philosophical hermeneutics 136, 140, 157, 182, 212–13
philosophical psychologists 33, 36
philosophy 92, 95, 100, 104, 196, 199, 212, 224, 236–8, 242–3, 249–50, 252, 255; and clinical theory 212; of Hans-Georg Gadamer 34–5, 92, 97–8, 103, 106, 136–8, 140–1, 176, 183, 196, 212, 236–7, 240, 247–9; and history 243; of inductive science 237; moral 240; psychological 10; of science 224, 226, 230, 235
political arrangements 2–3, 42–3, 72, 75, 77, 107, 109, 111, 115–16, 130–2, 135, 179, 182, 194; current 164, 183, 187; detailed 212; dominant 53; and expressions of the good that frame the clearing 115; structural 121
political functions 6, 124, 262
political resistance 49, 66, 92, 94, 98, 102, 146, 164, 175–202, 205; and critical thinking 94; importance of 98; motivation for 193; movement 193; shape of 176; in white communities 49
politics 1, 8, 32–3, 41, 116–17, 135–6, 156, 177, 212–13, 224, 230, 249–50, 256, 264; and economies 8; of the left 165; of mental health care 230; of psychological practice 224; of uncertainty 253–67
post-World War II 16, 61, 226; economy 12; era 10–12, 17, 19, 29, 81–2, 123, 213; families 18; middle-classes 12
postmodernism 44, 91, 93, 104, 106, 146, 176, 236, 257; feminist 182; and hermeneutics 91, 146, 236
power 17, 29, 31, 43, 48, 53, 69–70, 94–6, 99–103, 109, 147, 176, 208–10, 213; extreme 129; growing 242; hunger 89; increasing 20;

industrial 17; of the military 210; and personality 20; political 47; purchasing 190; relations 42–3, 53, 66, 74–5, 99, 141; restrictive 15

problems 12, 30–1, 55–6, 58–60, 62–3, 70–1, 75, 85–6, 101–2, 129–30, 199, 208–9, 218–19, 247; countable 216; economic 17; emotional 60; financial 211; human 190, 235; important 102; medical 60; mental 25; parenting 115; philosophical 68, 107, 121; political 111, 129, 178; psychological 55, 60, 130, 132; social 23, 29, 137, 263; and symptoms 64

proceduralism 121, 131, 148, 205, 216, 218, 220, 241, 243–5; authoritarian 151, 239; bureaucratic 131, 181, 204, 214; corporate 221; manualized 131; power of 131; scientistic 164, 196; and technicism 148

psychoanalysts 27, 93, 167, 170, 224, 250

psychological changes 108, 116, 193–4, 198, 251, 255

psychological practices 3, 89, 224, 230, 244, 249–51

psychological theories 2–3, 9, 189, 234, 250

psychologies 184; indigenous 2, 9; particular 108

psychology students 244, 246

psychotherapeutic modalities 26

psychotherapists 6, 20, 37, 40, 109, 137, 154; American 51

psychotherapy 6–8, 12, 25–8, 40–1, 53, 64–5, 72–4, 77, 121–2, 144–5, 168–9, 181–3, 217–18, 249–50; American 6, 176; hours 106, 119; normalizing function of 74; practices 26, 50, 55, 68, 135, 148, 150, 180, 217; profession of 51, 140, 200; theories 12, 70, 82, 125, 200, 217, 219, 257; unethical 153, 163

relational practices 182, 185, 200

relational psychoanalysis 92–3, 109, 138, 140, 167, 171, 173, 175–202, 245; continuing success of 93; important understandings of 138; interpersonal 167; and Jewish values 173; practices of 171, 187, 201

resolutions 229–30, 234; of conflict 198; psychological 65

Richardson, Frank 48, 58, 70, 72, 98–9, 118, 124, 140, 168, 176, 213, 236–7, 250–1

Ricoeur, Paul 227–8

Risser, James 98

Ritzer, George 80

Rosenberg, Joel 205

Safran, Jeremy D. 134–7, 142–3, 148, 150, 239

Sampson, Ed 2–3, 5–6, 11–13, 18, 22, 28–9, 32, 37, 129–30, 179, 237

Sandel, Michael 217

Sass, L. 2, 9, 15, 23, 28, 31

Sass, Louie 255

scientism 133, 137–8, 140, 144, 153–5, 163–4, 168, 184, 200, 205, 208, 235–8, 241–4, 256–7; allegiance to 164; circularity of 133; critics of 68, 137; demands of 236; interpretation of 237; mainstream 240; modern-era 144, 238, 240; objective 70; opposition to 140; practice of 238; procedural 221; and romanticism 140; and technicism 200

scientistic proceduralism 164, 196

Second Life (game) 125, 127–8, 214

self 1–3, 6–32, 36–8, 51–3, 80–3, 85–6, 123–5, 128–30, 142–6, 187–90, 192–3, 213–15, 217,

self *continued*
   261–3; bounded 10, 20, 28, 32; contained individualism 9–10, 28, 111, 124, 196, 237; deceit 4, 186–7; deep 123, 128; early-twenty-first-century 55; flattened 123, 128, 133, 143–4, 146, 151, 182, 215; fragmented 16, 21; individual 14, 18; in managed care 51, 61; masterful 8, 10–11, 31, 142; middle-class 14, 16; modern 12, 15; multiple 82–3, 86, 90, 123, 126, 130–1, 143, 178–80, 187, 189, 193, 197–8, 213–15, 226; particular 2, 19, 263; predominant 52, 123, 213, 240; true 21–2, 81; Western 13–14, 32, 142
self psychology 22, 193, 238; of Heinz Kohut 21, 81; in psychoanalytic theory 180
Seligman, Martin 87, 180–1, 224, 234
Severson, Eric 205
sexual orientation 60
Sheehy, Maura 159–61, 219
Simeon, Daphne 184
Singer, Margaret 26, 30
Slife, Brent 98, 140, 251, 255
smart phones 130, 177
social life 143, 217, 266
social practices 27, 35–8, 107, 111–12, 138, 148, 150, 164, 173, 179–80, 190, 247, 250, 258
social problems 23, 29, 137, 263
social sciences 11–12, 14, 26, 91–2, 213, 236, 241, 253, 255–6, 266; empirical 14; and humanities 91–2, 213, 253, 255–6, 266
society 22, 24, 28–9, 32, 46–8, 52–4, 77, 80, 117–18, 134–5, 139, 182, 230–1, 236; contemporary 131; current 89, 135; democratic 147, 186, 260; dominant 102; law-abiding 189; medieval 209, 256; multicultural 116; oppressive 104; psychological 124, 141

Soldz, S. 184, 226, 229, 232, 240
solutions 25, 55, 57, 61, 71, 75, 83, 85, 129–30, 139, 219, 254; coercive 211; cognitivist 131; current 26; decontextualized 218; developing political 24; explicit therapeutic 31; lifestyle 23–31, 123; one-dimensional 193; shallow 122–33
Steinbeck, John 1
Stern, D.B. 22, 119–20, 140, 150, 157, 177, 182–3, 194–7, 199–201, 205, 209–10, 214, 218, 250–1
Stigliano, Tony 3, 9, 98
Strenger, Carlo 134, 239
Strupp, H.H. 68, 138
students 33, 52, 94, 97, 137, 189, 205, 224, 243–6, 248, 252; doctoral 154, 246; and patients 137; psychology 244, 246
Suchet, Melanie 197
Sugarman, Jeff 98, 210, 226, 242, 249, 251, 255
Sullivan, W.M. 9, 18, 41, 150, 163, 178, 180, 193
Sully, Jake 146
surveillance 63, 220, 245
symptom-reduction modalities 122

Taylor, Charles 11, 14–15, 19, 23, 26, 28, 53, 70, 72, 100, 136, 178, 238, 251
teachers 4, 6, 91, 137, 170, 172, 189, 230, 244–5; religious 169; and spiritual healers 173; and storytellers 173
texts 3, 9, 92, 128, 138, 141, 176, 208–9, 245, 248, 266; cultural 2, 9; favorite 4; medical 236; and persons 141
theories 21, 23, 27, 30, 71, 74, 81, 93, 96, 167–8, 198–9, 205, 211–12, 233–4; and practices 71, 133; of process and change in psychotherapy 199

therapeutic 15–17, 26–31, 54–5, 58–69, 75, 94, 106, 109–11, 130, 145–6, 177, 194–7, 199–200, 215–18; practices 64, 75, 80, 94, 106, 110, 171, 181, 199, 216; processes 55, 64, 145, 195, 200; relationships 64, 66; settings 29–30; solutions 31
therapist-patient dyad 28
therapists 26–7, 29–30, 56–68, 86–7, 91, 105–10, 112–20, 132, 144–5, 148–9, 173–4, 188–9, 194–6, 244–6; calibrated 63; celebrity 68; compliant 66; and doctoral students 154; and doctors 161; family 27, 65; and graduate students 221; mainstream 123; in managed care 61, 64; and patients 53, 64–6, 112, 117–18, 148, 195, 244; practicing 73; white 40, 44, 47
therapy 6–7, 28–9, 56–61, 63–4, 66–8, 78–9, 113, 116–17, 119, 135, 141–5, 184, 218, 244–5; analytic 27; cognitive behavioral 61, 66, 250; correct 141; exploitive life-style 30; family 92; historical/political understanding of 135; individual 115; manualized 122–3; practices 73, 78, 80; radical 194; reflective 131; settings 29–30, 66; strategic 61; symptom-reduction 64; theories 8; well-conducted psychodynamic 31
therapy hour 40, 107, 196; *see also* psychotherapy hours
Tompkins, M.A. 58, 64, 66–7
torture 78, 92, 159, 200, 220, 223–52; and the Bush administration 232; definition of 228–9, 233; ethics of 224–5; morality of 224, 230; of patients 112; practices 184, 228–9, 234; and the US Department of Defence practice of 224

traditions 10, 12, 26–7, 35–7, 95, 97, 99, 102, 120, 124, 173, 176, 199–200, 247; academic 36, 41; critical 213; historical 198; Jewish 95–6, 165, 167, 205–6, 212; monocultural 95; moral 35, 100, 102, 104, 136, 151, 166, 231; rationalist 238; religious 222; scientist 36
trauma, wartime 155, 163
treatment 21, 40, 44, 48, 53, 55–60, 63–8, 71, 73–4, 86, 135, 142, 154–5, 218; contemporary psychotherapy 171; evidence-supported 216, 245; goals 67, 86; interventions 121; mainstream 163; managed care 63; manualized psychotherapy 214; medical 147; mental health 69; philosophy and practices of managed care 53–4, 153; plans 64, 85; practices 245; procedures 57; processes 63; protocols 63, 73; psychological 84; recommendations 56, 58; sessions 64; techniques 56
Trump, Donald 165, 263–4

unethical psychotherapy 153, 163
upper classes 15, 17, 87

Vietnam vets 155–8
virtual money 187
virtual worlds 125–6, 213
Vonnegut, Kurt 47
Walls, Gary 64, 114, 134, 181–3, 214, 251
war 17, 19, 89, 110, 124–5, 156–9, 163–4, 181, 184, 186–7, 200, 234, 249, 259
war machines 18, 214, 216
wartime trauma 155, 163
Weimer Germany 166; *see also* Germany
"Western self" 13–14, 32, 142
"What is Enlightenment?" 101

white guilt 40–50; counterproductive 44; generalized 49; political activity 39; and shame 49
"Why the Self Is Empty" 6
Wiesel, Elie 97, 172, 206
"Will Managed Care Change Our Way of Being ?" 240

Williams, Hank 8, 140, 153–4, 251
Williams, Richard 98
World War II 12, 17–18, 169

Zen Buddhism 108